Abboud Joseph   Designer

A Mao jacket cut from rough linen is worn over a hand-knitted waistcoat and collarless shirt. The buttons on each garment have a natural, artisanal quality which defies the urban slant used by most American designers. Of Lebanese descent, Joseph Abboud makes clothes for men and women which are an unusual combination of American sportswear and North African colours and textures. In the 1960s Abboud collected Turkish kilims and these have inspired his natural palette and the stylized symbols that recur in his work. He began his career as a buyer and in 1981 joined Ralph Lauren, later to become associate director of menswear design. He emerged four years later with a similar philosophy to Lauren: that clothing is as much about lifestyle as it is about design. In 1986 Abboud launched his own label and found a niche for his understated clothes with their rich colours and unusually crafted textures.

☞ Alfaro, Armani, Lauren, Ozbek

Joseph Abboud. b Boston, MA (USA), 1950. **Linen menswear. Spring/summer 1995.** Photograph by Randall Mesden.

Adolfo

Designer

This impromptu snap of society figures Mr and Mrs Wyatt Cooper is one of Adolfo's favourite pictures, and not just because both are wearing his refined clothes. He says, 'Getting dressed and going out is fun only because we don't do it often – it's good to feel glamorous once in a while.' But his glamour never strays into the realms of vulgarity. Adolfo worked first as a milliner, then trained at Chanel and Balenciaga, before setting up his New York salon. There, Adolfo provided his famous knitted suits, one of which is worn here by Gloria Cooper (aka Gloria Vanderbilt). Inspired by Coco Chanel's jersey sportswear and famous suits, they were bought by New York's old society. When his salon closed in 1993 his clientele were distraught, not least Nancy Reagan, who had worn Adolfo's clothes for two decades. She, perhaps more than anyone, embodied his assertion that, 'An Adolfo lady should look simple, classic and comfortable.'

☛ **Balenciaga, Chanel, Galanos, Vanderbilt**

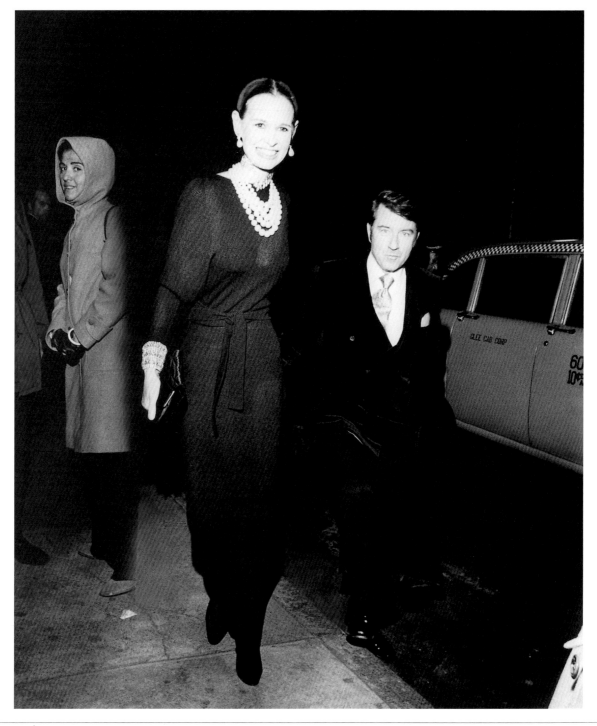

6

Adolfo (Adolfo Sardinia). b Havana (CU), 1933. **Mr and Mrs Wyatt Cooper.** Photograph by Bill Cunningham, American *Vogue*, 1972.

THE FASHION BOOK takes a fresh look at the fashion world and the people who created and inspired it. Spanning 150 years, the whole industry is represented; from pioneering designers including Coco Chanel and Issey Miyake to influential photographers such as Richard Avedon and Helmut Newton and the people they photographed. Easy to use and filled with inspirational images, it is an A–Z guide to 500 clothes and accessory designers, photographers, models and those iconic individuals who instigated or symbolize a whole fashion movement. It cuts through the usual classifications and creates juxtapositions that make fascinating and unlikely partnerships: René Lacoste sits opposite Christian Lacroix while Kate Moss rubs shoulders with Thierry Mugler. Each entry is illustrated with a photograph or drawing which shows a quintessential aspect of their work. An accompanying text describes where they fit into the fashion story and includes essential biographical information about the creator. In addition, THE FASHION BOOK uses a comprehensive cross-referencing system and glossary which explain the many collaborations and techniques used in fashion, that singular business which lives somewhere between art and commerce.

Abbe James   Photographer

James Abbe's choice of a simple, uncluttered backdrop and soft use of lighting accentuates the seductiveness of Gilda Gray, a dancer in *Ziegfeld Follies* and other Broadway revues. Like many fashion photographs of its time, it promotes a feeling that we are privy to something intimate – as if Gray has been captured unawares, dreamily caught up in her own thoughts with her eyes turned away from the lens. Taken in Paris in 1924, the photograph seizes the essence of mid-1920s eveningwear – a plumb line dress, possibly by Lanvin or Patou, in filmy, sensuous fabric trimmed with fringed tiers. In the early twentieth century, American photographer James Abbe favoured taking portraits of stage and screen actresses. His well-mannered work for American *Vogue* represented what Alexander Liberman called '...an underlying dream of a world where people act and behave in a civilized manner'.

☞ Lanvin, Liberman, Patou

James Abbe. b Alfred, ME (USA), 1883. d San Francisco, CA (USA), 1973. Gilda Gray, Paris. 1924.

Adrian Gilbert Designer

Joan Crawford wears Adrian's famed 'coat hanger look': a suit with padded shoulders and slim skirt which produces an 'inverted triangle' silhouette that has since intermittently returned to fashion – not least in the 1980s. Here, that shape is exaggerated further by triangular lapels which reach over the shoulders and taper, pointing at the waist. As Adrian told *Life* magazine in 1947, 'American women's clothes should be streamlined in the daytime.' He is also known for long, elegantly draped dinner gowns, like those he designed for Joan Crawford in *Grand Hotel*, and for his silver satin bias-cut dresses for starlet Jean Harlow. As a costume designer at Metro-Goldwyn-Mayer in the 1930s and 1940s, Adrian – born Adolphus Greenburg – found a vast audience for his work and became an influential fashion designer. In 1942 he retired as a costume designer to open his own fashion house, continuing to create his trademark suits and gowns.

☛ Garbo, Irene, Orry-Kelly, Platt Lynes

Gilbert Adrian (Adolphus Greenburg). **b** Naugatuck, CT (USA), 1903. **d** Los Angeles, CA (USA), 1959. **Joan Crawford.** c1940.

Agnès Madame   Milliner

During the 1930s, hats were literally the pinnacle of fashion, and a lady would no sooner go out without her hat than she would without her dress. In France millinery was an exclusively female occupation and Madame Agnès was the most popular milliner, famous for cutting her elegant brims while her clients were wearing them. Trained under Caroline Reboux, she established her own salon in 1917 on the rue du Faubourg Saint-Honoré in Paris among all the great couturiers. She worked in the same understated manner and combined this discrimination with an awareness of art and of the artistic trends of the 1930s, especially Surrealism. In particular, Madame Agnès brought a Surrealistic touch to that traditional millinery trim: the plumage of birds. The feathery touch and lightness of flight which represent Madame Agnès's interpretation of the movement is put into an eveningwear context with a jacket by Maggy Rouff.

☛ Hoyningen–Huene, Reboux, Rouff, Talbot

Madame Agnès. **b** (FR), late 1800s. **d** (FR). (Active 1910s–1940s.) **Hat of blue paradise plumes.** Photograph by George Hoyningen-Huene, *Harper's Bazaar*, 1935.

Alaïa Azzedine   Designer

Amazonian models in skintight dresses and high-heeled shoes embody the slick sex appeal of the dress-to-kill 1980s. Each wears an outfit from Azzedine Alaïa's 1987 spring/summer collection. 'The base of all beauty is the body,' says Alaïa, who was inspired by Madeleine Vionnet. 'There is nothing more beautiful than a healthy body dressed in wonderful clothes.' The 'King of Cling' is an expert manipulator of the female form, having studied sculpture when he was younger. He moved to Paris and worked briefly for Dior and Guy Laroche, and by the end of the 1960s had his own couture business on the Left Bank. Alaïa went on to produce the prototype for Yves Saint Laurent's famous Mondrian dress and worked for Thierry Mugler. In the early 1980s, his own stretchy dresses and bodysuits, constructed from thick knitted panels, came to define the Lycra revolution.

☛ Audibet, Bettina, Coddington, Léger, Vionnet

9

Azzedine Alaïa. b (TUN), c1940. **Paris presentation.** Photograph by Arthur Elgort, British *Vogue*, 1987.

Albini Walter   Designer

Striking disco poses, two women wear the Walter Albini hallmarks: fast, glamorous clothes which recall shapes from the 1930s. Albini started his luxury sportswear business in 1965 and became known for his fundamental allegiance to the early styles of Chanel and Patou, which were counterpointed by the global influences of the 1970s. Bold colours from Asian and African art, as well

as bright tartans, were employed on the jackets, skirts and other basic silhouettes. As much as any 1970s designer, Albini energized anti-establishment hippie layering and ethnicity and mixed it with the sophistication of the urbane sportswear pedigree. Albini's motto was 'Enjoy today and leave unpleasant things for tomorrow'. Ironically, premature death

obviated any tomorrows, but Albini's exuberant, aggressive and youthful sportswear was a significant contribution to the 1970s.

☞ Barnett, Bates, Chanel, Ozbek, Patou

10

Walter Albini. b Busto Arsizio (IT), 1941. **d** Milan (IT), 1983. **Black crepe outfits.** Photograph by Chris von Wangenheim, Italian *Vogue*, 1971.

Alexandre

Hairdresser

Alexandre de Paris, or 'Monsieur Alexandre', as he likes to be known, attends to Elizabeth Taylor's hair in 1962. Many legends surround the hairdresser, whose clients included the Duchess of Windsor, Coco Chanel and Grace Kelly. His parents, it is said, had wanted him to study medicine, but after a fortune-teller predicted that 'the wife of a king will do everything for you', they relented and let him pursue his ambition. He was apprenticed to Antoine, the Parisian stylist who invented the urchin cut. Alexandre took on his mantle and became the hairdresser of the European social set. His motif, a sphinx, was designed for him by Jean Cocteau in gratitude for the perm which restored to him 'the curly hair of a true poet'. In 1997, Jean-Paul Gaultier persuaded Alexandre out of retirement to design the hair for his first couture show, as he had done for Coco Chanel, Pierre Balmain and Yves Saint Laurent.

☛ Antoine, Cocteau, Gaultier, Windsor, Winston

Alexandre (Louis Alexandre Raimon). b St Tropez (FR), 1922. **Alexandre de Paris with Elizabeth Taylor.** Photograph by Eric Adjani, 1962.

Alfaro Victor   Designer

Victor Alfaro's first collection, launched in 1991, was dubbed by *Cosmopolitan* magazine 'a series of heat-seeking glamour missiles'. Reputedly the heir to Oscar de la Renta and Bill Blass, Alfaro has never sought to philosophize through his offerings; on the contrary, his mission is as simple as making the wearer look beautiful. This image shows a quintessential Alfaro creation in which vulgarity is proscribed, leaving room for bare simplicity skilfully counterbalanced by sexy, luxurious silk. The combination of a ball skirt and strapless top is typical of Alfaro's use of separates for cocktail - and eveningwear, acquired while working for American ready-to-wear designer Joseph Abboud. He uses slub silk as others use cotton, in keeping with the American sportswear tradition of evening clothes that quietly forgo decoration for practical statements, even on a ball gown.

☛ Abboud, Blass, de la Renta, Tyler

12

Victor Alfaro. b Chihuahua (MEX), 1965. **Silk bustier and evening skirt. Spring/summer 1996.** Photograph by Chris Moore.

Amies Sir Hardy   Designer

Her Majesty the Queen is photographed during the Silver Jubilee celebrations in 1977. She wears an eye-catching pink silk crepe dress, coat and stole by Sir Hardy Amies, dressmaker to Her Majesty since 1955 and the architect of her vivid, feminine and simple style. Sir Hardy, knighted in 1989, was designer and manager at Lachasse, a traditional British couture house, from 1934 to 1939.

As well as being lieutenant-colonel in charge of special forces in Belgium, he designed clothes under the Utility rationing scheme. In 1946 he founded his own dressmaking business, designing for Princess Elizabeth and eventually holding the royal warrant. In 1950, Sir Hardy started ladies' ready-to-wear and in 1961 began working with menswear chain Hepworths. His remark,

'A man should look as if he bought his clothes with intelligence, put them on with care, then forgot all about them', defines the Englishman's approach to fashion.

☛ Clements & Ribeiro, Hartnell, Morton, Rayne, Stiebel

13

Sir Hardy Amies. b London (UK), 1909. d Langford, Oxfordshire (UK), 2003. **Her Majesty Queen Elizabeth II wears pink Royal Jubilee outfit.** 1977.

Antoine

Hairdresser

Josephine Baker was one of Antoine's many famous clients – she wore his wigs like skullcaps for her stage performances. Born in Russian Poland, Antoine moved to work in the Parisian salon of hairdresser Monsieur Decoux. He acquired a following and, cannily, Decoux took his star stylist to the fashionable seaside town of Deauville; there Antoine was introduced to the society he would coif for decades. On his return to Paris, Antoine set up his own salon, selling his own haircare and cosmetics range – the first to do so. Although he is famed for his 'Eton crop', he always maintained he could not claim it as his own. At the time he said he was simply carrying out the orders of a client who returned three times to have her short bobbed hair cut progressively shorter to suit the increasingly sporty lifestyle enjoyed by women of that era. The peak of Antoine's career was the coronation of George VI, when he supervised 400 coiffures in one night.

☛ Alexandre, G. Jones, Kenneth, de Meyer, Talbot

Antoine (Antak Cierplikowski). b Sieradz (POL), 1884. d (POL), 1977. **Josephine Baker.** Photograph by Baron de Meyer, c1925.

Antonio

Illustrator

Antonio's watercolour model embraces a deconstructed mannequin for Italian *Vogue* in 1981. This surreal element, a tradition created by Dalí, Cocteau and Bérard in the 1930s, was a theme used by Antonio throughout his career. Texan Jerry Hall was painted with Lone Star emblems and cacti growing from her stetson and Pat Cleveland was metamorphosed into a stiletto boot.

Despite this visual play, Antonio worked from life, building sets as a photographer would. Antonio was inspired by the drawings of Boldini and Ingres, which becomes clear when looking at the fine finish on his pencil drawings. His work dominated fashion illustration for a decade, encouraging a discipline that had diminished throughout the 1950s. Antonio worked with a clique of international models and high-profile friends who converged on Paris in the 1970s. Tina Chow, Grace Jones and Paloma Picasso were regular sitters.

☛ Chow, G. Jones, Khanh, Versace

Antonio (Antonio Lopez). b (PR), 1943. d (PR), 1987. **Gianni Versace editorial.** Italian *Vogue*, 1981.

Arai Junichi   Textile designer

Junichi Arai has been described as the 'truly *enfant terrible*' of Japanese textiles...a naughty boy playing with high-tech toys'. His favoured toys are the jacquard loom and digital computer. The fabric illustrated here is typical of his work, which commonly uses metallic fibres and turns them into exquisite works of art destined only to be admired. The son and nephew of weavers, Arai was born in Kiryu, a historic centre for textiles. He initially worked with his father on kimono and obi cloths, which he developed, eventually acquiring three dozen patents for new fabrics. From 1970 Arai worked experimentally and began long-standing collaborations with Rei Kawakubo and Issey Miyake, who would suggest phrases such as 'like clouds', 'like stone' or 'driving rain' for Arai to magic into a representative fabric by using his idiosyncratic weaving techniques.

☛ Hishinuma, Isogawa, Jinteok, Kawakubo, Miyake

Junichi Arai. b Kiryu (JAP), 1932. **Crush-pleated fabric. Spring/summer 1990.** Photograph by Masanao Arai.

Arden Elizabeth — Cosmetics creator

In one of Baron de Meyer's famous advertisements for Elizabeth Arden, a model resembling a figure from a Modigliani painting wears the Arden face. The name behind one of the century's greatest cosmetic houses was inspired by Tennyson's poem *Enoch Arden* and a love of the name Elizabeth. Her real name was Florence Nightingale Graham and she worked as a beauty treatment girl for Eleanor Adair in New York where, in 1910, she opened her own salon on Fifth Avenue with her signature red door. One of the first beauty gurus to encourage exercise, she opened a spa and health retreat in Maine in 1934, and was passionate about horses. Arden developed a range of make-up for Hollywood which would not melt under the lights and was later used by women when they were out dancing. In 1935 she launched the legendary Eight Hour Cream, which remains to this day a cult beauty product.

☛ C. James, de Meyer, Morris, de la Renta, Revson

Elizabeth Arden. b Woodbridge, ONT (CAN), 1878. **d** New York (USA), 1966. **Advertising campaign.** Photograph by Baron de Meyer, c1927.

Armani Giorgio Designer

A man and woman wear the hallmarks of a great modernist: tailoring that trades stiff formality for assured relaxation. Giorgio Armani laid the groundwork for the easy, minimalist working uniform of emancipated 1980s women and blazed the trail for designers such as Calvin Klein, Donna Karan and Jil Sander. His menswear was equally mould-breaking: taking the stuffing and stiffness out of the suit, he made the laid-back style of southern Europe coveted around the world. Armani was assistant to Nino Cerruti before starting his own business in 1973. His name came to the fore in 1980 when he dressed Richard Gere for the film *American Gigolo*. Every scene was choreographed to work for Armani's clothes, prompting Gere to ask, 'Who's acting in this scene, me or the jacket?' A good question. Giorgio Armani's fashion shows never use famous models, the designer preferring that his clothes receive the audience's unclouded attention.

☞ Abboud, Cerruti, Dominguez, Etro

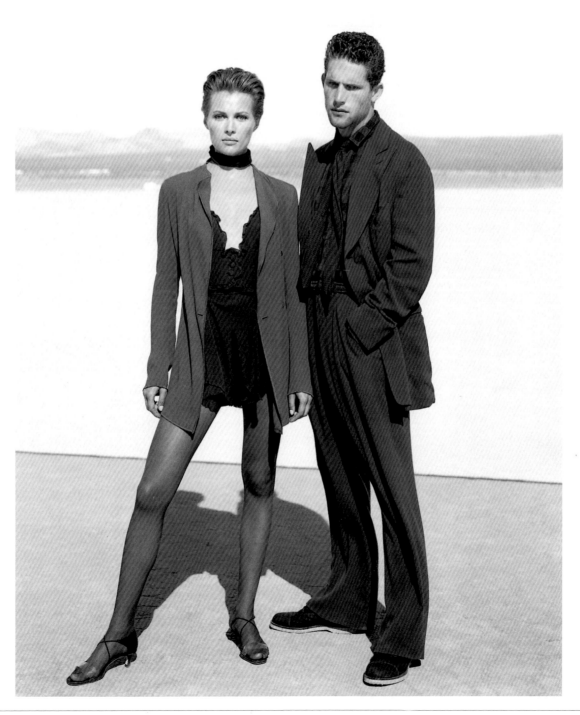

Giorgio Armani. b Piacenza (IT), 1934. **Unstructured tailoring. Spring/summer 1995.** Photograph by Peter Lindbergh.

Arnold Eve   Photographer

Eve Arnold's camera picks up the gold beaded skullcap, glossed lips and lacquered nails of a model backstage at a Lanvin show in 1977. Arnold rarely uses studios, relying instead on natural light and she is dependent on her hand-held Nikon. Her work is always respectful and sympathetic to its subject, background details are never an afterthought, and Arnold insists, 'You have to take advantage of the variables. It might be the smile, the gesture, the light. None of which you can predict'. She took pictures of black women modelling in Harlem fashion shows in 1948 and continued the project for two years, until *Picture Post* published her story. As a result, she was offered a job as the first female stringer for the Magnum Photos agency. A long friendship with Marilyn Monroe produced some of her best-known images. But Arnold's work covers a broad spectrum – 'everything from serious disaster to Hollywood hoop-la'.

☛ Lanvin, Lapidus, L. Miller, Stern

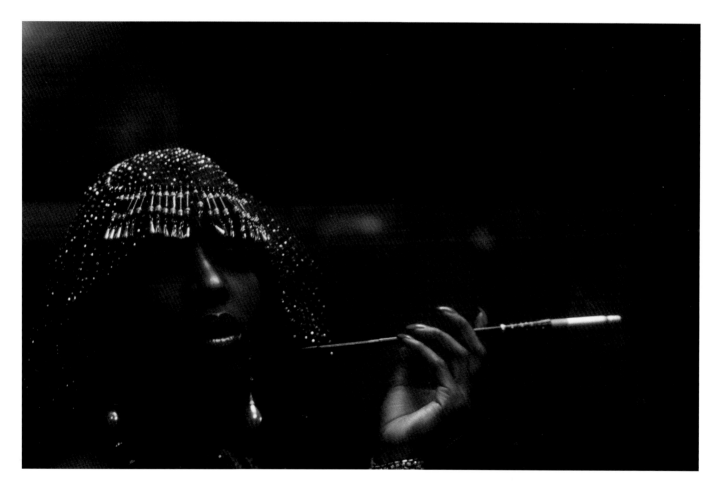

Eve Arnold. b Philadelphia, PA (USA), 1913. **Lanvin model at Mappins, Paris.** French *Vogue*, 1977.

Ascher Zika

Textile designer

In the long tradition of artists turning fabric designers, such as Dufy and Cocteau, the unmistakable sketches of Henry Moore are applied to silk by Zika Ascher. This design, which combines screen printing with batik painting, was selected for use by Nina Ricci. When *Vogue* asked in 1962, 'Which comes first, the chicken or the egg? The fabric or the fashion?' it could have had Ascher in mind. His innovative approach to fabrics revolutionized fashion from the 1940s. He started his own production company and silk-screen print works in London in 1942. In 1948 he approached artists such as Moore and Henri Matisse to design prints. His own inventive approach to textiles acted as a catalyst for fashion designers of that time: in 1952 his highly original large-scale floral prints were used by Dior and Schiaparelli, and in 1957 his shaggy mohair inspired Castillo to create huge enveloping coats.

☛ Castillo, Etro, Pucci, Ricci, Schiaparelli

Zika Ascher. b Prague (CZE), 1910. **Fabric designed by Henry Moore, 1945 (detail).** Photograph by Daniel McGrath.

Ashley Laura   Designer

A Victorian-inspired, white cotton dress worn under a floral pinafore sums up the mood of romantic rural idyll which made Laura Ashley a household name. She once said that she designed for women who wanted to look 'sweet': 'I sensed that most people wanted to raise families, have gardens and live as nicely as they can.' She used puffed sleeves, sprig prints, pin-tucking, lace trims and high collars to make romantic references to a pastoral lifestyle which in reality was a hard one for most. In a way that only fashion can, the look reinvented history and enabled women to dress for a role. It precipitated a movement known as 'milkmaidism'. In 1953, Ashley and husband Bernard began silk-screen printing textiles by hand in a small workshop in Pimlico, making table mats and napkins. In 1968 they opened their first shop, selling the basic Laura Ashley dress for £5. By the 1970s, it had become a symbol of femininity.

☛ Ettedgui, Fratini, Kenzo

Laura Ashley. b Merthyr Tydfil (UK), 1926. **d** Coventry (UK), 1985. **Dress with pinafore.** c1970.

Audibet Marc   Designer

This design is entirely about 'stretch'. There are no hooks, no eyes, no buttons and no zippers. It is a seamless, asymmetrical creation that clings to the body, following the lines of the model's figure. Audibet is both a fashion designer and an industrial designer, and is celebrated in the fashion world for his research into stretch fabrics. His expertise was acquired working as an assistant for Emanuel Ungaro and then as a designer for Pierre Balmain, Mme Grès and Nino Cerruti. An admirer of the work of Mme Vionnet and Claire McCardell, Audibet believes that fashion is a matter of anatomy and that innovation starts with fabrics. In 1987 he became textile adviser to the fabric and fibre company DuPont and together they created and launched single- and two-way stretch fabrics made from DuPont's 'Lycra' – the most important development in fashion in the 1980s.

☛ Alaïa, Bruce, Godley, Grès, Ungaro, Zoran

22

Marc Audibet. b Boulogne-sur-Seine (FR), 1958. **Stretch column.** Photograph by Tyen, American *Elle*, 1987.

Avedon Richard   Photographer

Penelope Tree is suspended in space, frozen in a joyful leap by Richard Avedon. It is an image that epitomizes the motion and emotion Avedon introduced into fashion photography, resisting the prevailing tradition of static poses. Instead he preferred the mood of street reality; a woman glimpsed on a busy pavement or the unexpectedness of his famous 'Dovima With Elephants'.

Influenced by photographer Martin Munkacsi, who explored the principle of the fashion figure in motion, Avedon established his images of dancing and swinging frenzy which have retained their freshness to this day. Avedon joined *Harper's Bazaar* in 1945, moving to *Vogue* in 1965. He never deserted fashion but, through his keen political convictions and intense interests in

subcultures, Avedon became a photographer in service to a vision larger than fashion *per se*.

☞ **Brodovitch, Dovima, Moss, Parker, Tree, Ungaro**

Richard Avedon. b New York (USA), 1923. **d** San Antonio, TX (USA), 2004. **Penelope Tree in Ungaro suit.** Paris studio, 1968.

Bailey David   Photographer

Jean Shrimpton, the face of the early 1960s, shares a confidence with Cecil Beaton, photographer, illustrator, costume designer and writer, whose influence on fashion spanned forty years. The photograph is by David Bailey. His shots of Jean Shrimpton, who he first met in 1960 and with whom he had a relationship for four years, let the world into an intimate bond between photographer and model. Bailey, who was regarded as a bad boy, used few models and developed long working relationships with them. His reluctance to be categorized as a fashion photographer is justified by time: those fashion shots now stand as legendary portraits in themselves. As Marie Helvin, model and former wife, put it, '...the very essence of Bailey's style is his refusal to allow his models to be simply clothes hangers or his pictures moments of fashion. He photographs women wearing clothes.'

☛ Beaton, French, Horvat, Shrimpton, Twiggy

24

David Bailey. b London (UK), 1938. Jean Shrimpton and Cecil Beaton. British *Vogue*, 1965.

Bailly Christiane　Designer

Christiane Bailly was part of the *prêt-à-porter* revolution of the 1960s. Her radical methods included experimenting with synthetic fabrics such as silver plastic and 'cigarette paper'. She took the stiff interlinings out of jackets for a more supple silhouette, and cut close-fitting clothes from black ciré in 1962. Bailly began her career as a model for Balenciaga, Chanel and Dior in 1957. Her interest in fashion developed and she entered design, working on more approachable clothes than those she had been modelling at the grand couture houses. In 1961 she started designing for Chloé and, after two years, moved on to work with Michèle Rosier. In 1962 Bailly formed a company with Emmanuelle Khanh, and both were assisted by a young Paco Rabanne. Their label, Emma Christie, produced revolutionary designs to critical acclaim and poor commercial success, but their role in the birth of French *prêt* was an important one.

☞ Bousquet, Betsey Johnson, Khanh, Lenoir, Rabanne

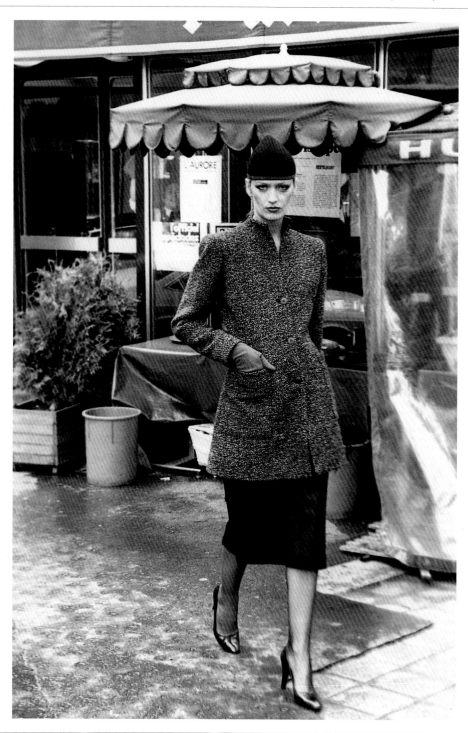

Christiane Bailly. b Lyons (FR), 1932. **Bouclé jacket and black wool skirt.** Photograph by Tim Jenkins, *Women's Wear Daily*, 1979.

Bakst Léon

Illustrator and designer

The overall effect of this costume is both classical and oriental. It reflects the current fashionable silhouette in its long, columnar shape. However, this severe line is softened by the lavish surface decoration, reminiscent of the East. Léon Bakst's contribution to the history of fashion came through the theatre. He collaborated with Sergei Diaghilev in the creation of the Ballets Russes which came to Paris in 1909. As its artistic director, Bakst designed the vibrantly coloured and exotic costumes. It was his designs for *Schéhérazade* which caused a sensation when it was performed in Paris in 1910. Orientalism in haute couture had already been successfully promoted by Paul Poiret. It was given further impetus by Bakst's sensual costumes, which had an extraordinary impact on Parisian fashion houses such as Worth and Paquin, who used his designs from 1912 to 1915. Bakst, like Erté, was a designer and an illustrator.

☛ **Barbier, Brunelleschi, Dœuillet, Erté, Iribe, Poiret**

26

Léon Bakst. b St Petersburg (RUS), 1866. **d** Paris (FR), 1924. **Design for Paquin.** Illustration, 1912.

Balenciaga Cristóbal

Layered bells form the sleeves of this cape, worn over a matching dress. They exemplify the shapely simplicity that made Cristóbal Balenciaga a great couturier. His genius lay in cut. The sack dress, the balloon dress, the kimono-sleeve coat and a collar cut to elongate the neck were a few of his fashion innovations, although his clothes also came with a disclaimer:

'No woman can make herself chic if she is not chic herself,' said Balenciaga. His Spanish severity contrasted with the light femininity of French designers; his favourite fabric was silk gazar, diaphanous but stiff, which satisfied his instinct for the sculptural. As early as 1938, Balenciaga's modern vision was influential, explained by *Harper's Bazaar* thus, 'Balenciaga abides

by the law that elimination is the secret of chic.' In 1968, after a battle against what he saw as the tide of vulgarity flowing through fashion, Balenciaga bowed out with the words, 'It's a dog's life.'

☛ Chow, Penn, Pertegaz, Rabanne, Snow, Thimister

27

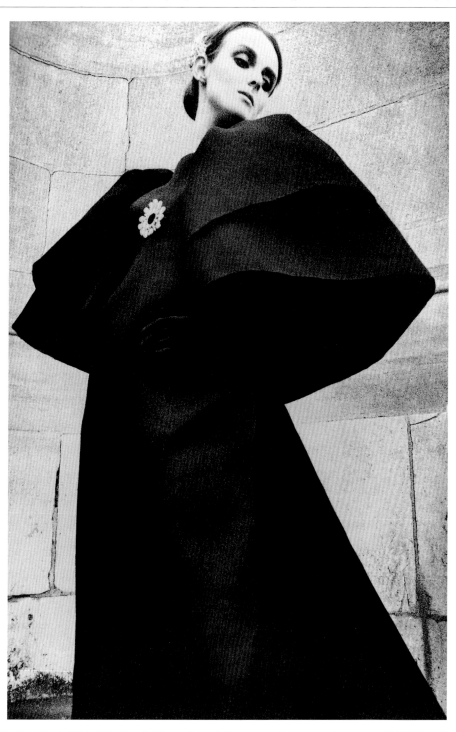

Cristóbal Balenciaga. b Guetaria (SP), 1895. **d** Valencia (SP), 1972. **Dress and cape. Autumn/winter 1964.** Photograph by Kublin.

Balla Giacomo   Designer

Although flat on the surface, this suit fuses movement, line and colour in a representation of the excitement of speed. Intrinsically forceful, the jagged strokes on the jacket, like storm-strewn palm leaves, mark high velocity and transmit energy. It gives us an image of an experimentalist at work. Balla, like fellow Futurists Severini and Boccioni, felt a positive need to extend his interests from the canvas to his environment, in this case exploring the subject of dress as a medium for expressing his Futurist ideas. Focusing more on male clothing, he stated the tenets of modernity in his 'Manifesto of Anti-Neutral Clothing', which aimed to bring disorder to the logic and communication of clothing. His ideas were based on asymmetry, clashing colours and juxtaposed forms that opposed tradition and convention. 'The past I so fiercely reject,' he said, embracing the industrial dynamics of modern art in his perception of fashion.

☛ Delaunay, Exter, Warhol

Giacomo Balla. b Turin (IT), 1871. d Rome (IT), 1958. **Sketch for men's suit, 1914.** Photograph by Giuseppe Schiavinotto, Rome.

Bally Carl Franz   Shoe designer

The continuity of fashion is illustrated by two examples of Bally's Mary Jane shoes, which are separated by fifty years. The delicacy of red suede, gold leather trim and diamond button was replaced by serviceable leather for the 1990s. Carl Franz Bally decided to mass-produce high-quality footwear after falling in love with a pair of shoes he found for his wife in Paris. The son of a silk ribbon weaver, Franz had taken over the family business, expanding the company to include an elastic tape that was used by shoemakers. While visiting one of his clients in Paris, he saw the inspirational shoes and bought the entire stock. 'Papa Bally' continued buying such shoes for his wife and later started to manufacture his own collections in his factory. The Bally style is a classic one and in the 1920s its Swiss quality made it an important player in the burgeoning ready-to-wear shoe market.

☛ Chéruit, Steiger, Vivier

Carl Franz Bally. b Schönenwerd (SW), 1821. d Schönenwerd (SW), 1898. Scarlet evening shoe, 1930, and brown leather reinterpretation, 1998.

Balmain Pierre   Designer

Mlle Laure de Noailles wears her debutante gown, with foaming tulle skirt, by Pierre Balmain. *Vogue* declared that 'eventful skirts' were his speciality; they were often embellished with embroidered motifs such as leaves, cherries or scrolls. Trained as an architect, Balmain believed that both professions worked to beautify the world, declaring couture to be 'the architecture of movement'. In 1931 he was appointed junior designer at Molyneux. He sold sketches to Robert Piguet, then worked at Lucien Lelong where he was joined by Christian Dior; they collaborated for four years. The pair nearly went into partnership together, but in 1945 Balmain left to establish his own house. Like Dior's New Look of 1947, Balmain's full-skirted silhouette was part of the new postwar luxury. His dresses were always carefully constructed. Signature details included drapery or a bow across the shoulders and fur hoods, muffs or trims.

☛ Cavanagh, Colonna, Dior, Lelong, Molyneux, Piguet

Pierre Balmain. **b** St-Jean-de-Maurienne (FR), 1914. **d** Paris (FR), 1982. **Mlle Laure de Noailles.** Photograph by Cecil Beaton, American *Vogue*, 1945.

Bandy Way

Make-up artist

Model Gia wears the perfect work of Way Bandy. Her light, translucent make-up was delivered with very few products. Usually working with liquid cosmetics, Bandy would mix his colours at home and tie them up in two small Japanese baskets. He was visionary in the formulations he used: his foundations were blended with eye drops that would tighten the pores, promoting the flawlessness he worked for. Blending was also very important to his work and Bandy named his dog Smudge after his refining technique. He was always perfectly made-up himself, turning up for fashion shoots wearing inconspicuous base and powder. For one night, however, Bandy demonstrated his skill by arriving at a Halloween party thrown by his friend Halston wearing the full, traditional kabuki face. As a friend remembered, 'He loved beauty and from those little bottles could come perfection in the form of lightness or the bizarre'.

☛ **Halston, Saint Laurent, Uemura**

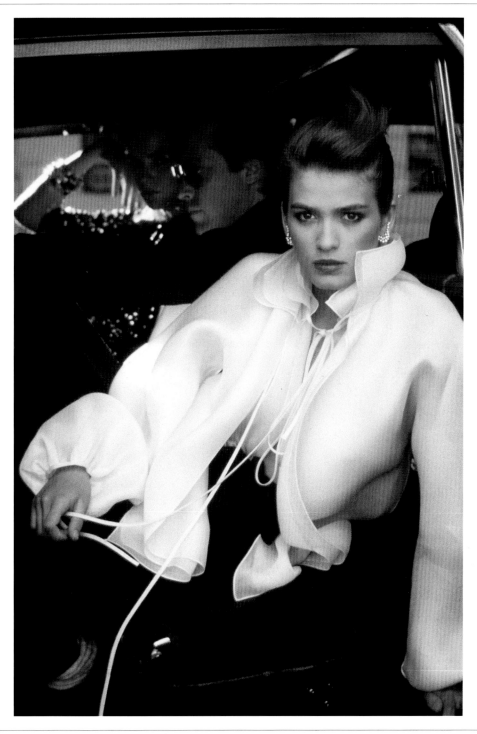

Way Bandy. b Birmingham, AL (USA), c1941. **d** (USA), 1986. **Gia.** Photograph by Arthur Elgort, 1978.

Banton Travis   Designer

Travis Banton's costume for Marlene Dietrich is from the film *Shanghai Express* (1932). He disguised her as a black swan in a costume of feathers, veiled and hung with ropes of crystal beads. Her handbag and gloves were specially made for her by Hermès; the hat was a John P. John creation. Banton regularly visited Paris; on one occasion, he bought up an entire stock of bugle beads and fish-scale paillettes reserved for Schiaparelli. In reparation, he sent her enough trim to complete her line for the season. Banton worked in couture in New York; his break came when he designed the costumes for Paramount's *The Dressmaker* from Paris in 1925, after which he became Paramount's designer-in-chief. He designed for Dietrich, Mae West, Claudette Colbert and Carole Lombard. One of his signatures was dressing women in men's clothes. He continued to run his successful couture business alongside costume designing.

☛ Carnegie, Hermès, John, Schiaparelli, Trigère

Travis Banton. **b** Waco, TX (USA), 1894. **d** Los Angeles, CA (USA), 1958. **Marlene Dietrich.** Still from *Shanghai Express.* 1932.

32

Barbier George   Illustrator

This fashion illustration shows two of Paul Poiret's models in a setting that represents one of his fashion houses. The evening coat on the right has a long train which falls from the shoulders and drops back at the sides like huge wings. It has an intricate design representing a stylized tree. A similar coat designed by Paul Poiret and called Battick was photographed by Edward Steichen and appeared in *Art et Décoration* in April 1911. The required headwear to be worn with the coat and equally exotic dress (with its high waistline reminiscent of the 'Directoire' line of late eighteenth-century France) was the turban, trimmed with pearls and surmounted by an aigrette. Barbier has united Poiret's simple classical line with the bold colours and design elements of his oriental style. Barbier was one of the great fashion artists, together with Paul Iribe and Georges Lepape, commissioned by Poiret to illustrate his fashions.

☛ **Bakst, Drian, Iribe, Lepape, Poiret, Steichen**

George Barbier. b Nantes (FR), 1882. **d** Nantes (FR), 1932. **Exotic coat and dress.** Cover of *Les Modes*. April 1912.

Barbieri Gian Paolo   Photographer

A woman in full, glamorous make-up wears the uniform of a meat market trader. It could be a reference to the model's work, but in a practical sense it is advertising a mesh vest which parodies the string version worn by working men. It is a typically dramatic example of Gian Paolo Barbieri's work. In 1997, he directed Vivienne Westwood's first-ever campaign which was based on the work of the sixteenth-century painter Holbein. For Barbieri this was more than fashion work. It was the creation of a filmic tableau which indulged all his passions: proportion, minute detail and a desire to seal the moment. In 1965 Barbieri photographed the first cover of Italian *Vogue*. His work for that magazine and others opened doors to advertising work for designers such as Valentino, Armani, Versace and Yves Saint Laurent. In 1978 the German magazine *Stern* named him as one of the fourteen most important image-makers of the time.

☛ Bourdin, Valentino, Westwood

Gian Paolo Barbieri. b Milan (IT), 1938. **Meat Market**. 1985.

Bardot Brigitte   Icon

Actress Brigitte Bardot sits under a tree, smoking moodily, her deshabille hair and au naturel appearance the epitome of amoral French sensuality. British *Vogue* called her 'the sensuous idol, a potent mixture of the sexy and the babyish, a seething milky bosom below a childish pout'. She was known simply as BB (the French pronounced it '*bébé*' – French for 'baby'), and the phrase 'sex kitten' was invented to describe her. Her narrow trousers and tight black sweater reflect the nonchalant beat style. She also popularized flat ballet pumps and set a trend for not wearing socks in her film *And... God Created Woman* (1956), for ruffles and ringlets, petticoats and prettiness in *Les Grandes Manoeuvres* (1955), and for Edwardian dress in *Viva Maria* (1965).

Jeanne Moreau wrote that Bardot, 'was the real modern revolutionary character for women'.

☞ Bouquin, Esterel, Féraud, Frizon, Heim

Brigitte Bardot. b Paris (FR), 1934. **Brigitte Bardot.** Photograph shot during the filming of *La Vie Privée*. 1961.

Barnett Sheridan Designer

A cool bride is transported to the church on a Harley Davidson. Her wedding outfit is by Sheridan Barnett, who graced the 1970s with lean, uncontrived fashion. Her cream jacket and skirt are spare of any detail other than Perspex buttons to fasten her jacket and patch pockets to carry her handkerchief. Barnett was almost architectural in his approach to clothes, demanding function and purity of line at a time when all around him were making additions – with embroidery, printing and appliqué fighting for space on dresses everywhere. Because function is more commonly found on menswear, Barnett often used it as a central theme. Although the bride's cloche hat is trimmed with net, a black pussy-cat bow is tied at her neck and her stockinged legs end in a pair of wedge sandals, that clean, masculine theme comes through in a jacket which is modelled on a classic, double-breasted blazer.

☛ **Albini, Bates, Wainwright**

Sheridan Barnett. **b** Bradford (UK), 1951. **Cream blazer and skirt.** Photograph by Peter Knapp, British *Vogue*, 1971.

Baron Fabien   Creative director

Fabien Baron's clean, clear layouts, allowing tangled graphics to float luxuriantly in vast areas of space, recall the power of Alexey Brodovitch's work and have set new standards in modern design. The son of a graphic designer, Baron started his career at *New York Woman* in 1982 and moved quickly to Italian *Vogue*. His first issue, September 1988, is now a collector's item.

He worked for eighteen months at *Interview* before being appointed creative director at Brodovitch's old home, *Harper's Bazaar*, of which he said, 'this was the only magazine left to do'. His style has been widely influential and Baron acknowledges, 'the look doesn't belong to me any more'. He directed Madonna's *Erotica* video and designed her metal-covered book, *Sex*.

The frosted vodka-bottle shape for Calvin Klein's unisex CK One perfume was also his creation. Klein says, 'We are on the same wavelength, except Fabien goes way beyond my capabilities of aestheticism.'

☛ Brodovitch, C. Klein, Madonna

Fabien Baron. b Antony (FR), 1959. **Collage of spreads.** From *Harper's Bazaar*, *Interview* and Italian *Vogue*. 1998.

Barrett Slim   Jewellery designer

In this swathe of chain links by Slim Barrett, jewellery becomes a garment with a piece which suggests both a draped necklace and a hood. Pierre Cardin and Paco Rabanne both used this theme by expanding dresses to become hybrids of fashion and jewellery, and here Barrett has done the same from his perspective as a jewellery designer. He returns intermittently to medieval themes – he helped Karl Lagerfeld by developing silver wire so fine that it could be knitted – and, in the 1990s, Barrett was responsible for the tiara's rise in popularity (particularly among brides). In his quest to extend the realm of costume jewellery, other catwalk collaborations (including those for Chanel, Versace, Montana and Ungaro), have resulted in the creation of plated body armour, waistcoats and skullcaps as vehicles for Barrett's work.

☛ Lagerfeld, Morris, Rabanne

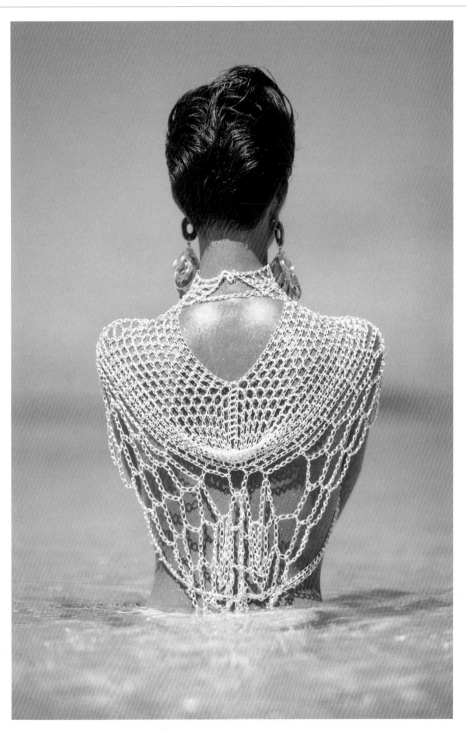

Slim Barrett. b Galway (IRE), 1960. **Chain mail torso in sterling silver.** Photograph by Philip Newton, British *Elle*, 1990.

Barthet Jean   Milliner

In a café scene from 1955, two women wear feminized boaters by Jean Barthet. They are coquettish yet formal accessories for tailored suits worn with gloves and pearls; a very proper combination for the period. While he designed in the traditional manner of the great French hat makers such as Caroline Reboux, who placed the emphasis on purity of line and structure, he also embellished his creations with trimmings that reflected his own imagination, in this case restrained velvet ribbons and bows. Barthet showed his first collection in 1949 and rose to become the most successful milliner in Paris, dressing the heads of Sophia Loren and Catherine Deneuve. His success was underlined by his membership of the Chambre Syndicale de la Couture Parisienne. He long collaborated with his colleagues, the fashion designers, including Claude Montana, Sonia Rykiel, Emmanuel Ungaro and Karl Lagerfeld.

☛ Deneuve, Hirata, Reboux

Jean Barthet. b The Pyrénées (FR), 1930. d 2000. 'Café Hats'. *La Donna*, 1955.

Bartlett John   Designer

A shirt is laid open at the throat and left untucked in the style of the 1950s. John Bartlett's aesthetic is a relaxed one. He thinks about clothing pictorially and his fashion shows have profound themes and narratives, often becoming essays in style. Bartlett trained at Willi Smith, a label historically known for its democratic attitude towards fashion, and he has developed a natural feel for sportswear. He began his menswear collections in 1992, adding womenswear five years later when he told *People*, 'My mission is to make women look sexy,' just as it is for men. He is said to be the American version of Thierry Mugler in sexy stories, but Bartlett adds something extra with his relish for the rhetoric of fashion, introducing his menswear collection for 1998 with the words, 'Imagine a world where *Forrest Gump* is directed by Otto Fassbinder...'

☛ Matsushima, Mugler, Presley, W. Smith

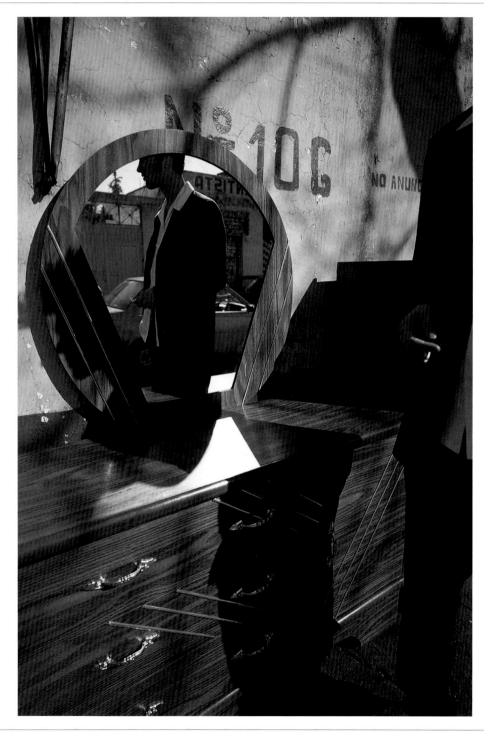

40

John Bartlett. b Cincinnati, OH (USA), 1963. **White open-neck shirt.** Photograph by Enrique Badulescu, *Arena*, 1997.

Bassman Lillian   Photographer

'I almost always focus on a long, elegant neck,' said Bassman of this photograph featured in *Harper's Bazaar*. Her shadowy, sensual pictures are known for their gentle intimacy: 'Women didn't have to seduce me the way they did male photographers. There was a kind of inner calm between the model and myself.' Her images were created by innovative printing techniques such as bleaching areas to give results that resembled charcoal drawings, recalling Bassman's early career as a fashion illustrator before being apprenticed to Alexey Brodovitch. Bassman's work is more evocative of moods than subjects and has not always been understood. Carmel Snow, former editor of *Harper's Bazaar*, once berated Bassman for photographing a diaphanous Piguet gown to resemble butterfly wings, saying, 'You are not here to make art, you are here to photograph buttons and bows' – a landmark in the debate about the purpose of fashion photography.

☛ **Brodovitch, Parker, Piguet, Snow**

41

Lillian Bassman. b New York (USA), 1917. **Barbara Mullen.** *Harper's Bazaar*, c1950.

Bates John   Designer

John Bates is photographed with two dramatic outfits from a 1979 collection. They both use silk cut away to reveal the torso – a charismatic theme based on shapes from the 1930s and 1940s. The black dress uses a geometrically bared midriff in a modern take on Carmen Miranda's trademark – a feature Bates had used in 1965 with his 'bikini dress', the two halves of which were joined with transparent netting. These squared-off shoulders minimize the hips and spaghetti ties are used as suggestively available fastenings. Decorative cocktail hats finish both outfits and lend them the highly co-ordinated, polished look of the 1930s. In the 1960s, Bates created 'the smallest dress in the world' and the black leather wardrobe for *The Avengers* television series.

His wide range of eveningwear, much of it ethnically inspired in the 1970s, was skilfully made and had a sophisticated youthfulness.

☛ Albini, Barnett, Burrows, N. Miller, Wainwright

John Bates. b Ponteland (UK), 1938. **John Bates with models. Spring/summer 1979.** Photograph by Chris Moore.

The Beatles Icons

The Beatles are credited with marketing the 'youthquake' look around the world. In 1962, while touring Germany, Stuart Sutcliffe's photographer girlfriend Astrid Kirchherr gave the group a co-ordinated image: matching 'moptop' haircuts like her own beatnik-style gamine cut. The following year, the Beatles' manager Brian Epstein contacted Soho tailor Dougie Millings, who recalled, 'I'd been experimenting with round collars. I did a sketch of one, showed it to Brian, and that was that. I've never claimed to have entirely "invented" it, I just came up with the suggestion.' In fact, the neat, collarless, high-neck, grey jackets with black trim had been inspired by Pierre Cardin. They became a trademark for the Beatles, worn with whip ties and pointed chelsea boots.

The Beatles hit the USA the following year and their girlfriends were credited with introducing America to the miniskirt.

☛ **Cardin, Leonard, McCartney, Sassoon, Vivier**

43

The Beatles. **John Lennon. b** Liverpool (UK), 1940. **d** New York (USA), 1980; **Ringo Starr (Richard Starkey). b** Liverpool (UK), 1940;
Paul McCartney. b Liverpool (UK), 1942; **George Harrison. b** Liverpool (UK), 1943. **d** Los Angeles (USA), 2001. **The Beatles, 1963.**

Beaton Sir Cecil   Photographer

Eight models in a spectacular neoclassical interior are wearing ball gowns by Charles James in this 1948 American *Vogue* editorial by Cecil Beaton. Its mood of elegant grandeur captures the spirit of Dior's New Look, which revolutionized fashion with its feminine romanticism and state-of-the-art construction. Dior claimed James had inspired the New Look and Beaton and James were lifelong friends. Beaton – photographer, illustrator, designer, writer, diarist and aesthete – captured the nuances of fashion and the fashionable from the 1920s until his death. In 1928 he began a long relationship with *Vogue*. Always in touch with the Zeitgeist, he developed accordingly, photographing the Rolling Stones, Penelope Tree and Twiggy in the 1960s. He was as much a part of Swinging London as they were. 'Fashion was his cocaine. He could make it happen. He sought the eternal in fashion,' wrote a friend after his death.

☞ Campbell–Walters, Coward, Ferre, Garbo, C. James

44

Sir Cecil Beaton. **b** London (UK), 1904. **d** Broadchalke (UK), 1980. **Dresses by Charles James, 1948.**

Beene Geoffrey   Designer

Geoffrey Beene is pictured with an outfit from 1975. His ivory shirt lies flat against the throat. The pleated trousers are 'not too wide, not too narrow' and the perfect coat to throw over it is a 'trench coat in beige cotton'. With their soft wrapping and pared-down functionality, Beene's creations were the epitome of simple elegance. While his dresses were sometimes seen as the American version of couture, Beene was ultimately a designer with a sportswear sensibility with a focus on comfort. Comfort was paramount and had been since his label was launched in 1963. His first collections used an easy fit for clothes designed for active women. Combining the simplicity of Vionnet with whimsy, he often worked with humble materials, including cotton piqué and sweatshirt fleece. Beene freely borrowed from menswear – collections included vests and fanciful ties – whilst the West met the East in his use of quilting, obi belts and layering.

☛ Blass, Miyake, Mizrahi, Vionnet

Geoffrey Beene. b Haynesville, LA (USA), 1927. d New York (USA), 2004. **Geoffrey Beene with model wearing stone mac and silk trousers.** Photograph by Deborah Turbeville, American *Vogue*, 1975.

Benetton   Luciano, Giuliana, Gilberto and Carlo   Retailers

Unusually for fashion advertising, the clothes in this photograph can barely be seen and are not the central focus of the picture. Two people of different races are handcuffed together but it is not clear who is handcuffed to whom, and why. 'I am not asked by Benetton to sell clothes' claims the photographer and former creative director Oliviero Toscani, 'The communication is a product in itself.' Such advertisements were an iconoclastic method of selling fashion. In the early 1980s Benetton's adverts had featured smiling young people of all nationalities, the 'United Colors of Benetton' catchline referring to both the cosmopolitan customers of their worldwide stores and the rainbow spectrum of knitwear and clothing.

Luciano Benetton, the family-run company's founder, admits these 1990s images contrast with its design philosophy: 'It is true our clothes are not at all extreme or controversial.'

☛ Fiorucci, Fischer, Strauss

46

Benetton. Luciano. **b** Treviso (IT), 1935; **Giuliana. b** Treviso (IT), 1937; **Gilberto. b** Treviso (IT), 1941; **Carlo. b** Treviso (IT), 1943. **Handcuffed.** Photograph by Oliviero Toscani, 1985.

Benito

Illustrator

Benito, one of the masters of fashion illustration of the Art Deco period, captured through his simple, supple strokes the statuesque women in their extravagant gowns who epitomized the 1920s. His outstanding characteristic was the extreme elongation of the figure to emphasize the elegance of the silhouette. His style was reminiscent of sixteenth-century Mannerist painting and of the Cubist paintings of Picasso and the sculptures of Brancusi and Modigliani. Benito was also noted for his inventive vignettes. The close links between fashion and interior decoration are shown with perfect clarity and create an Art Deco harmony of design, colour and line. Born in Spain, Benito went to Paris at the age of nineteen, where he established himself as a fashion artist. Along with Lepape, his illustrations for *Vogue* reflected the *haut monde* of the Jazz Age.

☛ **Bouché, Lepape, Patou, Poiret**

Benito (Eduardo García Benito). b Valladolid (SP), 1892. **d** Paris (FR), 1953. **Afternoon dress by Paul Poiret.** Drawing from *La Gazette du Bon Ton*, 1922.

Bérard Christian   Illustrator

As his painted caption reports, Bérard's subject in this rich watercolour sketch wears the train of her ruby velvet gown draped over a medieval chain slung around her hips. Like his close friend, Cocteau, Bérard was a master of many artistic media. He designed the stage-sets and costumes for several of Cocteau's plays. During the 1930s he turned his artistry to designing fabrics and to fashion illustration, becoming associated with Schiaparelli and Surrealism in fashion. His drawings appeared in *Vogue* for the first time in 1935. They were so well received that he worked for *Vogue* until his death in 1949. Also like Cocteau, Bérard's draughtsmanship is immediately recognizable by its very stumpy, spidery line that is liberally imbued with vivid colours. It was this lush style, enhanced by his vision of fashion as a kind of theatre, that he brought to his graphic work for *Vogue*. It was defined as romantic expressionism.

☛ Bouché, Cocteau, Creed, Dalí, Rochas, Schiaparelli

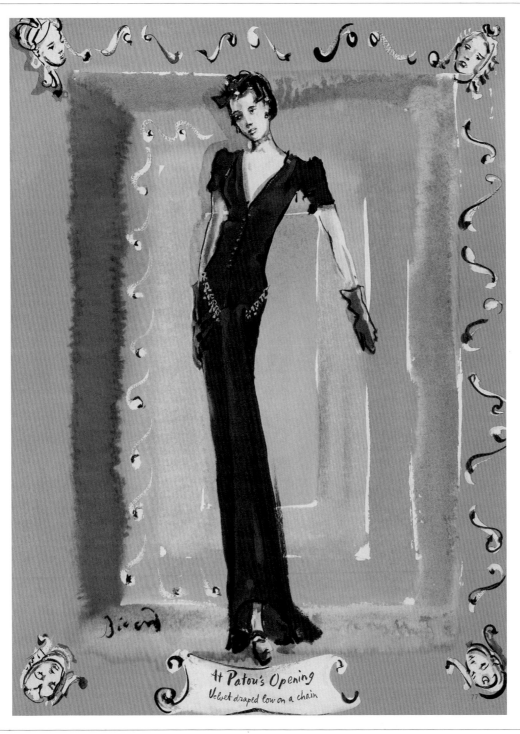

At Patou's Opening
Velvet draped low on a chain

Christian Bérard. b Paris (FR), 1902. d Paris (FR), 1949. **Dress by Patou.** American *Vogue*, 1938.

Berardi Antonio   Designer

Karen Elson wears a crepe dress smattered with astral embroidery. Its fluted, bias-cut skirt dips to the right to end in an asymmetric drape. Berardi's cutting techniques and decorative detailing have led him to be compared to John Galliano, with whom he trained for three years before finally being accepted as a student at Central Saint Martin's College of Art and Design in London (on his fourth attempt). Berardi's Italian roots manifest themselves in his love of traditionally crafted leather and hand-worked lace and macramé. Berardi's stunning leather pieces are decorated with embroidery and pierced with cutwork, specialist techniques that were reintroduced at a time when simplicity was being championed elsewhere. His light-as-air, lingerie-style pieces are intended to be flirtatious rather than vulgar. He describes his style as 'sensual, sexy and thought-provoking – and intrinsically feminine.'

☛ Chalayan, McDean, Pearl

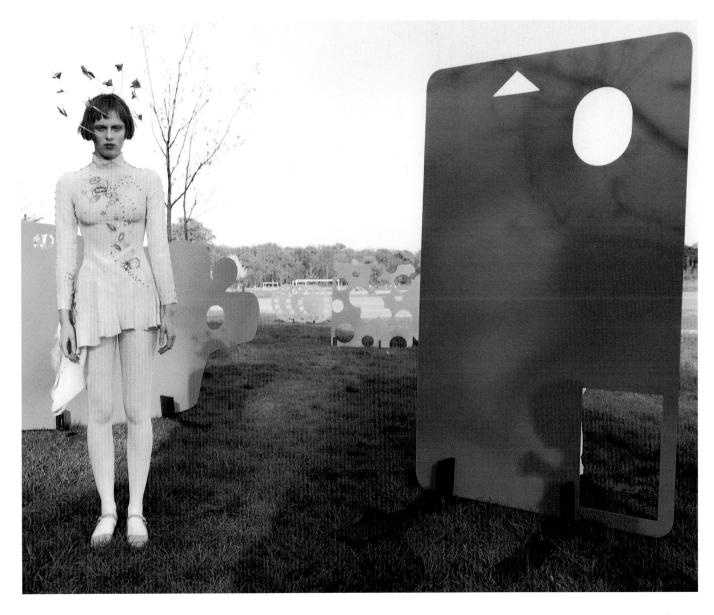

Antonio Berardi. b Grantham (UK), 1968. **Karen Elson wears pale blue, crepe dress.** Photograph by Craig McDean, Italian *Vogue*, 1997.

Beretta Anne-Marie Designer

In an abstract, graphic, red, white and black scheme, two leather coats are trimmed with Bs to signify the work of Anne-Marie Beretta. Her trademark is a play on proportions, from wide-collared coats to mid-calf-length trousers and asymmetrical lines, used here to break the conformity of these coats. The upper part of each letter is larger, throwing the emphasis onto the shoulders and thereby minimizing the widths of the models' hips. Beretta has used these techniques for many different collections, including ski-wear, but when she opened her own boutique in 1975 it was with business-like tailoring, similar in style to those collections she has since designed for the Italian label, MaxMara. Beretta wanted to pursue a career in fashion from an early age – by the time she was eighteen she was designing for Jacques Esterel and Antonio Castillo. In 1974 she established her own label.

☛ Castillo, Esterel, Maramotti

50

Anne-Marie Beretta. b Béziers (FR), 1937. **Leather 'B' coats.** *L'Officiel*, 1980.

Bergère Eric   Designer

These spare wrap dresses represent the self-assured work of Eric Bergère. Briefly apprenticed to Thierry Mugler, he arrived at Hermès aged just seventeen. It was Bergère who gave modernity to Hermès' luxury, using the then passé snaffle and H logo to add wit. In doing so, he famously created a camp, mink jogging suit. Bergère blends European humour and respect for tradition with the American sportswear sensibility. He has said, 'I like the work of Americans, like Anne Klein...very simple clothes, very elegant', and he keeps detail to a minimum, using a thin tie belt or a tiny bow on a knitted camisole top. His first collection under the Bergère label was tightly edited: twelve pieces of knitwear in three colours and one jacket in three different lengths. 'I want the jackets to be like cardigans, I try to make everything lighter – the finishings, the linings, the foundations – but they must still have a definite shoulder.'

☛ Evangelista, von Fürstenberg, Hermès, A. Klein

51

Eric Bergère. b Troyes (FR), 1960. **Shalom Harlow and Linda Evangelista wear black dresses.** Photograph by Mario Testino, *Visionaire*, 1997.

Bernard Augusta (Augustabernard)

During the 1930s there was a revival of interest in classical art and an evening gown was an especially suitable garment for re-creating the flowing movement of the draperies of Ancient Greek statues. It is this sculptural form and the long, floating line billowing out at the bottom that Man Ray captures in his photograph. Augusta Bernard enjoyed a successful career during the first half of the 1930s. A neoclassical evening gown she designed in 1932 was chosen by *Vogue* as the most beautiful dress of that year. Augusta Bernard belonged to that eminent band of couturières between the two World Wars which included Chanel, Vionnet, Schiaparelli, Louiseboulanger and the Callot Sœurs. Like Vionnet, she was a technician with a mastery of the bias cut. By cutting the fabric of the dress on the cross-grain, she achieved a fluidity which gave the evening gown great elasticity and a refined, draping quality.

☛ **Boulanger, Callot, Chanel, Schiaparelli, Vionnet**

52

Augusta Bernard. b Provence (FR). (Active 1930s.) **Bias-cut dress.** Photograph by Man Ray, *Harper's Bazaar*, 1934.

Berthoud François Illustrator

François Berthoud's startling illustration presents a woman in a stovepipe hat, her demonic eyes watching from the shadows. Berthoud uses linocuts and woodcuts for his melodramatic work. They are brave and unusual methods for fashion illustration, which usually demands flowing lines. But these approaches suit the sharp contours of contemporary fashion, lending strength and drama to the simplest garment. Berthoud studied illustration in Lausanne and, after receiving his diploma in 1982, moved straight to Milan where he worked for Condé Nast. He later became heavily involved in the visual appearance of *Vanity* magazine, a publication that showcased illustration, designing many of their covers. In the 1990s Berthoud's enduring illustrations have appeared in the New York-based style quarterly *Visionaire*.

☛ Delhomme, Eric, S. Jones

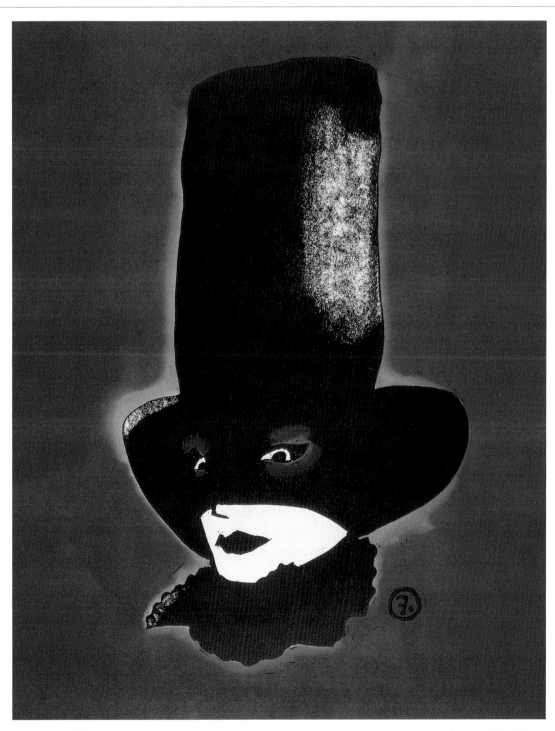

François Berthoud. b Lausanne (SW), 1961. **Woman with hat.** Woodcut, *Mondi*, 1993.

Bettina

Model

Wearing a sharply constructed black dress by Christian Dior, the French model gives a pose of polished *froideur*. Bettina's gamine beauty is unique in having inspired three designers over two generations. Born in Brittany, the daughter of a railway worker, Simone Bodin dreamed of becoming a fashion designer. She took her drawings to the couturier Jacques Costet, who took her on as his model and assistant. When the house closed, she moved to Lucien Lelong, employer of Christian Dior, who then invited her to join him in his own house. She refused, choosing to work for Jacques Fath instead. He renamed her Bettina and made her 'the face' of his scent Canasta, which was launched in 1950. Her fame took her to America where *Vogue* loved her 'Gigi' looks, and 20th Century Fox offered her a seven-year contract which she declined. In 1955 she left modelling, returning three decades later as muse (and best friend) of Azzedine Alaïa.

☛ Alaïa, Dior, Fath, Lelong

Bettina (Simone Bodin). b Laval (FR), 1925. **Christian Dior cocktail dress. Autumn/winter 1952.** Photograph by Frances McLaughlin-Gill.

Biagiotti Laura   Designer

The fluid spirit of Italy's 'Queen of Cashmere' is illustrated by René Gruau in 1976. His easy lines imitate the composed chic for which Laura Biagiotti is known: the sweater worn with lean tailoring and an open-necked shirt. Biagiotti read archaeology at university in Rome and worked in her mother's small clothing company after graduation. In 1965 she founded her company, with partner Gianni Cigna. It manufactured and exported clothing for the eminent Italian fashion designers Roberto Capucci and Emilio Schuberth. As the company grew, so did Biagiotti's aspiration to design herself. She presented a small but successful womenswear collection for the first time in 1972. Designing with comfort as a priority, Biagiotti became known for working with fabrics of exceptional quality, especially cashmere in the most subtle colours – a blueprint later used by Rebecca Moses.

☛ Capucci, Gruau, Moses, Schuberth, Tarlazzi

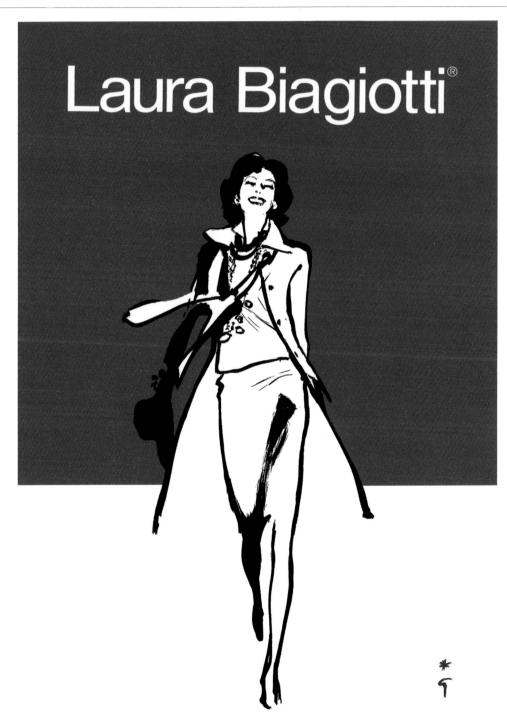

Laura Biagiotti. b Rome (IT), 1943. **Daywear.** Illustration by René Gruau, 1976.

Bikkembergs Dirk

Designer

'A classic suit which a businessman wears has nothing to do with fashion. For me, fashion should not be about business,' says Dirk Bikkembergs, whose own suits use unconventional cut and fastenings. This jacket has an asymmetric cut fastened with two distant buttons which suggests both militaristic and workwear themes. Having graduated with avant-garde contemporaries Ann Demeulemeester and Martin Margiela, Bikkembergs started out as a shoe designer in 1985. He made his name with a sturdy boot which has no eyelets and whose laces are threaded through the sole. The Bikkembergs aesthetic uses dark colours and heavy fabrics for his solid silhouettes, which lend them an urban appeal. He says, 'I design strong clothes for strong individuals rather than wrapping up pretentious nerds in sophisticated cashmere,' and his visual references often include macho stereotypes.

☛ Demeulemeester, Fonticoli, Margiela, Van Noten

56

Dirk Bikkembergs. b Bonn (GER), 1959. **Suit.** Photograph by Michel Comte, 1997.

Birtwell Celia

Textile designer

Actress Jane Asher sits amidst the jumble of accessories and kooky paraphernalia of a London boutique in 1966. She wears a printed paper minidress by Ossie Clark, another variation of which hangs on the wall behind her. The print is by Celia Birtwell, who decorated the fabric used by her husband Clark, and the 'paper' is a prototype of that used by Johnson & Johnson for J-cloths. Birtwell's stylized, sometimes psychedelic, florals with striped borders were also used for flowing fabrics resurrected from the 1930s, such as crepe and satin. Her lavish, two-dimensional style, which suited the fantastical and semi-historical fashion of the late 1960s and early 1970s, was part of a print explosion. Birtwell's bohemian mixture of Indian and traditional English themes was an expression of the wealthy, young Chelsea society around her, which was exploring the trail to Goa at the same time as inheriting the English countryside.

☛ Clark, Gibb, Pollock

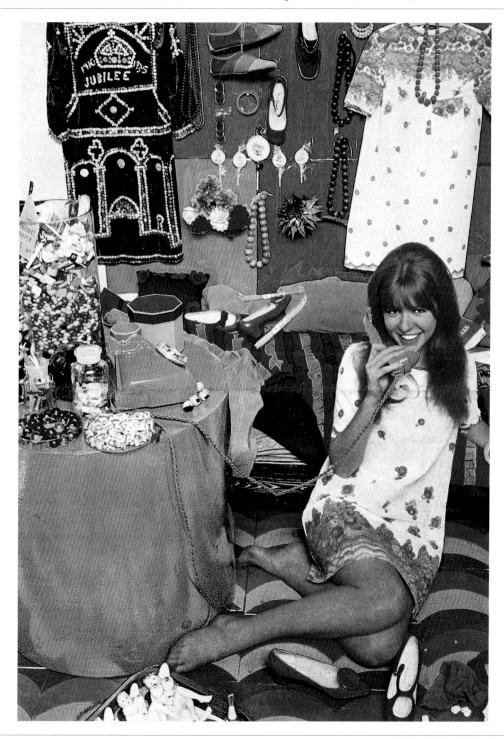

Celia Birtwell. b Bury (UK), 1941. **Jane Asher wears screen-printed paper minidress.** Photograph by Brian Duffy, 1966.

Blahnik Manolo Shoe designer

Rude and nude, but executed with as much refinement as a queen's coronation slipper, Manolo Blahnik's sexy sandal is made out of black leather. The transforming powers of Blahnik's shoes have become legendary. They are said to lengthen the leg from the hip all the way down to the toe cleavage. The secret lies in balance and taste; neither proportion nor degree of fashionability ever stray into vulgarity, thereby upsetting Blahnik's careful blend of beauty, style and function. He left the Canary Islands to study literature at the University of Geneva and art at the École du Louvre in Paris. During a trip to New York in 1973, an appointment with famous American *Vogue* editor Diana Vreeland inspired him to settle in London and open his first shop. Blahnik's influential shoe designs are, for many fashion designers such as John Galliano, the sole choice for catwalk collections.

☞ Coddington, Galliano, Tran, Vreeland

58

Manolo Blahnik. b Santa Cruz (CI), 1942. 'Lara'. Autumn/winter collection 1997. Illustration by Manolo Blahnik.

Blair Alistair   Designer

With deftness, Alistair Blair turns satin and velvet into a gracious evening outfit. The jacket rolls outward with the help of quilted facings and is cleverly cut to follow the waist inwards. Blair trained with Marc Bohan at Christian Dior, before moving on to assist Hubert de Givenchy and Karl Lagerfeld at Chloé. After six years in Paris, his ready-to-wear had taken on the quality and glamour of continental couture. Of his first own-label collection in March 1989, Blair said, 'The designing was absolutely the easiest part – it's what I enjoy'. He provided grown-up glamour during the eccentric streetwear boom of the 1980s. His use of luxurious fabrics such as cashmere, duchesse satin, grey flannel and kid leather brought a nostalgic quality to his carefully edited designs. Since 1995 he has designed for Louis Féraud, claiming, 'Today women want more than adoration from a designer – they want insight'.

☛ Bohan, Cox, Féraud, Tran

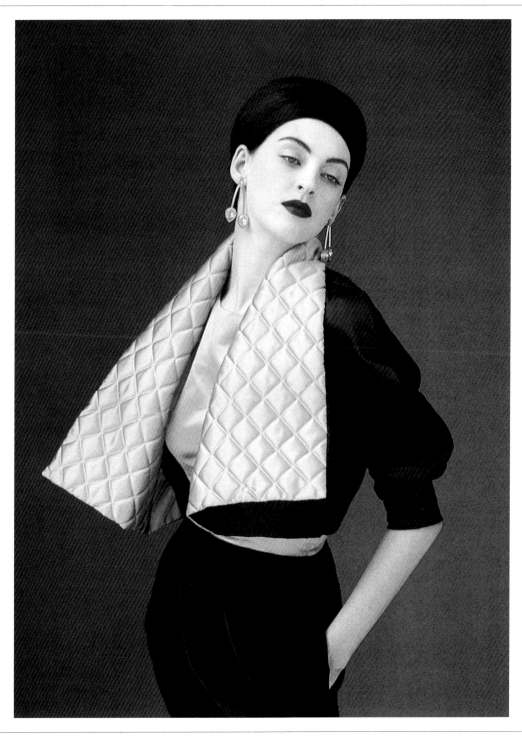

Alistair Blair. b Helensburgh (UK), 1956. **Quilted satin evening jacket.** Photograph by Ian Thomas, *Harpers & Queen*, 1987.

Blass Bill   Designer

Three distinctly American graces capture the essence of Blass's high-style sportswear. Urbane and Europe-aware, but definitely easy to wear and pared-down in ornament, Blass's separates for day and evening, and his dresses for what used to be called the cocktail hour captured the American spirit in functional, elegant clothing. Blass perpetuated the traditions of Norman Norell and Hattie Carnegie in providing smart, simplified sophistication for American women. Sweater dressing, even for evening gowns, was a Blass signature; layering and the harmony of rich materials, from silk to cashmere, are favoured. Witty references to menswear or vernacular dress were also frequent in Blass. Often referred to as the 'dean of American designers', Blass was one of the last of the designers consistently delivering classic good taste, filtering fashion's fluctuations through a fine sieve.

☞ **Alfaro, Beene, Roehm, Sieff, Underwood**

Bill Blass. b Fort Wayne, IN (USA), 1922. **d** New Preston, CT (USA), 2002. **Heavy, white, silk crepe dresses with bugle beads. Spring/summer 1984.** Photograph by Gideon Lewin.

Blumenfeld Erwin   Photographer

Legs are wrapped in damp muslin; this is not a fashion image but a beauty one. This photograph by Erwin Blumenfeld is reminiscent of his first art success, a suite of collages and altered images in the style of Berlin Dada. His late work in New York was equally cryptic, often obscuring the nude with smoke, mirrors and shadows, and implying spiritual forms through reference to the body. In between, in a series of photographs in *Vogue* and *Harper's Bazaar* in the 1930s through to the 1960s, he addressed fashion, but often subjected icons of beauty to his own obscurities and emendations. He allowed body parts to stand for the whole (most famously in a cover image of lips and eye for *Vogue* in January 1950), rendering fashion misty and mystical.

Blumenfeld came to fashion at the age of forty-one. He was an experimenter who reserved his admiration, and film, for the work of great designers such as Balenciaga and Charles James.

☛ Dalí, Hoyningen-Huene

61

Erwin Blumenfeld. **b** Berlin (GER), 1897. **d** Rome (IT), 1969. **Solarized Legs.** Paris, c1937.

Bohan Marc   Designer

In the preamble to Marc Bohan's show for Christian Dior, the designer and his model, wearing a slim cardigan jacket over a belted dress, pose for American *Vogue*. Bohan won plaudits for restoring haute couture to the tradition set by the grand couturiers, when he was appointed chief designer and artistic director of the house of Dior in succession to Yves Saint Laurent in 1960.

He was of his time, however, and was able to communicate a youthful spirit. His collection for winter 1966, influenced by the film *Doctor Zhivago*, started the craze for fur-trimmed, belted tweed coats worn with long, black boots. Marc Bohan gained valuable practical experience in fashion from his mother, who was a milliner. Between 1945 and 1958 he worked for the

fashion houses of Piguet, Molyneux and Patou. Having left Dior in 1989, he moved to London where he was enlisted in an attempt to revive the house of Norman Hartnell.

☛ Blair, Dior, Hartnell, Molyneux, Patou, Piguet

62

Marc Bohan. b Paris (FR), 1926. **Marc Bohan and model.** Photograph by Deborah Turbeville, American *Vogue*, 1975.

Bouché René   Illustrator

Working in pen and ink, Bouché was a master at blending fashion and society. Two attenuated figures are silhouetted against an empty background like a *tableau vivant*. They are linked by their large, fur muffs. With his vivacious and witty line, Bouché has revealed these fashionable women and their elegant clothes and has expressed their character, their manner and a sense of occasion. It is a throwaway style but the informal virtuosity of Bouché as a fashion illustrator was combined with a skilful training in painting, drawing and portraiture. Bouché illustrated the pages of *Vogue* during the 1940s, 1950s and early 1960s, and had a particular flair for communicating the relationship between clothes and wearers with accuracy and humour. The prestige of *Vogue* was due in large measure to the revival of fashion illustration by artists of the calibre of Benito, Eric, Christian Bérard, René Gruau and René Bouché.

☞ **Balmain, Benito, Bérard, Eric, Gruau**

René Bouché. b (FR), 1906. d (UK), 1963. **Two suits by Pierre Balmain.** Illustrated in American *Vogue*, 1945.

Boué Sylvie and Jeanne (Boué Sœurs)

A delicate lace and embroidered lawn tea gown is caught up on the hips with a threaded silk sash. Roses decorate the shoulders and, as was customary, the hem dips either side to create the impression of swags. The Paris couture house of the Boué Sœurs flourished at the beginning of the twentieth century, together with those of Paul Poiret, the Callot Sœurs and Mme Paquin. During the First World War the Boué Sœurs moved to New York, where John Redfern and Lucile had already opened branches of their businesses. The Boué Sœurs, who contributed much to the city's high fashion, were renowned for their romantic designs which often borrowed details from costume found in historical paintings. Their garments, sometimes reminiscent of underwear as here, were made in luscious fabrics such as paper taffetas and silk organdies and were ornately decorated.

☛ Callot, Duff Gordon, de Meyer, Paquin, Redfern

Sylvie Boué. b (FR), 1880; Jeanne. b (FR), 1881. (Active 1910s–1930s.) (Boué Sœurs.) **Tea dress.** c1920.

Boulanger Louise (Louiseboulanger)   Designer

Lace and tulle is projected as the backdrop for a dress whose bodice is so fine that it appears almost gaseous. Louise Boulanger was very much influenced by the work of her contemporary, Madeleine Vionnet. She imitated with finesse Madame Vionnet's use of the bias, cutting diagonally across the grain of the fabric to achieve a seamless, flowing movement. She was noted for launching graceful evening gowns that had skirts which were knee-length in front and reaching to the ankles at the back. Another of her trademarks was elegantly tailored suits worn with hats designed by Caroline Reboux. Louise Boulanger learned her craft as a thirteen-year-old apprentice with Madame Chéruit. In 1923 she opened her own fashion house, whose name was an amalgam of her first and last names. With her svelte figure, she was a couturière in the manner of Coco Chanel.

☛ **Bernard, Chéruit, Reboux, Vionnet**

Louise Boulanger. b Paris (FR), 1878. d c1950. (Louiseboulanger.) **Black tulle and corded silk dress.** Photograph by Cecil Beaton, British *Vogue*, 1935.

Bouquin Jean   Designer

'Hippie deluxe' is the phrase which will forever be linked with Jean Bouquin's clothes and lifestyle. Although he dabbled in fashion for just seven years, Bouquin captured the bohemian spirit of St Tropez's jet-set society at the end of the 1960s. This photograph from French *Vogue* epitomizes Bouquin's vision: a natural woman, draped with beads, who lives an ironically privileged hippie life wearing a luxurious interpretation of the nonconformist's uniform, all sold in Bouquin's boutique. Her printed panne velvet minidress uses drawstrings, borrowed from Indian pyjamas, at the cuffs, and ends just shy of the bikini bottoms she might have worn underneath it. After his success in St Tropez, Bouquin opened a second shop in Paris called Mayfair, which continued his theme of relaxed 'non-dressing'. He retired from the fashion business in 1971 to enjoy his social life.

☛ Bardot, Hendrix, Hulanicki, Porter, Veruschka

Jean Bouquin. b Paris (FR), 1936. **Panne velvet dress with beads.** Photograph by Henry Clarke, French *Vogue*, 1970.

Bourdin Guy

Photographer

An exercise of self-satisfaction, stimulated by the looks of John Travolta, mirrors the 1970s obsession with sex, individuality and status. The glamour of sheer fabrics and flashing make-up serves as a canvas for Guy Bourdin's cold yet unmistakably sexual vision. Daringly showing the symbiosis between savvy disco decadence and stardom, this image is finely in tune with the psyche of Bourdin's times. A Pop-Surrealist, he began to work for French *Vogue* in 1960, recommended by photographer Man Ray and couturier Jacques Fath. He concentrated on editorial work for this publication alongside advertising campaigns for Charles Jourdan shoes and Bloomingdales' lingerie range. An obsessive master colourist, Bourdin is said to have left actress Ursula Andress lying naked on a glass table for six hours while searching around Paris for the right shade of rose petals to match her skin.

☛ Barbieri, Fath, Jourdan, Man Ray

Guy Bourdin. b Paris (FR), 1928. d Paris (FR), 1991. **Advertising campaign for Charles Jourdan.** 1979.

Bourjois Alexandre Napoléon

Cosmetics creator

The fashionably blanched face of the 1920s is given colour by one of the first cosmetics companies, Bourjois, which was launched in Paris in 1863. Alexandre Napoléon Bourjois originally created his powders with the theatre in mind, and he sold them from a barrow. The dusty texture of his Rouge Fin de Théâtre was completely different from the greasepaint available at the time, and soon he was the official supplier to the Imperial theatres. Fashionable Parisiennes, taking their cue from actresses and courtesans, began to use his cosmetics. Bourjois repackaged his rice powder, Fard Pastels, in little card pots stamped with the legend 'Fabrique Spéciale pour la Beauté des Dames'. Bourjois set a precedent for printing phrases and quotes on the boxes and, famously, in 1947 it was 'Women will Vote'. One of the original colours, Cendre de Roses Brune, is still a bestseller, and the distinctive rose-water scent remains unchanged.

☛ Brown, Factor, Uemura

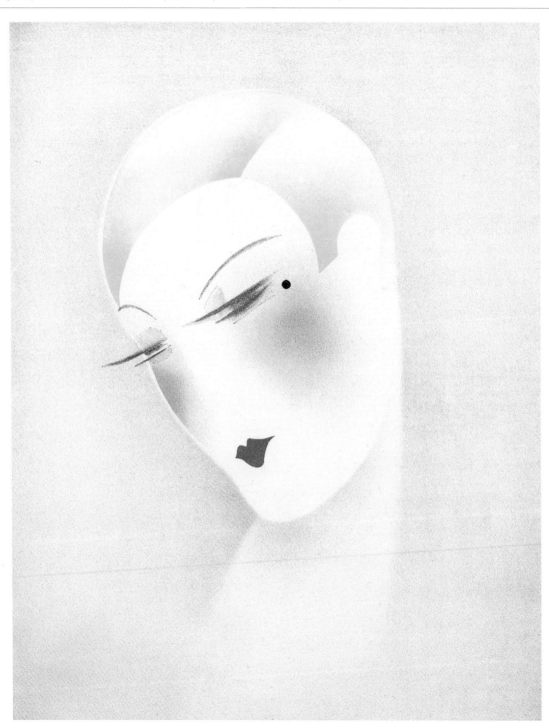

Alexandre Napoléon Bourjois. b Tours (FR), 1845. d Paris (FR), 1893. **Pastel face**. Illustration, 1927.

68

Bousquet Jean (Cacharel)

Designer

In a bizarre scene created by photographer Sarah Moon, a plaid pinafore by Cacharel is worn by a doll-like figure who lies on a vast sewing machine. The designer of the pinafore was Jean Bousquet, who named his company Cacharel after a species of wild duck. The company's aim was to represent a wild, free image which rejected the formality of clothing favoured by older generations. As such, Bousquet was part of the new ready-to-wear scene in Paris along with Christiane Bailly and Michèle Rosier. Emmanuelle Khanh, who went on to succeed in her own right, styled for Cacharel. In 1961 the company produced a blouse constructed without bust darts. The result was a best-selling fitted shirt. In 1965 Bousquet signed an agreement with Liberty to use its floral designs in his own contemporary colourways. Cacharel became known for semi-casual, matching separates which captured the Zeitgeist by bringing relaxed styles into broader use.

☛ Bailly, Khanh, Liberty, Moon, Rosier, Troublé

Jean Bousquet. b Nîmes (FR), 1932. (Cacharel.) **Plaid dress. Fashion show invitation, spring/summer 1982.** Photograph by Sarah Moon, 1982.

Bowery Leigh   Icon

Leigh Bowery approached dressing as a creative, artistic act, although whether his 'Redbeard with Aerosol Tops' from winter 1987 is 'art' or not is a matter of opinion. Part voodoo, part clown, Bowery's surreal and often disturbing costumes were always highly creative. 'I am in this odd area between fashion and art,' he said. He described his work as 'both serious and very funny'.

Bowery arrived in London in 1980 during the New Romantic era. He dressed up for the first time at an Alternative Miss World contest, and was delighted to find himself the centre of attention. Later he hosted the gay nightclub Taboo, continually reinventing himself and always trying to 'improve' on his previous outfit. An expert tailor, Bowery collaborated with Rifat Ozbek,

although posterity will remember him as a sitter for the painter Lucian Freud.

☛ N. Knight, Ozbek, Van Beirendonck

70

Leigh Bowery. b Melbourne (ASL), 1962. **d** London (UK), 1994. **Leigh Bowery.** Photograph by Nick Knight, *i-D* magazine, 1987.

Bowie David   Icon

Wearing a glittering knitted unitard, David Bowie plays Aladdin Sane. He used clothes as costumes for his stage personae, each one representing a phase and an album: from *Ziggy Stardust's* tight metallic spacesuits and wild plastic quilted bodysuits by Kansai Yamamoto to a sleek suit and tie for his 'plastic soul' disco album, *Young Americans*. He said of his inventions, 'The important fact is that I don't have to drag up. I want to go on like this long after the fashion has finished...I've always worn my own style of clothes. I design them. I don't wear dresses all the time either. I change every day. I'm not outrageous. I'm David Bowie.' At times he was a sexually ambiguous figure, using make-up and hair dye to achieve these characters and in doing so inspiring the New Romantic movement. Bowie's interest in fashion continued in the 1990s with his slightly less theatrical outfits designed by Alexander McQueen and his marriage to model Iman.

☛ **Boy George, Iman, McQueen, K. Yamamoto**

David Bowie (David Jones). b London (UK), 1947. **David Bowie.** Photograph by Bill Orchard, 1973.

Boy George

Icon

Boy George holds a home-made George doll given to him by a Japanese fan. Like him, it wears a theatrical outfit from 1984. With his Hasidic Jew's hat, dreadlocks, face of a geisha, loose-fitting Islamic-style shirt, checked trousers and hip hop shoes by Adidas, George represented an eclectic, home-styled approach invented in the squats and clubs around London. It was a fashion born of necessity. Students and the unemployed spent their days making ever-more exotic outfits to wear at night. The clubs, such as Taboo, had rigorous door policies – issuing humiliating rejections for those who had not made the effort – and they became a spawning ground for designers such as Body Map, John Galliano and John Flett. George, who was a central character, had been inspired by the androgynous costumes of David Bowie. He styled himself 'Boy George' to clear the confusion his dresses created amongst the wider public.

☛ Bowie, Dassler, Flett, Forbes, Stewart, Treacy

Boy George (George O'Dowd). b Bexleyheath (UK), 1961. **Boy George wears Dexter Wong.** Photograph by Brian Aris, 1984.

Brodovitch Alexey   Art director

Two cotton dresses are made exciting by placing them against a speeding foreground and background, like lambs playing amongst the rush-hour traffic. Alexey Brodovitch, who commissioned and laid out these pictures, brought a new informality and spontaneity to magazine design. Based on European graphic modernism, his years as art director of *Harper's Bazaar* (from 1934

to 1958), brought life to fashion photography. By creating complementary typographic images to put next to a picture, producing two-page spreads and using multiple images (a single woman photographed several times running across the page), Brodovitch invented the modern lexicon of art directors. His credo was 'Astonish me!' Richard Avedon, Hiro and Lillian Bassman were

a few of his favoured photographers and his Design Laboratory in Philadelphia was a workshop 'for studying new materials, new ideas...in order to establish new devices for the future'.

☛ Avedon, Baron, Bassman, Hiro, Snow

Uncommon Cottons—Embroidered and Marbled

• It takes an uncommonly knowing eye, these days, to know what's cotton and what isn't. The coat on our Junior cover, for instance: cotton looking uncommonly like tweed. And here, cotton embroidered so thickly it stands by itself or, above, cotton piqué, waffled and printed in marbly whorls. There's more here than just new surfaces, too: these cottons are ready to start spring now, ride on through Indian summer.
• The overall dress, opposite, in coppery red, encrusted with embroidery. About $25. And the properly workmanlike striped shirt that goes with it, about $7. Both by Loomtogs; Wamsutta cotton, Altman; Harzfeld's; Joseph Magnin; Sakowitz. Hat by Madcaps; M M satchel. The traffic: new 1955 Dodges.
• Print in three dimensions, above, black and white waffle piqué bound off in cotton satin. By Lanz Originals; cotton piqué by Everfast. About $35. Bonwit Teller; L. S. Ayres; Sakowitz. Hat by Madcaps.

HARPER'S BAZAAR, MARCH 1955

Alexey Brodovitch. **b** (RUS), 1898. **d** Le Thor (FR), 1971. **Fashion spread.** Design for *Harper's Bazaar*, 1955.

Brooks Daniel, John, Elisha and Edward (Brooks Brothers) Retailers

From Wall Street to Capitol Hill, the oldest retail clothing company in America has been catering to the Establishment since 1818. Brooks Brothers pioneered men's ready-to-wear, with an emphasis on soft construction and ease. Its unmistakable air of traditionalism has not prevented Brooks Brothers from introducing some of the principal innovations in American men's clothing.

Bermuda-length shorts and the classic pink shirt first hit the American shores through their stores. Brooks also brought over the button-down shirt collars worn by polo players in England, instituted madras fabric for shirts (originally designed for British officers in India), and introduced the Brooks Shetland sweater and their trademark Polo coat in white, camel or grey with

mother-of-pearl buttons and a full belt. Ralph Lauren's early work experience for Brooks Brothers was a crucial influence in shaping his own label's style.

☛ **Burberry, Hilfiger, Lauren**

Brooks. Daniel. b New York (USA), 1809. **d** (USA), 1884; **John. b** New York (USA), 1813. **d** (USA), 1899; **Elisha. b** New York (USA), 1815. **d** (USA), 1876; **Edward. b** New York (USA), 1821. **d** (USA), 1875. (Brooks Brothers.) **Button-down collars. Spring/summer 1998.**

Brown Bobbi

Cosmetics creator

In the early 1990s, Bobbi Brown provided an antidote to the exotic colours used throughout fashion. From beige to bitter chocolate, her earthy colours reflect natural beauty. They are achieved through a whole range of cosmetic products, without camouflaging ethnicity, age or skin tone. It is a method that looks to the skin for its lead: eye shadow that does exactly that and lipstick which accentuates rather than masks natural colour. Brown is simple, straightforward and basic. 'Make-up is not rocket science,' she says, downplaying the hype of make-up as an art form. With her degree in theatrical make-up and extensive catwalk and editorial work, Brown started on a small scale with ten neutral-toned lipsticks. While the beauty colourscape has radically altered, Brown remains true to her plain-spoken philosophy.

☛ Bourjois, Lauder, Page

Bobbi Brown. b Chicago, IL (USA), 1957. **Bridget Hall.** Photograph by Walter Chin, 1995.

Bruce Liza

Designer

Lisa Lyon, bodybuilding champion of 1979 and inspiration for Liza Bruce, braces herself in a strongwoman pose. Stretched across her muscular body is 'Liza', a black Lycra bikini which uses futuristic, graphic shapes to section her body. From the outset, Bruce determined to make experimentation a central theme of her work and her career has been punctuated by innovations which have found their way onto the high street. Initially a swimwear designer, she made a thick lustre crepe, designed by textile specialist Rosemary Moore, her signature material. They later developed a 'crinkle' crepe fabric which was widely copied throughout the swimwear business. Bruce is also credited with introducing leggings in the 1980s. Sport has been an enduring theme for Bruce, with function conspicuously dominating the design of everything from cycling shorts in the 1980s to an evening dress in 1998.

☛ Audibet, Godley, di Sant' Angelo

Liza Bruce. b New York (USA), 1955. **Lisa Lyon wears 'Liza' bikini.** Photograph by Robert Mapplethorpe, 1984.

Brunelleschi Umberto

Illustrator

Around the time of this drawing, a Paris critic wrote of Brunelleschi, 'His art has nothing realistic about it. He would not know how to evoke modern life with its huge factories and streets full of people. But the world of fiction, which is so much more beautiful than the world of men, that he makes real.' Parisian by adoption, Brunelleschi worked as a costume and set designer in the theatre, where the effects of the innovations made by Bakst and Poiret were still very much alive. The hallmarks of a Brunelleschi theatrical costume drawing are clear, strong, calligraphic lines, derived from his sound training at the Accademia di Belle Arti in Florence, and brilliant, jewel-like colours that bring a fairy-tale world to life, the influence of Bakst and Poiret. Like Bakst and Erté, Brunelleschi was both a designer and illustrator, making him a leading figure in the history of twentieth-century fashion.

☛ Bakst, Erté, Poiret

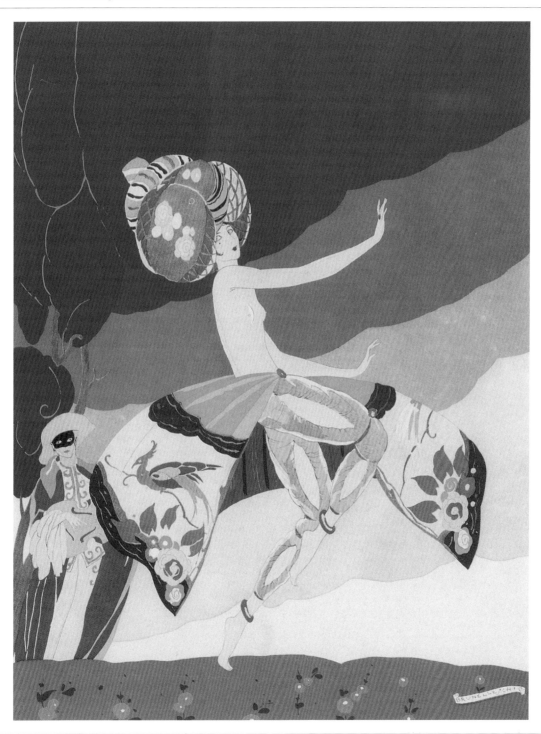

Umberto Brunelleschi. **b** Montemerio (IT), 1879. **d** Paris (FR), 1949. **'Danseuse Orientale'.** c1920.

Bruyère Marie-Louise Designer

The model wears a windbreaker coat from the Bruyère salon in the place Vendôme. It has a more feminine look than the simple, tailored styles seen in London in 1944. The shoulders have a softened, draped line, the waist is narrow, the sleeves are full, as is the hemline which has a swing to it. She is photographed outside the salon, opened in 1937 and decorated by Bruyère herself.

The window has been strafed with bullets and temporarily mended with brown paper, a detail that places this photograph between fashion photography and wartime reportage. Lee Miller, the photographer and journalist, was one of the first people to arrive in Paris on the liberation of the city in August 1944. Recording her impressions in *Vogue*, she wrote that, 'The French

concept of civilized life has been maintained.' Bruyère trained with the Callot Sœurs and worked as an apprentice with Jeanne Lanvin.

☛ Callot, Drecoll, French, Lanvin, L. Miller

78

Marie-Louise Bruyère. b (FR). (Active 1920s–1950s.) **Bruyère windbreaker coat.** Photograph by Lee Miller, 1944.

Bulgari Sotirio   Jewellery designer

A Bulgari collar and earrings modelled by Tatjana Patitz makes a statement worthy of a Medici, although the jewellery is a blend of traditional Italian forms and contemporary style. Andy Warhol once called the Bulgari store on Rome's via Condotti 'the best gallery of contemporary art'. The company was founded in Rome by silversmith Sotirio Bulgari. His sons, Constantino and Giorgio, developed the jewel and precious stone side of the business in the early twentieth century. In the 1970s, Bulgari drew on their Art Deco themes, in particular the rectangle-cut baguette work, to develop modern, graphically spare jewellery that put diamonds in geometric settings.

Precious jewellery was thus placed in the domain of young, fashionable society.

☛ Cartier, Lalique, Warhol

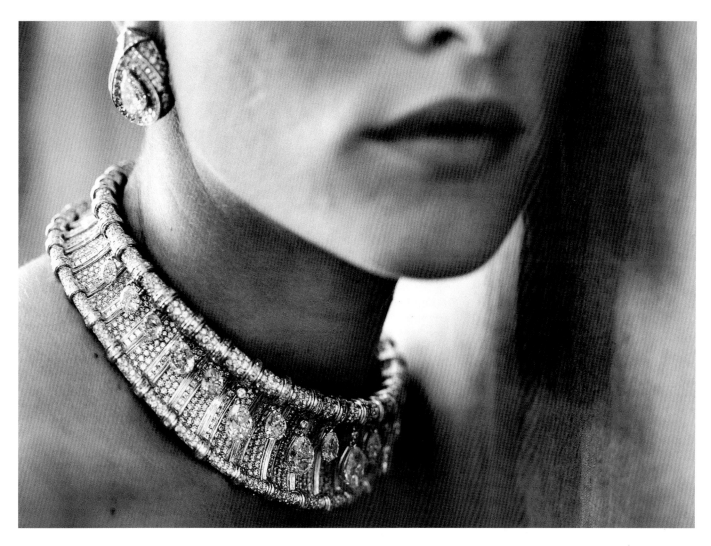

Sotirio Bulgari. b (IT). (Active 1880s–1930s.) **Tatjana Patitz wears a diamond collar and earrings.** Photograph by Fabrizio Ferri, 1989.

Burberry Thomas Designer

A geometric layout illustrates all the features that have made the Burberry check as British as the Liberty print or Scottish tartan. Thomas Burberry, a country draper, developed a water- and wind-proof fabric which he called gabardine; his first raincoat went on sale in the 1890s. Originally designed for field sports, the garment was used by officers in the trenches in the First World War and was dubbed the 'trench coat'. Many of the original features, from epaulettes and storm flaps to the metal D-rings, still appear on the coat today. The coat's shape slowly evolves to keep pace with broad fashion movements. Humphrey Bogart and other Hollywood stars later invested it with an aura of glamour. The distinctive beige and red check lining was first used in the 1920s.

Given new life by the Japanese Burberry-fever of the 1980s, it has since been applied to everything from umbrellas to silk underwear.

☛ **Brooks, Creed, Jaeger**

Thomas Burberry. **b** Dorking (UK), 1835. **d** Hook (UK), 1926. **Classic trench coat.** 1995.

Burrows Stephen   Designer

A matte jersey dress by Stephen Burrows is decorated with his trademark 'lettuce' edging. Deliberately created by closely spaced zig-zag stitching on raw seams, it is an example of how Burrows sparingly used machine techniques to decorate his fluid, sexy vision of modern femininity. The full cut of this dress will have produced a wake of rippling fabric, giving it sinuous movement.

Customers who visited his store-within-a-store, Stephen Burrows' World at Henri Bendel, in the 1970s, came for simple jersey and chiffon outfits which then defined New York style. In 1971, Halston told *Interview* magazine that Burrows was 'one of the unrecognized geniuses of the fashion world...Stephen gives the most original cut in America today. And the thing is really the cut.' One

of Burrows' favourite cuts is the asymmetric (where the hem is cut on the diagonal), about which he said, 'There's something nice about something wrong'.

☞ Bates, Halston, Munkacsi, Torimaru

Stephen Burrows. b Newark, NJ (USA), 1943. **Electric blue jersey wrap and matching pants.** Photograph by Oliviero Toscani, American *Vogue*, 1974.

Butler Nicky and Wilson Simon (Butler & Wilson) Jewellery designers

A face is framed by glittering diamanté jewellery, one eye obscured by an amusing lizard. Recognizing the potential for antique costume jewellery in the late 1960s, antique dealers Nicky Butler and Simon Wilson started selling Art Deco and Art Nouveau treasures at London's most fashionable markets. By the time they opened their first shop in 1972, Butler and Wilson had started designing themselves. Their eponymous period-inspired and often witty creations raised the profile of costume jewellery. The change in conventional attitudes towards genuine fakes, however, was never more conspicuous than in the opulently ornamental 1980s, when glamorous ambassadors of Butler & Wilson's style included Jerry Hall, Marie Helvin, Lauren Hutton and the Princess of Wales, who often wore their bejewelled designs for formal evening occasions.

☛ Diana, Hutton, Lane

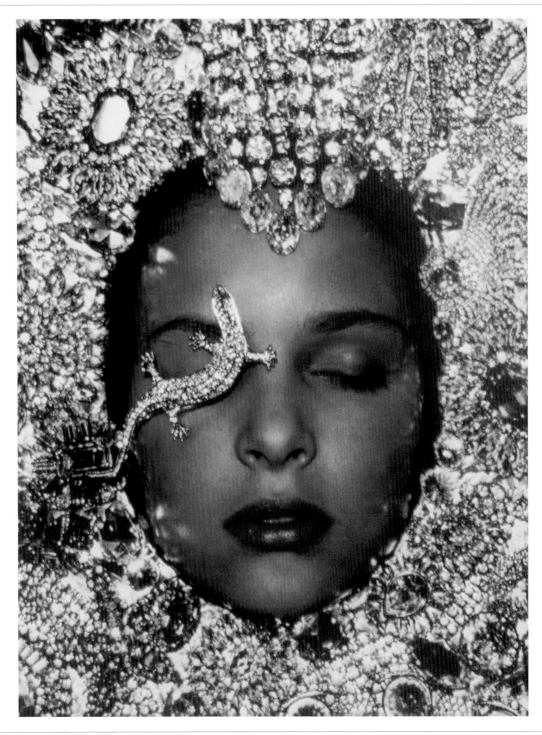

Nicky Butler. b (UK), c1950; **Simon Wilson. b** Glasgow (UK), 1950. (Butler & Wilson.) **Twenty-first birthday celebratory cover for Rough Diamonds: The Butler & Wilson Collection.** Photograph by John Swanell, 1989.

Callot Marie, Marthe, Regina and Joséphine (Callot Sœurs) Designers

This panniered taffeta evening dress, supported by a hoop, represents the exotic work of the Callot Sœurs. Its sheer vest is wrapped over a taffeta bodice and caught into a rose on the hip. The petalled skirt, inspired by an eighteenth-century dress, is appliquéd with green billows reminiscent of designs painted by Erté. The sisters worked with exquisite and unusual materials, including antique lace, rubberized gabardine and Chinese silks, with *Orientalisme* a favourite theme. They are remembered for introducing the fashion for the gold and silver lamé evening dresses which were popular in the 1910s and 1920s. The Callots were influential into the 1920s when Mme Marie Callot Gerber, the eldest sister, was referred to as the backbone of the fashion world of Europe.

Madeleine Vionnet said of her training at Callot Sœurs, 'Without the example of the Callot Sœurs, I would have continued to make Fords. It is because of them that I have been able to make Rolls-Royces'.

☛ Bernard, Boué, Bruyère, Dinnigan, Duff Gordon, Erté

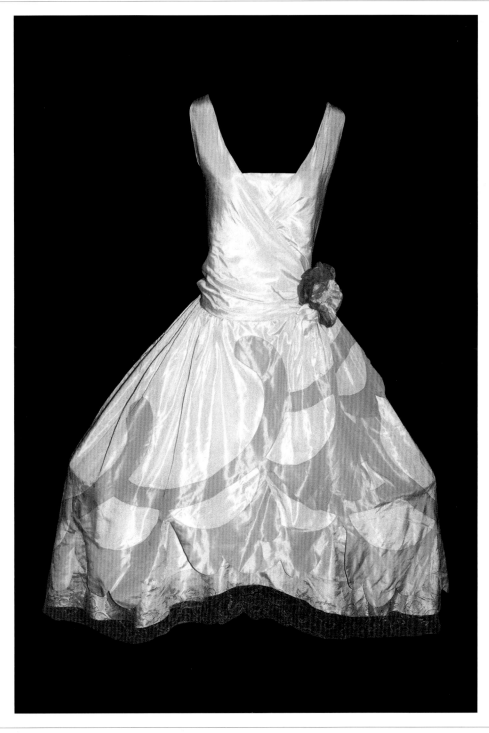

Callot. Marie, Marthe, Regina, Joséphine. (Callot Sœurs.) (Active 1890s–1920s.) **Ivory and chartreuse evening dress.** 1920s.

Campbell Naomi   Model

Herb Ritts casts Naomi Campbell as Pan, representing eternal spring. Her athletic body is regarded as being as near perfect as it is possible for a body to be – even in the fashion industry, a demanding audience. Azzedine Alaïa realized her potential early and dressed Campbell in his clothes, which are as equally demanding of perfection. She sought stardom from an early age, attending stage school in London, and has rarely been out of the news since she was hailed as a supermodel. Known for her diva-like qualities, she has a demanding, star-like ability to dominate a picture or catwalk. She was dubbed 'the black Bardot' for her full lips and sexy demeanour, although she claims to have encountered racial prejudice, saying, 'This is a business about selling – and blonde, blue-eyed girls are what sells.' However, Naomi Campbell's success has coincided with, and contributed to, a broader conception of the feminine ideal.

☞ Clements & Ribeiro, Jacobs, Kamali, Keogh

84

Naomi Campbell. b London (UK), 1970. **Norma Kamali bikini bottoms.** Photograph by Herb Ritts, British *Vogue*, 1990.

Campbell-Walter Fiona

Model

Fiona Campbell-Walter wears the duchesse satin ball gown, stole and gloves of an aristocrat, the society she represented in the 1950s. Born the daughter of an admiral in the Royal Navy, she was encouraged by her mother to become a model at eighteen, and was photographed by Henry Clarke, John French, Richard Avedon and David Bailey. She attended modelling school and soon became a *Vogue* regular, chosen for her aristocratic looks. She was also Cecil Beaton's favourite. Always in the gossip columns, Campbell-Walter married Baron Hans Heinrich Thyssen-Bornemisza, an industrialist. Together they were prolific art collectors, living mainly in Switzerland. They had two children but divorced in 1964. A high point of the Baroness's career in 1952 was to feature on the front cover of *Life* magazine – a surprising but understandable source of aspiration for fashion models, given its intellectual gravitas.

☛ Beaton, Clarke, McLaughlin-Gill

Fiona Campbell-Walter. b (UK), c1932. **Duchesse satin ball gown.** Salle des Glaces, Versailles. Photograph by Frances McLaughlin-Gill, 1952.

Capasa Ennio (Costume National)

Described as a 'mix of couture and the street', Ennio Capasa's dress uses cutaway armholes to reveal the shoulders and a simple tie at the neck. These are its only details. Its focus is the fabric: shimmering Lurex which highlights the curves of the body. Capasa's work is dictated by material. 'I always start designing a collection from the fabrics,' he says. 'I love the interplay between matt and shine. The fabrics are where you really experiment in fashion.' He trained with Yohji Yamamoto in Japan in the early 1980s, where the practice was to pare details away from a design and to take inspiration from traditional cutting techniques. On his return to Milan in 1987, Capasa started his own label, Costume National. It combines his perception of Japanese purism with a sexier, more close-fitting silhouette influenced by street fashion – a 1990s imperative epitomized by Helmut Lang and Ann Demeulemeester.

☛ Demeulemeester, Lang, Y. Yamamoto

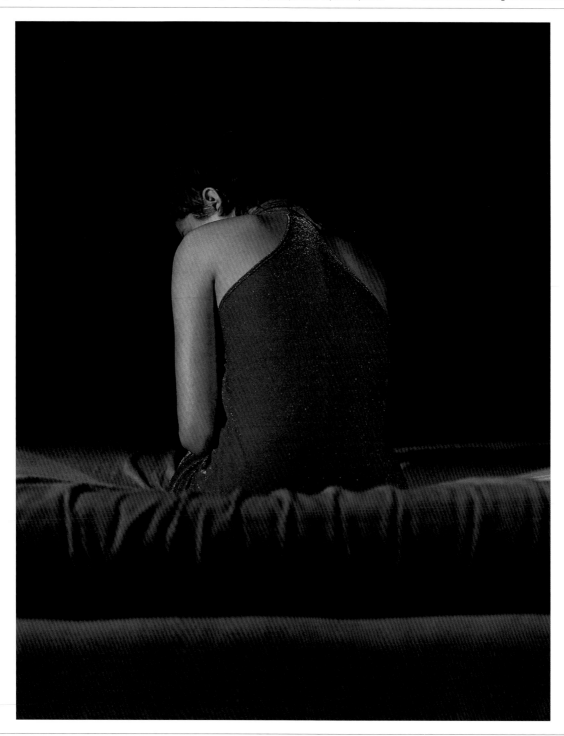

Ennio Capasa. b Lecce (IT), 1960. (Costume National.) **Lurex dress. Spring/summer 1997.** Photograph by Nathaniel Goldberg.

Capucci Roberto   Designer

Two immense ball gowns are assembled from an acre of pleated rainbow taffeta. The backs are constructed in such a way that they appear to be shoulder-to-floor bows. They are an example of engineering from Roberto Capucci who, in 1957, was called the 'Givenchy of Rome' by fashion writer Alison Adburgham. She continued, 'He designs as though for an abstract woman, the woman we never meet.' Such is the extravagance of some experiments that the wearer becomes secondary to the gown. For ten years Capucci showed in Rome before decamping for six years to Paris in 1962, and showing alongside fashion's other architect, Cristóbal Balenciaga, with whom he is often compared. The purity of Capucci's work extended to his selling technique. His fashion shows would be conducted in silence and he refused to replicate an outfit, so that any woman buying from him would have to do so from the show collection.

☛ Biagiotti, Exter, Givenchy, W. Klein

Roberto Capucci. b Rome (IT), 1929. **Pleated gowns. 1985.** Photograph by Fiorenzo Niccoli.

Cardin Pierre   Designer

In what could be a still from *Star Trek*, men, women and even a boy, strike poses to accentuate their tomorrow's wardrobe. In the mid-1960s Pierre Cardin spun off into deep space with Courrèges and Paco Rabanne. He offered utopian clothes to a new generation. Graphic symbols were cut from his jersey tunics; men's jackets were given military epaulettes. The silver shine of asymmetric zips, steel belts and buckles brought couture into the space age. Cardin's training had been a traditional one – at the houses of Paquin, Schiaparelli and Dior – but his mind was on the future. In 1959 he was the first couturier to design ready-to-wear and was expelled from the Chambre Syndicale. Cardin became fashion's scientist, developing his own material, Cardine, a bonded fibre that would rigidly hold his geometric shapes, and experimenting with metals to produce dresses. In later years, Cardin put his name to everything from pens to frying pans.

☛ Beatles, de Castelbajac, Courrèges, Rabanne, Schön

Pierre Cardin. b Sant'Andrea di Barbarana (IT), 1922. 'Space' collection. Autumn/winter 1967/8. Photograph by Yoshi Takata.

Carnegie Hattie   Retailer

C.Z. Guest, an American social figure, wears a simple gown by Hattie Carnegie. Although she has a reputation as a revered designer, Carnegie never actually made a dress. She was a retailer who delivered a current look, such as this strapless, wasp-waisted silhouette derived from Dior, a shape that formed the hourglass figure of the 1950s. Carnegie's reputation was legendary. She employed designers of the calibre of Norman Norell, Travis Banton, Jean Louis and Claire McCardell; the 'Carnegie look' was a sophisticated simplification of European design that was favoured by American society and high-profile clients such as the Duchess of Windsor. In 1947, *Life* declared Carnegie (née Kanengeiser, but she took the name of the richest American of the time) to be the 'undisputed leader' of American fashion, with more than one hundred stores selling her product and her imprimatur the keenest sign of prestige in American clothing.

☛ Banton, Daché, Louis, Norell, Trigère, Windsor

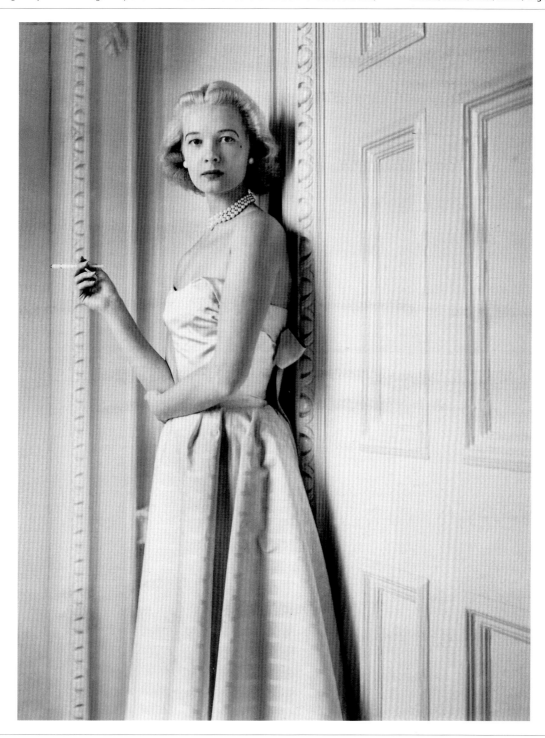

Hattie Carnegie. b Vienna (AUS), 1889. d New York (USA), 1956. C.Z. Guest. Photograph by Cecil Beaton, 1952.

Cartier Louis François Jewellery designer

This brooch, designed as a flamingo in characteristic pose, has plumage set with calibré-cut emeralds, rubies and sapphires. Cabochon citrine and sapphire are used for the beak, a sapphire for the eye, with the head, neck, body and legs pavé-set with brilliant-cut diamonds. It was created in 1940 by Jeanne Toussaint for the jewellery firm Cartier, founded in Paris in 1847 by Louis François

Cartier. This jewel was designed for the Duchess of Windsor, who owned one of the finest jewellery collections of the 1940s. It was chosen for her by the Duke of Windsor, who spent a great deal of time choosing jewels to adorn her clothes, often designed as a setting for a particular gem. Pieces such as this one (resold in 1987 for $470,000) were still considered

avant-garde many years after their design and were the precursors of a new vocabulary in *bijouterie* after the Second World War.

☛ **Bulgari, Tiffany, Windsor**

90

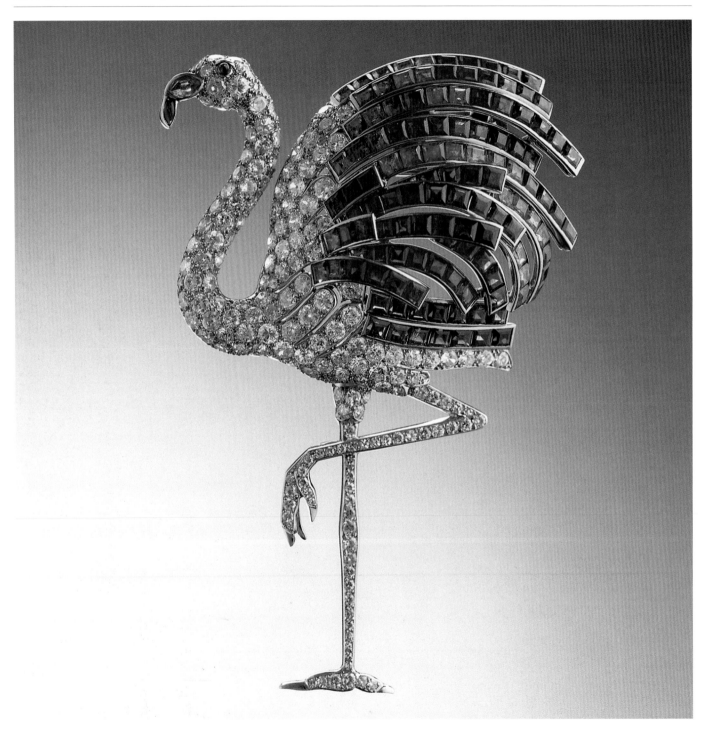

Louis François Cartier. b (FR), 1819. d Paris (FR), 1904. **Flamingo brooch created for the Duchess of Windsor, 1940.** Photograph by Louis Tirilly.

Cashin Bonnie   Designer

A capacious, grey cashmere poncho trimmed in leather typifies Bonnie Cashin's distinctive contribution to American sportswear. Attuned to dancers and their motion, the variable weather and outdoor life of California, and to Hollywood and the movies (she was a designer for 20th Century Fox), Cashin created ingenious sportswear. She often used global references but always remained faithful to the pragmatic and contemporary woman. Separates were versatile and luxurious; sizing was easy, given that most tops, dresses, skirts and trousers wrapped or tied, allowing for accommodation for many body types. Cashin used layering before it became an accepted and expected part of women's lives. Toggles and luggage hardware became practical fastenings for her bags and leather-trimmed wools. Cashin is regarded, along with Claire McCardell, as the mother of American sportswear.

☛ A. Klein, McCardell, Schön

91

Bonnie Cashin. **b** Oakland, CA (USA), 1915. **d** New York (USA), 2000. **Cashmere shawl.** Photograph by Francesco Scavullo, 1966.

Cassini Oleg — Designer

In the 1960s, Cassini was the American designer most identified with Jacqueline Kennedy as First Lady, an evening dress for whom is illustrated here. Stung by criticism of her costly wardrobe (largely from Balenciaga and Givenchy), even before her husband was elected president, Mrs Kennedy chose to consider Cassini her official designer. Although her mother-in-law and aides secretly helped Mrs Kennedy to continue to acquire clothes by Grès, Chanel and Givenchy, Cassini's sleek minimalism supplemented that elite wardrobe and the American designer was publicly acclaimed. By the conspicuous association with Kennedy, Cassini became a powerful figure in 1960s style, offering youthful, smooth modernity; his A-line dresses and suits of a semi-fitted top over a slim skirt corresponded to Parisian designs. Cassini respected Mrs Kennedy's demureness, while letting each garment stand out in a manner appropriate for a First Lady.

☛ Givenchy, Grès, Kennedy

Oleg Cassini. b Paris (FR), 1913. d Manhasset, NY (USA), 2006. **Evening dress for Jacqueline Kennedy.** 1961.

De Castelbajac Jean-Charles — Designer

The deadpan expression on the model's face contradicts Jean-Charles de Castelbajac's joke: a square-cut dress that imitates the front-opening of a huge pair of blue jeans. De Castelbajac uses a deceptively childlike sense of form in this way – bearing in mind Cervantes' phrase, 'Always hold the hand of the child you once were.' His simple, enveloping clothes remain true to the uncut cloth. Thick, felt-like fabrics have preoccupied him since he was at boarding school, where he cut his first garment out of a blanket. He was one of France's new age of ready-to-wear designers in the 1960s and has worked with Pop Art themes such as Warhol's Campbell's soup can, which he printed onto a cylindrical dress in 1984. Inspired by the work of Paco Rabanne and Pierre Cardin, which he said surpassed the work of artists working on the theme of futurism, he has been called 'the space-age Bonnie Cashin'.

☛ Cardin, Ettedgui, Farhi, Rabanne, Warhol

93

Jean-Charles de Castelbajac. b Casablanca (MOR), 1950. **'Jeans' dress.** Photograph by Denis Malerbi, 1984.

Castillo Antonio   Designer

The risqué potential of the black lace used in Castillo's A-line dress is at once removed by its stately aura. A black hat, moulded into the shape of a mantilla comb, lends grace, while the model maintains an imperial pose, turning her back to the camera as if to shake hands with foreign heads of state. Born of a noble Spanish family, regality and dignity surround every one of Antonio Castillo's designs – his training was as accessory designer for Chanel and as designer at the distinguished fashion houses Piguet and Lanvin. Castillo left Spain for France in 1936 at the onset of the Spanish Civil War. He was no Courrèges, indulging in avant-garde couture for the younger generation of customers in the1960s; instead, he subtly instilled a sense of innovation into mature, seemingly classic looks, which resulted in a quiet, exceedingly tidy style.

☞ Ascher, Beretta, Lanvin, Piguet, G. Smith

94

Antonio Castillo. **b** Madrid (SP), 1908. **d** c1984. **Lace Cage.** Photograph by Seeberger Brothers, 1965.

Cavanagh John Designer

John Cavanagh is photographed with a model wearing his full, yet immaculately tailored coat. Its black cuffs, plain collar and geometric configuration of buttons are its only details beyond top-stitched, princess-line seams into which the pockets disappear. His was an international training, firstly with Molyneux on his return from Paris and then at Pierre Balmain. In 1952

Cavanagh opened his own couture house in London, making clothes with international appeal. He noted, 'A couturier worth his name must design in the world-stream of design change, but direct it to the lives of his clients that make this business exist.' Cavanagh was at the centre of London's small made-to-measure society which continued to dress the English season, despite

becoming engulfed by cheap imitations. In 1964 he said, 'Couture will and must continue. It is the lifeblood of the ready-to-wear.'

☛ Balmain, Molyneux, Morton

95

John Cavanagh. b (IRE), 1914. **John Cavanagh and model wearing cream wool coat.** Photograph by John French, 1962.

Cerruti Nino   Designer

Jack Nicholson wears loose linen separates by Cerruti in the film *The Witches of Eastwick*. 'Fashion, ultimately, is a way of describing the world we live in,' says Cerruti, a philosophy that applies itself not only to the world of fashion but also to film – Cerruti has designed costumes for over sixty movies. Cerruti initially studied philosophy and had wanted to become a writer, but in 1950 he took over the family textile business in northern Italy. His launch of a menswear range, Hitman, in 1957 was the start of the company's transformation into a luxury label. A women's ready-to-wear collection followed in 1977. Epitomizing the aspirational dressing of the 1980s, the Cerruti label was used in films such as *Wall Street*. In the 1990s, Cerruti's womenswear enjoyed a period of success while it was designed by Narciso Rodriguez, who introduced contemporary themes such as transparent, embroidered fabrics worn with precise tailoring.

☛ Armani, von Etzdorf, Rodriguez

Nino Cerruti. b Biella (IT), 1930. **Jack Nicholson.** Still from *The Witches of Eastwick*. 1987.

Chalayan Hussein   Designer

Katerina Jebb, known for her photocopier art, depicts a dress trimmed with gold chains by Hussein Chalayan. He describes his innovative designs as 'an evolution of ideas'; his first collection was made from reinforced paper which he had buried with iron filings in his back garden to create a rusted effect. Chalayan is known for his intricate detail – be it delicate beading, glittery flight-pattern charts or flashing LED lights. Each of his collections is based around a narrative plot and customers are provided with booklets outlining the story. There is often a darkness to his themes: vampires, tombs and constriction have all featured in the past. Chalayan maintains that, 'Trends are boring and transient. I am interested in clothes, not fashion.' With McQueen and Berardi in the 1990s, he pioneered the sharp, angular tailoring that became known as the 'London look'.

☞ Berardi, Clements Ribeiro, Dell'Acqua, Isogawa

Hussein Chalayan. **b** Nicosia (CYP), 1970. **'Lands Without'. Spring/summer 1997.** Photograph by Katerina Jebb.

Chanel Gabrielle (Coco)

Designer

Coco Chanel is strolling in the Tuileries in Paris, a short distance from the rue Cambon where she lived and had her maison de couture, which she closed in 1939 and re-opened in 1954. She is wearing all the hallmarks of her signature style: suit, blouse, pearl jewellery, scarf, hat, gloves and handbag with gilt chains. She was a perfectionist, and the way she gestures to Alexander Liberman with her right arm manifests one of her fixations – a comfortable arm movement. She would rip off the sleeves of her suit time and again to get a perfect fit. The basic idea for her suits came from the concept of military uniforms. As the mistress of the Duke of Westminster, she had taken many trips on his yacht where the crew wore uniforms. The essence of her style was rooted in a masculine model of power, a direction that has dominated twentieth-century fashion.

☛ Cocteau, Dalí, Lagerfeld, Liberman, Parker, Verdura

Gabrielle (Coco) Chanel. b Saumur (FR), 1883. d Paris (FR), 1971. **Coco Chanel wearing Chanel suit.** Photograph by Alexander Liberman, 1951.

Charles Caroline   Designer

In an early design, Caroline Charles uses a chequerboard pattern jacket, worn with long socks. During the 1960s, Charles also worked as a broadcaster and journalist but she stayed with fashion. 'Does it fit? Is it useful? Does it create the feeling that someone wants to get close to you?' These practical questions are considered for every piece of Caroline Charles clothing. Charles recalls wanting to be a dress designer from an early age. After graduating from Swindon Art School, she headed to London, which was in full 1960s swing. Following a spell at Mary Quant, she launched her own collection in 1963. Charles's occasion- and eveningwear were an instant hit with the entertainment trendsetters of the day, including Cilla Black and Barbra Streisand. However, it has been her knack of creating very British clothes – and, latterly, accessories and interiors – that has allowed her career to span three decades.

☛ Courrèges, Foale & Tuffin, Quant

Caroline Charles. b Cairo (EG), 1942. **Check weave wool jacket and black wool skirt**. Tatler, 1964.

Chéruit Madeleine Designer

Monochromes forge a vintage ambience, illuminated by porcelain skin set against dazzling sequins under transparent organza. Marion Morehouse wears a deep V neckline, then considered risqué, that runs down to a beltless waist, indicating the move away from the curvaceous prewar silhouette to a relaxed contour. Trained in the 1880s at the couture house Raudnitz,

Chéruit was a Parisian designer who, like Lelong and Louise Boulanger, transformed high fashion into the reality of ready-to-wear. She refined the excessiveness of couture for her aristocratic Parisian clientele, who favoured her richly ornamented dresses. Fascinated by the effect of light on fabric, she worked with taffeta, lamé and gauze. With Chanel's move towards simple

fashions in the 1920s, her opulent taste lost appeal. She retired in 1923, but her design house continued until 1935 when Schiaparelli famously took over her premises.

☛ Bally, Boulanger, Lelong, Morehouse

Madeleine Chéruit. b (FR). (Active 1900s–1930s.) **Marion Morehouse.** Photograph by Edward Steichen, 1927.

Choo Jimmy   Shoe designer

A powder-blue suede sandal is trimmed with feathers, an example of the dainty, seductive work of Jimmy Choo, who was born into a family of shoemakers and made his first pair aged eleven. Previously all Choo shoes were handmade; he has recently adapted his perfectionist craftsmanship for an additional ready-to-wear line. They are never overtly fashionable, yet are equal in elegance to the designer clothes they are usually worn with. He attended London's Cordwainer's Technical College with a fresh generation of cobblers, including Patrick Cox and Emma Hope. Of his style, Choo says, 'There is an elegance, a femininity, maybe a sexiness.' It was one that came to be favoured by the Princess of Wales, who would buy one style in several colours for eveningwear and to co-ordinate with her day suits. Choo's Malaysian roots account for his signature palette: a range of crystalline colours which includes aqua blue, fuchsia pink and bright orange.

☛ Cox, Diana, Hope

Jimmy Choo. b Penang (MAL), 1961. **Feathered sandal. Spring/summer 1997.** Photograph by Simon Archer, *E.S.* magazine, 1998.

Chow Tina   Icon

Tina Chow strikes an elegant, demure pose. A supreme model in the 1970s, she went on to become one of the great fashion connoisseur-collectors of the twentieth century. An Asian-American, Chow represented the new diversity and universalism of modern beauty, but her fashion intelligence was even greater than her beauty. One of the most important collectors of couture clothing, Chow's practised eye is still regarded as the paradigm of collecting and connoisseurship. Chow knew the great designers of her time, but demonstrated her interest in the past by choosing works by Madeleine Vionnet, Cristóbal Balenciaga and Christian Dior for her astute collection. Her initial collecting interest was Mariano Fortuny, whose 'Delphos' dresses, capes and mantles were a syncretist interpretation of East and West.

☛ Antonio, Balenciaga, Fortuny, Vionnet

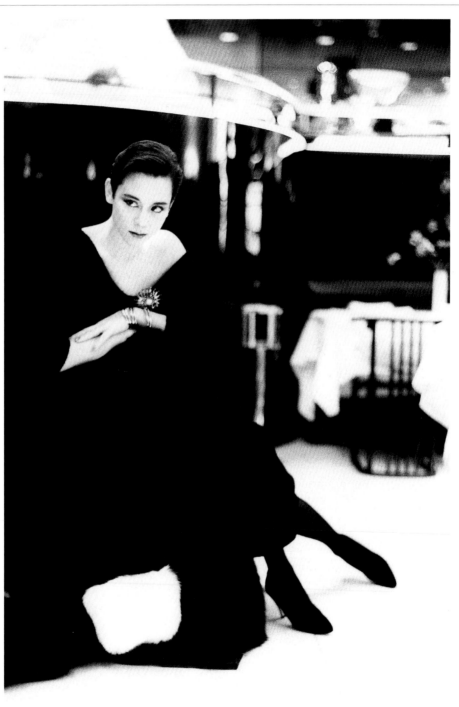

102

Tina Chow. b Cleveland, OH (USA), 1950. **d** New York (USA), 1992. **Tina Chow.** Photograph by Arthur Elgort, 1982.

Clark Ossie

Designer

In this wild scene photographed at London's Chelsea Town Hall in 1970, Ossie Clark shows his clothes under the name Quorum, a company set up by Alice Pollock. It was, said *Vogue*, 'more a spring dance than a show'. The spaced-out models wear Clark's chiffon dresses (each with a secret pocket into which a key and a £5 note would fit – his trademark), both printed by his wife, textile designer Celia Birtwell. The couple were immortalized in a portrait entitled *Mr and Mrs Clark and Percy* by their friend, painter David Hockney, who can be seen on the far right of this picture. 'I'm a master cutter. It's all in my brain and fingers,' Clark had said, and that talent became one of the most sought-after in the late 1960s and early 1970s. Singer Marianne Faithfull and Anita Pallenberg, then the girlfriend of the Rolling Stones guitarist Keith Richards, shared an 'Ossie' snakeskin suit, now one of the most precious reminders of the age.

☛ Birtwell, Fratini, Hulanicki, Pollock, Sarne

Ossie Clark. b Liverpool (UK), 1942. **d** London (UK), 1996. **Printed chiffon dresses.** Photograph by Annette Green, 1970.

Clarke Henry   Photographer

The citrus colours of summer are given a fresh, literal interpretation. Photographer Henry Clarke was first drawn to fashion photography by watching Cecil Beaton photograph Dorian Leigh. He created animated photographs, but Clarke was also naturally inclined to elegance, and his images of French fashion in the 1950s, in particular, exemplify the balance he sought between the formal, almost statuesque, dress of the epoch and the casual effect of snapshot instantaneity. Artful and artless at the same time, Clarke's photographs benefited from the licence given him by Diana Vreeland at *Vogue* and the exotic locations they used for photo shoots. Skilfully moving from 1950s high style to the dazzling colours and layering of the 1960s, he made the flamboyant and ethnographic clothes come alive in the context of Mayan archaeological sites and various settings in India, Sicily and around the world.

☛ Campbell–Walters, Goalen, Pertegaz, Vreeland

104

Henry Clarke. **b** Los Angeles, CA (USA), 1918. **d** Le Cannet (FR), 1996. **Fruit sweaters.** French *Vogue*, 1957.

Clements Suzanne and Ribeiro Inacio (Clements Ribeiro)

Clements Ribeiro's graphically patterned cashmere has become its trademark: from bold rainbow stripes to this striking Union Jack insignia, which symbolized the 1990s upswing in British fashion fortunes known as 'Cool Britannia'. Ribeiro has said, 'We do simple cuts with strong fabrics; we call it clumsy couture'. Bright prints define the themes of each collection; from traditional tartans and windowpane checks to bohemian paisleys and mottled florals. Luxurious materials are used for daywear – dusty-coloured suedes, cashmere, silk taffeta and sequins. Clements Ribeiro favour neat separates and simple styling. Their collections are inspired by an ever-changing female role model: punk, gypsy, suburban housewife or mermaid. They met at Central Saint Martin's College of Art and Design, married and moved to Brazil after graduating. They designed their first joint collection in London in 1993.

☛ Amies, Campbell, Chalayan

Suzanne Clements. b London (UK), 1969; **Inacio Ribeiro. b** São Paulo (BR), 1963. (Clements Ribeiro.) **Union Jack cashmere sweater. Autumn/winter 1997.** Photograph by Chris Moore.

Cobain Kurt   Icon

Cobain was to grunge what Johnny Rotten was to punk. His greasy, bleached hair, pale waify body and thrift-shop clothes created the image of a strung-out, moody adolescent. The garments of grunge bands such as Cobain's Nirvana, Pearl Jam and Alice in Chains were cheap and casual; washed-out jeans and rock T-shirts. It started as an anti-fashion formula that dressed a generation of disaffecteds known as Generation X, but, predictably, was 'cleaned up' to become a mainstream movement known as 'Heroin Chic': an affected representation of an addict's wardrobe. Rebelling against his upbringing among homophobic lumberjacks in his home town, he would sometimes try harder by wearing his partner's flowery dress and painting his nails red. That partner, Courtney Love, came to personify a feminized version of the look which inspired Marc Jacobs to create his 'grunge' collection of 1993.

☛ **Dell'Acqua, Jacobs, Rotten**

Kurt Cobain. b Hoquaim, WA (USA), 1967. **d** Seattle, WA (USA), 1994. **Kurt Cobain and daughter, Frances Bean.** Photograph by Stephen Sweet, 1994.

Cocteau Jean Illustrator

The legend on this fashion drawing reads, 'Paris 1937. Schiaparelli made this tapering sheath dress for dining and dancing. Jean Cocteau drew it for the readers of *Harper's Bazaar*. Cocteau was a writer, film-maker, painter, print-maker, stage-, fabric- and jewellery-designer and fashion illustrator. His *entrée* into the world of fashion came through the theatre. Cocteau met Diaghilev when the Ballets Russes came to Paris in 1910 and he designed posters for him. Some of Cocteau's most important work for the theatre and fashion included his collaborations with Chanel. Between 1922 and 1937 she designed costumes for a whole cycle of his plays, including *Le Train Bleu* of 1924. He often sketched her and her fashions in his characteristic form of outline drawing with its sharp line and elegant simplicity. Cocteau was also closely associated with Surrealism and fashion. For Schiaparelli he designed fabrics, embroideries and jewellery.

☛ Bérard, Chanel, Dessès, Horst, Rochas, Schiaparelli

Jean Cocteau. b Paris (FR), 1889. d Paris (FR), 1963. **Schiaparelli dress.** Illustrated in *Harper's Bazaar*, 1937.

Coddington Grace

Editor

'Grace Coddington is the eye – the eye...I never saw a wrong dress she chose...Grace was without a doubt the fashion editor.' says Manolo Blahnik. Coddington has influenced fashion in many different ways. In 1959 'The Cod', photographed here wearing all-over prints by Jacques Heim, was spotted by Norman Parkinson. She constantly reinvented her image by changing her distinctive red hair from a chunky Vidal Sassoon bob to a halo of frizzy curls – a formula that would later be used by Linda Evangelista. In 1968 she moved to British *Vogue*, taking Calvin Klein's modern aesthetic to a 1970s European audience. Her style inspired designers such as Kenzo and Pablo & Delia and she later championed the talents of Azzedine Alaïa and Zoran. Coddington moved to American *Vogue* in 1987. She said of her time there, 'You're either having dinner with 300 people or grovelling on the floor with pins in your mouth.'

☛ Alaïa, Blahnik, Heim, C. Klein, Sassoon, Zoran

108

Grace Coddington. b Holyhead (UK), 1941. **Grace Coddington wears Jacques Heim.** Photograph by John French, 1965.

Coffin Clifford   Photographer

For the June 1949 issue of American *Vogue*, Clifford Coffin photographs four models wearing swimsuits as polka-dots on a sand dune in a customarily strong composition. Coffin's main contribution to fashion photography in the 1950s was his use of ring-flash lighting – a circular bulb which wraps around the lens and casts a directional light onto the model, thereby creating an indistinct shadow. A technique which 'blasts' light onto the subject, highlighting shiny fabric and make-up, it was widely used in tandem with a wind machine in the 1970s and 1990s. Coffin was a fashion personality whose early ambition was to be a dancer. He was also an 'out' homosexual, who was close to society writer Truman Capote. His work for American, British and French *Vogues* secured his own position in that society and he was described as 'the first photographer to actually think fashion, sometimes more than fashion editors'.

☞ Gattinoni, Gernreich, Goalen

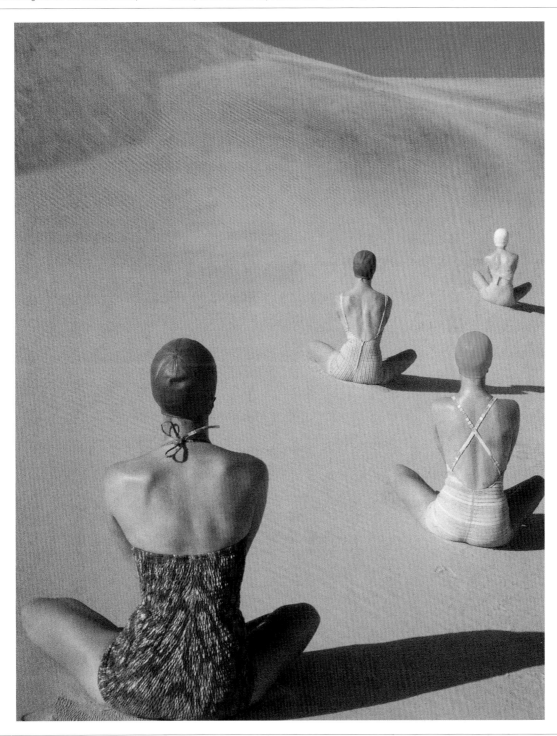

Clifford Coffin. **b** IL (USA), 1913. **d** Pasadena, CA (USA), 1972. **Swimsuits.** American *Vogue*, 1949.

Colonna Jean   Designer

Imagine the dark backstreets of Paris, a flashing neon sign and a hidden door opening to an underground world inhabited by women who sleep during the day and dress for the night in leopard prints, stretchy sheer lace, skimpy skirts and little else. This is the world of French designer Jean Colonna, whose fashion shows conjure up the world of the Pigalle district after dark. He came to prominence during the 'deconstruction' trend of the early 1990s, upsetting the establishment by creating clothes that people could actually afford. The manufacturing methods that allowed him to do this included overlocked hems and edges, doing away with the need for finishing. He also used unashamedly cheap fabrics such as PVC. Colonna trained in Paris and spent two years at Balmain, before launching his own label in 1985. Colonna's philosophy has always been that 'a piece of clothing must be simple – to make, to sell and to wear'.

☛ **Balmain, Dolce & Gabbana, Topolino**

Jean Colonna. b Oran (ALG), 1955. **Backstage. Spring/summer 1998.** Photograph by Thierry Ledé.

Connolly Sybil   Designer

Photographed in her Dublin home, Sybil Connolly wears a dress made from her famous pleated linen. The tailored shawl covers a simple bodice and typically understated skirt. The doyenne of Irish fashion in the 1950s, Connolly specialized in adapting traditional Irish fabrics for modern, easy dressing. Her forward-thinking designs transformed thick mohair, Donegal tweed and linen, which she hand-pleated for delicate blouses and dresses. Like her American contemporary, Claire McCardell, she was a pioneer in the creation of smart shapes that used informal fabrics and a relaxed attitude during the 1950s and 1960s. Connolly moved to London to learn dress design, but returned to Ireland upon the outbreak of the Second World War. At the age of twenty-two she became design director of the Irish fashion house Richard Alan, going on to launch her own couture label in 1957 at the age of thirty-six.

☛ Leser, McCardell, Maltézos

Sybil Connolly. b Swansea (UK), 1921. **d** Dublin (IRE), 1998. **Sybil Connolly at home, Merrion Square, Dublin.** Photograph by Perry Ogden, 1987.

Conran Jasper   Designer

In an exercise in contrast, a scarlet poppy hat, designed by Jasper Conran and made by Philip Treacy for a production of *My Fair Lady*, explodes above an unadorned black dress from Conran's mainline collection. Jasper Conran regarded Jean Muir as his mentor and his own work carries her hallmarks of modern sophistication. Lit from behind, his dark dress comes to life as a silhouette,

a graphic sculpture beneath an organic one. Having studied at Parson's School of Design in New York, Conran set up his own label at the age of nineteen. He relies on a monochrome palette interspersed with stimulating bursts of striped fabric or salvos of colour: bold orange, cerise or cobalt blue. He likes his clothes to have 'speed and life... For me it's always about the cut and the shape'.

Conran's work is also wearable. Some garments, such as a fitted leather jacket reminiscent of Marlon Brando's 'biker' jacket, have remained in his collection for ten years because of their flattering shapes.

☛ Muir, Treacy

112

Jasper Conran. b London (UK), 1959. 'Poppy'. Hat designed for *My Fair Lady* stage production. Photograph by Tessa Traeger, 1992.

Courrèges André   Designer

A former civil engineer, André Courrèges placed the meticulous cut of fashion he had practised in Balenciaga's atelier in the 1950s in the service of the 1960s idealism of youth and the future. Along with Pierre Cardin and Paco Rabanne, Courrèges led the cult of visionary fashion design in Paris. It was a movement that cut away superfluous material, banned decoration and established geometry and new materials for fashion. 'I think the women of the future, morphologically speaking, will have a young body,' said Courrèges at the time. His miniskirts were stiff and square and advocated a minimum of body coverage, enjoying those 'young' bodies that became visible in the 1960s. His most characteristic symbol, often covering his dresses and bare body parts, was the youthful daisy. Unisex was another Courrèges theme. He predicted that womenswear would become at least as practical as menswear.

☛ **Cardin, Charles, Frizon, Quant, Rabanne, Schön**

André Courrèges. b Pau (FR), 1923. **Space-age designs.** Photograph by William Klein, 1964.

Coward Noel   Icon

The playwright and entertainer Noel Coward strikes a classic pose in this photograph by Horst. A flawless Prince of Wales check, accessorized with polka-dot silk and woven checks, epitomizes his peerless sophistication. After his first theatrical success in 1924, Coward remarked, 'I was unwise enough to be photographed in bed wearing a Chinese dressing gown as an expression of enhanced degeneracy. I indulged in silk shirts, pyjamas and underclothes...coloured turtleneck jerseys...and started a fashion.' It was the look for the glamorous, brittle 1920s aesthete. For the first time since Oscar Wilde, a writer's appearance seemed as important as what he wrote. 'All sorts of men suddenly wanted to look like Coward – sleek and satiny, clipped and well groomed,' observed Cecil Beaton. Cary Grant was one of them, remarking that he based his own urbane style on, 'a combination of Jack Buchanan and Noel Coward'.

☛ Beaton, Horst, Wilde

114

Noel Coward. **b** London (UK), 1899. **d** Blue Harbour (JAM), 1973. **Noel Coward. Paris, 1934.** Photograph by Horst P. Horst.

Cox Patrick

Shoe designer

A model wears the python-skin Wannabe shoe that became an icon and raised the average male spend on footwear. In 1993 Patrick Cox realized that his collection needed a lightweight summer shoe. His answer was the Wannabe, a moccasin-constructed loafer. In 1995 his Chelsea shop was besieged by customers wanting a pair, some of whom attempted bribery. When he launched the range in 1993, Cox acknowledged his debt to the white loafers worn by the American comedian Pee Wee Herman. An indispensable accessory of the rave culture, the Wannabe is one half of Cox's shoe business – the other comprises a collection of styles that develops with fashion trends. Born in Canada, Patrick Cox moved to London in 1983 to study at Cordwainer's Technical College. His first success was a customized Dr Marten shoe in 1984, and he went on to work with a long list of designers.

☛ Blair, Choo, Flett, R. James, Marteans, Westwood

115

Patrick Cox. b Edmonton, AB (CAN), 1963. 'Python' Wannabe loafer. Autumn/winter 1995. Photograph by François Rotger.

Crahay Jules-François Designer

Jules-François Crahay poses with Jane Birkin who wears a matte jersey dress pulled into a lazy handkerchief knot at the shoulder. Crahay learned the techniques of dressmaking at his mother's shop in Liège and at the fashion house of Jane Régny in Paris. After these apprenticeships he became a designer at Nina Ricci in 1952, then at the house of Lanvin in 1963. While he was fêted for his refined eveningwear, Crahay was also one of the leading fashion designers to promote the peasant and gypsy styles which dominated fashion at the end of the 1960s. As early as 1959, his collections contained full, flounced skirts worn with low-cut, elasticated blouses and scarves worn around the head, neck and waist. All were made in vividly coloured, lightweight materials which produced the light, feminine style for which Crahay is remembered. He characterized his own work by saying that he wanted to have fun making his dresses.

☞ Lanvin, Pipart, Ricci

Jules-François Crahay. b Liège (BEL), 1917. **d** Monte Carlo (MON), 1988. **Jules-François Crahay and Jane Birkin.** Photograph by Jacques-Henri Lartique, French *Vogue*, 1976.

Crawford Cindy   Model

Cindy Crawford works on her multi-million-dollar body, the marketing of which is still controlled by its owner, who says, 'I see myself as a president of a company that owns a product that everybody wants.' Her defined physique, honed in the fitness market, welded the connection between health and beauty for a generation of women. A shoot for *Playboy* was also part of the

business strategy: 'I wanted to reach a different audience...let's face it, most college guys don't buy *Vogue*.' While conservative in the fashion sense (she kept the same hairstyle for ten years), Crawford was a commercial supermodel. Her popularity is attributable to her clean sex appeal and 'multicultural' appearance. It adds up to the perfect cover face: a beauty that

alienates nobody. Crawford remains a pragmatist, an example of the new model breed that has learned to separate fact from fantasy.

☞ P. Knight, Lindbergh, Schiffer

Cindy Crawford. b De Kalb, IL (USA), 1966. **Cindy Crawford.** Still from *Shape your Body Workout* video. Photograph by Tim Rooke, 1992.

117

Creed Charles   Designer

This outfit is typical of the 1930s. The suit has a boxy-style jacket with a broad shoulder line and wide lapels, while the skirt is straight and the hemline stays well below the knees. It foreshadows the masculine, military style of the Second World War, but details such as the buttons and the hat anchor the outfit firmly in the prewar era. Charles Creed belonged to an English family of tailors who were known for their understated tweeds, popular in nineteenth-century Paris. The family established a tailoring firm in London in 1710 and in Paris in 1850, launching womenswear in the early 1890s. During the Second World War, Creed designed women's suits and coats while on leave from the army and was also involved in the Utility scheme. He set up his own fashion house in London in 1946 and enjoyed success in America where his restrained English tailoring found a ready market.

☛ Bérard, Burberry, Jaeger, Morton

Charles Creed. **b** Paris (FR), 1906. **d** London (UK), 1966. **Travel coat.** Illustration by Christian Bérard, 1935.

Crolla Scott Designer

Using rich colours, opulent brocade and blooming prints, Scott Crolla's early work was an historical fantasy. Crolla trained in art and sculpture, but grew bored of the discipline, moving to fashion because it is 'the honest side of the whole artistic discourse'. In 1981 he formed a partnership with fellow artist Georgina Godley. This tableau, styled by Amanda Harlech, who went on to work for John Galliano and Chanel, suggests the ecstasy of an eighteenth-century poet – a scene that epitomizes Crolla's fanciful work. Brocade trousers worn with silk stockings and tail coats dominated a time when fashion became costume and men rediscovered the vain pleasure of peacockery – a historical tendency that puts this outfit into context. Despite its fancy-dress connotations, Crolla's work was instrumental in encouraging men and women to wear ruffled shirts and brocade trousers.

☛ Godley, Hope, Wilde

Scott Crolla. b Edinburgh (UK), 1955. **Ruffled shirt.** Photograph by Andrew Macpherson, *The Face*, 1984.

Daché Lilly   Milliner

Lilly Daché decorates a half-hat with feathers, autumnal berries and dried flowers for American *Vogue*. Towering turbans, draped toques and snoods, and knitted or openwork nets which enclosed the hair at the back of the head were other millinery confections characteristic of Daché. Trained at Caroline Reboux's atelier in Paris, she emigrated to the United States and in 1924 became, like Hattie Carnegie before her, an assistant in the millinery department at Macy's. Two years later she set up her own establishment in New York and became one of the most eminent milliners in America, challenging Paris for the title of millinery capital. She adorned the heads of New York high society and of Hollywood stars such as Betty Grable and Marlene Dietrich – as well as Carmen Miranda. Her most outstanding discovery was Halston, who designed pillbox hats for Jacqueline Kennedy before moving into fashion.

☛ Carnegie, Kennedy, Sieff, Talbot

Lilly Daché. b Bégles (FR), 1907. **d** Louveciennes (FR), 1989. **'Autumnal Berry' hat.** Photograph by Edward Steichen, American *Vogue*, 1946.

Dahl-Wolfe Louise

Photographer

Beneath the Cairo sun, model Nathalie shades herself in a cotton robe by Alix Grès. Louise Dahl-Wolfe, the photographer, often cast her images in bright sunlight. Beaches, deserts and sunny plains were her natural domain, first for compositions in black and white and later for some of the most sumptuous photographs ever taken of swimwear, playsuits and the exoticism of modern fashion. Her most frequent editor-stylist was Diana Vreeland. The unpretentious Dahl-Wolfe and the extravagant Vreeland were an odd couple in style, but together they became collaborator-adventurers in seeking out an ambient naturalism for the modern woman. Vreeland's flamboyance and artifice were sweetly tempered by Dahl-Wolfe's interest in portraiture and in landscape. Even in the most glamorous image, Dahl-Wolfe displays her inquiring mind and analytical insight, giving photography character and idiosyncrasy.

☛ Grès, Maxwell, McCardell, Revillon, Snow, Vreeland

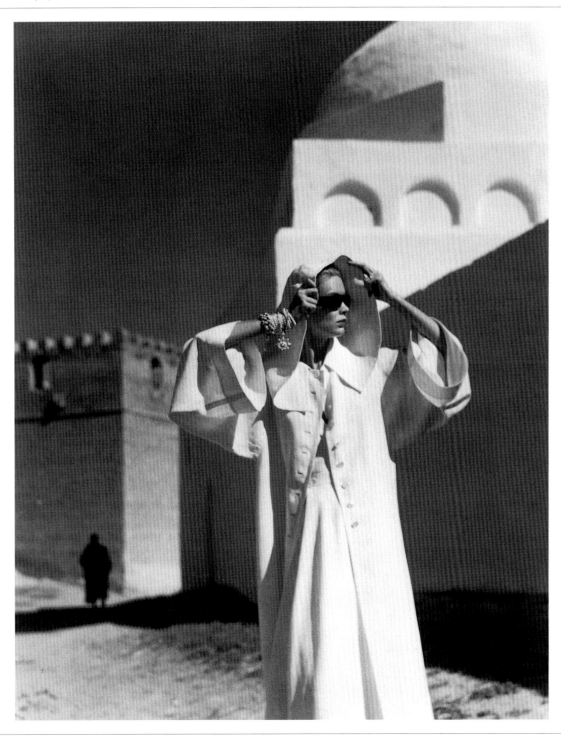

Louise Dahl-Wolfe. b San Francisco, CA (USA), 1895. d New York (USA), 1989. Grès coat, Egypt. 1950.

Dalí Salvador Illustrator

In this dream sequence by Salvador Dalí, the spectator's attention is fixed on the figure wearing a bold red dress very fashionably cut on the bias, the fabric falling in smooth, vertical folds from the hips. Dalí described his pictures as 'hand-painted dream photographs' and his juxtaposition of the real and unreal presented fashion in a new way, bringing out its elegance and seduction.

During the 1930s, with economic and political pressures mounting, fashion and fashion illustration took an escapist route, venturing into Surrealism, the dominant art movement of the decade. Cecil Beaton, Erwin Blumenfeld and George Hoyningen-Huene captured Surrealism's bizarre elements in their work. *Vogue* also commissioned artists such as Dalí, who collaborated

with Schiaparelli in the design of fabrics and accessories, to make 'photo-paintings', presenting fashion's relationship with Surrealism.

☛ Bérard, Blumenfeld, Cocteau, Man Ray, L. Miller

Salvador Dalí. **b** Figueres (SP), 1904. **d** Figueres (SP), 1989. **I Dream About an Evening Dress.** Illustration for American *Vogue*, 1937.

Dassler Adi (Adidas)   Designer

Sport met fashion and music in 1986 when hip hop group Run DMC recorded its devotion to streetwear on the track 'My Adidas'. Sweatshirts, track pants and trainers were appropriated by a generation of men and women who threw away the laces and decorated themselves with heavyweight gold jewellery. In the 1970s, Adidas trainers had been an anti-establishment fashion statement worn with jeans, but in the defiant, label-aware 1980s branding took over and an unsuspecting sportswear company found itself at the heart of a fashion movement. At the 1936 Olympics, Jesse Owens, a black American runner, won four gold medals wearing a pair of trainers made by cobbler Adi Dassler and his brother, Rudolf. They had seen a gap in the market for high-performance athletic shoes in 1920 and they started to build what was to become a label as important to street fashion as it was to sport.

☛ Boy George, Hechter, Hilfiger, P. Knight, Lacoste

Adi (Adolf) Dassler. b Herzogenaurach (GER), 1900. **d** Herzogenaurach (GER), 1978. (Adidas.) **Run DMC in 'Superstar' shoes.** Photograph by Michael E. Heeg, 1986.

Day Corinne   Photographer

In this picture, from the series that introduced Kate Moss to the world, photographer Corinne Day aims to capture 'a teenage sexuality which I love. I want to make my images as documentary as possible, an image of life that is real'. Day's style rejects everything that fashion photography has traditionally stood for – glamour, sexiness, sophistication – by shooting skinny girls in cheap nylon knickers amidst squat-like squalor. Her anti-fashion attitude exemplifies the mood of the 1990s. Herself an ex-model, Day discovers her subjects in the street, preferring 'cocky English girls with a strong identity'. She launched the career of Kate Moss by photographing her aged fifteen for *The Face*, shown here. The best known of the 'grunge' photographers, Day is credited with starting the trend for pre-pubescent-looking waifs. *Vogue* editor Alexandra Shulman, however, defended her work as 'a celebration of vulnerability and joyousness'.

☛ Moss, Page, Sims

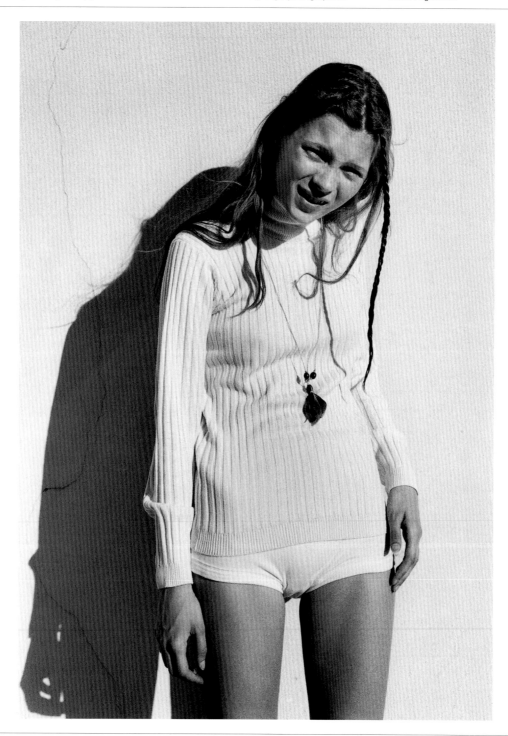

Corinne Day. b (UK), 1950. (Active 1980s–1990s.) **Kate Moss.** 1990.

Dean James   Icon

James Dean, the original teenage rebel, leans against a wall smoking. Dean was the role model for generations of disaffected youth who immediately related to his portrayal of lost adolescence and emulated his wardrobe because of it. Andy Warhol called him 'the damaged but beautiful soul of our time'. His status as a handsome movie star far outshone his acting talents, and in his short-lived career he made only three films: *East of Eden* (1955), *Rebel Without a Cause* (1955) and *Giant* (1956). Dean said, 'Being a good actor isn't easy; being a man is even harder. I want to do both before I'm done'. But, tragically, he was killed at the age of twenty-four, crashing his Porsche Spyder on the way to a race meeting. He is now suspended forever in adolescence. The basics that Dean wore are still popular today as the uniform of youth: Levi's jeans, white T-shirt and zip-up bomber jacket.

☛ Presley, Strauss, Warhol

James Dean. b Fairmount, IN (USA), 1931. **d** Route 466 CA (USA), 1955. **Bomber jacket and Levi's.** *Rebel Without a Cause* publicity shot. 1955.

Delaunay Sonia   Designer

Brilliantly coloured and sharply patterned geometric designs are lavishly displayed on this 'simultaneous' coat. Sonia Delaunay, a leading Parisian artist of Orphism, a movement which developed out of Cubism and which made colour the primary means of artistic expression, has here merged art with fashion. In 1912 she began a series of non-figurative paintings called *Contrastes* *simultanés*, combining geometric forms with bright, prismatic hues. This work was based on the theory of the simultaneous contrast of colours of the nineteenth-century chemist Michel-Eugène Chevreul. Her simultaneous fashions had their origins in these paintings, since she moulded the fabric to the shape of the garment to ensure that the application of the colours remained intact. Her new concept of fabric pattern, whereby the cut and decoration of the garment were created at the same time, perfectly complemented the unstructured clothes of the 1920s.

☞ Balla, P. Ellis, Exter, Heim

126

Sonia Delaunay. **b** Odessa (RUS), 1884. **d** Paris (FR), 1979. **Embroidered 'simultaneous' coat created for Gloria Swanson. 1923.**

Delhomme Jean-Philippe
Illustrator

The supermodel, the hairstylist, the photographer and the assistant interact in a familiar scene from the fashion world. Such familiarity, however, becomes a novelty when painted in the form of a comic-style strip. An accessory to Jean-Philippe Delhomme's wit, fashions are blurred in favour of visually comforting satires of the affectations of those who lead their everyday lives

in this industry. This bright, hand-painted gouache, which belongs to Delhomme's own one-page column published monthly in French *Glamour* since 1988, reveals a knowing artist. While drawing inspiration from his friends in the fashion trade, he claims to operate in, 'a *décalage*, a kind of jet lag, that appears between life written up in magazines and what's happening in the

real world'. Delhomme's highly stylized and spontaneous caricatures recall the work of Marcel Vertès who, in the 1930s, fondly satirized the foibles of fashionable society.

☛ Berthoud, Vertès

Jean-Philippe Delhomme. b Nanterre (FR), 1959. **Modes de Vie.** Illustrated for *Glamour*, 1993.

Dell'Acqua Alessandro

How to make something delicate and romantic appear hard-edged and punky: this dilemma is at the centre of Alessandro Dell'Acqua's work. While his clothes have a softness and sensuality defined by materials such as chiffon, shown here on a T-shirt with fluted, bias-cut sleeves, his outfits are often styled with aggression. Long leather gloves and broad sweeps of violet eye shadow lend edge to what would otherwise be a dainty shirt. Dell'Acqua claims rock star Courtney Love, widow of Kurt Cobain, as his heroine and her own style reflects his blend of aggressive femininity. His mix-and-match, layered pieces are modern in their versatility and wearability. His signature palette is contrasting colours (nude and black being two of his favourites). Initially Dell'Acqua specialized in knitwear and he worked with a small group of artisans in Bologna. His collections carry reminders of this period through fragile knits of delicate, lacy mohair.

☛ Cobain, Chalayan, Sarne

128

Alessandro Dell'Acqua. b Naples (IT), 1963. **Silk chiffon T-shirt. Autumn/winter 1997/8.** Photograph by Chris Moore.

Dell'Olio Louis   Designer

Dogtooth check and black leather is a blend of fashion and function, sass and shrewdness by Louis Dell'Olio, called 'the designer for everywoman'. The fitted, single-breasted jacket follows a body-conscious line without alienating his conservative clientele. This outfit was created under Anne Klein's label which he had taken over with Donna Karan, a friend from college, after Klein's death in 1974. Dell'Olio said of the experience, 'We didn't know enough to be terrified' but together they forged a style that suited the working women of America. In 1984 Karan left to set up her own label and Dell'Olio continued what they had started until Richard Tyler took over the company in 1993. One fan of Dell'Olio's work told *Vogue*, 'I don't want to be gussied up to the ears...the jackets hide a multitude of sins, the pants have a fabulous fit, the clothes are clean.'

☞ **Karan, A. Klein, Tyler**

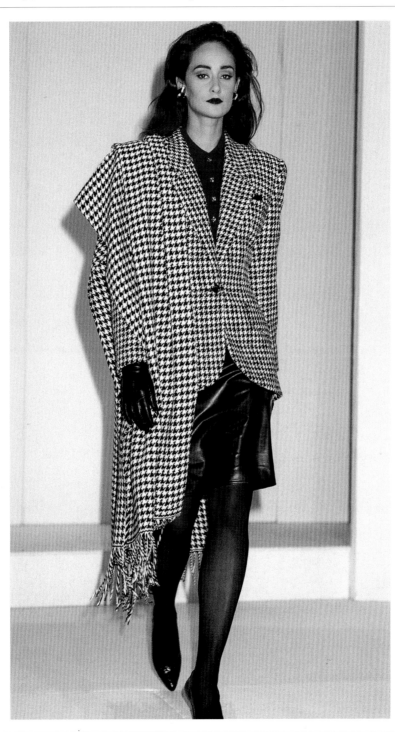

Louis Dell'Olio. b New York (USA), 1948. **Dogtooth check and black leather for Anne Klein.** Photograph by Chris Moore, 1988.

Demarchelier Patrick

Photographer

Patrick Demarchelier catches Nadja Auermann mid-spin, her aigrette adding to an aura of costume history. Though relentlessly modern, Demarchelier's work also has a grand quality usually associated with the great couture photographers of the 1950s. He left Paris for New York in 1975 and started a long relationship with America's magazines, in particular the Condé Nast titles *Vogue*, *Glamour* and *Mademoiselle*. In 1992 he joined *Harper's Bazaar*, recruited by Liz Tilberis, for his clear, graphic photographs. It was the perfect material for the spreads designed by creative director Fabien Baron. Though dealing largely with the vicissitudes of fashion, Demarchelier's work has also explored other territories. *Harper's Bazaar* said of his work, 'For people who want to look really beautiful, Demarchelier has become the photographer of choice, perhaps the most sought-after shooter of the 1990s'.

☛ Baron, Chanel, Lagerfeld, Wainwright

Patrick Demarchelier. b Le Havre (FR), 1943. **Nadja Auermann wears haute couture by Karl Lagerfeld for Chanel.** *Harper's Bazaar*, 1994.

Demeulemeester Ann   Designer

It could be a music video or a science fiction film: the subject's hard-edged image, punk make-up and black leather dress alienate her from the natural environment she inhabits. Belgian designer Ann Demeulemeester's 1970s rock star-style tailoring and leatherwear draw inspiration from strong female icons of music, such as Patti Smith, Janis Joplin and Chrissie Hynde. 'The things that meant something to you when you were sixteen stay with you forever. They are your roots,' she says. From cobweb knitwear to oversized masculine 'slouch' suits, Demeulemeester designs clothes with attitude. Jackets are worn back to front or have just one sleeve; trousers are oversized, slung around the hips; knitwear is shrugged off the shoulder. In the same way that Helmut Lang has earned his copyists, Demeulemeester's ideas have been translated onto many other catwalks. Her work has that highly marketable quality: cool.

☞ Bikkembergs, Capasa, Kerrigan, Thimister, Van Noten

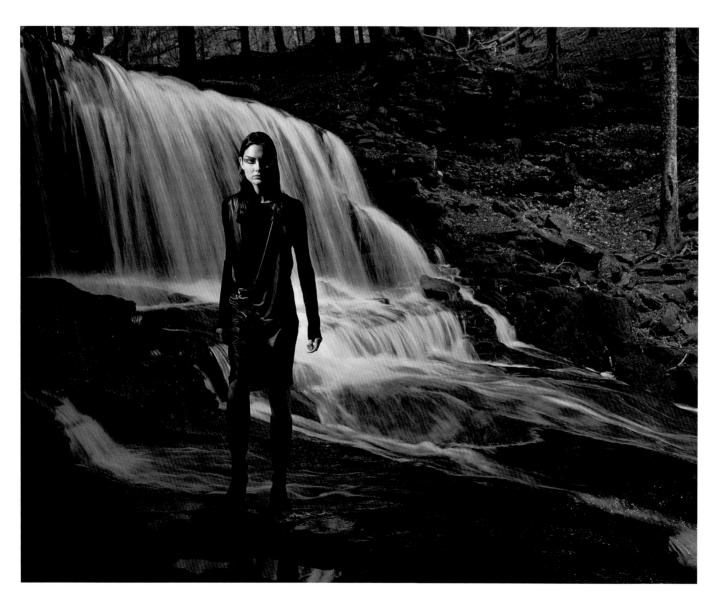

Ann Demeulemeester. **b** Courtrai (BEL), 1954. **Black leather draped tunic dress and jersey shirt.** Photograph by Philip-Lorca diCorcia, *Harper's Bazaar*, 1997.

Deneuve Catherine Icon

Catherine Deneuve leaps for Francesco Scavullo's camera, a consummate model as well as an icon of French elegance, *froideur* and sensibility. Deneuve is also a long-term muse to Yves Saint Laurent, whom she met when he dressed her for *Belle de Jour*. Saint Laurent says of her, 'She is a woman who makes me dream... As a friend she is the most delightful, warmest, sweetest and most protective.'

As French *Vogue*'s most featured cover face, Deneuve represents the legendary chic femininity of French womanhood and as such was also the face of Chanel No.5. Here, she wears a suit made of calfskin printed with cheetah spots and trimmed with mink, a powerful combination brought together by Arnold Scaasi. When she talks about the de-feminized roles played by actresses in modern films, Deneuve outlines her own style, 'Superficially, it may appear that the women now are stronger, but they are not stronger, only more masculine.'

☞ Barthet, Chanel, Saint Laurent, Scaasi, Scavullo

Catherine Deneuve. b Paris (FR), 1943. **Calfskin and mink cheetah print suit by Arnold Scaasi.** Photograph by Francesco Scavullo, 1970.

Dessès Jean — Designer

The roses at the hem of this chiffon dress were only usually exposed as the wearer walked. They are a charming addition to a classically inspired gown. The fashions of Dessès were inspired by his Greek heritage and Egyptian place of birth. He was a master of draped chiffon and muslin evening dresses that were derived from ancient robes. He was also noted for dresses made in the form of fitted jackets in plain colours with voluminous skirts in a contrasting patterned print. He established his own maison de couture in Paris in 1937. Dessès participated in the Théâtre de la Mode, the fashion doll exhibition organized by the Chambre Syndicale de la Couture Parisienne under its president, Lucien Lelong. Some forty couturiers designed haute couture in miniature for these little mannequins made of wire. They were placed in sets depicting scenes of Parisian life designed by artists involved in fashion, such as Cocteau and Bérard.

☛ Cocteau, Laroche, Lelong, McLaughlin-Gill, Valentino

Jean Dessès. **b** Alexandria (EG), 1904. **d** Athens (GR), 1970. **Black chiffon dress with pink silk roses on underskirt.** Photograph by Frances McLaughlin-Gill, American *Vogue*, 1952.

Diana Princess of Wales Icon

'Clothes are now not as essential to my work as they used to be', Diana, Princess of Wales, told *Vogue* in 1997. It was a confident statement from a woman who had come to realize that a pair of jeans wouldn't compromise her effectiveness. And it showed. Towards the end of her life, Diana's wardrobe finally took a back seat to the person she was and the work she did; an utterly modern concept. Here she wears an artfully uncomplicated navy lace dress by Catherine Walker for a charity film premiere in 1997. From the day Lady Diana Spencer was first caught on film in the early 1980s wearing archetypal British upper-class clothing, the ensuing developments in her wardrobe and the colour of lipstick she chose were closely watched and widely copied. Particular attention was given to her hair, sleeked and simplified in the 1990s by Sam McKnight.

☛ Choo, Emanuel, Fratini, Oldfield, G. Smith, Testino

134

Diana, Princess of Wales. b Sandringham (UK), 1961. **d** Paris (FR), 1997. **Catherine Walker dress.** Photograph by Kelvin Bruce, 1997.

Dinnigan Colette Designer

Colette Dinnigan's dress has the charm of an antique gown, yet possesses a modern sensuality, suspended as it is from two spaghetti straps. Its lace tiers and train belong to the romantic, early twentieth-century designers such as Paquin, Lucile and Dœuillet. Dinnigan launched her career designing and selling lace and chiffon lingerie. Her success allowed her to open a shop in 1992, and begin designing a ready-to-wear line. Her use of womanly fabrics and attention to the female form resulted in clinging slip dresses which gave sophistication to the trend for wearing underwear-as-outerwear. The preciousness of her designs is reminiscent of haute couture detailing and was a contrast to the prevailing use of undecorated fabrics cut into graphic forms. The simple shapes of underwear are wrought in lace and placed over contrasting satins to achieve the luminescence illustrated here.

☞ Dœuillet, Duff Gordon, Moon, Oudejans, Paquin

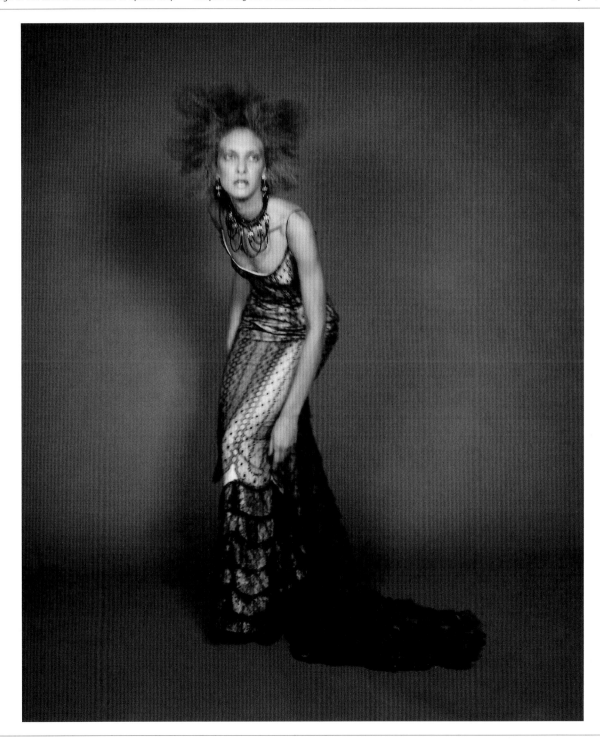

Colette Dinnigan. **b** Durban (SA), 1965. **Satin dress overlaid with lace.** Photograph by Gerald Jenkins, Australian *Style*, 1997.

Dior Christian

Designer

Reading the faces of this salon audience, it is possible to gauge the breadth of reaction which greeted Christian Dior's first collection, which was dubbed the 'New Look' after this show by Carmel Snow, editor of *Harper's Bazaar*. As they gaze at an hourglass jacket of cream tussore over a skirt constructed from a decadent yardage of black wool, the audience registers shock, disapproval and deep yearning. At a time of postwar austerity, the New Look tempted women back into the nostalgic femininity of corsets and, most controversially, flowing skirts that would use up to fifty yards of material. Dior, who had wanted to be an architect but turned to fashion, working for Piguet, Lelong and Balmain, said that it was one of the happiest moments of his life: 'I created flower women with gentle shoulders and generous bosoms, with tiny waists like stems and skirts belling out like petals.'

☛ Bohan, Ferre, Galliano, Molyneux, Saint Laurent

136

Dœuillet Georges Designer

The fashion plates of André Marty have a very evocative quality. Fastidiously stylish, Marty has created a pictorial witticism to depict the character of the dress. He has juxtaposed the delicacy and fragility of the *robe de lingerie* against the foreboding figure of Cupid and the dark, sinister landscape. It is an example of haute couture providing a stimulating atmosphere for the rejuvenation of fashion illustration, a combination of luxurious design and texture with artistic excellence that captured the spirit of the times. The exquisitely intricate workmanship of this immaculate dress came from the Paris couture house of Dœuillet, which was founded in 1900. Noted for its use of magnificent fabrics, Dœuillet was a prestigious fashion house that provided the *bon ton* with some of the most opulent clothes of the early years of the twentieth century. It merged with the salon of Jacques Doucet on his death in 1929.

☛ **Bakst, Dinnigan, Doucet, Poiret**

137

Georges Dœuillet. d (FR), 1929. (Active 1890s–1920s.) **Broderie anglaise boudoir dress.** Illustration by André Marty, *La Gazette du Bon Ton*, 1913.

Dolce Domenico and Gabbana Stefano (Dolce & Gabbana)

This photograph of Italian actress/model Isabella Rossellini could almost be a still from one of her father, Roberto Rossellini's, black-and-white films of the 1940s. This cinematic sensuality is typical of Dolce & Gabbana's style. Their idealistic vision of Italy revolves around specific themes: 1940s screen sirens (leopard prints and corsetry à la Sophia Loren), Catholicism (Sunday best suits and rosary beads) and various Italian stereotypes, from Mafioso machismo (pinstripe suits and trilbys) to the simplicity of Sicilian widows (little black dresses, headscarves, fishing village baskets). But beneath this puritanical patriotism there are also hints of subversion: cross-dressing and suits cut with integral corsetry or lace panels are favourites. Although the religious imagery is strong, it is glamorized almost to the point of pastiche, from sequined icons to rosary beads worn as jewelled necklaces.

☛ Colonna, McGrath, Matsushima, Meisel, Nars

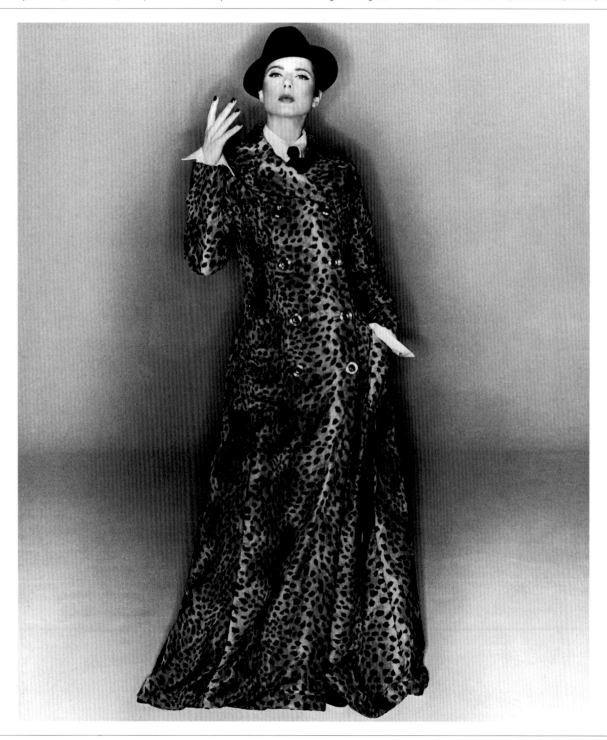

Domenico Dolce. b Palermo (IT), 1958; **Stefano Gabbana. b** Milan (IT), 1962. (Dolce & Gabbana.) **Isabella Rossellini wears leopard-print coat. Autumn/winter 1994.** Photograph by Michel Comte.

Dominguez Adolfo

Designer

A bodice is formed from a swathe of iridescent fabric, the only decoration being the shine picked out by the light on its folds. As with the work of Mitsuhiro Matsuda, the material dictates the shape and creates a garment somewhere between shawl and jacket. Adolfo Dominguez is the Spanish answer to Giorgio Armani. In the 1980s he was famously called 'King of the Wrinklies' for his tailored but unpressed, crinkled suits for men. Like Armani, he is known for using fabrics that direct his work and lend themselves to a simpler, softer look. These visual preoccupations come from the fact that he is not a traditionally trained fashion designer. Dominguez studied cinematography and aesthetics in Paris, before returning to his father's drapery shop in Orense, northern Spain. Dominguez launched his first men's ready-to-wear collection in Madrid in 1982, and followed it with womenswear in 1992.

☛ Armani, Matsuda, del Pozo

139

Adolfo Dominguez. b Orense (SP), 1950. **Metallic shawl jacket.** Photograph by Manuel Madarnas, 1988.

Doucet Jacques   Designer

Doucet's gown is beautifully illustrated by Magnin for *La Gazette du Bon Ton* in 1914. The illustration reflects not only the high-waisted style in vogue before the First World War but also the way Doucet worked with artists. Together with his contemporary Poiret, he helped revive the art of fashion illustration in France. He was also a patron of the fine arts and in 1909 bought Picasso's avant-garde painting *Les Demoiselles d'Avignon*, installing it at the head of a crystal staircase in a specially built wing of his house. The grandson of a lace merchant, Doucet expanded the family business by opening a couture department in 1871. With his gowns of rare gros-point de Venise, bodices of paper-thin ivory chamois and opera capes lined with swans' down or chinchilla, Doucet's style epitomized the opulent femininity of the *belle époque*.

☛ Dœuillet, Iribe, Poiret

Jacques Doucet. b Paris (FR), 1853. **d** Paris (FR), 1932. **Afternoon dress.** Illustrated by J. Magnin for *La Gazette du Bon Ton*, 1914.

Dovima

Model

Dovima, made-up with the painted kohl lids and expressive pencilled brows of the 1950s, strikes an artful pose from behind white tulle. She and Richard Avedon broke new ground in fashion photography. Modelling with elephants or in front of the pyramids, they took fashion out of the whitewashed studio and into the 'real' world for the first time. Dovima was talent-spotted on the street outside the offices of *Vogue* in New York and was soon in front of Irving Penn's lens. She told him her name was Dovima (the first letters from her real names, Dorothy Virginia Margaret) because that was how she signed her paintings. Charging an hourly rate of $60, she became known as the dollar-a-minute girl. After twelve years at the top, she appeared alongside Audrey Hepburn in one of the most famous fashion films, *Funny Face*. Dovima's graceful, arch poses are now regarded as the *sine qua non* of haute couture presentation.

☛ Avedon, Lauder, Penn

Dovima (Dorothy Virginia Margaret Juba). b New York (USA), 1927. **d** Fort Lauderdale, FL (USA), 1990. **Dovima behind tulle.** Photograph by Cecil Beaton, 1950s.

Von Drecoll Baron Christoff

Designer

The house of Drecoll spanned the years from 1905 to 1929 and shows two distinct styles. In the *belle époque* period, Drecoll specialized in promenade gowns and evening dresses with boned bodices, tight waists and full skirts, which produced the S-shaped figure of the period. Photographs in *Les Modes* show that Drecoll ensembles were fussier and trimmed with more confection than comparable outfits from other couture houses. In the 1920s the house was known for chic, short, low-waisted gowns teamed with the cloche, a tight-fitting hat shaped like a bell and pulled low over the forehead. These flapper outfits were illustrated in luxury fashion magazines such as *Art*, *Goût* and *Beauté*. The house of Drecoll was founded by Christoff von Drecoll in Vienna. It opened in Paris in 1905 under the ownership of M and Mme de Wagner, a Belgian couple, who also supported Marie-Louise Bruyère.

☞ **Bruyère, Gibson, Poiret, Redfern, Rouff**

Baron Christoff von Drecoll. (Active 1890s–1920s.) **Afternoon dress.** *Les Modes*, 1914.

Drian Etienne   Illustrator

'Evening dress in moon-blue sequined silk' is the caption accompanying this watercolour illustration by Drian. His loose and simple technique successfully conveys the soft and fluid texture of silk. Drian was an artist who worked in Paris for the illustrated fashion magazine *La Gazette du Bon Ton*, from its foundation in 1912 until its closure in 1925. He illustrated articles and also produced fashion plates. His graphic style was brisk and clear, with the *bon ton* depicted in fluid movement in anecdotal settings which give a picture of contemporary life. He was very adept at bringing out the intricate workmanship of the haute couture of the period, in the fashions, for example, of Paul Poiret. Among his contemporaries at *La Gazette du Bon Ton* were Georges Barbier and Georges Lepape. Drian was also well known in the 1920s and 1930s for his sanguine portrait drawings and for his decorative murals.

☛ **Barbier, Lepape, Poiret, Sumurun**

Etienne Drian (Etienne Adrien). **b** Bulgneville (FR), 1885. **d** Paris (FR), 1961. **Evening dress in moon-blue sequined silk.** *Costumes Parisiens*, 1914.

Duff Gordon Lady (Lucile)

Designer

Lucile, who started out in 1890 by dressmaking for her friends, opened her own fashion house in 1891. Her marriage to Sir Cosmo Duff Gordon in 1900 catapulted her into designing for the upper echelons of international society, with branches in New York (1909), Chicago (1911) and Paris (1911). Like the Callot Sœurs, she designed romantic dresses made of silk and lace. Her speciality was picturesque tea gowns in pastel shades worn with mild corsetry, the fitting of which is being conducted here. Like her countryman Worth, she held fashion shows for her clients. Like Poiret, she was an innovator, designing clothes which were startling for the time – such as draped skirts which revealed the legs. She was also involved in the entertainment world, designing costumes which became popular fashion, such as those for Lily Elsie, star of the *The Merry Widow*. Her other clients included the dancer Irene Castle and actress Sarah Bernhardt.

☛ Boué, Callot, Dinnigan, Molyneux, Poiret, Worth

144

Lady Duff Gordon (Lucy Sutherland; Lucile). b London (UK), 1862. d London (UK), 1935. **Lucile with client and mannequin at a fitting.** 1912.

Dufy Raoul

Textile designer

This lush silk is decorated with silver lamé work. The oriental motifs in sky blue, royal blue and rose reflect the imagery of the woodcuts Dufy executed for Guillaume Apollinaire's *Le Bestiaire* of 1911. Rose-coloured horses frolic amongst waves, scallops, dolphins and froth, all spectacularly taking on silver highlights in the light. This fabric was chosen by Poiret for an evening dress he displayed at the Exposition des Arts Décoratifs in Paris in 1925. It was produced by the textile company Bianchini Férier, with whom Dufy had an exclusive contract from 1912 to 1928. His use of colour came from his association with the Fauves (a group of artists who developed a new style of painting characterized by a bold handling of vivid colours). Dufy collaborated with Poiret in establishing the Petite Usine for fabric-printing. Even though it closed at the end of 1911, it had a great impact on Dufy's career as a fashion artist.

☞ Patou, Poiret, Rubinstein

Raoul Dufy. b Le Havre (FR), 1877. **d** Forcalquier (FR), 1953. **'Shells and Marine Horses'**, produced by Bianchini Férier, 1925 (fabric detail).

Eisen Mark   Designer

Model Jodie Kidd is picked out in a catwalk line-up at the end of Mark Eisen's show. She is wearing a mix of animal skin, wholesome wool and shiny silk. Born in South Africa, Eisen studied at the University of Southern California, where he not only learned business and achieved fame by designing a football helmet for 'Trojans' fans, but also gained the sensibility for streamlined, no-nonsense dressing that stresses contemporary materials. Eisen's flirtatious, but simple silhouettes and intense materials are relaxed versions of contentious European fashion, giving wearability to otherwise challenging schemes. Even natural materials get coated so that they literally shine. He has shown 'couture denim' and other signs of the street in a style former *New York Times* journalist Amy Spindler called 'driven by the spirit of techno music, repetitive, strong and stripped down'. Eisen provides the clothes for the spirit of 'California dreamin'.

☛ **Kors, Oldham, Rocha**

Mark Eisen. b Cape Town (SA), 1960. **Catwalk line-up. Autumn/winter 1998.** Photograph by Chris Moore.

146

Ellis Perry   Designer

Ellis, who launched his own label in 1978, created a strong brand of American sportswear by emphasizing colour, often in stripes and blocks, and by using the textures of natural fibres. Here, linen is used for a T-shirt and skirt, joined in the middle by an outsize belt. His inspirations included Sonia Delaunay, Patou and Chanel in the 1920s and contemporary culture. Capacious summer linen trousers and skirts were often matched with cotton sweaters or blouses. Sweaters were a staple for Ellis throughout the year. Winter wools were luxurious and, like all the clothes, cuddly and easy to wear. Ellis began in fashion sales; his design was conceptual and often devoted to stories or ideas that readily translated to the consumer: the winter 1985 sweaters seized unicorns, decorative foliage and sleek greyhounds from medieval tapestry, and his slouchy looks of the 1980s were exaggerated to create the look of a picturesque hobo.

☛ Delaunay, Jackson, Jacobs, Patou

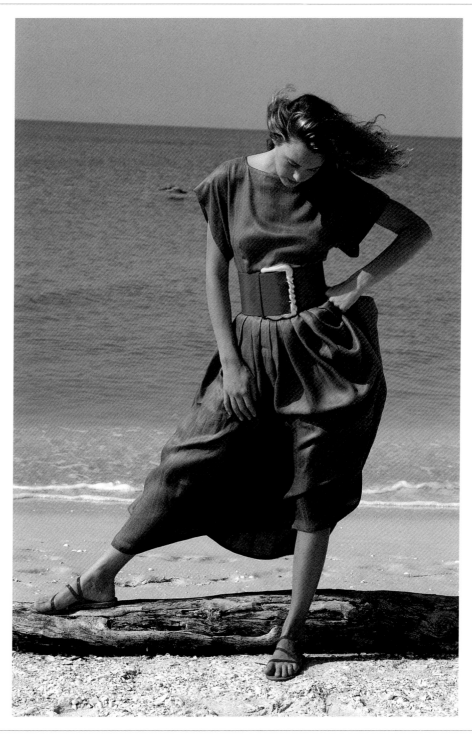

Perry Ellis. b VA (USA), 1940. d New York (USA), 1986. **Blue linen dress with scarlet belt. Spring 1983.** Photograph by Erica Lennard.

Ellis Sean

Photographer

In a fashion shoot for *The Face*, Sean Ellis re-creates a fantasy based on a supernatural storyline about voyeurism and death. It gives meaning to the phrase 'fashion story', which is used by magazines to explain a theme which runs through a multi-page shoot. In this case, the angelic character's eyes are made luminous to signify contact lenses which allow her tormentor to see himself as she would. The red dye which stains her snowy chiffon top signifies blood. Such stories put fashion into an anomalous context rather than simply showcasing clothes. It is a challenging method of fashion photography which has come to the fore in the 1990s, although other photographers such as Guy Bourdin and Helmut Newton developed sophisticated story-telling techniques around sex and death themes in the 1970s. Ellis explains his narrative pictures as 'not necessarily fashion pictures – they just happen to be fashionable'.

☛ Macdonald, Pearl, Tennant

148

Sean Ellis. b Brighton (UK), 1970. **'White Dragon' shirt by Tristan Webber.** *The Face*, 1998.

Emanuel David and Elizabeth

A spontaneous moment is snapped on 31 July, 1981. The Princess of Wales is dressed in the romantic counterpoint to her husband's uniform. The flashlight throws into relief the yards of silk taffeta ruffles at her neck and the delicate, specially made Nottingham lace cuffs at her wrist. Unseen is the eight-metre train decorated with pearls. It was called 'a dress for a real fairy princess'. David and Elizabeth Emanuel, who designed the dress for the Princess, had created a popular movement in womenswear which reflected the moment it was designed for – one that reached a record television audience around the world. The married couple originally met at the Royal College of Art. They graduated in 1978, the year they also launched their Mayfair boutique. They garnered a celebrity following, with Joan Collins and Bianca Jagger among those who wore their extravagant and quixotic visions of femininity.

☛ Diana, Fratini, Tappé

Emanuel. David. b Bridgend (UK), 1952; Elizabeth. b London (UK), 1953. The Prince and Princess of Wales on their wedding day. 1981.

Eric

Illustrator

Using the broad mirror of a powder room, Eric is able to describe the jewelled details of Jean Patou's evening dress from both front and rear. He had a deft, calligraphic style whereby the model and the clothes she was wearing were minutely examined. To get such accuracy of observation, Eric drew from life and insisted the models remain static in their settings for long periods. To him, fidelity to detail was all-important. Born in America of Swedish parents, Carl Erickson studied at the Academy of Fine Arts in Chicago, where he acquired the training and discipline required for working with the figure. His first fashion illustrations for *Vogue* appeared in 1916. By 1925 he was settled in France, and, apart from the period during the Occupation of Paris (when he returned to America), he provided *Vogue* with fashion illustrations on the modes and manners of the Parisian beau monde right up to the mid-1950s.

☞ Antonio, Berthoud, Bouché, Patou

150

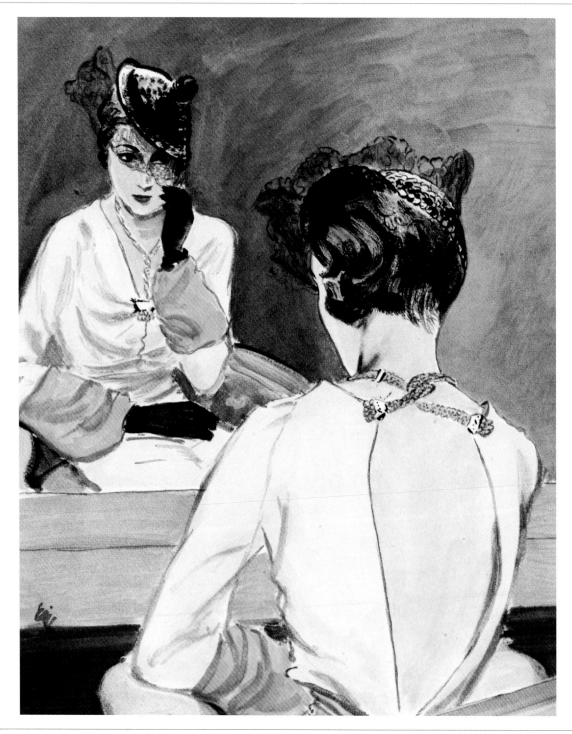

Eric (Carl Erickson). b Joliet, IL (USA), 1891. d Senlis (FR), 1958. **Dress by Jean Patou.** American *Vogue*, 1933.

Von Etzdorf Georgina

Textile designer

Colour and texture meet on an outfit by the textile design partnership, Georgina von Etzdorf. Golden sunbursts are embroidered onto a woollen gauze vest and devoré velvet is used to give a shadowy, raised pattern to a bias-cut skirt. Foliage and flower motifs, evoking the atmosphere of rural England, typify the work of a company that is inspired by natural imagery. In 1981 Georgina von Etzdorf

entered into a partnership with two art school contemporaries, Martin Simcock and Jonathan Docherty. The hand-printing method they developed involves screen-printing supplemented by hand-applied paint strokes, a process which lends individuality to each garment. Georgina von Etzdorf's contribution to fashion has been to stimulate the use of handmade fabrics,

especially for scarves. Velvet and silk is printed with abstract shafts and blocks of colour, the result being a wearable piece of conceptual textile design.

☛ Cerruti, Lloyd, Mazzilli, Williamson

Georgina von Etzdorf. b Lima (PER), 1955. **Hand-embroidered camisole and velvet devoré skirt. Autumn/winter 1998.** Photograph by Howard Sooley.

Eula Joe

Illustrator

Free, vivid colour captures a woman mid-step in a sketch that typifies the art of modern fashion illustration. Eula was a keeper of the graphic tradition of fashion at a time when photography dominated. His fashion illustrations for Italian and French *Harper's Bazaar*, from 1979, used impressionistic watercolour. Eula began his career in the 1950s on the fashion and social pages of the *Herald Tribune*, then worked for *The Sunday Times* in London. Back in New York in the 1960s, he worked on fashion stories for *Life* and designed sets and costumes for the New York City Ballet under George Balanchine. He diversified into television, directing 'fashion specials' for movie stars such as Lauren Bacall. In the 1970s he also worked with Halston, illustrated fashion for *Vogue* and assisted Diana Vreeland, who was then head of the Costume Institute at the Metropolitan Museum of Art in New York.

☛ **Halston, Missoni, Vreeland**

Joe Eula. b Norwalk, CT (USA), 1925. **d** Kingston, NY (USA), 2004. **Knitwear by Missoni. Spring/summer 1985.** Illustration for *Harper's Bazaar*.

Evangelista Linda Model

Linda's haircut transformed a model into not just a supermodel, but *the* supermodel. In October 1988 *Vogue* photographer Peter Lindbergh persuaded her to have her hair cut short. Evangelista cried throughout, but the crop made her career. Over the following six months, she appeared on the covers of every edition of *Vogue*. Linda knew that the key to longevity was

versatility, so she continued to change her haircut and colour every couple of months – and fashion followed. Evangelista's professionalism put her at the top and she became famous for her audacious statements. 'We don't *Vogue* – we are *Vogue*,' was surpassed by a comment that defined the supermodel era: 'We don't wake up for less than $10,000.' While the 'supers' were inevitably

equalled by the 1990s beauty cult – that of Stella Tennant and Kate Moss – Evangelista's fame gave her the longevity she was looking for.

☛ Bergère, Garren, Lindbergh, Moss, Twiggy

Linda Evangelista. b St Katherine, ONT (CAN), 1965. **Velvet tank by Kenar. Autumn/winter 1997.** Photograph by Rocco Laspata.

Exter Alexandra   Designer

Alexandra Exter, an artist/fashion designer, brings the two disciplines together with *Dama al Ballo*, the painting of a dress which lives somewhere between both. After studying art in Kiev, she went to Paris where she met Pablo Picasso, Georges Braque and Filippo Martinetti. From 1900 to 1914 she travelled between Paris, Moscow and Kiev, spreading the doctrines of Cubism and Futurism among the Russian avant-garde. By 1916 she was working in theatrical costume design in Moscow and in 1921 she became a teacher at the Higher Artistic and Technical Workshops there. She promoted the idea that art and fashion could enhance everyday life and began working in fashion design. She designed proletarian dresses in brightly coloured geometric patterns analogous to the work of her friend, Sonia Delaunay. In the traditions of haute couture, she made sumptuously embroidered dresses inspired by peasant art.

☛ Balla, Capucci, Delaunay

Alexandra Exter. b Kiev (RUS), 1882. **d** Paris (FR), 1949. **'Dama al Ballo'.** Costume design for a Russian production of the ballet *Romeo and Juliet*, 1921.

158

Factor Max   Cosmetics creator

Known as 'Hollywood's make-up wizard', Max Factor oversaw Jean Harlow's *maquillage* – he created a star and started a beauty revolution when he dyed her hair platinum blonde. Harlow's heavy scheme of oily, blackened lids and lips was typical of that used for black-and-white films which required strong contrasts. Pancake make-up base was created to even out skin tone as films were transformed in the age of colour. It was cosmetics that created the glamorous images of the movie stars and, as they testified to the quality of the products they were using on a daily basis, the general public clamoured for them. Factor's products coincided with an acceptance of coloured cosmetics for women. The studios sent their budding starlets to him for grooming, and in 1937 the Max Factor Hollywood Make-Up Studio opened and Max Factor set about bringing the make-up of the stars to the public.

☛ **Bourjois, Lauder, Revson, Uemura**

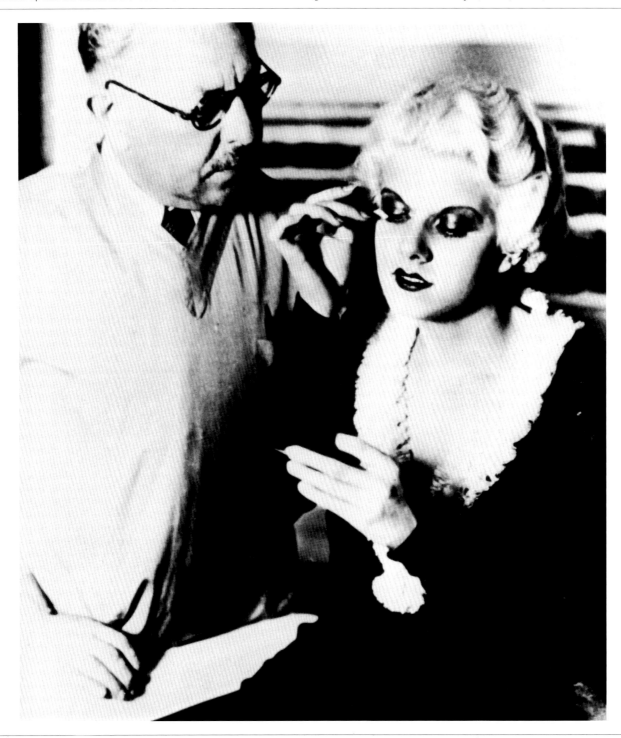

Max Factor. **b** Lodz (POL), 1872. **d** Los Angeles, CA (USA), 1938. **Max Factor with Jean Harlow.** 1931.

Farhi Nicole   Designer

Easy, wearable, comfortable linen is the fabric most associated with the work of Nicole Farhi. When she launched her own label in 1983, Farhi's clothes became the epitome of understated fashion for women – all based on the kind she likes to wear. They are not intended to make major fashion statements. Instead, they drift with the differing times, staying in touch with them but always bearing the wearer in mind. Farhi described herself in the *Guardian* as 'a feminist in a soft way', and her clothes appeal to women who are looking for approachable tailoring and casual clothes which have Farhi's own dressed-up European attitude. Farhi studied fashion in Paris and freelanced for de Castelbajac before moving to Britain in 1973 to design for the French Connection chain. In 1989 she introduced menswear to the Farhi label, blending British tailoring and her European unstructured style.

☛ de Castelbajac, Kerrigan

160

Nicole Farhi. b Nice (FR), 1946. **Elasticized linen dress. Spring/summer 1998.** Photograph by Kelly Klein.

Fath Jacques   Designer

A negative image accentuates a perfect hourglass figure created on a soft line with a curving, structured shape. This evening dress evokes the heady exuberance and gaiety of the early 1950s, when Jacques Fath, called the 'couturier's couturier', was in the same haute couture firmament as Christian Dior. He was famed for his feminine evening dresses, whipped up for royalty and movie stars. This golden era was described by his muse, Bettina, in an interview in 1994. She recalled the extremely creative atmosphere when he worked with assistants who were to succeed in their own right, such as Guy Laroche and Hubert de Givenchy. Fath worked in tandem with the model. He moulded the fabric directly onto her body without any preliminary drawing. Standing in front of a mirror, he would ask her to strike a pose, creating a *théâtre de la mode*, which became the source for the design in the collection.

☛ **Bettina, Bourdin, Head, Maltézos, Perugia, Pipart**

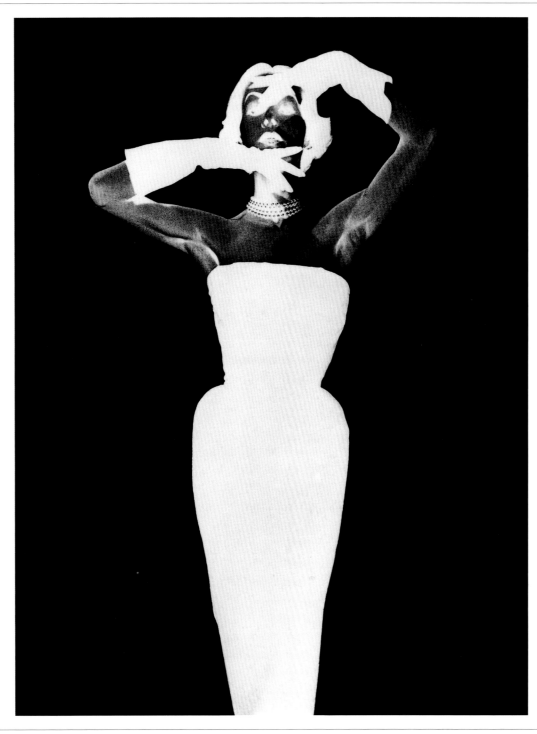

Jacques Fath. b Maisons-Lafitte (FR), 1912. **d** Paris (FR), 1954. **Cocktail dress.** Photograph by Maurice Tabard, *Jardin des Modes*, 1950s.

Fendi Adele and Eduardo

Fendi's great achievement was to update fur's traditional image by giving it a fashion edge. Fox is seen here fashioned into a punky coat. Adele Casagrande founded the company in 1918, changing its name when she married Eduardo Fendi in 1925. Since then Fendi has remained a family-run business, now managed by Adele's five daughters and directed by her granddaughter at board level, although Karl Lagerfeld has designed the collections since 1965. He has used fur for casualwear, creating mink-trimmed denim jackets and fur-lined sporty raincoats. In 1969 he introduced a leather and accessories line, which features the family's double-F motif. Lagerfeld continues to make innovations in fur today, combining his high fashion aesthetic with high-tech developments – tiny perforations that make the coats lighter to wear, speckled colouring techniques for a more intense shade and unusual furs such as squirrel and ferret.

☞ Lagerfeld, Léger, Revillon

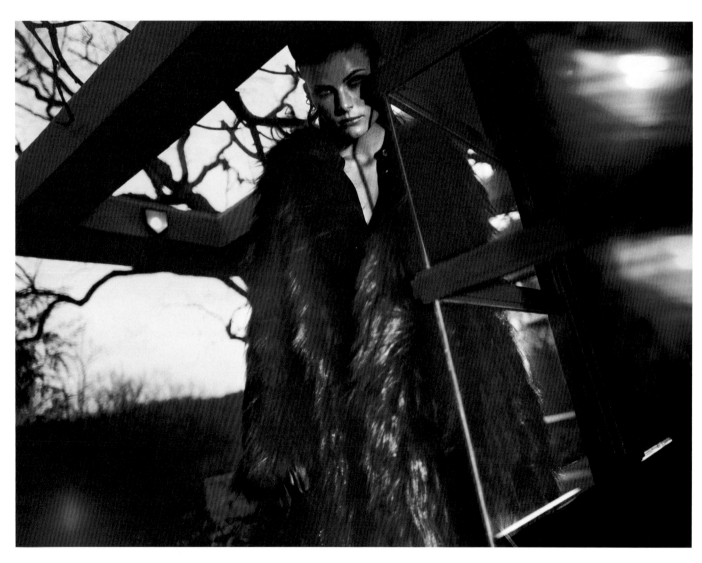

Fendi. Adele. b Rome (IT), 1897. d Rome (IT), 1978; Eduardo. b Rome (IT). (Active 1920s–1950s.) d Rome (IT), 1954. 'Feather fox' coat. Autumn/winter 1997/8. Photograph by Jerome Esch.

Féraud Louis   Designer

Sunny, heavily embroidered clothes are Louis Féraud's métier. The designer says of his work, 'I live in the joy of being surrounded by women, of somehow directing their destiny, in so far as their destiny depends on a note of excess'. In 1955, Féraud opened a boutique in Cannes. He had dressed the young star Brigitte Bardot in an off-the-shoulder, white piqué frock; 600 copies of this dress were sold and Féraud's success was established. Grace Kelly, Ingrid Bergman and Christian Lacroix's mother were also customers. He opened a boutique in Paris where he began to produce couture alongside prêt-à-porter, and he and his wife were dubbed 'The Gypsies' because of their bright, Midi-inspired look. In the 1960s, Féraud's work was characterized by simple, architectural shapes with graphic detailing; Twiggy modelled the collections and Féraud designed the costumes for the cult television serial *The Prisoner*.

☛ Bardot, Blair, Esterel, Ley

Louis Féraud. b Arles (FR), 1920. d Paris (FR), 1999. **'Golden Sun' dress. Haute couture. Spring/summer 1997.** Photograph by Sylvie Lancrenon.

Ferragamo Salvatore

Shoe designer

This shoe, which marries glamour with imagination, is made of gilded glass mosaic, satin and kid leather. Salvatore Ferragamo was a shoemaker of great originality whose choice of materials made him unique. When leather was in short supply during the Second World War, he experimented with cellophane for the body of his shoes. For soles he revived the use of cork and wood. Amongst his other cobbling innovations were wedge heels, platform soles and the steel shaft that stabilizes spike heels. Ferragamo's heyday was after the War, when Italian fashion was recovering and film production was booming. Film stars, rich tourists and socialites such as the Duchess of Windsor flocked to his Florence shop. He also earned himself the soubriquet 'shoemaker to the stars' by decorating the feet of two Hollywood generations, stretching from Gloria Swanson in the 1920s to Audrey Hepburn in the 1950s.

☞ Gucci, Levine, Louboutin, Pfister, Windsor

164

Salvatore Ferragamo. b Naples (IT), 1898. d Flumetto (IT), 1960. **Golden 'orthopaedic wedge' shoe.** Gilded glass mosaic, satin and kid leather. 1935.

Ferre Gianfranco   Designer

The dramatic play on proportions – exaggerated sleeves and cuffs and carefully structured corset – of this white taffeta shirt link fashion with Gianfranco Ferre's training as an architect. 'I use the same approach to clothes as I did when I designed buildings,' he says. 'It is basic geometry: you take a flat form and revolve it in space.' Ferre originally worked as a jewellery and accessories designer, before launching a ready-to-wear label in Milan in 1978. In 1989 he was appointed artistic director at Christian Dior; his first collection was inspired by Cecil Beaton's black-and-white costumes for *My Fair Lady*. Ferre prefers a neutral palette with dashes of his signature bright red. A perfectionist, his technical skill is shown in his precision tailoring, with a love of proportion-play revealed in his constant reinvention of the white shirt. It has been worn with jodhpurs and evening skirts, but under Ferre's direction it always has been glamorized.

☛ Beaton, Dior, Turlington

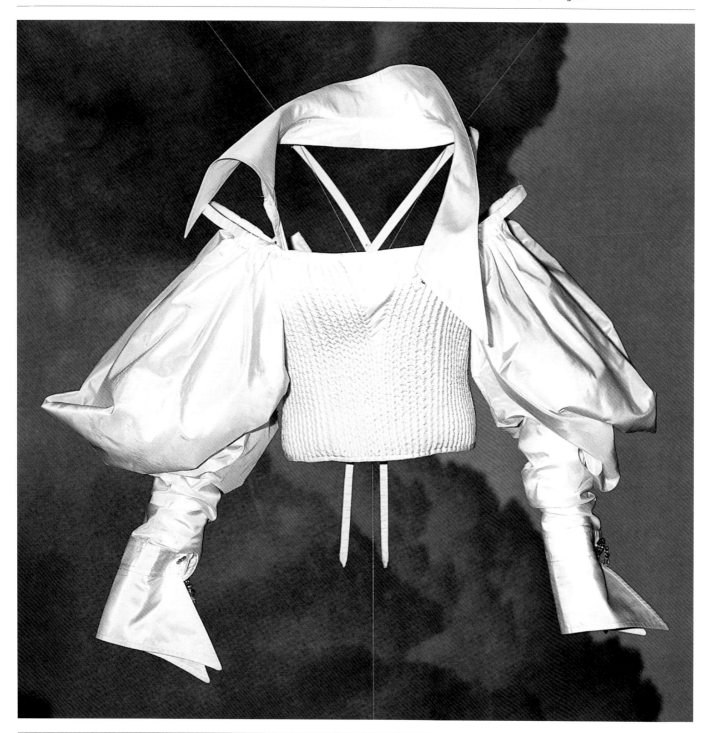

Gianfranco Ferre. b Legnano (IT), 1944. **Taffeta shirt. Spring/summer 1994.** Photograph by Kazuo Oishi.

Ferretti Alberta   Designer

Two women recline on a chaise longue in ethereal chiffon dresses. The overall effect is one of old-fashioned prettiness, yet their gaze and pose are self-assured, undermining any sense of passivity that prettiness might imply. 'I like to think I design feminine clothes,' says Ferretti. 'Everything is created by a woman for women, understanding what they want.' That vision is a particularly delicate one. Ferretti developed a special appreciation of textiles, especially daintily beaded or embroidered chiffons and sari silks, through watching her couturière mother at work. A young entrepreneur, she opened her own designer clothes shop at the age of seventeen. At the end of the twentieth century, Ferretti was one of the most powerful businesswomen in Italy, manufacturing not only her own collections but those of Narciso Rodriguez and Jean-Paul Gaultier.

☛ Rodriguez, Roversi

Alberta Ferretti. b Riccione (IT), 1950. **Chiffon dresses. Autumn/winter 1997/8.** Photograph by Paolo Roversi.

Fiorucci Elio   Designer

Oliviero Toscani's colourful, sexy images for Fiorucci defined the disco era of the 1970s and early 1980s. The label's skintight Buffalo '70 jeans, worn here by Manhattan modelling queen Donna Jordan, were popular with New York's clubbing crowd. Jackie Kennedy, Diana Ross and Bianca Jagger were all fans. Elio Fiorucci is credited with inventing the concept of designer denim, a theme taken up by Gloria Vanderbilt, Calvin Klein and virtually every label-aware designer since. Fiorucci refused to design for women above a size 10, claiming his clothes suited these sizes better. Fiorucci also set out to make fashion fun, creating glittery Plexiglas jewellery and strawberry-scented carrier bags. His cheeky graphics included Vargas-style pin-ups and cherubs wearing sunglasses. He made his name in 1962 with rainbow-coloured Wellington boots. This was Fiorucci's forte: turning function into fashion without losing a sense of fun.

☛ Benetton, Fischer, Kennedy, T. Roberts

Elio Fiorucci. b Milan (IT), 1935. **Donna Jordan in 'Buffalo '70' advertising campaign.** Photograph by Oliviero Toscani, 1973.

Fischer Donald and Doris (Gap)

Retailers

Born in 1969 during the disillusioned post-hippie era, Gap offered a reactionary-chic approach to the cultural phenomenon of the time. Immaculate, harmonious and unpretentious, it bridged societal fissures, notably the generation gap from which it drew its name. Founded by Donald and Doris Fischer, the company initially sold Levi jeans and records before creating their own label of basic, modest merchandise in an extensive array of colours and sizes. Serving the homogeneous American masses with its brand of clean, white modernism cast in neatly piled, prismatic shades, Gap has become a widely copied retail phenomenon. In recent decades, it has developed the idea of gender integration, selling wardrobe basics with few differences between the men's and women's lines and thus pioneering the 1990s concept of 'androgynous chic'.

☞ Benetton, Fiorucci, Strauss

168

Fischer. Donald. b San Francisco, CA (USA). Doris. b San Francisco, CA (USA). (Active 1960s–) (Gap). 'Khaki' campaign. Spring/summer 1998. Photograph by Walter Chin.

Fish Michael (Mr Fish) Designer

Matching shirt, tie and waistcoat exemplify the work of Michael Fish. He was Swinging London's fey fashion boy and image-maker, whose camp, outrageous style defined 'flower power'. In 1965 he dressed the actor Terence Stamp in matching Liberty prints for the cult movie *Modesty Blaise*. One-inch ties were fashionable; Fish made Stamp's four inches wide. The following year he opened his men's boutique, Mr Fish, in London's Clifford Street near the heartland of tailoring, Savile Row. The clothing ranged from outfits cut from voile, sequins and brocade to flower-printed hats and 'mini-shirts' (as famously worn by Mick Jagger for the Rolling Stones' Hyde Park concert). Other clients included Lord Snowdon and the Duke of Bedford. 'The people in my shop don't dress to conform to any given image', said Fish. 'They dress as they do because they're confident in themselves. They're blowing their minds.'

☛ Gilbey, Liberty, Nutter, Snowdon, Stephen

Michael Fish. b London (UK). (Active 1960s–1970s.) **Chevron striped waistcoat and giant peaked cap.** Photograph by Bill King, *Queen*, 1970.

Flett John   Designer

A wide-shouldered business jacket, sliced at the chest, is worn over a shirt and gauze skirt and the shoes are turned inside-out. John Flett's clothes were known for their complexity of cut: circular seams, abundant drapes and cavalier shapes which made theatrical figures of those who wore them. Widely respected and admired for his work, Flett was a central figure in the 1980s club scene in London, where he partied with other designers of the time including his former boyfriend John Galliano. They both created theatrical fashion which challenged the status quo but which matured into distinctive, directional styles. Flett started his own label in 1988 but closed it down a year later to go freelance. He moved to Europe to work with Claude Montana at Lanvin in Paris and then at Enrico Coveri in Milan, but died of a heart attack, aged twenty-seven, before his promise could be fulfilled.

☞ Boy George, Cox, Galliano, Montana

John Flett. b London (UK), 1964. **d** Florence (IT), 1991. **Tailored jacket and gauze trousers.** Photograph by Jill Furmanowsky, *The Face*, 1985.

Foale Marion and Tuffin Sally (Foale & Tuffin)   Designers

Wearing a miniskirt, the uniform of the time, Twiggy swings her fringed sleeves for Cecil Beaton in 1967. 'We made Swinging Sixties clothes,' says Marion Foale of the fashion company she set up in 1961 with Sally Tuffin. The pair were taught at the Royal College of Art by Janey Ironside, who was an influential force in British fashion. After graduating in 1961 and deciding that they didn't want to make 'elderly clothes', the two designers set to work in their bedsits on a range of bright, fun dresses, skirts and tops. They were picked up by a London store which had just established a 'young' department, and David Bailey photographed Foale and Tuffin's clothes for *Vogue* just as London's 'youthquake' movement took hold. They opened a shop on Carnaby Street and became allied to a group of British designers, including Mary Quant, which was dedicated to producing affordable fashion for teenage and twenty-something customers.

☛ Bailey, Charles, Betsey Johnson, Quant, Twiggy

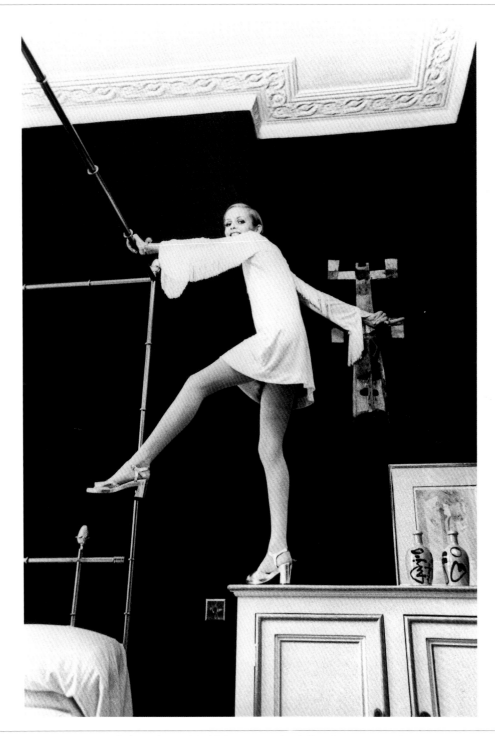

Marion Foale. b London (UK), 1939; Sally Tuffin. b London (UK), 1938. (Foale & Tuffin.) Twiggy wears a white minidress. Photograph by Cecil Beaton, 1967.

Fonssagrives Lisa

Model

Photographed by her husband Irving Penn, Lisa Fonssagrives wears a 'harlequin' opera outfit from 1950. Once described as 'the highest paid, highest praised, high fashion model in the business', Fonssagrives used to call herself simply 'the clothes hanger'. In the 1930s she moved to Paris from Sweden to train for the ballet. Here she met and married another dancer, Fernand Fonssagrives, who took some pictures of her to *Vogue*. She was immediately sent to see Horst; his assistant, Scavullo, later recalled, 'She had a marvellous profile and moved like a dream'. Fonssagrives was famous for her grace and poise, learnt from her ballet background. She called modelling 'still-dancing' and referred to her poses as 'arrested dance movements'. She became one of the most sought-after models in Paris in the 1930s and 1940s and in New York in the 1950s.

☛ **Horst, Penn, Scavullo**

172

Lisa Fonssagrives. b Gothenburg (SWE), 1911. **d** New York (USA), 1992. **Harlequin dress.** Photograph by Irving Penn, 1950.

Fontana Zoe, Micol and Giovanna (Sorelle Fontana) Designers

A monkishly simple, white satin dress, with half-sleeves, boat neck and gently belled skirt, is decorated with embroidery formed from cord. It plays on the cotton dresses worn by gamines such as Audrey Hepburn and Brigitte Bardot but the Fontana sisters were always associated with the aristocracy and society figures such as Jackie Kennedy, for whom they provided evening gowns and tailored suits. Roman couture also appealed to movie stars. Their most famous client was the film actress Ava Gardner, whom they dressed for *The Barefoot Contessa* in 1954. One of their most memorable outfits was the impish Cardinal outfit, which featured a black hat and black dress with a white collar set off by a jewelled cross. The fashion house of the Fontana family was founded in Parma, Italy, in 1907. The three Fontana sisters, Zoe, Mical and Giovanna, moved to Rome in the 1930s. There they established their own house in 1943.

☛ Galitzine, W. Klein, Schuberth, Watanabe

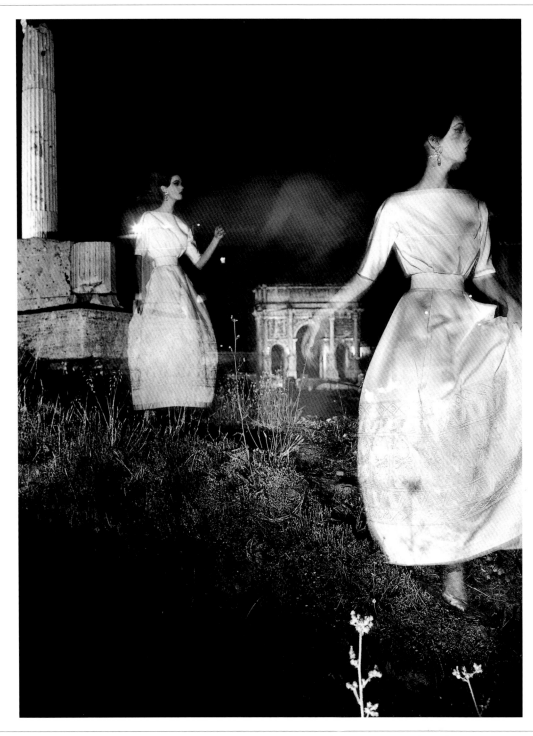

173

Fontana. Zoe. **b** Parma (IT), 1911. **d** Rome (IT), 1978; **Micol. b** Parma (IT), 1913; **Giovanna. b** Rome (IT), 1915. **d** 2004. (Sorelle Fontana.)
Dorothy McGowan wears Fontana, Rome. Photograph by William Klein, 1962.

Fonticoli Nazareno and Savini Gaetano (Brioni) Tailors

This 1971 high-waisted, double-breasted dinner suit, together with a car coat, describes the progressive tailoring of Rome's extrovert menswear house, Brioni. From the 1954 futuristic space-age suit to the Maharajah styles, which were popular in mid-1960s London, and the elegant tailoring devised for Pierce Brosnan's role as James Bond, Brioni left no avenue unexplored in men's couture. Its colourful silks and metallic threads, rarely seen since the eighteenth century, heralded the 'male peacock revolution' in the late 1950s. Even though the use of tunics, bolero jackets, lace and macramé clearly contrasts with the Anglo-Saxon tradition, a Brioni blazer epitomized elegance and flaunted wealth in preppie, early 1980s California. Having been responsible for the first ever men's catwalk show in 1952, Brioni inaugurated prêt-couture six years later, resolving flow production methods within a made-to-measure system.

☛ Bikkembergs, Gilbey, Nutter, Versace

174

Nazareno Fonticoli. **b** Penne (IT), 1906. **d** Penne (IT), 1981; **Gaetano Savini. b** Rome (IT), 1910. **d** Rome (IT), 1987. (Brioni.) **Evening suit and car coat, 1971.**

Forbes Simon   Hairdresser

This stark, androgynous image of hair fashion is the work of Simon Forbes, owner of Antenna, the salon famous for developing hair extensions. The picture represents hair as sculpture and created a cutting-edge, 'anti-beauty' statement which followed on from the punk and new wave proclivity for making hair an intrinsic part of the costume. Forbes invented the Monofibre Extensions technique which allowed greater creativity for stylists to do this. Synthetic hair was grafted onto real hair to give it instant and dramatic length. It was often dyed with vivid colours and wrapped with rags. With this and his electric clippering and precision razoring, Forbes became the directional hairdresser of the early 1980s and his salon became a fashion venue. Extensions, which were inspired by the urban street style of Rastafarians, were sported by musicians such as Boy George and Annie Lennox.

☛ Boy George, Ettedgui, Stewart, Van Noten

175

Simon Forbes. b London (UK), 1950. **Fibre dreadlocks for Antenna.** Photograph by Mike Owen, 1982.

Ford Tom   Designer

Pinstripes for a man and woman, a gilt-trimmed clutch bag, body-conscious shirts and, most telling of all, a golden 'G' shining from her waistband. These are all the elements which go to make up Tom Ford's image for Gucci. As creative director he took styling from the 1970s, when Gucci represented flashy European style, and created a culture of seasonal icons: handbags and shoes that shine brightly for six months but become redundant through their high-fashion visibility. Ford's success is rooted in his American blend of sexy, market-aware commercialism married with Italian craftsmanship. As John Fairchild, owner of the fashion trade paper *Women's Wear Daily*, wrote in 1989, the year before Ford joined Gucci, 'If American designers were working in Europe with the...eagerness to be different for novelty's sake...they could be better style leaders than anyone.' In 2004 Ford left Gucci and, with his colleague Domenico de Sole, launched a new company eponymously called Tom Ford.

☞ Gucci, Halston, Testino

Tom Ford. b Austin, TX (USA), 1962. **Evening outfits for Gucci. Autumn/winter 1996/7.** Photograph by Mario Testino.

Fortuny Mariano   Designer

The Delphos was constructed from four to five widths of silk that were sewn into a tubular shape and secured at the shoulder, as Lillian Gish demonstrates. The cord around her neckline added finish to the gown and also served to adjust the fit. Fortuny started to design his Delphos around 1907 when a nostalgia for Classical Greece was beginning to be felt in fashion, art and theatre. However, what made Fortuny's Delphos unique was its pleating, a secret process which he patented in 1909. Named after the Ancient Greek sanctuary of Delphi, Fortuny's garment derived from the *chiton*, a tunic worn by Classical Greek charioteers which focused on the natural shape of the body. Since the Delphos emphasized the female form in movement, it was popular among actresses and dancers such as Isadora Duncan. Trained as an artist, Fortuny advocated a timeless form of dress and continued to create the Delphos right up to his death.

☛ **Chow, Lester, McFadden, Poiret**

Mariano Fortuny. **b** Granada (SP), 1871. **d** Venice (IT), 1949. **Lillian Gish wears a Delphos dress.** c1920.

Fratini Gina

Designer

The range of Byronic details used on this gown distinguishes it as the work of Gina Fratini. Unafraid of romantic themes, she trimmed cuffs with rosebuds and edged frills with lace on her chiffon, lawn and silk gauze dresses. Historical references, such as off-the-shoulder 'Winterhalter' necklines and pin-tucked bodices usually seen on Victorian nightgowns, added to that charm. For this reason her wedding dresses were particularly popular. Fratini's romanticism came to the fore in 1971 when Norman Parkinson delivered samples of her work to Princess Anne in preparation for her twenty-first-birthday portrait. She chose a classic Fratini gown with a lace-trimmed ruff which co-ordinated with her pretty, tawny pink make-up. After her own business closed, Fratini designed lingerie with Ossie Clark as well as collections for Norman Hartnell and for private clients, including the Princess of Wales.

☛ Ashley, Clark, Diana, Emanuel, Hartnell, Parkinson

178

Gina Fratini. b Kobe (JAP), 1934. **Cream chiffon dress.** Photograph by Norman Parkinson, British *Vogue*, 1973.

French John   Photographer

A formal velvet coat is given a surreal treatment by John French. Originally a graphic designer, he believed, 'You have to compose a picture in the view-finder exactly as if it were an artist's picture on the canvas.' His black-and-white portraits were always perfectly arranged. 'Fill in the space. The space round the subject is as important as the subject itself,' he would say. French's apparently impromptu style contrasted with the posed formality of fashion photography in the early 1950s. One of Britain's first model talent-spotters, he encouraged Barbara Goalen and others to develop their own personalities in front of the lens. The hand intruding at the bottom of the picture doesn't belong to French. He never actually released the camera shutter himself; instead he would direct set, lighting and model, then tell his assistant (at times David Bailey or Terence Donovan), to take the photograph.

☛ Bailey, Bruyère, Goalen, Morton

John French. b London (UK), 1907. **d** Surrey (UK), 1966. **Fur-trimmed velvet coat by Digby Morton.** *Daily Express*, 1955.

Frissell Toni   Photographer

Toni Frissell's fashion photographs of the 1930s through to the 1950s captured the idyllic sense of the rich at play. Here, a model swims in her gown to illustrate its flowing material. With the innate nonchalance of an aristocrat, Frissell documented her world of wealthy playgrounds. Some of her vivid fashion images were of the beach, featuring playful swimwear and recreation dresses, and crisp tennis outfits. Frissell loved the outdoor setting and sunlight's play at least as much as the clothes or model, and let that casual naturalism permeate photographs for *Vogue* and *Harper's Bazaar*. Frissell's images appear effortless, whether of dogs, children, fox-hunting, war or fashion. She mingled the snapshot's vitality and compassion with traditional composition. Frissell recorded a charmed life in every way, including radiant photographs of the 1953 wedding of John F. Kennedy and Jacqueline Bouvier.

☛ **Kennedy, McLaughlin–Gill, Vallhonrat**

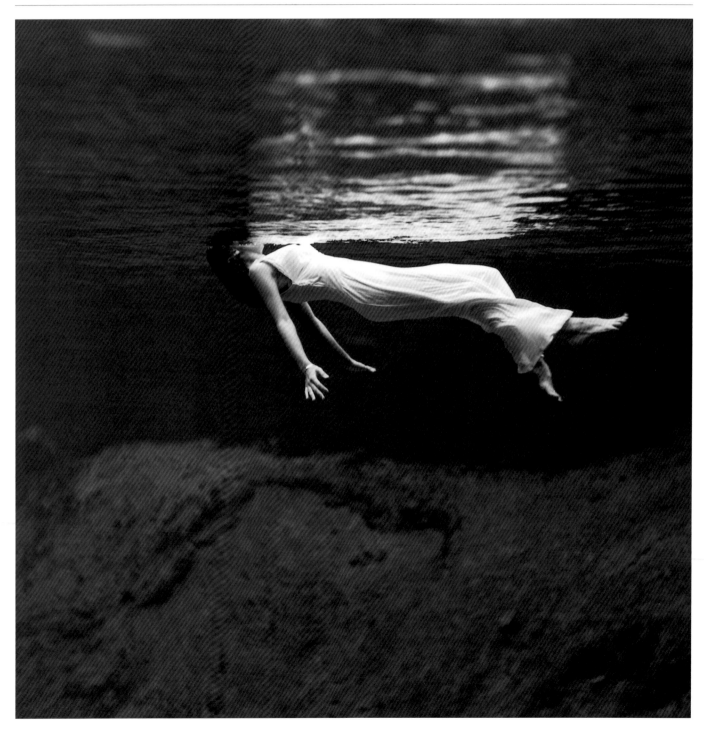

180

Toni Frissell. **b** New York (USA), 1907. **d** New York (USA), 1988. **Weeki Wachee Spring, Florida.** *Harper's Bazaar,* 1947.

Frizon Maud   Shoe designer

Maud Frizon is known for her shoes with cone-shaped heels, a black suede pair of which are the only garments worn in this picture. The role of the man is to communicate the sexual intention of Frizon's work. 'A shoe has to make you look beautiful. You can be wearing a simple dress, but if you have something exquisite on your feet, it becomes a perfect look,' said Frizon, who gained this understanding as a model for Courrèges, Nina Ricci, Jean Patou and Christian Dior. She decided to design shoes when she was unable to find styles to go with the designers' clothes on her modelling assignments (in the 1960s models were expected to provide their own shoes). In 1970 she created her first collection of witty, sexy shoes, all hand-cut and finished.

There were queues outside her tiny shop on Paris's rue Saint Germain. Brigitte Bardot was a fan, particularly of Frizon's innovative, zipless, high-heeled Russian boots and simple girlie pumps.

☛ Bardot, Courrèges, Kélian, Patou, Ricci

Maud Frizon (Maud Frizon De Marco). b Paris (FR), 1941. **Heeled pumps.** Photograph by Dominique Issermann, 1989.

Von Fürstenberg Diane

Designer

Diane von Fürstenberg wears her own fashion phenomenon for the cover of *Newsweek*. The real appeal of her wrap dress was its wearable shape and endless versatility. Smart yet sexy, it looked as good at the disco as it did at the office. The designer called it, 'Simple one-step dressing. Chic, comfortable and sexy. It won't become dated after one season. It works around the clock, travels across the world and fits all a woman's priorities.' An ex-model, von Fürstenberg partied at Studio 54, dated Warren Beatty and was briefly married to Fiat heir Prince Egon von Fürstenberg. The glamorous divorcée's jet-set lifestyle contributed to the cachet of her dresses (which prominently bore her signature). Originally launched in 1972, the DVF wrap dresses contrasted with the unisex trouser suits of the time and the swing tickets attached made this point with the words, 'Feel like a woman. Wear a dress.'

☞ Bergère, de Ribes, Vanderbilt

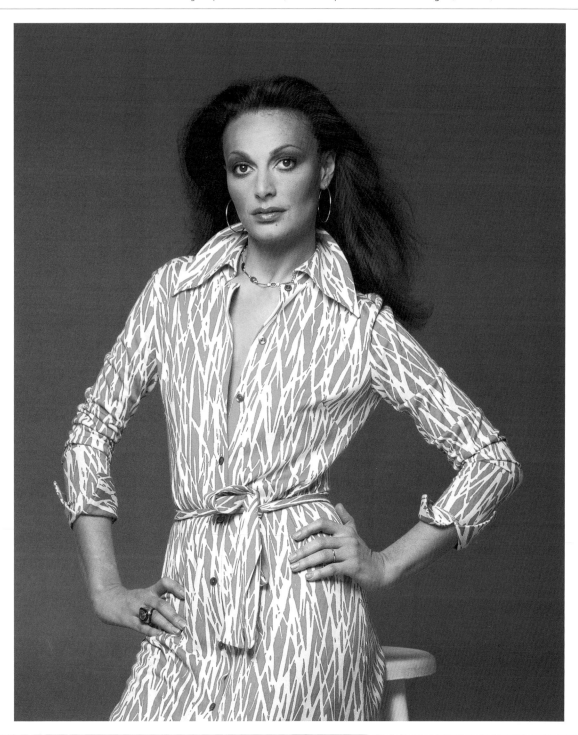

Diane von Fürstenberg. b Brussels (BEL), 1946. **Wrap dress.** Photograph by Francesco Scavullo, *Newsweek* cover, 1976.

Galanos James   Designer

With this perfectly plain, wool dress, Galanos displays the reason why he was dubbed 'America's couturier'. 'I never deviated from what was most important, which was quality,' said Galanos, who actually produced the highest class of ready-to-wear. Nancy Reagan claimed, 'You can take one of Jimmy's dresses and just wear it inside out, they're so beautifully made.' The simplicity of his designs was deceptive and he used couture-standard dressmaking techniques which made his pieces expensive. Galanos worked in Hollywood with John Louis, head of costume design at Columbia, who soon found his fledgling designer's clothes were as popular with the stars as his own. Having later trained with Robert Piguet in Paris, Galanos opened a small shop in Los Angeles in 1951. His designs were discovered by a senior buyer at Neiman Marcus, who claimed she had found 'a young designer from California who would set the world on fire'.

☛ Adolfo, Louis, Piguet, Simpson

James Galanos. b Philadelphia, PA (USA), 1925. **Black wool dress.** Photograph by Kourken Pakchanian, American *Vogue*, 1973.

Galitzine Irene   Designer

William Klein arranges a party of variously uniformed men as accessories for Irene Galitzine's evening trouser outfits. They are variations of her famous wide-leg trouser suits which were dubbed 'palazzo pyjamas' by Diana Vreeland, then at *Harper's Bazaar*. Galitzine's aristocratic Russian family fled the Revolution in 1918. She studied art in Rome, English at Cambridge and

French at the Sorbonne. Galitzine finished her broad education as an assistant to the Fontana sisters in Rome. Her own collection, first designed in 1959, suggested an international, yet easy way of dressing. It blurred the distinction between day- and eveningwear and made a relaxed alternative to formal cocktail dresses. It was a look that immediately appealed to the Italian aristocracy.

Her draped sari-style tunics could be worn for day or evening, and were favoured by Elizabeth Taylor, Greta Garbo and Sophia Loren.

☛ Fontana, Garbo, W. Klein, Pulitzer, Vreeland

184

Irene Galitzine. **b** Tiflis (RUS), 1916. **d** Rome (IT), 2006. **'Palazzo pyjamas'.** Photograph by William Klein, 1962.

Galliano John Designer

John Galliano has chosen this picture of his 'seamless' dress, worn by Carla Bruni during his autumn/winter 1995/6 ready-to-wear collection in Paris. It is representative of his work, even though it looks simpler than most of his designs. In truth, the structure is anything but. The seams and darts have been banished into the outline of the black flowers, the first time such a complicated technique has been used outside haute couture. It leaves an apparently seamless dress, a luxurious, almost mythical item. Throughout his career, Galliano has looked to the work of great couturiers such as Madeleine Vionnet and Paul Poiret to resurrect special techniques which have been neglected in the rush of mass-manufacture. In particular, he has become the unequalled master of the bias cut, Vionnet's speciality. A rocky but high-profile career was crowned by his appointment in 1996 as designer, at Givenchy and then at Christian Dior.

☛ **Dior, Givenchy, LaChapelle, Poiret, Vallhonrat, Vionnet**

John Galliano. b Gibraltar (SP), 1960. **'Seamless dress'. Pink and black silk crepe.** Photograph by Chris Moore. 1995.

Garbo Greta Icon

Called the 'greatest star of all', Greta Garbo wears a masculine jacket, cut with sexual ambiguity, in a portrait by Cecil Beaton. Beaton wrote of his subject, 'Perhaps no other person has had such an influence on the appearance of a whole generation...the secret of her appeal seems to lie in an elusive and haunting sensitivity...Garbo has created a style in fashion which is concerned with her individual self'. Garbo arrived in Hollywood aged nineteen in the entourage of Mauritz Stilla from Sweden. Signed up by Metro-Goldwyn-Mayer, she went on to star in *Queen Christina*, *Camille* and *Anna Karenina*, dressed by Adrian. Famed as a recluse, she said in 1932, 'I am awkward, shy, afraid, nervous and self-conscious about my English. That is why I built a wall of repression about myself and lived behind it'. The director George Cukor said that she reserved 'her real sensuousness for the camera'.

☛ Adrian, Beaton, Galitzine, Sui

186

Greta Garbo. b Stockholm (SWE), 1905. d New York (USA), 1990. **Greta Garbo.** Photograph by Cecil Beaton, 1946.

Garren

Hairdresser

From the strawberry-red, Sophia Loren bouffant to the boyish, platinum, Andy Warhol bob, Garren has been the architect behind all of supermodel Linda Evangelista's publicized, chameleon-like hairstyle changes. His directional approach has been witnessed not only in the high-glam look he achieved in collaboration with photographer Steven Meisel in the late 1980s, but also in the spiky 'chicken do' (his trademark punk-inspired style seen earlier that decade), which he modified in the softer, more feminine gamine cut seen in the wake of the waif look. His extreme work in editorial and on the catwalk for Marc Jacobs and Anna Sui is tempered in the salon where he gives reality a chance. As he told American *Vogue*, 'As soon as a client comes in...I'm checking out the way she moves, her shoes, her handbag, body language. That tells me what her needs are.'

☞ Evangelista, Jacobs, Meisel, Sui, Warhol

Garren. (Active 1970s–.) **Garren with Linda Evangelista.** Photograph by Peter Lindbergh, *Harper's Bazaar*, 1997.

Gattinoni Fernanda Designer

The serene allure of Gattinoni's brilliant green, brocade evening coat is captured by Clifford Coffin in a photograph for American *Vogue* in 1947. Hinting at Imperial Chinese influences, its Zen-like dignity anticipates the refined ethnicity of Romeo Gigli. Gattinoni trained at the Rome fashion house Ventura, before opening her own atelier. Here she attracted the likes of Audrey Hepburn, Ingrid Bergman and Anna Magnani – film-star clients renowned for their highly photogenic mix of thoroughbred grace and soft femininity. In the 1950s, with the great success of films such as *Roman Holiday*, Rome became synonymous with the glamour of cinema and Gattinoni came to epitomize cultured European sophistication and romance. She also offered indulgent escapism – twenty-five full-time embroiderers were employed to decorate wedding dresses – for a clientele weary of postwar realities.

☛ Coffin, Gigli, Molyneux

Fernanda Gattinoni. b Cocquio (IT), 1907. d Rome (IT), 2002. **Brocade evening coat.** Photograph by Clifford Coffin, American *Vogue*, 1947.

Gaultier Jean-Paul   Designer

A man and woman mirror one another in near-identical outfits from Jean-Paul Gaultier's 1994 women's collection, 'The Big Journey'. That he is wearing her clothes comes as little surprise, since Gaultier has been dressing men in skirts since 1985. On this occasion, their rich, quilted satin coats, long hems and geisha-style platforms suggest a trip through the Far East. Since he started his label in 1978, Gaultier has been influenced by global costume, both old and new, such as that worn by London's punks. Sexual ambiguity has also been an enduring theme. While his men have worn skirts and even tutus, pipe-smoking women have trodden his catwalk in pinstriped business suits. His menswear was influenced by the wave of gay men coming out in the 1970s, using camp clichés that included macho bodybuilders and butch sailors. Like these outfits, Gaultier's whole style is a humorous, eclectic challenge to the French establishment.

☛ Alexandre, Madonna, Margiela, Pita, Van Beirendonck

Jean-Paul Gaultier. b Arcueil (FR), 1952. 'The Big Journey' collection. Autumn/winter 1994/5. Photograph by Jean-Marie Périer, French *Elle*, 1994.

Gernreich Rudi   Designer

The topless bathing suit, worn here by Peggy Moffit, Rudi Gernreich's favourite model, was developed to meet the trend for topless bathing. It was also intended to be something of a feminist statement, as was his no-bra bra of 1964, which was the first to allow the natural shape of a woman's breasts. Gernreich also invented the high-cut, buttock-baring, thong bathing suit. His radical body-based clothes of the 1960s and 1970s reflected the social revolution of women's liberation and his early designs provided unprecedented freedom of movement. In the 1950s he produced knitted swimwear without the usual boning and underpinning and he developed the concept into tube dresses. It was Gernreich's early influences that helped to develop our relationship between stretch and comfort; Rudi joined several modern dance companies and became fascinated by the leotards and tights of the dancers.

☛ Coffin, Heim, Rabanne, Sassoon

190

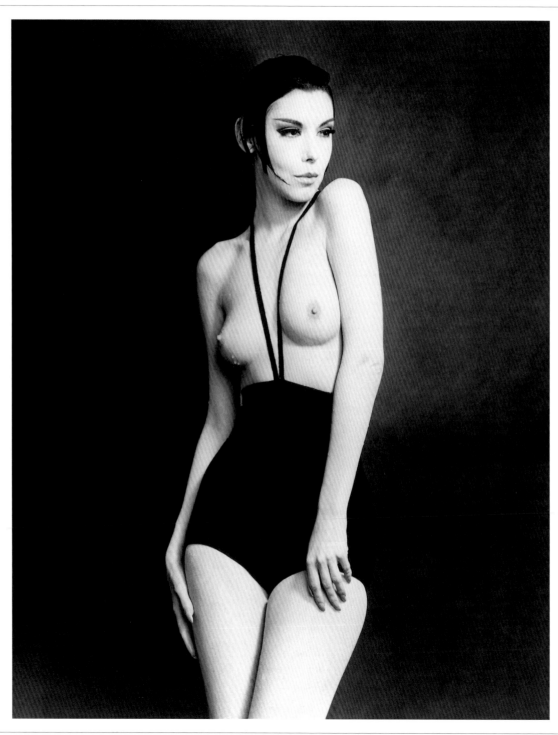

Rudi Gernreich. b Vienna (AUS), 1922. **d** Los Angeles, CA (USA), 1985. **Peggy Moffit wears a topless swimsuit, 1964.** Photograph by William Claxton.

Gibb Bill

Designer

'Miles of untouched forest hand-printed onto silk... the Bill Gibb environment, rich fabrics with richer decorations – marbled, hand-painted, feathered, piped...flower-faced beauty.' As it is, the words that accompanied this editorial picture left out a few of the techniques used on Gibb's lavish, layered and fantastical dress. He claimed to have an aversion to 'the tailored thing' and his grand vision was an alternative to the lean trouser suits of the 1970s. Gibb came from a farming family, but was encouraged by his grandmother, a painter, to enjoy his hobby of copying pictures of historical costume, especially that of the Renaissance era. This influence has affected his most spectacular work. He often incorporated knitwear into his collection by collaborating with Missoni and knitting specialist Kaffe Fassett, saying, 'What women want to wear in the daytime is beautiful knits.'

☛ Birtwell, Mesejeán, Missoni, Porter

Bill Gibb. b Fraserburgh (UK), 1943. **d** London (UK), 1988. **'Forest' dress.** Photograph by Penati, British *Vogue*, 1972.

Gibson Charles Dana Illustrator

Before television and movies, Gibson identified an essential character as deftly and as unforgettably as any novelist. His 'Gibson Girl' was the personification of America's modern woman. Probably seen wearing the fashionable shirtwaist (a masculine-styled blouse of the early twentieth century), her S-curve figure and loosely constructed mound of hair gave shape to the new woman. Her face varied slightly, but she was the icon of twentieth-century fashion embodied in an active life in such Gibson books on the middle and upper-middle classes as *The Education of Mr Pipp* (1899), *The Americans* (1900) and *The Social Ladder* (1902). Gibson had studied at the Art Students' League in New York and worked for late nineteenth-century magazines that required illustrations for news and stories, but ultimately he invented his own story of the fashionable, independent woman of the twentieth century.

☛ Drecoll, Paquin, Redfern

192

Charles Dana Gibson. **b** Roxbury, MA (USA), 1867. **d** (USA), 1944. **Gibson Girls on the beach**, 1901.

Gigli Romeo

Designer

Benedetta Barzini is photographed enjoying Romeo Gigli's extravagant coat. Gold flowers and embroidered leaves collect around the shawl collar, cuffs and hem, with a velvet scarf finishing with a golden tassel. Gigli's childhood was saturated in art history and antiquarian books, over which he pored. It gave him an appreciation of beauty, history and travel which underlies his work – he plays with clothes from history and non-European cultures. The Gigli look was, and still is, one of the most distinctive in fashion. In the 1980s, Gigli's vision had a grandeur only equalled by that of Christian Lacroix. Silk suits, with either stovepipe trousers or long, narrow skirts, were worn with shirt collars that framed the wearer's face (as here) and placed under velvet coats that enveloped the figure in luxury. The impression was similar to that created by Poiret: a richly decorated, giant bloom growing from a narrow stalk.

☛ **Gattinoni, Iribe, Meisel, Poiret, Roversi, Vallhonrat**

193

Romeo Gigli. b Faenza (IT), 1949. **Benedetta Barzini wears an embroidered coat.** Photograph by Steven Meisel, French *Vogue*, 1989.

Gilbey Tom   Designer

This is classic Tom Gilbey. With his trademark simplicity and an almost militaristic neatness, Gilbey was an important force in menswear in the 1960s. Here, he uses both traditionally masculine details and softer, experimental methods, such as sleeves gathered into cuffs. Despite their feminized aspects, these outfits are strong, angular examples of the new wave of British tailoring. Gilbey began designing for John Michael and in 1968 opened his own shop, in London's Sackville Street. Gilbey is one of fashion's visionaries. In 1982 he launched a waistcoat collection which suited the aspirational yuppie. Around the same time, and pre-dating the transatlantic sportswear boom by fifteen years, he said, 'I'm influenced by the American campus look, it's so classic and immaculate. Jeans and a T-shirt, big bumper shoes, Bermuda shorts...I hate fuss. I love things to be clean, strong and aggressive.'

☛ Fish, Fonticoli, Nutter, Stephen

Tom Gilbey. b London (UK), 1938. **Winter coats.** 1971.

194

Givenchy Hubert de Designer

Snap! Audrey Hepburn, playing a model, is captured in a still from the 1957 film, *Funny Face*. Her dress, a floral cotton gown, is by the man who became a lifelong friend and collaborator. 'It was as though I was born to wear his clothes', said Hepburn of Hubert de Givenchy. When she was first sent to his house, Givenchy was expecting the other 'Miss Hepburn' – Katharine. His disappointment gave way to adoration. He had already worked at Lelong, Piguet, Fath and Schiaparelli, before opening his couture house at the age of twenty-five. Encouraged by Balenciaga, he specialized in clothes for the new era of air travel and grand eveningwear. In 1956 Givenchy banned the press from his shows, saying, 'A fashion house is a laboratory which must conserve its mystery'.

He retired in 1995, making way for two of the most publicity-aware designers – John Galliano and Alexander McQueen – to design under his name.

☛ Horvat, Lelong, Pipart, Tiffany, Venet

195

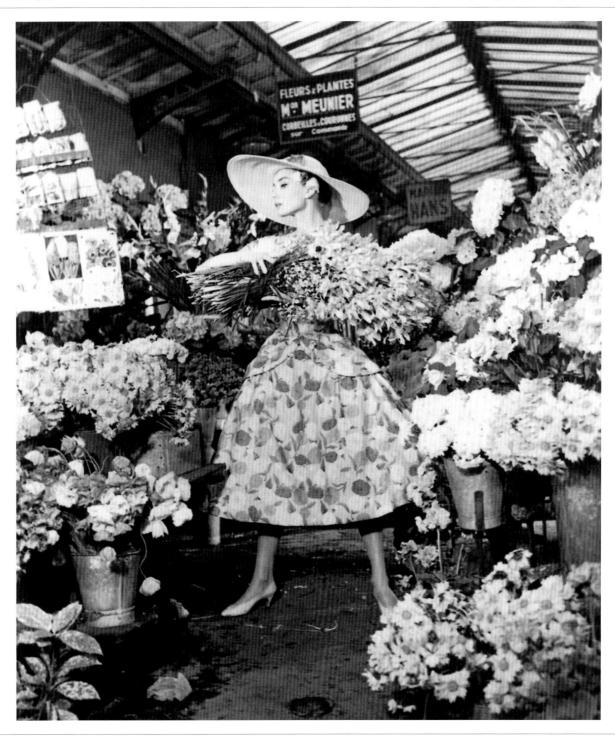

Hubert de Givenchy. b Beauvais (FR), 1927. **Audrey Hepburn.** Still from *Funny Face*. 1957.

Goalen Barbara   Model

The archetypal 1950s aloof and haughty mannequin, the well-bred Goalen was chauffeur-driven to assignments in a Rolls-Royce. Careful to protect her image, she said, 'I always did high fashion and I never touched anything that wasn't high quality'. The photographer Henry Clarke said, 'You put the dress on Barbara and she made it sing.' At one time she was almost exclusively photographed by John French and was Coffin's favourite model. She was the first British model to be sent to the Paris shows by British *Vogue*. At the height of her fame, she toured Australia and was mobbed in the North of England. Like many models in the 1950s, she married well – to Lloyd's underwriter Nigel Campbell. Her hips were too slender for sample sizes, so she rarely did catwalk modelling.

She only worked for five years, before retiring while still very much in demand.

☛ Clarke, Coffin, French

196

Barbara Goalen. b (UK). (Active 1950s.) Strapless evening dress. Photograph by John French, 1954.

Godley Georgina   Designer

An otherwise utterly plain, jersey T-shirt dress springs away from the average with the introduction of organza into the hem and neck. An experimental purist, Georgina Godley uses sculpture to introduce avant-garde shape into her work. 'We are dealing with a woman who is an individual now,' she told *Vogue*. 'Fashion is so retrograde, putting people down. It's not a designer's personality you're buying, it's yours. I believe in a reappraisal of sexual roles.' Her contemporary work is in contrast to the historicism explored during her partnership with Scott Crolla. Their cult shop, Crolla (opened in 1981), stocked romantic men's clothes in velvet and brocade which matched the New Romantic mood. After parting from him in 1985, Godley developed her own line, favouring a one-to-one relationship with the client, in which her creativity could be displayed by women who relish her individual experiments.

☛ **Audibet, Bruce, Crolla**

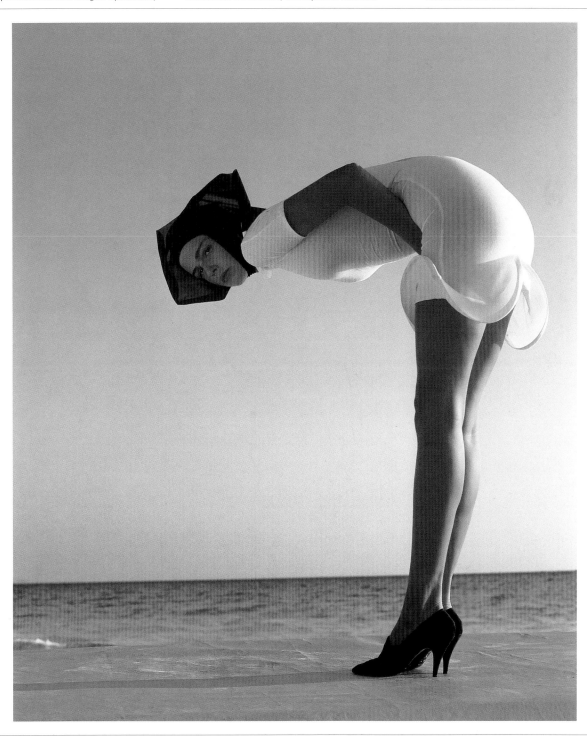

Georgina Godley. b London (UK), 1955. **Cotton jersey body-and-soul dress.** Photograph by Alex Chatelain, British *Vogue*, 1986.

Grès Madame   Designer

The white, silk jersey fabric of this evening gown has been moulded onto the figure as if it had the properties of the piece of sculpture standing next to the model. Even the play of light and shade in its deep pleats echoes the sculpture. Silk jersey is a material that lends itself to pleating in precise, fluid folds and it was a mainstay in the classicism of Madame Alix Grès, one of the great couture artists. *Harper's Bazaar* proclaimed in 1936 that, 'Alix stands for the body rampant, for the rounded, feminine sculptural form beneath the dress'. She had been trained as a sculptress and it was her feeling for Classical Greek sculpture that enabled her to capture its timeless elegance in her evening gowns. Hers was an individualistic, uncompromising style where the sculptural cut of her gowns had the liquid effect of the 'wet' drapery of Classical Greek sculpture that turned fashionable women into living statues.

☛ **Audibet, Cassini, Lanvin, Pertegaz, Toledo, Valentina**

198

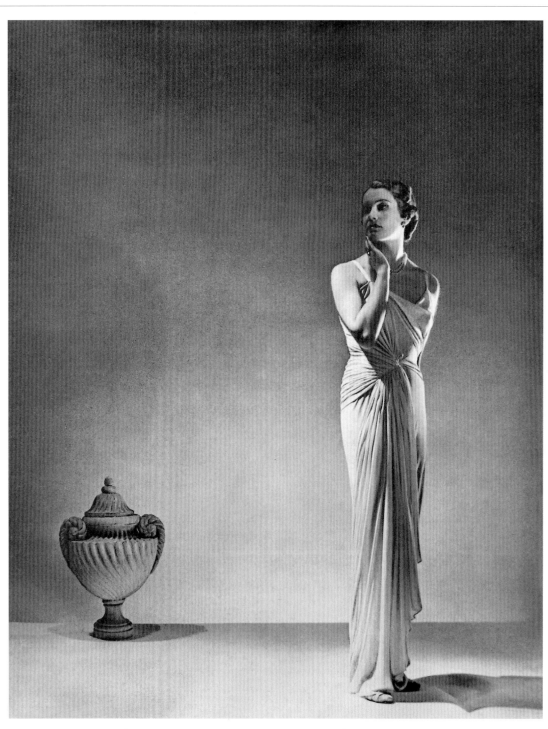

Madame Alix Grès (Germaine Krebs). b Paris (FR), 1903. **d** (FR), 1993. **Grecian column dress.** Photograph by Eugène Rubin, *Femina*, 1937.

Griffe Jacques   Designer

In a picture from an American *Vogue* sitting in 1952, the model's seated pose makes a display of Jacques Griffe's diaphanous pin-tucks. The entire evening dress grows from a flamboyant pink tulle bow which uses the fabric of both bodice and skirt. It finishes ten inches from the floor – a younger look for ball gowns at the time and known as the ballet length. Griffe trained with Vionnet where he learned the techniques of draping and cutting fabrics, such as this luscious chiffon, from the Lyons textile firm Bianchini-Férier, noted for its fluid materials in brilliant colours. After the Second World War, Griffe worked for Molyneux before opening his own maison de couture in 1946. Like Vionnet, he worked directly with the material, modelling it on a wooden dummy. Griffe's tailoring work was distinguished by the use of seams and darts as decorative details and by his invention of the boxy jacket.

☞ **McLaughlin-Gill, Molyneux, Vionnet**

Jacques Griffe. b Carcassonne (FR), 1917. **d** 1996. **Tulle dress.** Photograph by Frances McLaughlin-Gill, American *Vogue*, 1952.

Gruau René   Illustrator

In this suggestive advertisement for Christian Dior, the sinuous lines of a woman's hand are placed on a panther's paw against an infinite background, reflecting a spirit of graceful worldliness and glamour. Noted for his strong silhouettes and tonalities of colour, Gruau's images became prestigious icons of elegance. He was an outstanding graphic artist of the period after the Second World War, when his swift, expressive line was chosen by Dior's couture and perfume company to illustrate their perfume advertisements. Together with Bouché, Gruau also brilliantly illustrated haute couture of the era in French *Vogue*. Influenced by the posters of Toulouse-Lautrec, he used strong outlines – a technique that perfectly accentuates fashion's shape and form. He was one of the last grand magazine illustrators before the creative possibilities of fashion photography made it equal to the fantasy of illustration.

☛ **Biagiotti, Bouché, Dior**

René Gruau. **b** Rimini (IT), 1908. **d** Rome (IT), 2004. **Panther Paw.** Advertisement for *Miss Dior* perfume. 1949.

Gucci Guccio   Accessory designer

On a terrace in Cannes, Romy Schneider caresses the classic Gucci loafers worn by Alain Delon. The snaffle loafer has been an icon of wealth and European style since it was designed in 1932 by the company's patriarch, Guccio Gucci. After rebelling against joining his family's ailing straw hat-making business, Gucci ran away to London. He found a job as maître d'hôtel at the Savoy where he looked after the wealthy guests, paying particular attention to their baggage. He returned to Florence and opened a small shop selling saddlery, later expanding into leather bags and shoes which were decorated with a horse's snaffle. In 1933 Aldo, his son, joined the business and designed the iconic Gucci logo using the interlocking double Gs of his father's initials.

Intermittent periods of stunning success were counterpointed with family squabbles and even murder, marring the extraordinary Gucci story.

☛ Ferragamo, Ford, Hermès

Guccio Gucci. **b** Florence (IT), 1881. **d** Milan (IT), 1953. **Alain Delon wears Gucci loafers.** c1959.

Halston

Designer

Halston is surrounded by eleven models for a 1972 *Vogue* sitting. Their fluid, silk jersey dresses and svelte clothes made from Ultrasuede are pure Halston: utterly simple and an eternal antidote to fussy dressing. These are the hallmarks of classic American design, and Halston was recognized as a master of the art. His popularity in the 1970s made him a social figure, most famously among the set that frequented Manhattan's Studio 54 club. Bianca Jagger and Liza Minnelli were friends and clients, and both were Concorde-class models for his draped jersey dresses and lean trouser suits. Halston designed for his friends, saying in 1971, 'Fashion starts with fashionable people... No designer has ever made fashion alone. People make fashion.' Although he died in 1990, Halston's influence has continued to grow. Tom Ford, designer at Gucci, acknowledged his Studio 54 look as crucial to uncluttered fashion in the 1990s.

☞ Bandy, Daché, Ford, Maxwell, Peretti, Warhol

202

Halston (Roy Halston Frowick). b Des Moines, IA (USA), 1932. d San Francisco, CA (USA), 1990. **Halston with models, 1972.** Photograph by Duane Michals, American *Vogue*.

Hamnett Katharine Designer

'At last! An original,' was Prime Minister Margaret Thatcher's response to Katharine Hamnett's anti-missile message when the two met at a British government reception in 1984. Such an easily copied idea (deliberately so, claimed Hamnett, who wanted her messages to be read by as many people as possible) meant that her slogan T-shirts became a symbol of the 1980s. Hamnett has since fostered the connection between cloth and politics, most notably by using and helping with the development of organic cotton. Practicality and youth have always been important to the label – parachute silk, cotton jersey and denim are some of the relaxed and functional fabrics that have been trademarks for Hamnett over the years. She has said of her clothes, 'There is a real utility in them...they're functional, they're easy to look after and they last a long time.'

☛ Stiebel, Teller, von Unwerth

Katharine Hamnett. **b** Gravesend (UK), 1948. **Katharine Hamnett with Margaret Thatcher, 10 Downing Street.** 1984.

Hartnell Norman   Designer

Princess Margaret's picturesque white evening gown, with its scooped neckline, tight bodice and full skirt, recalls the gowns Charles Frederick Worth made for the Empress Eugénie and which were immortalized in the portraits of her painted by Winterhalter. This distinctively British romantic revival interpretation was the creation of the royal couturier, Norman Hartnell. Its origins can be traced back to the royal visit to Paris in 1938, when King George VI specifically requested Hartnell to design a wardrobe for his queen based on the royal portraits painted by Winterhalter in the 1860s that hung in Buckingham Palace. Hartnell exquisitely used white silk, satin, chiffon and tulle for evening gowns and decorated them sumptuously with embroidered and beaded motifs.

This style of evening dress gained an international reputation as a British fashion classic. It remained a constant in the royal wardrobe throughout the postwar period.

☞ Bohan, Rayne, Sumurun, Worth

204

Norman Hartnell. b London (UK), 1901. **d** Windsor (UK), 1979. **HRH Princess Margaret wears sequined butterfly gown for her nineteenth birthday.** Photograph by Cecil Beaton, 1949.

Head Edith

Designer

Perhaps the most honoured of Hollywood's costume designers, Edith Head was also the most versatile. She excelled at recognizing the trends in contemporary fashion and in creating movie costumes realistic for their age, as in Elizabeth Taylor's wardrobe, inspired by Christian Dior and Jacques Fath, for *Elephant Walk* (1954). In her years at Paramount Pictures, Head designed for Mae West, created the sarong for Dorothy Lamour and made Barbara Stanwyck *The Lady Eve* (1941), but her real gift was an 'eye' – a keen sense for what was happening in contemporary fashion. She wrangled with fashion designers (most notably, Hubert de Givenchy) over design credits, and she gave her films a timely sense of fashion, unlike the grand picturesque of Hollywood Golden Age fashions, and anticipating 1980s and 1990s films where fashion is chosen from the marketplace.

☛ Fath, Givenchy, Irene, Louis, Travilla

Edith Head. b Los Angeles, CA (USA), 1907. **d** Hollywood, CA (USA), 1981. **Elizabeth Taylor.** Still from *Elephant Walk*. 1954.

Hechter Daniel   Designer

Daniel Hechter's leaping tracksuit represents the age of performance fashion. His reality-check womenswear emerged in the 1960s, with function dominating style. Hechter is realistic about his role: 'Fashion is not art. It can be artistic, but it is not art. I'm really a stylist. I respect designers who create fashion, like Chanel, Poiret. Or Levi's...[but] if you dress a billion people, that's phenomenal.' The first prêt-à-porter womenswear collection, co-designed with friend Armand Orustein, was launched in 1963. Perfectly pitched for the 'youthquake' market, he persuaded Twiggy to model clothes that were targeted at young women who aspired to a designer lifestyle. He integrated pop culture into his scheme, creating accessible clothes which were designed to be worn out and then replaced. His maxi coats, trouser suits and divided skirts were counterpointed with menswear that mixed separates in the 1970s.

☛ Dassler, Kamali, P. Knight, Strauss, Twiggy

Daniel Hechter. b Paris (FR), 1938. **Tracksuit.** Photograph by Jim Greenberg, *L'Officiel*, 1980.

Heim Jacques   Designer

Heim will be forever known as the couturier who promoted the bikini. He featured it in his 1946 collection under the name 'atome'. When, in the same year, atomic bomb tests were conducted by the United States at Bikini Atoll, the swimsuit's name was changed to bikini. This bathing suit shot to fame when Brigitte Bardot was photographed in 1956 wearing one made of gingham adorned with frills. Heim entered the world of fashion through his parents' fur business, founded in 1898. He also collaborated with Sonia Delaunay, designing dresses, coats and sportswear which were exhibited at the Art Deco exhibition in Paris in 1925. He established his own fashion house in the 1930s, his forte being beachwear and sportswear. Between 1946 and 1966 he opened a series of boutiques which specialized in these garments. Heim was president of the Chambre Syndicale de la Couture Parisienne from 1958 to 1962.

☛ Bardot, Coddington, Delaunay, Gernreich, Jantzen

207

Jacques Heim. b Paris (FR), 1899. d Paris (FR), 1967. **Slip-over top and cotton bikini.** 1950.

Hemingway Wayne (Red or Dead)

Loud and opinionated, just like this line-up of his team's work, Wayne Hemingway doesn't care about high fashion. Beyond showing his collections at the normal times, Hemingway's company, Red or Dead, rejoices in its desire to please nobody but its young, clubby customers. It started life in 1982 as a second-hand clothing and shoe stall at London's Camden Market. In 1995 it demanded press reaction when models wielding bloody knives and knitting needles prowled along the catwalk in a pastiche of Alfred Hitchcock's thrillers. Hemingway's fashion philosophy is based around the desire to reinterpret youth culture, using socio-political sloganeering as a hook. 'I design for a free-thinking British youth culture,' he has said. In other words, he gives them what they want, be it Bollywood, Punk, Mod, Britpop, Grandad or 1980s trash.

☛ Hamnett, Leroy, Rotten

208

Wayne Hemingway. b Morecambe (UK), 1961. (Red or Dead.) Catwalk montage, 1989–96. Photographs by Chris Moore and Suresh Karadia.

Hendrix Jimi   Icon

Hendrix was as individualistic in his stage wardrobe as he was in his stage act. His clothes, old mixed with new, clothes of war and the tie-dye fabrics of war protesters, were as loud and chaotic as his electric guitar playing. His own sense of style was manifest at eight years old when he was ordered out of a Baptist church for being dressed too extravagantly. Expelled from school at fifteen, he drifted into juvenile delinquency, stealing flashy clothes from stores. He wore his hair in a wild, unkempt version of the Afro hairstyle adopted by the 'Black Pride' movement of the late 1960s. His clothes were often an eclectic mix of almost fop-like finery and hippie ethnicity. He often wore his trademark black felt fedora. His psychedelic clothing – multicoloured patchwork shirts, flower-print jackets and swirly scarves – was reminiscent of the drug-induced hallucinations that inspired the lyrics of his songs.

☞ Bouquin, Ozbek, Presley

209

Jimi Hendrix. b Seattle, WA (USA), 1942. d London (UK), 1970. **Jimi Hendrix.** Photograph by Gered Mankowitz, 1967.

Hermès Thierry Accessory designer

Princess Grace of Monaco attends to a young Caroline. In her other hand she carries a handbag big enough for a mother, yet courtly enough for any member of royalty. On the occasion of her marriage to Prince Rainier, the Hermès bag Grace Kelly had carried throughout their engagement was renamed in her honour. The 'Kelly bag' has been fashionable ever since and involves a three-month waiting list. Modelled on a '*sac haut à courroie*' or 'high-handle', which was used as a carrying case for saddles, the flap is fastened with horizontal straps and a twisting clasp. Hermès was founded in 1837 by Thierry Hermès. In 1920 his grandson Emile brought modern design and luxurious clothes to the label, but Hermès continues to prosper from its image as a high-quality saddler, using snaffles and stirrups as themes for its printed silk scarves. In 1997, the company appointed avant-garde designer Martin Margiela.

☛ Banton, Bergère, Gucci, Lacroix, Loewe, Margiela

Thierry Hermès. **b** Crefeld (GER), 1797. **d** Paris (FR), 1878. **Princess Grace with 'Kelly bag' and her daughter, Caroline.** Monaco, 1958.

Hilfiger Tommy   Designer

'Check it out...check out Tommy...Tommy Hilfiger...' raps Treach as he models for a Hilfiger catwalk show in 1997. Hilfiger's name dominates his streetwise sportswear and turns his customers into advertisements. The distinctive red, white and blue logo came about after he noticed that counterfeiters were taking the discreet insignia of his competitors and enlarging them on T-shirts and caps.

It was effortless advertising. Thus Hilfiger sold the idea back to those who invented and bought it. He started producing his logo-aware designs and was soon being name-checked in hip-hop songs – and worn by those who listen to them. In the 1970s Hilfiger's New York shop, People's Place, became a celebrity draw. In the 1980s his clothing assumed a preppie style similar in feel to that of

Ralph Lauren's, but it was his mastery of the street market which made an impact on fashion.

☛ Brooks, Dassler, Lauren, Moss

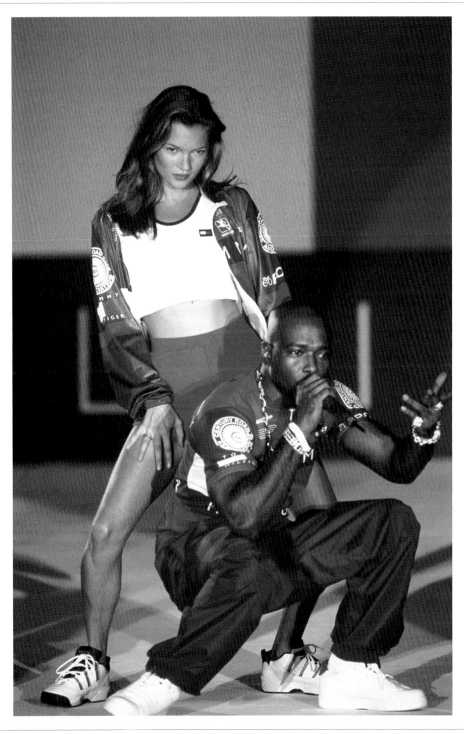

Tommy Hilfiger. b Elmira, NY (USA), 1952. **Rapper Treach and Kate Moss. Spring/summer 1997.** Photograph by Chris Moore.

Hirata Akio   Milliner

With its delicate sculptural form and body-encompassing loops circling the shoulders, this hat challenges our preconceived ideas about millinery work. Akio Hirata, Japan's most influential milliner, has collaborated with many avant-garde Japanese designers including Yohji Yamamoto, Comme des Garçons and Hanae Mori. His passion for European fashion magazines encouraged him to tour France in 1962. There he met French milliner, Jean Barthet, with whom he trained for three years at his Paris salon and perfected his craft. He returned to Japan and founded his own house, Haute Mode Hirata, in 1965. Every design in his boutique, Salon Coco in Hiroo, was handmade. He worked on commissions for Pierre Balmain and Nina Ricci and designed for the wives of Japanese heads of state, who brought his work to the attention of a wider international audience during state visits abroad.

☛ Barthet, Kawakubo, Mori, Ricci, Sieff, Y. Yamamoto

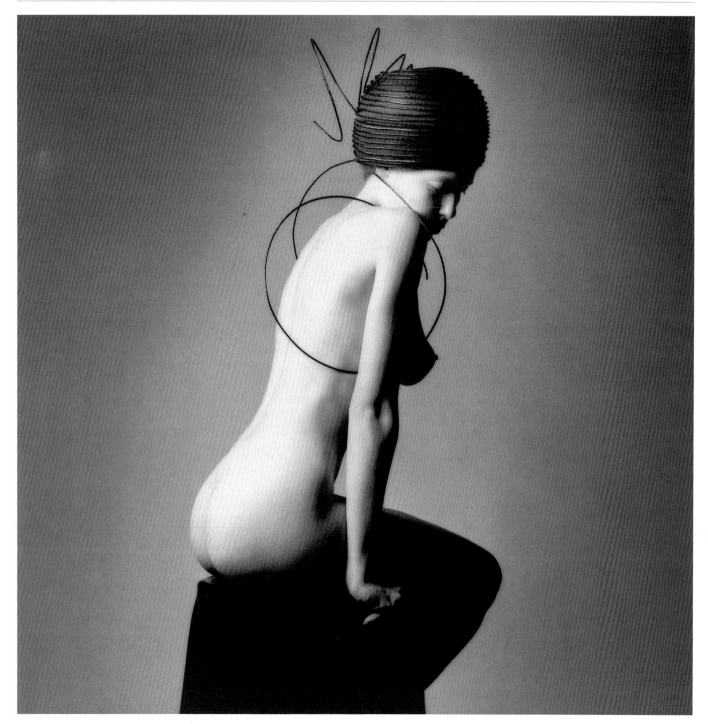

Akio Hirata. **b** Nagano Prefecture (JAP), 1925. **Black cord hat.** Photograph by Jeanloup Sieff, 1992.

Hiro

Photographer

In a stunning removal of fashion from its accepted context, Harry Winston's diamond and ruby necklace is placed on a cloven hoof. Attention is centred on the contrast between bestial nature and the glamour of Winston's work – usually associated with Hollywood – with all its amusing connotations. Hiro has applied the same humour to other subjects, including a silver bangle by New York society's favourite fashion jeweller, Elsa Peretti, which he placed on a bleached bone. Taken for the December 1963 issue of *Harper's Bazaar*, this image exemplifies both the technical and artistic brilliance of the photographer known as Hiro. Born in Shanghai to Japanese parents, he moved to New York in 1954, working with Richard Avedon and becoming a member of Alexey Brodovitch's Design Laboratory. In 1958 he became a photographer at *Harper's Bazaar*, where he defined the decade through his still-life compositions.

☛ Brodovitch, Peretti, Winston

213

Hiro (Hiro Wakabayashi). b Shanghai (CHN), 1930. **Harry Winston necklace.** New York, 1963.

Hishinuma Yoshiki

Textile designer

Using a mixed technique known as *shibori*, Yoshiki Hishinuma creates a negative silhouette on polyester. Japanese textile designers are amongst the most exciting pioneers in fashion's most scientific field, pushing the practical and aesthetic boundaries of material. Hishinuma's training at Issey Miyake's Design Studio gave him a solid background in experimental fabric technology. Belonging to the Japanese school of avant-garde fashion, Hishinuma was able to launch his own Tokyo-based label in 1984, but not before his freelance work earned him the New Designer's Prize at Tokyo's Mainichi Fashion Grand Prix. Today he has his own textile studio, specializing in isolated, neck-to-ankle fabric effects. 1998 looks include otherworldly chiffon, wrapped about the body like crumpled white tissue paper, and clipped feathers knitted tightly into a sweater.

☛ Arai, Milner, Miyake

Yoshiki Hishinuma. b Sendai (JAP), 1958. 'Shibori' technique, polyester fabric. Spring/summer 1995. Photograph by Noboru Iwahashi.

Hope Emma   Shoe designer

Emma Hope's shoes are romantic and individual in style, as this brocade buckled slipper shows to perfection. She established her company in 1985 after graduating from Cordwainer's College in London's East End, and began by selling a small range of brocade mules which were worn with Scott Crolla's ornate, antiquarian clothes. Hope's desire is to evoke 'the deliciousness of the first pair of shoes you really wanted', and make them a joy both to wear and behold. She makes bespoke and ready-to-wear shoes, and brides, in particular, buy her amazingly delicate slippers, which are covered in seed pearls and beads or decorated with fine embroidery. Hope creates nostalgic shoes, which recall the work of nineteenth-century cobblers such as Pinet. Those made from silk are especially precious, with memories of a time when a lady's foot would rarely meet the pavement.

☛ Choo, Cox, Crolla, Pinet, Yantorny

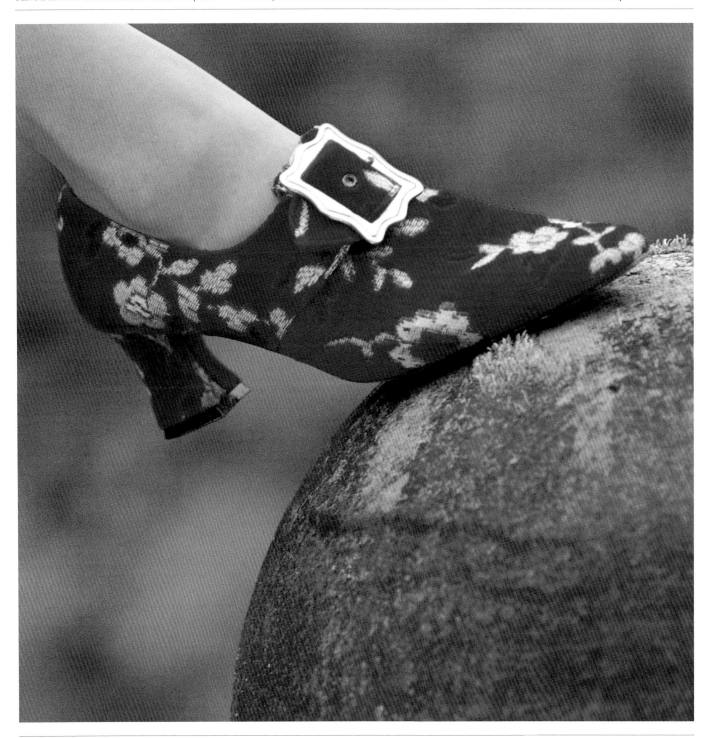

215

Emma Hope. b Portsmouth (UK), 1962. **Shoe with buckle.** Autumn/winter 1994/5. Photograph by John Swannell, *Woman's Journal*, 1994.

Horst Horst P.   Photographer

Despite an illustrious career spanning over sixty-five years, photographer Horst P. Horst will forever be linked with his portraiture of the inter-war years. He began by working with George Hoyningen-Huene at *Vogue* in 1932 and, within a few years, had developed an unmistakable fashion style that fused elements of Greek sculpture with the decadent elegance of the time. His early black-and-white images mixed subtle contrast with mood and sensitivity, achieved with carefully positioned lighting that could take three days to perfect. 'I like taking photographs, because I like life,' he once said. Picasso, Dietrich, Dalí, Cocteau, Gertrude Stein and the Duchess of Windsor were his friends and the subjects of his portraiture. His work has remained timeless and iconographic – as proved by the singer Madonna who copied his 1939 picture, *Mainbocher's Pink Satin Corset*, for her 'Vogue' video in 1989.

☛ **Cocteau, Coward, Dalí, Fonssagrives, Parker, Piguet**

216

Horst P. Horst. b Weissenfels (GER), 1906. **d** Palm Beach, FL (USA), 1999. **Helen Bennett wears a cape dress by Jean Patou.** French *Vogue*, 1936.

Horvat Frank   Photographer

Peering out from between an organic swathe of organza and a milliner's cascade of petals, the model seems to float on a background of racegoers. Male and female, black and white, this 1958 shot for *Jardin des Modes* is an exercise in contrast. Considering its composition, it is perhaps unsurprising that Frank Horvat went on to make his name outside fashion with his photographs of trees. His fashion work in 1960, however, was seminal for fashion photography, using natural make-up and pastoral backdrops rather than the prevailing mood of urban formality. Originally a photojournalist, Horvat's first colour photograph appeared on the cover of the Italian magazine *Epoca* in 1951. His wide-ranging experience benefited his fashion work, adding a broad quality to technically adept images that catch the eye.

☛ Bailey, Givenchy, Milner, Stiebel

Frank Horvat. b Abbazia (IT), 1928. **Givenchy hat, Paris.** *Jardin des Modes.* 1958.

Howell Margaret   Designer

In this gentle fashion image, Margaret Howell's tailored navy shorts resemble those worn in the 1930s. Her clothes blend memories of England with the pleasure of wearing worn-in country clothes. The look was revolutionary when she began in the early 1970s, inspired by nostalgic icons of British style, such as brogues, gymslips, sturdy tweed skirts and her father's gardening mac hanging on the back of a door. Howell's menswear and womenswear collections were launched in 1972, with an emphasis on tailoring. Howell has been so copied, it almost obscures her contribution but her linen duster coats, shirt dresses, floor-sweeping raincoats and tweed suits for women have an enduring appeal. 'When I started out, I was only thinking about what I wanted,' she told *Vogue*. 'I liked quality and comfort... I was probably responsible for the move towards using men's tailoring tweeds for women's clothes.'

☞ Jackson, Jaeger, de Prémonville

218

Margaret Howell. **b** Tadworth (UK), 1946. **Cotton sweater and crepe shorts. Spring/summer 1992.** Photograph by Koto Bolofo.

Hoyningen-Huene George   Photographer

George Hoyningen-Huene's fashion photographs were inspired by Classical Greek sculpture. He posed his models with props so that they resembled the figures in a frieze. His technique of back- and cross-lighting, to achieve line and volume and to give the models, the clothes and the settings texture and sheen, is unique. During the Russian Revolution, Hoyningen-Huene fled to England and went on to Paris in 1921. He studied painting under André Lhote and began to draw fashion. After collaborating with Man Ray, he became chief photographer for French *Vogue* in 1926, moving on to New York and American *Vogue*. Hoyningen-Huene worked at *Harper's Bazaar* in New York from 1935 to 1945. He then moved to Los Angeles where he taught photography at the Art Center School and worked on sets and costumes for Hollywood movies.

☛ **Agnès, Blumenfeld, Mainbocher, Morehouse**

George Hoyningen-Huene. b St Petersburg (RUS), 1900. **d** Los Angeles, CA (USA), 1968. **Gold reefer jacket by Mainbocher, gloves by Hattie Carnegie.** *Harper's Bazaar,* 1939.

219

Hulanicki Barbara (Biba)

A woman and child in identical maxi, panne velvet dresses are the essence of the Biba look. Barbara Hulanicki, a fashion illustrator, had dreamed of bringing decadence to the masses. She began with a 'postal boutique' in 1963, opening her first shop, named after her sister, Biba, a year later. It was a treasury of exotic accessories and fabrics and, despite its cheapness which made it accessible to students and teenagers, dressed stars including Twiggy and Julie Christie. Biba was, in the words of Ossie Clarke: 'Disposable glamour shrouded in purply, mulberry shades...' Hulanicki's style lived somewhere between Art Deco and Art Nouveau: slim, often cut from satin and velvet and highlighted with lean lurex knitwear. In 1973 Biba moved into a department store building. This 'nickelodeon land of Art Deco with potted palms and mirrored hall' only lasted until 1975, but Hulanicki's ideal is still admired.

☞ Bouquin, Clark, Kamali, Moon, Twiggy

220

Barbara Hulanicki. b Warsaw (POL), 1936. (Biba.) **Mother and daughter.** Photograph by Sarah Moon, 1969.

Hutton Lauren   Model

Lauren Hutton, with her rare beauty and alluring gap-toothed smile, has graced a record twenty-five *Vogue* covers and countless editorial campaigns. Her most newsworthy career move was the contract she signed with Revlon in 1974. The first of its kind, this exclusive agreement set a precedent for supermodels' fees, changing them from hundreds to thousands of dollars.

Over the following ten years, while modelling exclusively for Revlon, Hutton made a name for herself on screen. Born in Charleston, South Carolina, she grew up mainly in Florida and, after dropping out of college, moved to New York where she began modelling to pay for the life of travel she had originally planned. Her return to modelling in the 1990s has been a proud achievement

for Hutton, who has inspired debate about the size and age of models. Her example, she hopes, will encourage a broader view of beauty.

☛ Butler, C. Klein, Revson

Lauren Hutton. b Charleston, SC (USA), 1943. **Lauren Hutton.** Photograph by Fred Seidman, 1972.

Iman

Model

A slender sculpture in black velvet and white taffeta, Iman was dubbed Black Pearl for her ebony-black beauty. The contours of her feline figure, boasting a perfect *physique du rôle* to flaunt the 1980s' opulence, ensured that she was a true supermodel of her time. Her exotic presence on the catwalk made her a fetish model for Azzedine Alaïa, Gianni Versace and Thierry Mugler. Born

Iman Abdulmajid in Somalia to a diplomat, she studied political science in Nairobi before being discovered by Peter Beard, the photographer who took her into the New York fashion spotlight. A multimillion-dollar contract with Revlon in the late 1970s, as well as her marriage to rock star David Bowie and the launch of her own make-up range (especially devised for black

women), have conferred on her almost mythical status among black models, a reputation shared only by Naomi Campbell and Beverly Johnson.

☞ Bowie, Beverly Johnson, Revson

222

Iman (Iman Abdulmajid Haywood). b (SOM), 1955. **Formal evening gown and feather headdress.** Photograph by Arthur Elgort, 1993.

Irene

Designer

This film still from the 1940 film *Seven Sinners* shows the work of the costume designer known as 'Irene of California'. She started making clothes on the campus of the University of Southern California, where Dolores del Rio became a client. Her connections took Irene into the Beverly Hills sphere, where she became involved with actresses and their personal wardrobes. She moved to Hollywood to continue her trade. From 1942 she took over from Adrian as head costumer at Metro-Goldwyn-Mayer, making outfits for, among others, Marlene Dietrich and Marilyn Monroe. Her signature style always remained slim, curvy and tailored for daywear; eveningwear, however, was lavish and dramatic, with feathers, frills and sparkle. Here, Marlene Dietrich wears an outfit embellished with the trappings of a romantic vamp: polka-dot veil, net gloves, ostrich-trimmed handbag and chiffon corsage.

☞ Adrian, Head, Louis, Travilla

Irene (Irene Lentz Gibbons). **b** MT (USA), 1907. **d** Los Angeles, CA (USA), 1962. **Marlene Dietrich.** Still from *Seven Sinners*. 1940.

Iribe Paul

Illustrator

The simple lines and brilliant colours of Poiret's oriental style are beautifully evoked in this fashion illustration, published a year before the arrival of the Ballets Russes and Bakst in Paris. The Hispahan coat in the centre, made in green cotton velvet, has embroidered Persian palms sharply outlined in bold yellow and white. This coat is framed by two others in shades of yellow and mustard, trimmed with fur. Further contrasts of colour are provided by the dresses visible beneath the coats and by the headwear. With its format of clear, flat areas of colour and the asymmetrical arrangement of the models, the fashion illustration shows the influence of Japanese prints. In order to obtain such jewel-like colours, Iribe used a special technique called the *pochoir* process, whereby a monochrome print was hand-coloured using a series of bronze or zinc stencils, enabling him to capture an image as close as possible to the original.

☛ Bakst, Barbier, Doucet, Gigli, Lepape, Paquin, Poiret

224

Paul Iribe. b Angoulême (FR), 1883. **d** Paris (FR), 1935. **'Three Coats'.** From *Les Robes de Paul Poiret* racontées par Paul Iribe. 1908.

Isogawa Akira   Designer

Against a background of pattern pieces (the building blocks from which fashion takes shape), Akira Isogawa's model wears a vest contructed from bronze jacquard silk. Its seams, brought together as an abstract, asymmetric puzzle, are stitched on the outside, leaving their frayed edges to become part of the exterior decoration. Isogawa left his native Japan for Sydney, Australia, to escape becoming a 'salary man'. He trained in fashion and in 1996 showed his first collection as part of Australian Fashion Week. It was an exotic *mélange* of Japanese vintage kimonos, delicate and translucent floral-print dresses and modern leather and wool tailoring, all layered together to create a new aesthetic in fashion. The attraction of Isogawa's clothes lies in his passion for fabric. 'I have a connection, a Zen thing with material', he has said. His delicate handprints, antique fabrics from Japan and form-fitting tailoring make a sharp, yet individual statement.

☞ Arai, Chalayan, Kobayashi, Lloyd

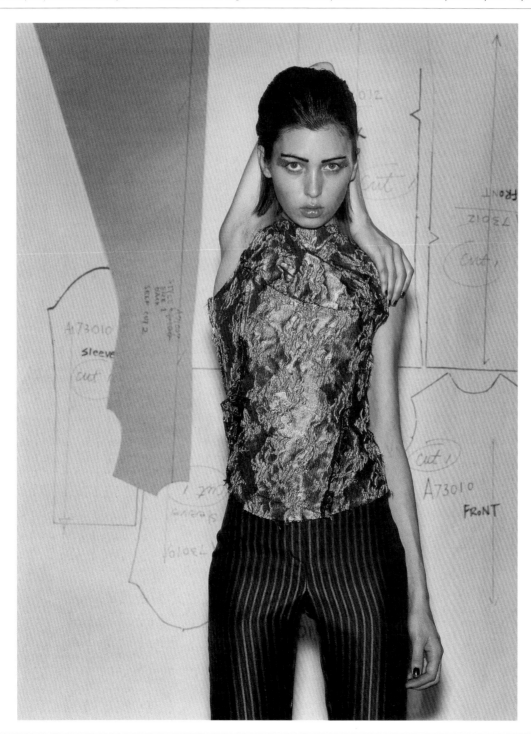

Akira Isogawa. b Kyoto (JAP), 1964. **Deconstructed bronze brocade top and pinstriped trousers.** Photograph by Eddy Ming, 1998.

Jackson Betty   Designer

Square, linen shapes, styled for *Vogue* by Vera Wang, represent the work of Betty Jackson, who is known for her thoughtful balance between fashion and comfort. Consequently, her designs appeal to women whose working and leisure wardrobes tend to be interchangeable – a relaxed, modern concept. She originally wanted to become a sculptor, an aspiration which was thwarted by an allergy to plaster of Paris. Instead, she freelanced as an illustrator, before turning her attention to fashion in 1973, working for Wendy Dagworthy and then at Quorum. Jackson and her French-born husband, David Cohen, founded their own company under her name in 1981. The core of her easy, fluid collections consists of boldly coloured, simple and versatile shapes; a style that allows elements of high fashion to be represented without compromising her notion that fashion belongs to women of any age.

☞ P. Ellis, Howell, Pollock, Wang

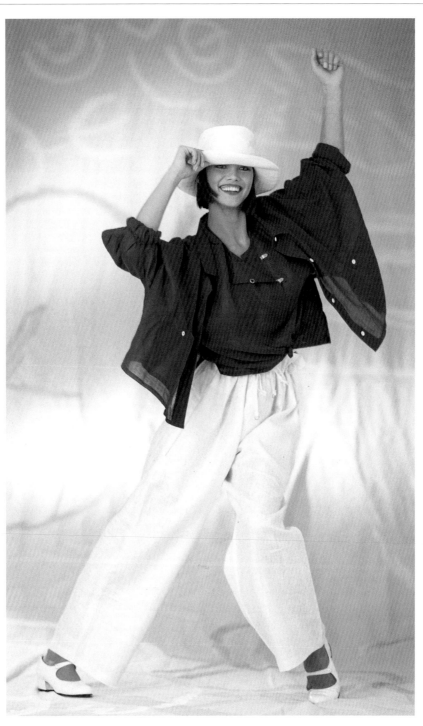

226

Betty Jackson. b Bacup (UK), 1949. **Linen shirt and drawstring trousers.** Photograph by Tony McGee, American *Vogue*, 1984.

Jacobs Marc   Designer

Naomi Campbell is caught laughing, mid-pose, in a sitting for American *Vogue*. Her powder-grey, cashmere vest and flat-fronted trousers are by Marc Jacobs, examples of what the *New York Times* has called his 'caviar clothes'. The simplicity of her outfit is given an edgier profile with a pair of sharp stilettos, a contradiction that Jacobs uses in his own work.

His proclivity for luxurious materials and modern references recommended the one-time designer for Perry Ellis to the position of creative director at Louis Vuitton, the French luggage company. Jacobs has introduced pop and kitsch elements to its traditional image; 'Deluxe hip' was Suzy Menkes' summary in the *International Herald Tribune*. Jacobs addresses his own age group: rich women in their thirties are attracted by his witty update of a brand that has been the accessory of choice for generations.

☞ Campbell, Cobain, Garren, Kors, Moses, Vuitton

Marc Jacobs. b New York (USA), 1963. **Naomi Campbell wears cashmere vest and flat-fronted trousers.** Photograph by Wolfgang Tillmans, American *Vogue*, 1997.

Jacobson Jacqueline and Elie (Dorothée Bis) Designers

Fun, funky knitwear was the key to the Dorothée Bis style. Their 'total look' often incorporated knitted tights and hats and unconventional layering such as skirts over trousers or, as seen here, thigh-clinging shorts worn with over-the-knee socks. Jacqueline and Elie Jacobson founded the label with the desire to create wearable versions of high-fashion styles, producing clothes that were ideal for the youth-inspired period of short-lived fashion trends in the 1960s. The label was always commercially minded, reflecting their backgrounds in the fashion trade (in the 1950s, Jacqueline owned a childrenswear shop and Elie worked as a wholesale furrier). Each decade they defined the key looks, from knitted maxi coats and skinny-rib sweaters in the 1960s, to voluminous layering in the 1970s and tight, shoulder-padded graphic knits in the 1980s.

☛ Khanh, Paulin, Rykiel, Troublé

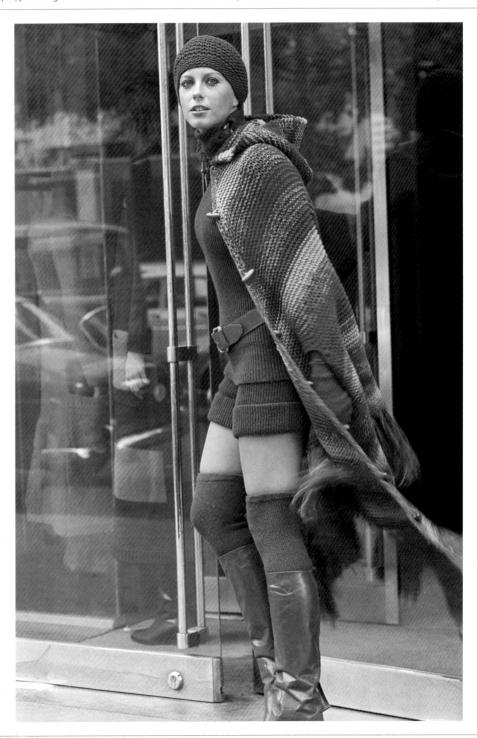

Jacobson. Jacqueline. b Lens (FR), 1928; **Elie. b** Paris (FR), 1925. (Dorothée Bis.) **Hooded poncho and shorts.** Photograph by Peter Knapp, French *Elle*, 1970.

Jaeger Dr Gustav   Designer

Dr Gustav Jaeger, a German dress reformer who believed that animal hair made the most healthy fabric, stands erect, wearing close-fitting, woollen breeches. Unlikely as it seems, Jaeger inspired a classic British label which was patronized by George Bernard Shaw and Oscar Wilde. The company was founded in 1883 by Lewis Tomalin, the London businessman who translated and published Jaeger's thoughts. Tomalin went on a health crusade to convert the public to the benefits of wearing wool next to the skin as advocated by the doctor from Stuttgart, securing his rights and name. It wasn't until the 1920s that fashion was embraced by Jaeger, and then it was used to popularize the appeal of 'healthy' materials through a style that came to represent British, dependable design. Jean Muir, who made her name with her draped wool jersey dresses, was Jaeger's most celebrated designer.

☛ Burberry, Creed, Howell, Muir, Wilde

Dr Gustav Jaeger. b Börg am Kocher (GER), 1832. d Stuttgart (GER), 1917. **Dr Gustav Jaeger.** c1880.

James Charles   Designer

Charles James was working for Elizabeth Arden when he created the couture dress that is the sculptural centre of this John Rawlings photograph. Every James dress was a *tour de force* of sculptural imagination; the pyramid shape on the left and the black-and-white figure on the right confirm his penchant for sculpture. The evening dress (c1944) anticipates the postwar silhouette, especially that of Christian Dior's New Look. A corseted bodice emphasizes the supported bust and narrowed waist, while the flaring fabrics just below the waist float out from the body to construct fictive hips that make the waist seem even slimmer. Irascible and self-destructive, James couched his designs in pseudo-systems and supposed geometries, but made his name as the maker of the extravagant concoctions that defined the conservative picturesque in post-Second World War fashion.

☞ Arden, Beaton, Scaasi, Steele, Weber

230

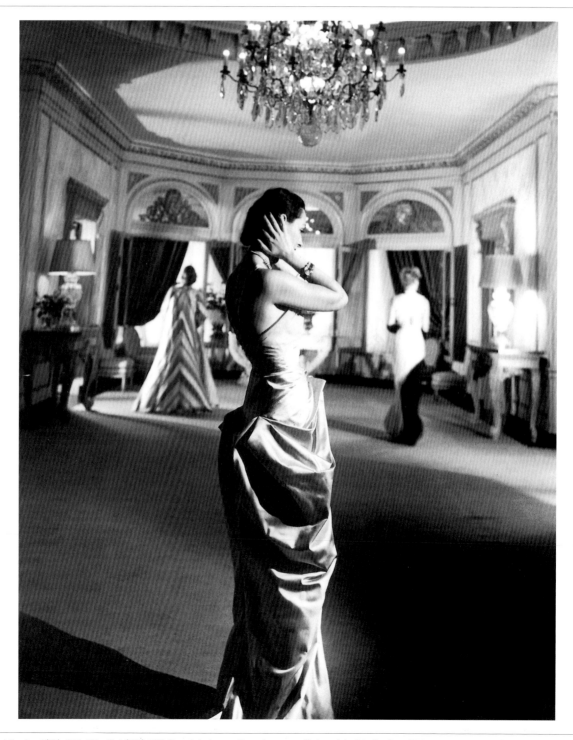

Charles James. b Sandhurst (UK), 1906. d New York (USA), 1978. **Draped duchesse satin couture gown.** Photograph by John Rawlings, 1944.

James Richard   Tailor

Actor Edward Atterton is laid out in a country house 'whodunnit' spread for *Elle*, much to the entertainment of the tourists. The photographer, David LaChapelle, maximizes the tongue-in-cheek appeal of Richard James' lilac wool suit. Since 1976, when he launched his label, James has been regarded as the 'light player' of Savile Row, using vivid colours instead of sombre greys and eccentric checks rather than traditional tweed. His choice of such exclusive fabrics gave British bespoke and tailored, ready-to-wear menswear a contemporary feel, drawing comparisons with Tommy Nutter and his contemporaries from the 1960s. A-list film stars and pop stars (and their girlfriends) patronize James, who says, 'Many of the suits made along the row are beautiful but bland. We are trying to add a youthful spirit and excitement, while maintaining the propriety that Savile Row stands for.'

☞ Cox, LaChapelle, Nutter, P. Smith

231

Richard James. b Ely (UK), 1953. **Edward Atterton wears lilac wool suit and woven stripe shirt.** Photograph by David LaChapelle, British *Elle*, 1996.

Jantzen Carl   Designer

Swimming champion Johnny Weissmuller poses poolside in a pair of 'Jantzens', the world's first elasticized trunks. Invented by knitwear designer Carl Jantzen, who experimented with the machines which made sweater cuffs, this innovation prompted the world to stop merely 'bathing' and start 'swimming'. Jantzen founded the Portland Knitting Co with John and Roy Zehntbauer in 1910. Their heavy wool sweaters, socks and gloves, produced on a few knitting machines and sold from the company shop, were phenomenally successful. The trunks soon became known as 'Jantzens', and the company changed its name accordingly in 1918. Three years later, the Red Diving Girl motif was added. Jantzen's early designs were unisex (although women wore theirs with stockings), but the developments resulted in streamlined swimwear for women. By 1925 Jantzen was one of the first clothes companies to export its work.

☛ Gernreich, Lacoste

232

Carl Jantzen. **b** Aarhus (DK), 1883. **d** (USA), 1939. **Johnny Weissmuller wears wool tanksuit, Olympic Games, 1924.**

Jinteok

Designer

Jinteok is known for simple designs crafted from luxurious fabrics which meld traditional elements of her cultural heritage with Western influences. Here, she uses Chinese red silk for an apron dress. Its bodice and hem are decorated with naturalistic forms in the tradition of oriental silk garments. The underskirt, cut from roughly assembled denim, lends this potentially glamorous garment a rustic, hobo feel. Such subtle themes, inspired mainly by nature, are evident throughout her collections. Since she opened her first shop in Seoul in 1965, Jinteok has played a pioneering role in contemporary fashion in her native country, South Korea. She founded the Seoul Fashion Designers Association, which encourages young Korean designers, and presented her womenswear collection on the catwalks in Paris for the first time in 1994.

☛ Arai, Kim, Rocha

233

Jinteok (Jin Teok). b (KOR), 1938. **Red embroidered gown. Spring/summer 1995.** Photograph by Marcio Madeira.

John John P.   Milliner

Although this outfit is heavily accessorized, the pieces are so carefully matched that at first glance they are barely noticeable, camouflaged against the co-ordinated clothing. During the 1930s no fashionable outfit was complete without matching hat, gloves, shoes and bag. At that time, New York's accessory designers were moving into the limelight, and John P. John was one of America's top proponents. Also known as Mr John, he had a career in Hollywood for fifty years, working with Adrian and Travis Banton. With Frederic Hirst he formed the John-Frederics label, creating perfectly co-ordinated outfits. This picture shows how a puff-sleeved, tartan shirt and cream skirt is complemented with formal accessories, including a matching bag. The cream broad-brimmed hat is covered in black net and tones with the gloves. Unusually, a long band hangs from the hat, encircling the blouse and literally pulling the outfit together.

☛ Adrian, Banton, Daché, Simpson

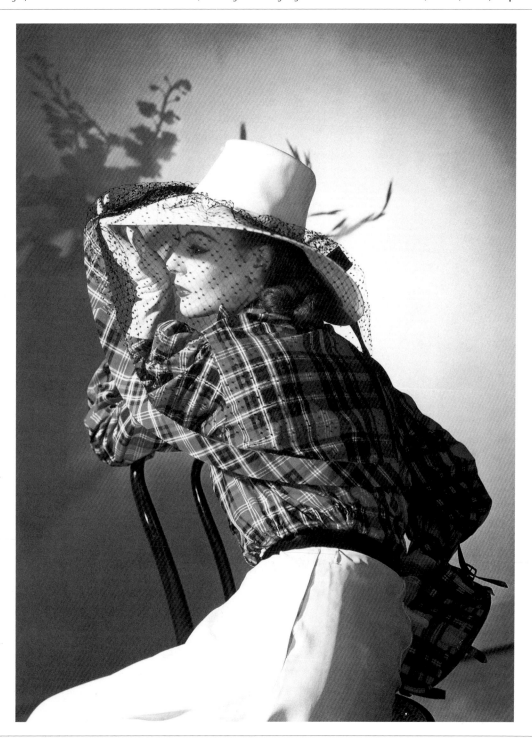

John P. John. b (GER), c1906. **d** Los Angeles (USA), 1993. **Veiled panama hat, plaid blouse and pocket book.** Photograph by Horst P. Horst, 1939.

234

Johnson Betsey   Designer

'Fashion is all about having fun and these are clothes to have fun in,' says Betsey Johnson, who wears her own kooky combination of floral dress and fishnet tights. Johnson's attitude to fashion is summed up by the cartwheels she performs along the catwalk at the end of her shows. Best known for her brightly coloured, madcap prints, she started designing in 1965 and her imaginative designs took full advantage of the new synthetics and mini-lengths. Her dresses were decorated with jangling shower-ring hems and her fluorescent underwear was packaged in tennis ball cans. Johnson also sold plastic dresses in kit form for the wearer to arrange as she wanted. It was a dress with a ten inch, extended collar that made her name. Worn by British actress Julie Christie, it sold in the tens of thousands. Johnson's career was launched by New York's Paraphernalia boutique, a champion of youth-inspired fashion in the 1960s.

☛ Bailly, Foale, Rabanne

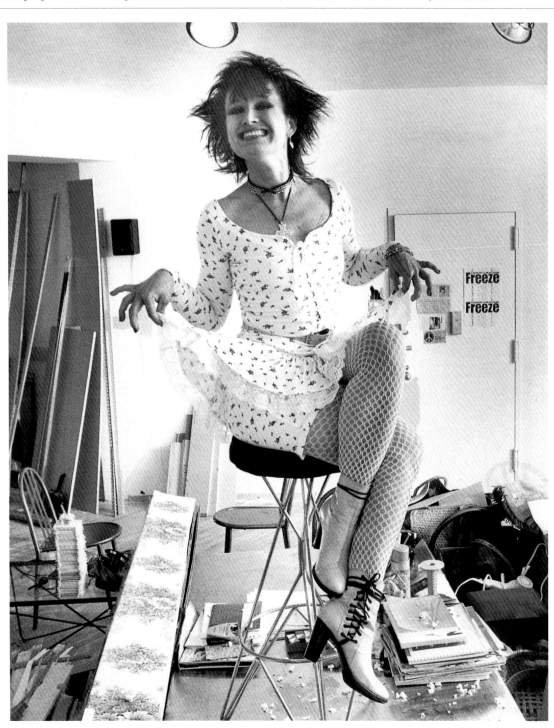

Betsey Johnson. b Hartford, CT (USA), 1942. **Betsey Johnson in her design studio, New York, 1982.** Photograph by Harry Benson.

Johnson Beverly   Model

Beverly Johnson has a place in fashion history, not only as the first black model to be featured on the cover of American *Vogue*, but also for paving the way for black women the world over to feel part of the fashion industry. Johnson began modelling while a student at Northeastern University in Boston, receiving assignments for *Vogue* and *Glamour* despite having no portfolio.

Fashion editors were impressed by her fresh beauty. When Scavullo photographed her for the *Vogue* cover in August 1974, the magazine was taking a chance. Little did they know that its circulation for that month would double. Johnson said at the time, 'The participation of black models ... is unjust in proportion to the amount of money that is put into the industry by black people'.

Her career spanned the 1970s and early 1980s and also included film roles, records and two books.

☞ Iman, Nast, Turbeville

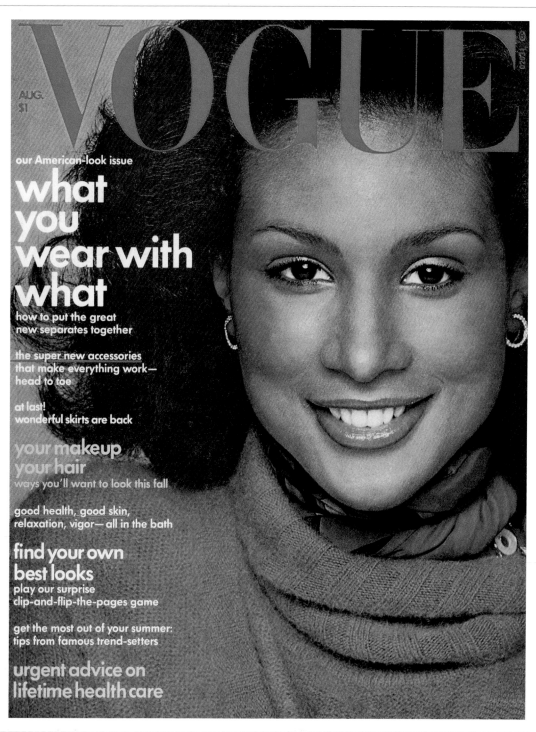

Beverly Johnson. b (USA), 1953. **Beverly Johnson.** Photograph by Francesco Scavullo, American *Vogue*, 1974.

Jones Grace   Model

Grace Jones poses for a Polaroid taken by her friend Antonio Lopez in his bathroom. Jones, with her Amazonian figure and shorn hair, was the antithesis of femininity. The daughter of a Pentecostal minister, she rebelled against her strict upbringing and pursued a modelling career in Paris at a time when her theatrical attitude perfectly suited the extremes of 1970s fashion:

'Glitter? Uh-huh. Platform shoes? Yeah... It was sort of old Hollywood star stuff.' Fashion centred on the flashy nightclub scene at Paris's Club Sept, where Jones partied every night. Together with friend Jerry Hall, Jones brought outrageous performance to modelling and, as a result, created a second career for herself. In the 1980s she turned to music, cultivating an aggressive look of

sharp, angular, leather clothes and a razored quiff to clothe her image as a modern diva.

☞ Antoine, Antonio, Price

237

Grace Jones. b Spanish Town (JAM), 1954. Grace Jones. Photograph by Antonio Lopez, 1980.

Jones Stephen   Milliner

The model camps it up for Mario Testino's camera. On her head she wears a miniature topper by milliner Stephen Jones, known for his innovative, witty and gregarious hats. Boaters, caps and bowler hats have all been reduced to create millinery caricatures. He was a central figure in London's New Romantic movement in the early 1980s, making hats for his friends Steve Strange and Boy George. In 1984 his work was noticed by Jean-Paul Gaultier and Thierry Mugler, who both asked him to design hats to accessorize their collections, making him one of the first British milliners to work in Paris. Jones has since collaborated with a succession of international fashion designers. As with the shoe designer Manolo Blahnik, his work as an accessory designer lends itself to collaborative ventures because of its sympathy with the clothes, as well as a sharpness that makes it a punchy punctuation mark.

☛ Berthoud, Galliano, Testino, Van Beirendonck

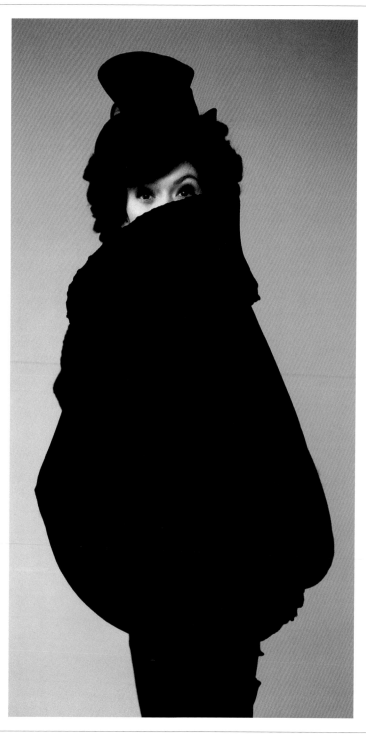

Stephen Jones. b West Kirby (UK), 1957. **Top hat.** Photograph by Mario Testino, *Harpers & Queen*, 1988.

238

Jourdan Charles   Shoe designer

In the 1930s, Charles Jourdan was the first shoe designer to advertise in fashion magazines. In the 1970s, his advertisements, such as the one below, were photographed by Guy Bourdin and became legendary. Bourdin lent the shoes wit and mystery by placing them in surreal scenes, making them components of a larger story. Here, two women are escaping over a wall, leaving three of their platform sandals behind. Jourdan had introduced low-priced diffusion lines to his handmade collection after the Second World War. He sold simple designs in a multitude of colours and fits, for a developing ready-to-wear business. In 1958 Maxime, a low-heeled, square-toed court shoe with a satin bow, became his best-selling style. In the 1960s, a collaboration with André Perugia added a touch of glamour, but Jourdan's collaboration with Bourdin remains the most exciting impression of his work.

☛ **Bourdin, Oldfield, Perugia**

Charles Jourdan. b Bourg-de-Péage (FR), 1883. **d** Romans-sur-Isère (FR), 1976. **Summer sandals.** Photograph by Guy Bourdin, 1974.

Kamali Norma   Designer

In the tradition of American fashion, Norma Kamali formed an entire wardrobe from utilitarian material. When she launched her own range of clothes, Kamali created a fashion phenomenon by using sweatshirt fleece fabric for clothes such as leggings, kick skirts and wide-shouldered dresses. Her outfits addressed a problem felt by millions of American women: how could they get away with comfort when fashion dictated structure and ostentatious formality? She was also one of the first to offer the unitard. Kamali's fashion career began in 1968, when she opened a boutique with her husband Eddie in New York. At the time, she was an air stewardess and sourced many European fashions, particularly from Biba in London. In 1978, after her divorce, Kamali set up OMO (On My Own) and her new-found independence was reflected in her clothes, which have continued to provide a modern response for modern women.

☛ Campbell, Hechter, Hulanicki

240

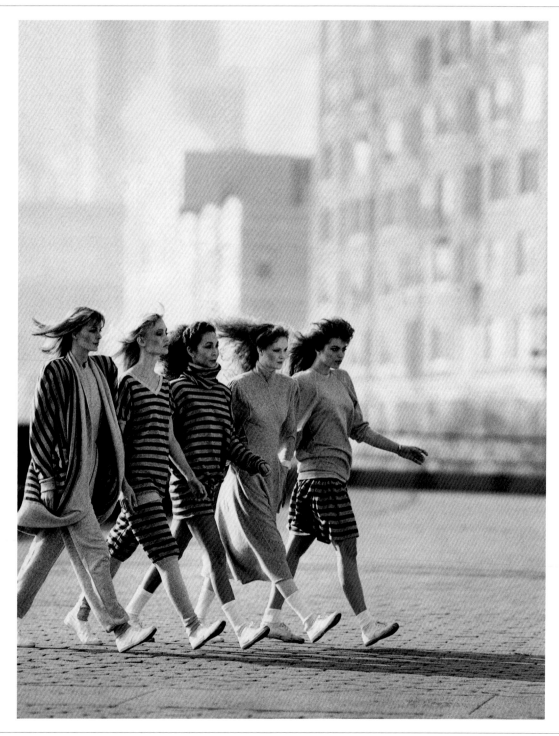

Norma Kamali. b New York (USA), 1945. **Sweatshirt collection. Spring/summer 1980.** *Women's Wear Daily.*

Karan Donna   Designer

'What do I need? How can I make life easier? How can dressing be simplified so that I can get on with my own life?' Donna Karan's own thoughts could be running through the head of the 'first woman president', who represents her own ideal: ultimately powerful and urban. Professional wearability dictates Karan's work. Her first collection was a wardrobe of separates based around the 'body' – a practical, stretchy, leotard shape with poppers at the crotch. Karan also designs to flatter the normal woman, saying, 'You've gotta accentuate your positive to delete your negative', and only designs clothes that she would wear herself. Karan trained with Anne Klein, taking over the design with Louis Dell'Olio when Klein died. Karan's fidelity to Klein's easy-to-wear never waned, but in the 1990s she became increasingly interested in spiritual philosophies, and began producing looser, more sensual clothing.

☛ Dell'Olio, A. Klein, Maxwell, Morris

241

Donna Karan. b New York (USA), 1948. **'In Women We Trust' advertising campaign.** Photograph by Peter Lindbergh, 1992.

Kawakubo Rei (Comme des Garçons) Designer

In this classic photograph of work by Rei Kawakubo for her label Comme des Garçons, shredded sweaters are patchworked together. The mishmash of knitwear is held together by visible, rough over-stitching and deliberately careless seaming. The model's make-up feigns bruising, she wears jersey bandages around her wrists and her hair is razored into a brutal crop. In the early 1980s, Kawakubo's aesthetic changed the way clothes were seen. Called 'post-nuclear chic', it supplanted the assumption that fashion was always to be approached with the intention of creating perfectly made clothes in the old tradition of those that flatter the body. Kawakubo is a conceptualist, using Japanese rather than European clothing traditions. She challenges her customers to wear her ideas even when they resemble a work of art – as was the case in 1997 when she padded them with cushions to re-contour the body shape.

☛ Arai, Hirata, Lindbergh, Miyake, Vionnet, Watanabe

242

Rei Kawakubo. b Tokyo (JAP), 1942. (Comme des Garçons.) **Knitwear. Autumn/winter 1984/5.** Photograph by Peter Lindbergh.

Kélian Stéphane   Shoe designer

A pair of bronze sandals epitomizes the work of one of France's most enduringly fashionable shoe designers. Basket-woven leather has been a feature of Kélian shoes since Georges and Gérard Kélian opened a workshop to design and manufacture classic men's shoes in 1960. In the mid-1970s, Stéphane entered into partnership with his two older brothers, bringing a new fashion spirit to their traditional shoe company. In subsequent collections, he continued to feature the specialist weaving techniques used by his brothers, but modernized the designs and introduced a panoply of shimmering colours into the colour palette. Stéphane presented his first collection of women's shoes in 1977 and the opening of the first of many international boutiques followed a year later in Paris. Kélian is known for his design collaborations with fashion designers and other cobblers, including Martine Sitbon and Maud Frizon.

☛ Frizon, Sitbon, Steiger

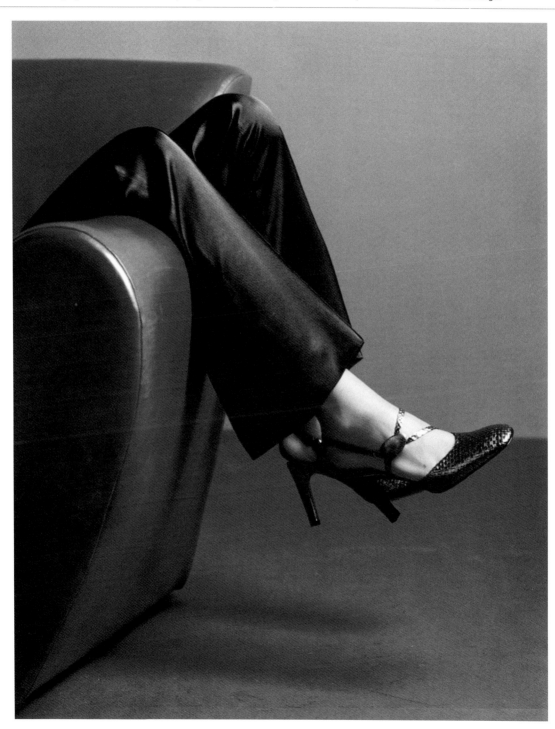

243

Stéphane Kélian (Stéphane Kéloglanian). b Romans-sur-Isère (FR), 1942. **Basket-weave sandals. Autumn/winter 1997/8.** Photograph by Roberto Badin.

Kelly Patrick   Designer

Shining out amidst the backstage chaos are symbols that characterize one of the most exuberant designers of the 1980s. A committed Francophile, Patrick Kelly describes the Eiffel Tower in rhinestones for a black dress, uses it for clunking gilt earring charms and even on high-heeled shoes. Journalist Bernadine Morris noted Kelly's 'collection of lively, unpretentious clothes that made fashion look like fun...an unforced feeling of happiness'. His work always contained an element of the theatrical and his catwalk shows combined the largesse of a rural Southern American culture with the camp bravado of Moulin Rouge entertainment. Affordable ready-to-wear clothing was gaily decorated with buttons, and black rag dolls, once a sign of oppression, were festooned over a coat. Between 1985 and 1989, Kelly seemed an irrepressible force for dynamic fashion, involving young people and black experience.

☛ W. Klein, Moschino, Parkinson, Price

244

Patrick Kelly. b Vickysburg, MI (USA), 1954. **d** Paris (FR), 1990. **Backstage.** Photograph by William Klein, 1987.

Kennedy Jacqueline Icon

Ladylike but youthful, formal but fashionable, the 'Jackie' style caught America's attention and made the young woman a fashion icon. This picture illustrates Jackie's trademarks: the simple coat, the white gloves, the hair by Kenneth. In 1961 Oleg Cassini became her designer, telling her that she could only wear his clothes – although she would occasionally consult with Diana Vreeland at *Harper's Bazaar*. In return, Cassini created a wardrobe for the First Lady. It had a pared-down elegance and an informal spirit that was unusual. She rarely wore patterns and stuck to simple shapes: sleeveless, boxy shift dresses with matching coats and accessories. Halston was her milliner, creating her famous style. Jackie always wore gloves and rarely wore jewellery, except for occasional pearls. As with her clothes, Jackie liked her shoes 'slender...but not exaggerated – no tricky...business – timeless and elegant'.

☛ Cassini, Daché, Lane, Pulitzer, Vanderbilt, Vreeland

Jacqueline Kennedy. b New York (USA), 1929. **d** New York (USA), 1994. **'Raja' coat in dupion silk by Oleg Cassini.** Photograph by Art Rickerby, *Life*, 1962.

Kenneth

Hairdresser

In 1963, an article in American *Vogue*, entitled 'The Kenneth Club', described the lengths to which women would go for an appointment with the hairdresser Kenneth Battelle. He attended to Jackie Kennedy's bouffant bob, copied across America. He created the perfect domed bobs on Veruschka and Jean Shrimpton for *Vogue* covers when Diana Vreeland was editor. She called it the 'Dynel period' because of the enormous quantities of synthetic hair that were used for ever more elaborate wigs and extensions. Famously, in Tahiti, they used Dynel not just on the models but on a real white horse to create a fairy-tale ponytail. However, for Kenneth, the cut rather than the dressing was the most important element to a hairstyle: his teased and backcombed precision bobs defined an era. 'I defy a woman to wear a Courrèges dress without really great make-up and a hairdo,' he is quoted as saying.

☛ Antoine, Kennedy, Shrimpton, Veruschka, Vreeland

246

Kenneth (Kenneth Battelle). b New York (USA), 1927. **Bouffant bob.** Photograph by Art Kane, American *Vogue*, 1962.

Kenzo

Designer

Her layered, floral, prairie cottons swing to life; an earthy, retrospective look that dominated much of the mid-1970s. The dress and jacket use the Victorian details such as a fitted bodice and billowing sleeves caught into deep cuffs. Kenzo Takada, its designer, opened his first shop in Paris in 1970. Since it was decorated with jungle prints, he called it Jungle Jap, a name which soon became popular with young, fashionable models who were looking for fresh, spirited clothes. Inspired mostly by traditional Japanese shapes, Kenzo's early, highly desirable collections included easy-to-wear smocks, tunics, oriental blouses and wide-legged trousers. They were predominantly made from cotton and quilted. Kenzo also specialized in knitwear which was added to the cottons to produce an eclectic, comfortable look. His refreshing use of colour, pattern and print have made him one of the most durable of the 1970s designers.

☞ Ashley, Ettedgui, Matsuda

Kenzo (Kenzo Takada). b Hyogo (JAP), 1939. **Tiered floral print dress, Spain.** Photograph by Peter Knapp, 1973.

Keogh Lainey   Designer

'Lainey's knitwear,' said Hamish Bowles in American *Vogue*, 'challenges all one's preconceptions of the woolly jumper.' Here, her friend Naomi Campbell wears an intricately knitted dress which is light as air, clingy and revealing. Knitting is one of Ireland's oldest cottage industries and although Keogh's style is modern – with details such as the quirky, asymmetric hem and shoulder – this dress is also ethereal and romantic. The emerald green hand-work conjures up images of mermaids and the fishing nets used on the west coast of Ireland. Lainey Keogh says her hand-knitted clothes are 'like food or sex: intimate and personal'. This poetic sensibility is her signature; she claims to have discovered her talent through knitting a jumper for her lover. She loves the 'exquisite feeling of the lightest textures against the skin' and her fabrics are created using feather-light cashmere and iridescent chenille.

☛ Campbell, Kobayashi, Macdonald

Lainey Keogh. **b** (IRE). (Active 1990s–.) **Lace knitwear. Autumn/winter 1997/8**. Photograph by Chris Moore.

Kerrigan Daryl   Designer

A Daryl K dress is hitched up in a movement which corrects a predicament known as the 'Daryl dip'. Daryl Kerrigan's problematic but highly fashionable strapless tops, worn with tomboyish hipster trousers, blend sportswear with tailoring for women who aren't ready to commit to a suit. She studied fashion at the National College of Art and Design in Dublin, before moving to

New York in 1986. Kerrigan was determined to design the perfect pair of jeans. Her boot-cut, hipster jeans, dubbed 'low riders', were partly inspired by a pair of 1970s hip-huggers she had found in a vintage warehouse. The jeans were to make her name and become the mainstay of her collections, alongside her stretchy tube tops, drawstring nylon skirts and zip-up jersey sweat-jackets. She says,

'Women want something new and don't want to feel like they're dressing in a period play.'

☛ Demeulemeester, Farhi, Lang

Daryl Kerrigan. b Dublin (IRE), 1964. **Strapless dress.** Photograph by Jon Mortimer, 1998.

Khanh Emmanuelle Designer

'Haute couture is dead,' proclaimed Emmanuelle Khanh in the 1960s. Her French street fashion paralleled Mary Quant's during the 'youthquake' movement. Her radical designs, tightly modelled on the curves of the body, drew inspiration from the pop scene. A former model for Balenciaga and Givenchy, Khanh reacted against the stiff sophistication of 1950s couture by reflecting and modernizing the loose, feminine frame of the 1930s. Her relaxed style, shown here, was a mixture of low-waisted culottes, fitted jackets with narrow shoulders and dog-eared collars. These flattering innovations were adapted from her earlier knitwear for Missoni, Cacharel and Dorothée Bis. Her own label, created in 1972, echoed the ethnic look of the period in Romanian hand embroidery and peasant-style dresses. Khanh represented the young face of French fashion, together with Christiane Bailly and Paco Rabanne.

☞ Antonio, Bailly, Ettedgui, Jacobson, Quant, Rosier

250

Emmanuelle Khanh. b Paris (FR), 1937. **Ready-to-wear womenswear**. Illustration by Antonio López, French *Elle*, 1967.

Kim Christina (Dosa)   Designer

The featherweight gauze shirt worn over silk trousers is representative of Christina Kim's almost spiritual work. The designer behind the Dosa label launched in 1983, Kim was born in Korea but has lived much of her life in Los Angeles. The Dosa philosophy was born when her t'ai chi teacher's traditional Chinese jacket caught her eye and inspired her to make a similar one but in heavy, washed linen. Kim has since perfected the art of melding simple shapes, inspired by her Korean heritage, with fabrics from diverse cultures, in a palette of soothing, often iridescent colours. In 1997 Dosa – the Korean word for 'sage' and Kim's mother's nickname – was heralded as the hottest label to come out of the USA and into Europe. Mindful of the environment, Kim also uses the by-products of the clothing manufacturing process for home accessories.

☛ Jinteok, Matsuda, Zoran

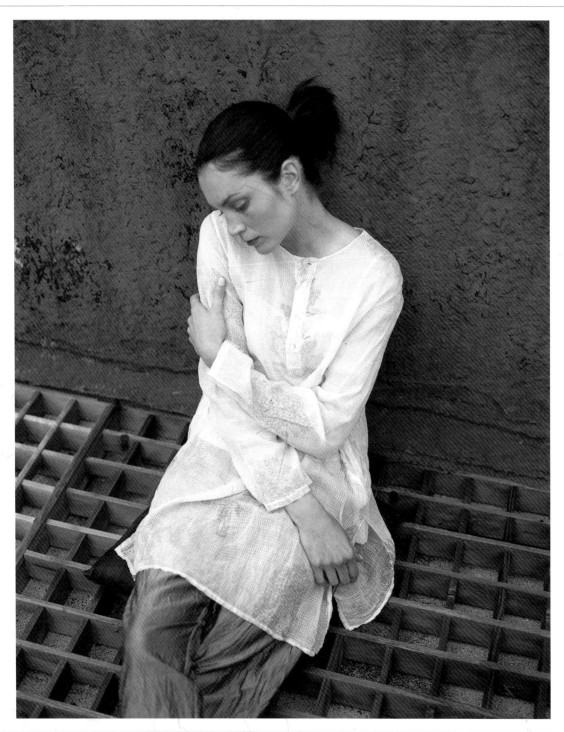

251

Christina Kim. b Seoul (KOR), 1957. (Dosa.) **Diaphanous shirt with silk trousers.** Photograph by Don Freeman, *Joyce*, 1997.

Klein Anne

Designer

A belted, white playsuit over a long-sleeved T-shirt epitomizes every practical detail used by Anne Klein. Klein only just missed inventing American designer sportswear. Following the pioneers of the 1930s and 1940s – McCardell, Leser, Maxwell *et al* – she came to represent the ethos of contemporary sportswear, creating clothes that suited modern women. Beginning with her work at Junior Sophisticates in 1948, she always thought in terms of carefree and casual forms, soft materials (especially jersey for evening), mixable separates (for sensible wardrobe-building) and forgiving tunics and outer wraps. Her bodysuits and derivations from active sportswear determined the basic canon of American designer sportswear in the 1950s and 1960s.

Klein's lead was followed by Donna Karan and Louis Dell'Olio who both excelled (and still do in Karan's case) at fashion that is friendly towards a multitude of figure shapes.

☛ Dell'Olio, Leser, Maxwell, McCardell, Rodriguez

Anne Klein. b New York (USA), 1923. **d** New York (USA), 1974. **Cream shorts suit.** Photograph by Kourken Pakchanian, American *Vogue*, 1972.

Klein Calvin   Designer

Lauren Hutton wears a simple blouson jacket, mannish pleated trousers cinched with a silk tie, and a clean, white top. The styles may have changed but the adjectives have followed Calvin Klein's work through three decades. 'I made a lot of things that go with things,' said Klein, whose sophisticated sportswear in natural fabrics and colours came to define the versatility of modern fashion. In the 1970s, Klein produced branded jeans, thereby creating the modern-day designer label as a branding tool. Klein is also known for his clever marketing: when Brooke Shields purred sexily in his adverts, 'Nothing comes between me and my Calvin's', it scandalized New York and ensured fame for Klein – as did the pin-up, billboard posters for his men's and women's underwear in the 1980s. Klein is often credited as being most in tune with the Zeitgeist and mostcapable of understanding what the modern woman wants to wear.

☞ Baron, Coddington, Hutton, Moss, Turlington, Weber

253

Calvin Klein. b New York (USA), 1942. **Lauren Hutton wears cream.** Photograph by Francesco Scavullo, American *Vogue*, 1974.

Klein William   Photographer

The viewer always has the best seat in the house for Klein's spectacle. In a 1960 meeting of Roberto Capucci dresses on the Piazza di Spagna in Rome, Simone d'Aillencourt almost steps into the viewer's lap; Nina de Vos, walking the other way, looks back as if to notice that the two dresses are so Op Art and so alike. Only the 'chance' presence of the guy on the Vespa tells us that this is the street and not a commissioned runway. Klein exalted the artifice of a fashion photograph, defying many of his contemporaries in the 1950s, who preferred naturalism or its simulation. Klein sought the startling effect. Later a film-maker, Klein let out some of his fashion contempt in the satirical film, now a fashion legend, *Qui êtes-vous, Polly Magoo?* (1966). Klein appeared to care little about the dresses; he was always a maker of eccentric, visual melodramas.

☛ Capucci, Courrèges, Fontana, Kelly, Paulette

William Klein. b New York (USA), 1928. **Black-and-white dresses by Roberto Capucci.** American *Vogue*, 1960.

Knight Nick   Photographer

Devon, the young model, looks vulnerable and fragile. She is scarred and seemingly half-blind, her face transformed by make-up artist Topolino. Although her stance and expression are aggressively defiant, the image is a deeply disturbing vision by photographer Nick Knight. It is fashion photography *in extremis*. 'If you want reality, look out of the window,' says Knight. Like many 1990s photographers, he manipulates his images by computer to heighten their impact. Knight's photographs, which have appeared in *Vogue* and *i-D*, usually have a fairy-tale aspect to them, often contrasted with disturbing touches of violence, as here. His pictures focus on form as well as fashion, as demonstrated by the geometric shapes in the photograph. His unconventional view of beauty has led him to photograph a size 14 model for *Vogue* and a septuagenarian teacher for a Levi's advertising campaign.

☛ McQueen, Strauss, Topolino

Nick Knight. **b** London (UK), 1958. **Brocade cowl dress by Alexander McQueen.** 1996.

Knight Phil and Bowerman Bill (Nike)   Designers

The famous 'Swoosh' tick is the designer logo of the sportswear market. One of Nike's two founders, Phil Knight, was a middle-distance runner at the University of Oregon. He founded a company called Blue Ribbon Sports in 1971, importing the Japanese Onitsuka Tiger trainer. Soon afterwards, he started manufacturing his own range, called Nike after the Greek winged goddess of victory. Much of the key to Nike's success lies in the marketing of its image, with advertisements that push the brand rather than the product. The company's slogans, including 'Just Do It', are unapologetically uncompromising; Nike was criticized by the Olympic Committee for its 'You don't win silver – you lose gold' advertisements. Nike took advantage of the sportswear-as-streetwear trend of the 1980s and 1990s, producing fashion-conscious designs in limited editions which have since become collectors' items.

☛ Crawford, Dassler, Hechter, Lacoste

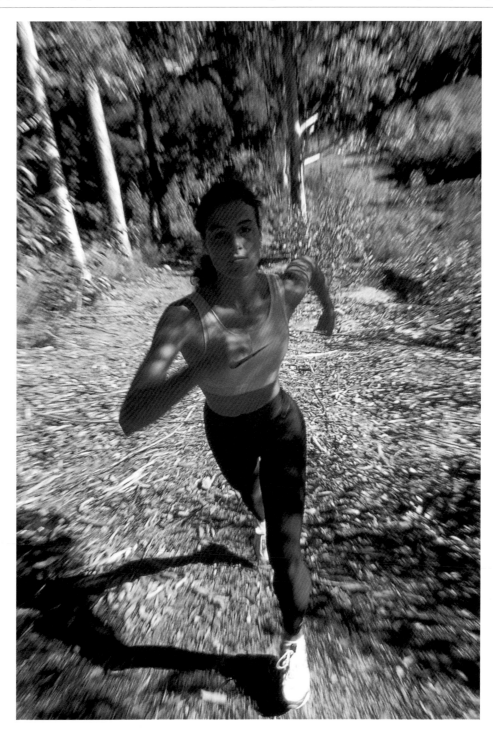

256

Phil Knight. b Portland, OR (USA), 1938; **Bill Bowerman. b** Portland, OR (USA), 1911. **d** Fossil, OR (USA), 2000. (Nike.) **Sportswear, South Africa, 1997.** Photograph by Anton Want.

Kobayashi Yukio   Designer

This photograph by the legendary photographer of New York's drug culture, Nan Goldin, was taken in 1996 as part of a series entitled *Naked New York – Nan Goldin meets Yukio Kobayashi*. Kobayashi had been designer of the Matsuda menswear line since 1983, and took on the role of chief designer of womenswear in late 1995. This photograph is from the autumn/winter 1996 Matsuda collection and was taken to capture its 'raw energy and artistic foundation'. Kobayashi is unusual in his mission to create clothes that break free of conventional style and offer an 'ageless' and 'genderless' alternative, using highly developed sewing and decorative techniques, such as 'needle punch' and quilting. 'From my perspective', he says, 'fashion and art are inseparable...both need to be nurtured and developed to ensure they prosper over time'. Here translucent prints on bare skin simulate intricate tattoos.

☛ Isogawa, Keogh, Matsuda

257

Yukio Kobayashi. b Niigata (JAP), 1951. **Yukio Kobayashi for Matsuda. Autumn/winter 1996.** Photograph by Nan Goldin.

Kors Michael   Designer

Michael Kors is a designer of modern American sportswear. His aspiration is to design clothes that can be both shown off and worn for everday life. Kate Moss wearing this strapless, black outfit on a racing track and holding a helmet bearing the US flag epitomizes his style: it is sexy, fun and practical. Kors had two career aims as a child – to be a movie star or a fashion designer. He chose fashion and studied it briefly, but learnt his trade by working at a boutique where he eventually became a designer. He established his label in 1981, incorporating menswear in 1990. Kors works with neutral and bright colours; his clothes are minimalistic in shape and luxurious to touch. He layers his silhouette and uses luxury fabrics, preferring cashmere, kid leather, silk and organza over cheaper alternatives. In 1998 he also began designing for deluxe French house, Céline, a parallel to Marc Jacobs' move to Louis Vuitton.

☛ Eisen, Jacobs, Mizrahi, Moss, Tyler

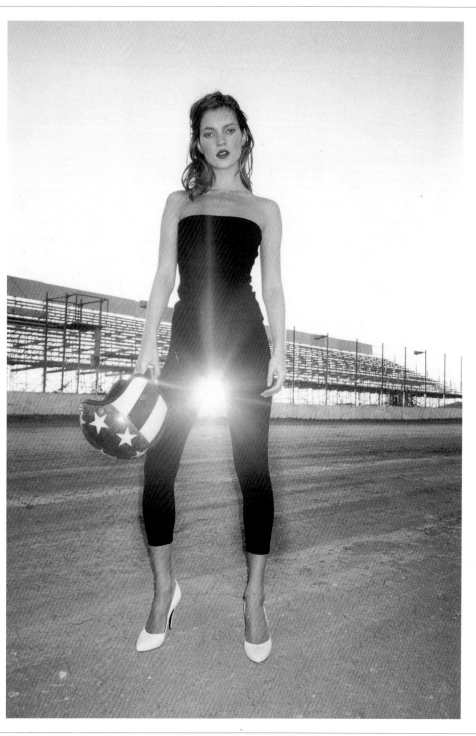

Michael Kors. b New York (USA), 1959. Kate Moss wears stretch tube top and pedal pushers. Photograph by Terry Richardson, *Harper's Bazaar*, 1997.

LaChapelle David Photographer

'I love drama and outrageousness. I love crazy scenes,' says LaChapelle, who creates an unforgettable interpretation of John Galliano's outfits for his two 'Milkmaids' here. When he was young, his mother organized elaborately staged photographs: 'In the family albums we look like the Vanderbilts. My mom remade her reality through snapshots.' Their move from conservative Connecticut to the brashness of Carolina encouraged LaChapelle to 'celebrate the artificial'. He left home at fifteen and moved to New York where he worked as a busboy at the legendary New York nightclub, Studio 54 – 'a big influence...all that pop imagery'. He met Andy Warhol at a Psychedelic Furs concert and was employed by him at *Interview*. 'For me, taking photographs, planning them and working on them, is a big escape,' he says. LaChapelle likes his subjects to be equally dramatic. 'Exhibitionists make the best models.'

☛ Galliano, R. James, Vanderbilt, Warhol

259

David LaChapelle. b Hartford, CT (USA), 1963. 'Milkmaids'. *Stern*, 1996.

Lacoste René   Designer

The French tennis star, René Lacoste, launched his polo shirt in 1933, six years after he had earned the nickname 'le crocodile' for winning a crocodile-skin suitcase in a bet. 'A friend drew a crocodile,' he said, 'and I had it embroidered on the blazer I wore on the courts.' His polo shirts were the first example of sportswear as fashion. The Lacoste empire now includes leisure-, golf- and tennis-wear for men, women and children. As such, it was a precursor to the sportswear phenomenon that accelerated throughout the century. Lacoste's crocodile, one of the most famous fashion emblems, is sold across the world to brand-conscious youth. When logo mania boomed in the 1980s, Lacoste became a major label, worn from Laos to Liverpool; it was in this city that Casuals, working-class football supporters, began wearing upmarket labels such as Lacoste as an emblem of personal success.

☛ Dassler, Jantzen, P. Knight

René Lacoste. b Paris (FR), 1904. **d** Saint Jean-De-Luc (FR), 1996. **René Lacoste wears blazer with a crocodile motif, 1927.**

Lacroix Christian   Designer

This printed leotard, smattered with beading and worn with grandiose costume jewellery – not least a beaten gold and chain belt – epitomizes Christian Lacroix's role as an ornate antidote to monochrome power dressing. His grandfather, a dandy who lined his suits with green silk and painted his bicycle gold, inspired Christian's love affair with the eighteenth century, introducing him to Boucher, Madame de Pompadour and Louis XIV. An *ancien régime* opulence influences much of his work, which is also coloured by his hot, southern French roots. Having designed for Hermès, Lacroix joined Patou in 1981. His 1984 couture collection for that house, inspired by the bohemians and aesthetes of prewar Paris and London, injected life back into the couture scene. Having opened his own house in 1987, Lacroix became famous for his fearless confusion of fabric, colour and surface decoration.

☛ Etro, Gigli, Hermès, McCartney, Patou, Pearl

Christian Lacroix. b Arles (FR), 1951. **Marie Sophie wears printed and embroidered catsuit.** Photograph by Mario Testino, 1990.

Lagerfeld Karl   Designer

'I am not interested in the future or the past; now is the interesting time', Karl Lagerfeld said in 1986. Yet this photograph, taken by the designer himself, suggests yesterday's Paris with her deconstructed pompadour hairstyle. Lagerfeld's modern influence is evident in the New York street scene and in the sharp cut of her dress, an enduring theme for his label. The son of wealthy parents, Lagerfeld moved to Paris, aged fourteen. His love of history, particularly eighteenth-century costume, has influenced his work and his style – Lagerfeld's ponytail and fan have almost become trademarks. Describing himself as a 'professional dilettante', his portfolio has included collections for Chanel, Fendi, Chloé and his own label. His work at Chanel took Coco Chanel's traditional leitmotifs, including gilt buttons and the chains used to weight her jacket hems, and turned them into design features.

☞ Fendi, Léger, Lenoir, Macdonald, Paulin, Tennant

Karl Lagerfeld. b Hamburg (GER), 1938. **Nadja Auermann wears empire-line dress, New York.** Photograph by Karl Lagerfeld, 1994.

262

Lalique René Jules   Jewellery designer

A gold and diamond tourmaline dragonfly brooch displays Lalique's precise copying techniques and delicate pictorial detailing. Master goldsmith René Lalique led the Art Nouveau jewellery movement of the 1890s, and later became a premier glass-maker. Unconventionally, Lalique worked with materials for their aesthetic value rather than their preciousness. Decoration was the purpose of the pieces and elaborately ornate hair combs were especially popular. Many of the pieces had references to nature, such as insects, animals or flora, and many featured pictorial scenes, such as a forest clearing, with a single pearl suspended below. Often impractically large in order to increase the visual impact, the pieces were favoured by extroverts such as Sarah Bernhardt. Lalique moved into glass jewellery in the 1920s and 1930s, creating all-glass rings, and pendants on silk cords.

☛ **Bulgari, Tiffany**

René Jules Lalique. **b** Aÿ (FR), 1860. **d** Paris (FR), 1945. **Diamond tourmaline pendant brooch, c1900.**

Van Lamsweerde Inez

Photographer

A Van Lamsweerde photograph is instantly recognizable. Turn the pages of a style magazine such as *The Face*, *Vogue*, *Arena* or *Visionaire* and it will be impossible to miss the hyper-real and highly technical images made with her creative and live-in partner Vinoodh Matadin. This image, for example, taken from a *Face* fashion shoot and featuring clothes by French designer Véronique

Leroy, uses computer manipulation to create a fantastical situation: two women on a surreal bicycle ride are surrounded by phallic imagery which includes a space shuttle launch. It is staged, it is ridiculous, but most of all this image is humorous pastiche, and this is the main characteristic of their work – satire. The pair met at Rietveld Academy of Arts in 1991, and have

worked together since on academic, fashion and advertising projects which include campaigns for Yohji Yamamoto and Louis Vuitton.

☛ Leroy, Molinari, Vuitton, Y. Yamamoto

264

Inez van Lamsweerde. **b** Amsterdam (NL), 1963. 'Well basically, Basuco is coke mixed with kerosene ... '. 1994.

Lancetti Pino   Designer

Two models tread Pino Lancetti's catwalk. Their richly detailed gowns serve to reinforce their sleek-haired conspicuousness, a style that belongs to the wealthy society for which he caters. Both dresses fall from raised waistbands and are accessorized with co-ordinating wraps to maintain their decorum. Initially a painter, Lancetti became involved in fashion when he moved to Rome and began sketching 'for fun' for the couturiers there. In 1963 he launched a seminal 'Military Line' collection which transferred the uniform into fashion. His designs, unsurprisingly, tended to be painterly, their inspiration ranging from Modigliani to Picasso to Impressionism. The look was often 'folksy', using soft, printed fabrics. Even the Military Line showed ethnic touches within the braiding. Lancetti avoided the trappings of the international fashion world and was best known in Japan and Italy.

☛ Lapidus, McFadden, Scherrer, Storey

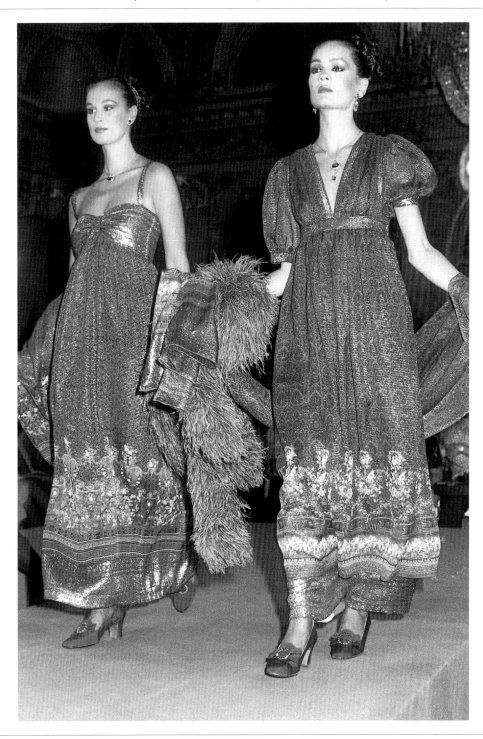

Pino Lancetti. b Bastia Umbra (IT), 1935. d 2007. **Gilded evening dresses**, *Women's Wear Daily*, 1977.

Lane Kenneth Jay   Jewellery designer

Dubbed 'the undisputed king of costume jewelry' by *Time* magazine, Kenneth Jay Lane believes every woman has the right to look glamorous – no matter what her income or status. Lane eschews the elitist stance of many designers. Early in his career, Lane designed shoes for Christian Dior, where he worked under the tutelage of Roger Vivier. By 1963 Lane had decided costume jewellery was his future and spent his spare time covering cheap plastic bangles with stripes, patterns and crystals. He was celebrating the possibilities of non-precious materials. Lane would place demonstrably artificial plastics next to glass approximations of diamonds. This has been an enduring formula that was widely copied in the 1980s and 1990s. His clients, all of whom were famous for their real jewels, have included Jackie Kennedy, Elizabeth Taylor, Babe Paley, Barbara Bush and Joan Collins.

☛ **Butler & Wilson, Kennedy, Leiber, Paley, Vivier**

266

Kenneth Jay Lane. b Detroit, MI (USA), 1932. **Paulette Stone.** Photograph by Norman Eales, 1967.

Lang Helmut   Designer

A backstage snap, capturing a theatrical headdress, worn with plain white vests, epitomizes the work of the most copied designer of the 1990s. Technology and bare fabrics that are rarely made from natural fibres, are joined in his collections. Lang's watchwords are 'now', 'urban', 'clean' and 'modern'. His clothes reflect a downbeat style which is instantly recognizable.

He describes his clothes as conveying 'the sort of anonymous status that the truly knowing admire' – indeed, they are adored by fashionable aesthetes the world over. Lang launched his own label in 1977. His first Paris show, in 1986, was an immediate success and his popularity continued throughout the 1990s, affording him cult status. The essence of his design ethos is to create a simple silhouette for both sexes; this is then made more complex with textural combinations – sheer/opaque, shiny/matt – and flashes of bright colour.

☛ **Capasa, Kerrigan, Sander, Teller, Tennant**

Helmut Lang. b Vienna (AUS), 1956. **Kirsten Owen wears feather headdress.** Photograph by Juergen Teller, 1997.

Lanvin Jeanne   Designer

Keeping the waisted, full-skirted dress alive was a speciality of Jeanne Lanvin, as the mannequin and the sketches on the floor and in the hand of the couturière attest. Famous for her *robes de style* and frocks that recalled earlier times, Madame Lanvin promoted romantic clothes when other couturiers such as Madeleine Vionnet, Coco Chanel, Alix Grès and Jean

Patou were modernizing with their vertical aesthetic. Opening her maison de couture just before the First World War, Jeanne Lanvin was already fifty-one when the war ended. Rather than initiate revolutionary trends, she clung to that era – designing on the lines of the full skirt of 1915–16 with only slight adjustments. Fittingly, when romantic clothes thrived in the theatre, her

favourite client was the star, Yvonne Printemps. Madame Lanvin was also famous for her mother/daughter outfits and for introducing, in 1926, a line of menswear.

☞ **Abbe, Arnold, Castillo, Crahay, Grès, Montana**

268

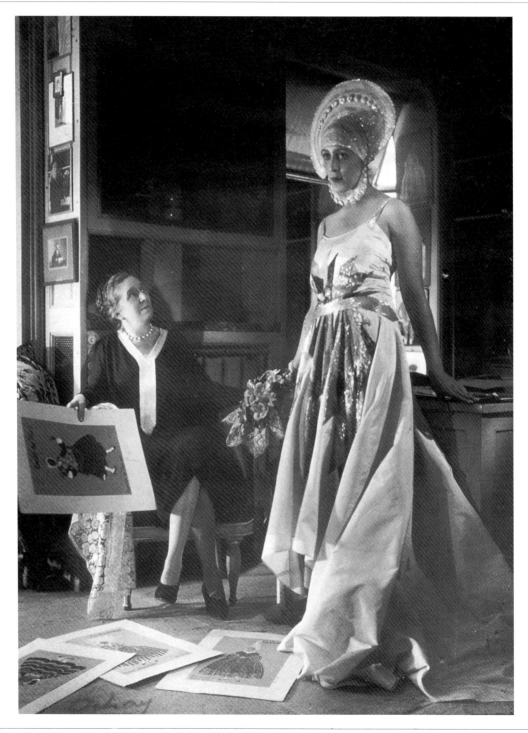

Jeanne Lanvin. **b** Brittany (FR), 1867. **d** Paris (FR), 1946. **Jeanne Lanvin with mannequin in her Paris studio, 1921.**

Lapidus Ted   Designer

Ted Lapidus and his model Lilo pose for Eve Arnold backstage at his winter show in 1977. Lilo wears a typically romantic, crepe georgette dress by Lapidus. Despite its heavy embroidery and beading, it is a relaxed shape which is dressed down with a peasant neckline and a tiered skirt – details usually found on daywear. Lapidus's design education began with an engineering diploma taken in Tokyo in 1949, but he was inspired by his Russian tailor father to take up fashion instead. Using the principles learnt from both disciplines, Lapidus attracted a reputation as a master of pattern-cutting. Inspired by his experience of high technology in Japan, he felt that it was important to integrate science with fashion. Consequently, he became involved with mass-manufacture at the same time as applying his precision techniques to his couture collections.

☛ Arnold, Lancetti, McFadden

Ted Lapidus. b Paris (FR), 1929. **Ted Lapidus with Lilo wearing a beaded dress.** Photograph by Eve Arnold, French *Vogue*, 1977.

Laroche Guy   Designer

Guy Laroche's career began at a hat-maker's in Paris, then in New York, on Seventh Avenue. On returning to Paris, he found employment in the maison de couture of Jean Dessès. His successful apprenticeship encouraged him to open his own house in 1957. Laroche was renowned for his mastery of cutting and tailoring. His early work was influenced by the architectural cutting of Cristóbal Balenciaga, but he later gave that formality a lively freshness, cultivating popularity with younger women – this meant diversifying his couture business by moving into ready-to-wear in 1960. Laroche is remembered from that time for lending an almost girlish attitude to formal clothes – especially with his empire-line dresses with material gently gathered into raised waistbands. In the following decade, his trouser suit, itself a symbol for liberated women, was required wearing.

☛ Dessès, Fath, Miyake, Paulette, Valentino

270

Guy Laroche. b La Rochelle (FR), 1923. d Paris (FR), 1989. **Tweed suits and woollen accessories.** Photograph by Chris Moore, 1971.

Lauder Estée   Cosmetics creator

The Estée Lauder look from 1961 is a constructed scheme using shading, lighting and lashings of liquid eyeliner. Lauder, who founded her company in 1946, was one of the queens of New York cosmetics. Born there, she was the daughter of a well-to-do Hungarian mother and Czechoslovakian father. Her interest in skincare was inspired by her Uncle John, a dermatologist, who,

when he came to stay in America, admonished her for washing her face with soap. With him, the family set up a laboratory and produced creams which became favourites with their friends and friends of friends. The real business began when Estée was invited to sell the products at a Manhattan salon. Lauder encouraged women to buy scent for themselves and was one of

the first names to develop a full range of cosmetics. The company is now a giant, encompassing other brands: Aramis, Clinique, Prescriptives, Origins, Aveda and Bobbi Brown.

☛ Brown, Dovima, Factor, Horst, Revillon

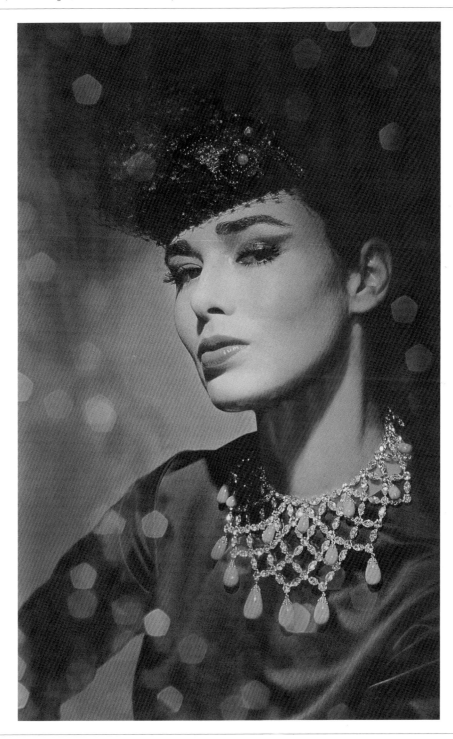

Estée Lauder. b New York (USA). **d** New York (USA), 2004. (Active 1940s–) **Estée Lauder make-up.** Photograph by Horst P. Horst, American *Vogue*, 1961.

Lauren Ralph

Designer

A Californian ranch is the setting for Ralph Lauren's advertisement from 1988. His vision, conjured by Bruce Weber, is of a measured, monied society which has a home in Connecticut and a ranch in Pasadena. Lauren, apart from being one of the most famous fashion product designers in the world, is a clever marketing man; a purveyor of a Waspish, all-American lifestyle, dressing every aspect of it, from exotic travel to business suits for Wall Street. Since 1968, when he launched his menswear label, Polo, Lauren has created a brand that is known throughout the world and clothes which are status symbols. His style, borrowed from vintage clothing, evolved from a desire to give new relevance to nostalgic elegance. It was an aesthetic summed up in the films *The Great Gatsby* (1974) and *Annie Hall* (1977), for which Lauren worked on the actors' wardrobes. In later years, he has made the look his own.

☞ **Abboud, Brooks, Hilfiger, Wang, Weber**

272

Ralph Lauren. b New York (USA), 1939. **'Polo' advertising campaign, Pasadena.** Photograph by Bruce Weber, 1988.

Léger Hervé   Designer

These rainbow dresses, formed from hand-stitched elastic bandages, are little more than extended swimsuit shapes. Hervé Léger learned his craft working with Karl Lagerfeld, designing swimwear first for Fendi, then Chanel. His forte is remoulding the body and Léger is more concerned with perfecting the female form than he is about passing trends. He claims that the woman he designs for is 'fed up with the vagaries of fashion. She does not give a damn about trends, she refuses to be a feminine clothes hanger.' His use of stretchy bands for his 'bender dresses' means his clothes are often compared with those of Azzedine Alaïa, his 1980s predecessor. Both designers greatly admired the silhouette-enhancing work of Mme Vionnet, and Léger's ankle-length column dresses have a glamorous simplicity and an uninterrupted line. His swimwear continues to be regarded as flattering, correcting the body like foundation-wear.

☞ Alaïa, Chanel, van Lamsweerde, Model, Mugler

273

Hervé Léger. b Bapaume (FR), 1957. **Joanna.** Photograph by Inez van Lamsweerde and Vinoodh Matadin, 1995.

Leiber Judith   Accessory designer

A glittering Judith Leiber evening bag has been the focus of Hollywood outfits since the 1960s. Despite its high-voltage sparkle, the example carried by Elizabeth Hurley is understated. 'I like to do things that look crazy, yet are practical', says Leiber, who sent First Lady Hillary Clinton a bag modelled on Socks, the White House cat. Ladybirds, teddy bears, fruit and Fabergé eggs have all been fashioned into such rhinestone whimsies. Though Leiber was offered a place to read chemistry at London's King's College in 1939, the Second World War forced her to stay in her native Budapest, where she was apprenticed to a master handbag maker. Leiber moved to New York in 1947, starting her own business in 1963. Her handbags are collected by customers such as American social queen Pat Buckley, who displays them as works of art. Leiber is less reverent about her own work, saying, 'The bag is really an object to be worn.'

☛ Lane, Mackie, Wang

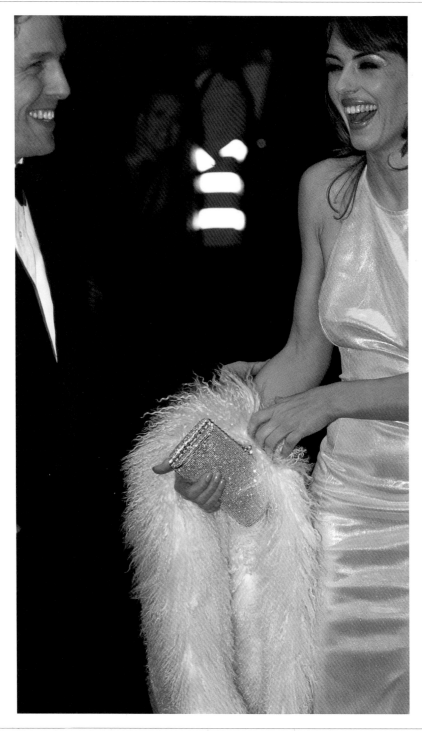

Judith Leiber. b Budapest (HUN), 1921. **Liz Hurley with diamanté minaudière and Hugh Grant.** 1997.

Lelong Lucien   Designer

The sleeves of this black, silk velvet evening gown are intricately cut, in the style of a medieval robe, withpointed cuffs which swoop like swallows' wings. The gown closely follows the shape of the figure, moulding the waist and the hips before widening into a skirt which flows softly into a train, like the outspread feathers of a bird's tail. The birdlike character of the dress is associated with the imagery of Surrealism, the dominant art movement of the 1930s. Lelong, who opened his own couture house after the First World War, was president of the Chambre Syndicale de la Couture Parisienne from 1937 to 1947. He persuaded the occupying Germans to allow French couture houses to remain in Paris rather than be transferred to Berlin or Vienna. Through his efforts, at least one hundred fashion houses were kept running throughout the Occupation of Paris from 1940 to 1944.

☛ **Balmain, Bettina, Chéruit, Dessès, Givenchy**

Lucien Lelong. **b** Paris (FR), 1889. **d** Danglet (FR), 1958. **Black, silk velvet gown.** Photograph by Hoyningen-Huene, French *Vogue*, 1934.

Lenoir Jacques and Aghion Gaby (Chloé)   Designers

Chloé's name, meaning 'young, green shoot', is particularly appropriate, given that the label pursues modernity. Yet Chloé retains an ethereal, whimsical femininity that is not always followed by its eclectic choice of designers, including the late Guy Paulin and Martine Sitbon. Launched in 1952 by Jacques Lenoir and Gaby Aghion, Chloé's intention was to approach *prêt-à-porter*

with the finesse of haute couture, elevating the more directional ready-to-wear to an art form. The most catalytic example – Lagerfeld's 'Woodstock couture' of the 1970s, which he revived in 1993 with Linda Evangelista as his muse – evoked the flower-child mood with free-flowing, pale chiffon, swirly patchwork maxiskirts and full bloomed, silk roses. However, second

time round public reaction to Lagerfeld proved inconsistent, and Chloé replaced him in early 1997 with Stella McCartney, who stuck to Chloé's house style with vintage lace, pastel satin and glass buttons.

☛ Bailly, Lagerfeld, McCartney, Paulin, Sitbon, Steiger

276

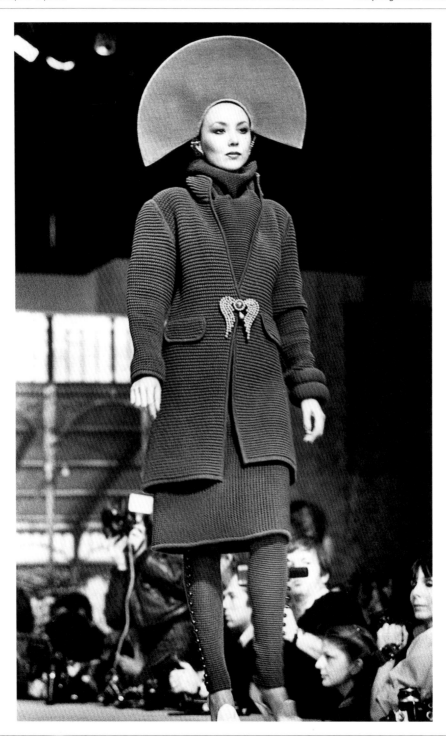

Jacques Lenoir. b Paris (FR), 1920. **Gaby Aghion. b** Alexandria (EG), 1921. (Chloé.) **Wool outfit by Karl Lagerfeld for Chloé.** Photograph by Chris Moore, 1979.

Leonard

Hairdresser

For one of Leonard's striking hair designs, a hairpiece is looped under the chin and caught in a hand-painted hair slide by Pablo and Delia. Leonard's extreme colouring techniques were developed by him for Stanley Kubrick's *2001: A Space Odyssey* in 1968. 'I had to push things as far as they would go,' says Leonard. 'The coloured hair, the crazy colours, the unnatural ones, they started there.'

His work was innovative and directional in the 1960s and 1970s: he cut the Beatles' mopheads and when Justin de Villeneuve delivered his young prodigy Twiggy to Leonard for a haircut, he made the best business move of his life. Leonard, who had started out with de Villeneuve on a Shepherd's Bush Market fruit barrow, asked Twiggy to model a new haircut invented by him. After eight

hours of snipping, a talent honed during his training with Vidal Sassoon, Twiggy's waifish crop was born and so was her career.

☛ Beatles, Mesejeán, Sassoon, Twiggy

Leonard (Leonard Lewis). b London (UK), 1938. **Hair coloured by Leonard.** Photograph by Barry Lategan, 1970.

Lepape Georges   Illustrator

These 'Fashions of Tomorrow' most certainly live up to their name. Poiret's pantaloon gowns, illustrated here by Georges Lepape, were considered shocking at the time, but anticipated the move towards greater physical freedom in women's fashion. This illustration is one of the plates from *Les Choses de Paul Poiret vues par Georges Lepape*. The sculptural simplicity of Lepape's illustrations captures perfectly the silhouette of Poiret's clothes. Poiret was the first couturier to relate fashion successfully to the other arts and was innovative in commissioning the artists Georges Lepape and Paul Iribe to compile limited-edition albums of his designs. Lepape contributed illustrations to *La Gazette du Bon Ton*, a folio of fashion news and drawings in the twentieth century, and regularly appeared on the cover of *Vogue* in the 1920s. Lepape was instrumental in bringing art movements such as Cubism into the realm of fashion.

☛ **Barbier, Benito, Drian, Iribe, Poiret**

278

Georges Lepape. b Paris (FR), 1887. **d** (FR), 1971. **'Fashions of Tomorrow'.** From *Les Choses de Paul Poiret vues par Georges Lepape*. 1911.

Leroy Véronique Designer

Véronique Leroy was once described as 'the unchallenged reigning queen of the Paris sexy-tack scene'. This sportswear-meets-eveningwear outfit is typical of Leroy's flirtation, and often unashamed love affair, with bad taste. Her method is to use recently outmoded references. Here she used gilt chain and nylon mesh at a time when the memories of their misuse in the hands of the mass-market were still fresh. The chain, a reference to Chanel's handbag handles, suspends an Op Art patchwork of artificial sportswear fabrics. These thrift store-inspired collections dabble in different themes, each one rich in its potential for anti-taste, including *Charlie's Angels*, Pop Art and science fiction. Before starting her own label, Leroy worked with Azzedine Alaïa, who taught her how to handle body-hugging Lycras and synthetics, and Martine Sitbon from whom she learned about the art of catering for the rock-chick market.

☛ **Hemingway, van Lamsweerde, Sitbon**

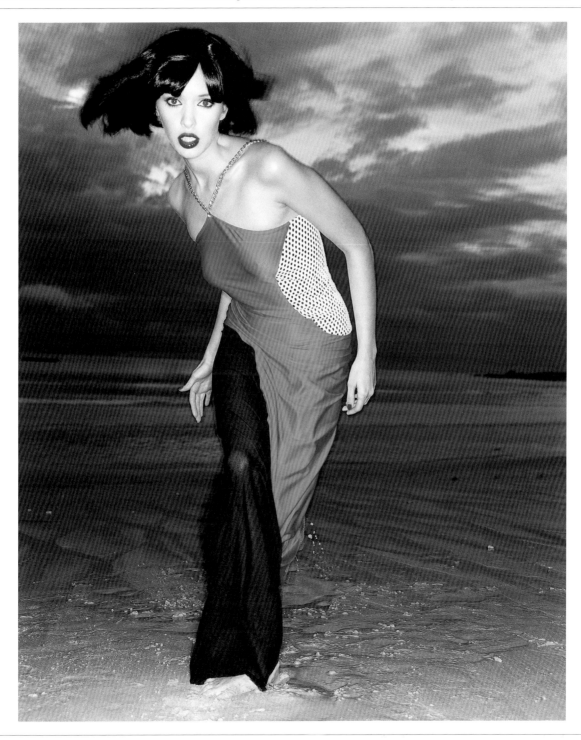

279

Véronique Leroy. b Liège (FR), 1965. **Blue halterneck dress.** Photograph by Christophe Kutner, British *Elle*, 1995.

Lesage Albert   Embroiderer

This bolero jacket, lavishly embroidered with a parade of elephants, is from Schiaparelli's 'Circus' collection of 1938. Not since Poiret had a fashion designer shown such an instinctive flair for the use of embroidery, making it a glamorous adjunct to haute couture. Collaborating with the celebrated Maison Lesage, which had been founded in 1922 by Albert Lesage, *maître brodeur*, and in particular with his young son, François, Schiaparelli designed her collection especially to offset the sumptuous embroidery. Her basic silhouette of wide shoulders and neat waist enabled Lesage to adorn her jackets with embroideries that enhanced her whimsical dreams. Here, the spotlight is on performing elephants, their threads richly complementing the encrustations in gold. Maison Lesage, renowned for its jewel-studded embroidery, let loose all the capriciousness of Schiaparelli's Surrealism.

☛ Schiaparelli, Wang, Yantorny

Albert Lesage. **b** Paris (FR), 1888. **d** (FR), 1949. 'Circus'. Elephant embroidery for Schiaparelli. 1938.

Leser Tina

Designer

A cute, teenager outfit of turned-up, denim jeans and striped cotton shirt epitomizes the freshness of American fashion after the Second World War. Tina Leser was among the new wave of designers unique to American culture who concentrated on sportswear as fashion. Her clothes, designed for a manufacturer (until 1952 when she formed her own company), were informed by everyday shapes such as play-suits, sarong dresses, smocks, swimsuits and shrug-on jackets, but they were almost always influenced by a more formal aesthetic, as is evident here. Leser's mother was a painter and the designer studied art, painting, design and sculpture in Philadelphia and Paris. Leser moved to Honolulu and opened a boutique in 1935, moving to New York in 1942. During the 1950s she designed cropped and harem pants before any other designers; she is also thought to have been the first designer to make dresses from cashmere.

☛ Connolly, A. Klein, McCardell, Simpson

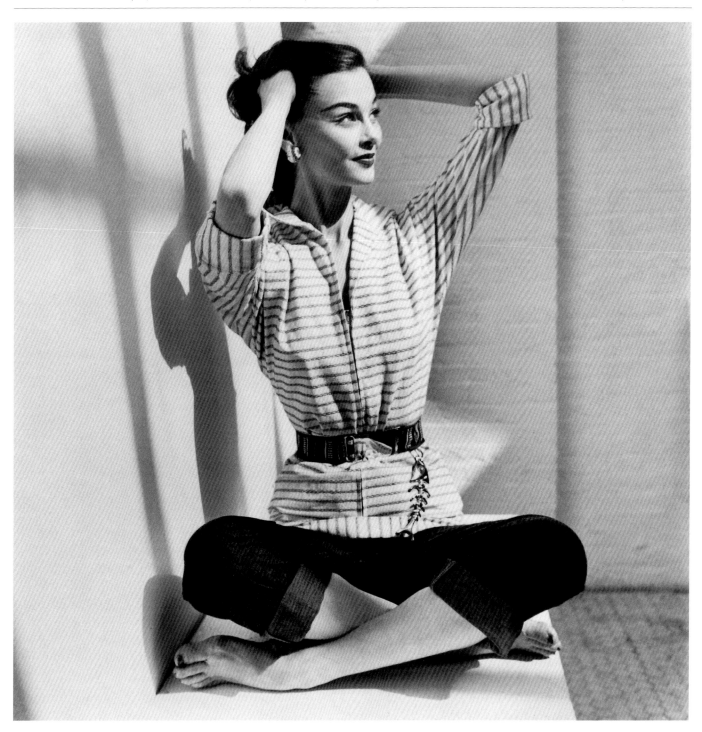

Tina Leser (Christine Wetherill Shilland–Smith). b PA (USA), 1910. d Sands Point, NY (USA), 1986. **Mexican cotton shirt and denim jeans.** Photograph by John Rawlings, *Harper's Bazaar*, 1951.

Lester Charles and Patricia

A golden, hand-pleated silk dress is set against antique fabrics. It recalls the Delphos style designed by Fortuny eighty years earlier, but it is the work of designers Charles and Patricia Lester, who were unaware of his work when they started their experiments in the 1960s. Years of research go into the techniques used by the Lesters: designs are burnt out of velvet to form devoré and others are hand-painted to produce unique cloth which is used for tunics, dresses and robes. The historical perception of these techniques has an attraction which sets their work apart from the less enduring elements of high fashion. Consequently, it has been used for opera productions and for the film adaptation of Henry James' novel *The Wings of a Dove*, in which Helena Bonham Carter wafts around pre-First World War Venice. Her pleated silk dresses and velvet coats, however, were taken from the Lesters' 1990s collection.

☛ Fortuny, McFadden

282

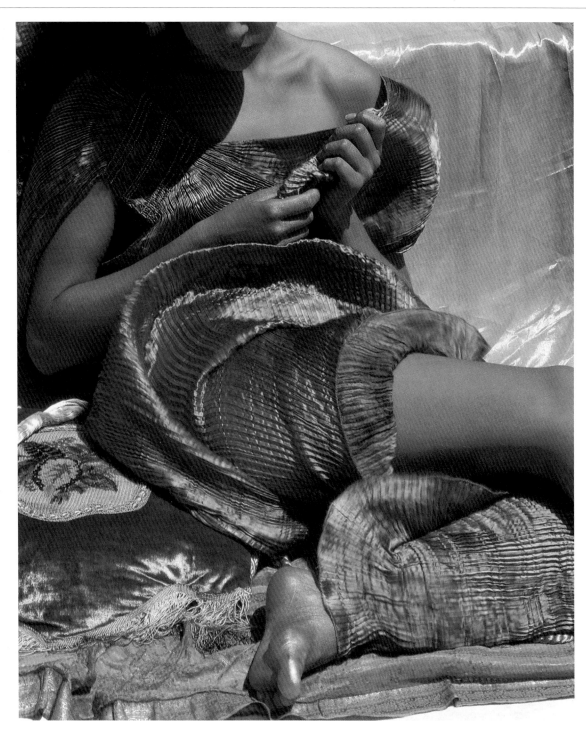

Lester. **Charles. b** Banbury (UK), 1942; **Patricia. b** Nairobi (KEN), 1943. **Gold pleats.** Photograph by Alex Chatelain, British *Vogue*, 1985.

Levine Beth   Shoe designer

Freedom of movement and freedom from the conventions of footwear are provided by Beth Levine's innovative stocking boots. All Levine's shoes gave the potential for motion, from the elasticated sole of her Spring-O-Lator mule, to the aerodynamic curves and rounded 'rock-a-bottom' sole of her Kabuki pumps, the prototype for which was carved from a teak salad bowl (a shape later reinvented by Vivienne Westwood for her 'rocking horse' platforms). Levine was known for her sexy, stretchy boots, including pairs made for Nancy Sinatra who sang 'These Boots Were Made for Walking'. She conjured imaginative heels, from a rolled scroll shape to chunky cuboid blocks, and favoured unconventional materials such as Astroturf and frog skin. Originally untrained in shoe design, Levine pushed the physical possibilities of footwear – her high-heeled 'topless' shoe was a satin sole stuck to the foot using spirit gum.

☞ Ferragamo, Parkinson, Westwood

283

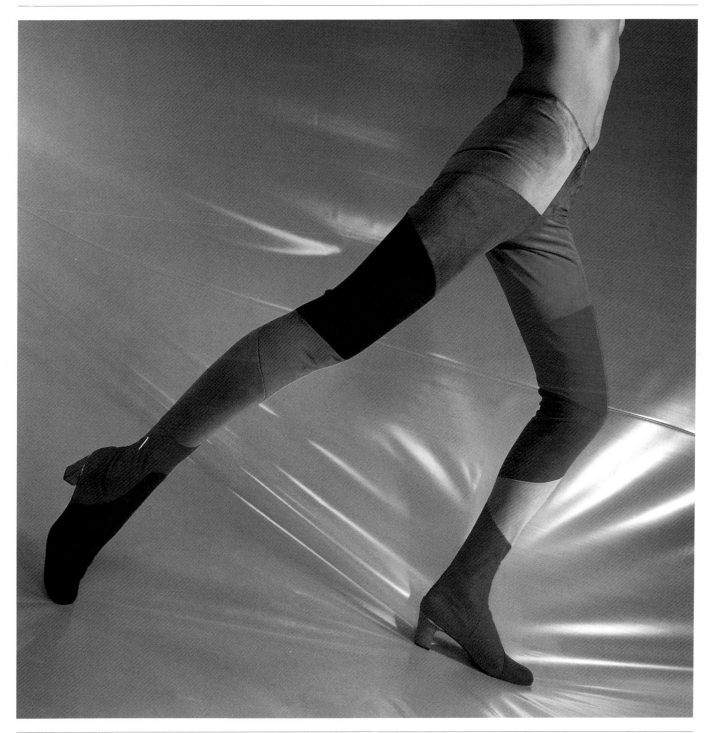

Beth Levine. b New York (USA), 1914. d 2006. **Suede boots.** Photograph by Norman Parkinson, American *Vogue*, 1969.

Ley Wolfgang and Margaretha (Escada)

Designers

The affectations of this image are stereotypical of the 1980s: strong-shouldered siren with sharp, glittery skirt, big hair and bigger attitude. What Escada meant for women far surpassed their angst-ridden boundaries as working mothers and wives – it symbolized the triumph of ostentatious glamour at a time when image dominated substance, and even taste. Launched in 1976 by Wolfgang and Margaretha Ley, Escada was aptly named after a winning racehorse. Their sexy, chiselled suits, leopard-print blouses and nautical-striped sweaters, all offset with gold buttoning and braid, eulogized a 'bourgeois chic' look. It was a hugely popular style. Wealth was counted in sequins which were applied to every surface – even sweaters were taken out of their casual context with a smattering of sparkle. With Todd Oldham hired as creative consultant in 1994, Escada took a fresh approach and embraced the spirit of the times.

☛ Féraud, N. Miller, Norell, Oldham

Ley. Wolfgang. **b** GA (USA), 1937. **Margaretha. b** Västernorrland (SWE), 1933. **d** Berlin (GER), 1992. (Escada.) **Sequined sweater and skirt for Escada.** Photograph by Albert Watson, 1984.

Liberman Alexander Photographer and art director

Alexander Liberman photographs Christian Dior, Bettina Ballard, fashion editor of American *Vogue*, and Despina Messinesi, also from *Vogue*, in the early 1950s. This image, taken during one of the legendary Sundays that a few privileged people spent at the French couturier's country house, bears witness to the intimate relationship that Liberman had with the fashion world for almost six decades. After working for Lucien Vogel on *Vu*, a photo-journalism magazine published in Paris, Liberman moved to New York, where he became art director of *Vogue* in 1943. In 1962 he was appointed editorial director of all Condé Nast's publications, thus acquiring a unique insight into every aspect of the fashion journalism trade. He maintained that its appeal lay in providing the viewer with a ticket of escape from her surroundings, 'into the heaven of fashion and the unbelievable nirvana of luxe and elegance.'

☛ Abbe, Chanel, Dior, McLaughlin–Gill, Nast

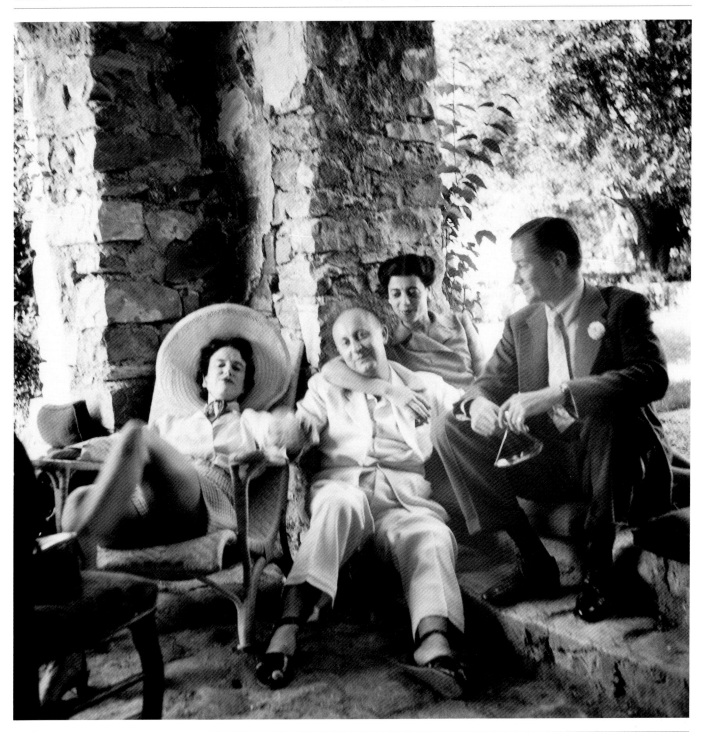

Alexander Liberman. **b** Kiev (RUS), 1912. **d** Miami Beach, FL (USA), 1999. **Bettina Ballard, Christian Dior, Despina Messinesi and Bettina Ballard's husband.** Photograph by Alexander Liberman, 1950.

Liberty Arthur Lasenby Retailer

Just as the work of Liberty has reflected the times ever since it was founded in 1875, this lawn dress, speckled with flowers, was perfectly in tune with the mood of its age. It is bright, simple and, with its co-ordinated accessories, captured young British fashion (and the Rolling Stones). It was designed by The Ginger Group, a label founded in 1963 by Mary Quant, the quintessential fashion designer of the 1960s. She was one of the leading lights of 'Swinging London', a term coined by the American *Time* magazine in 1964, the date of this dress. Arthur Lasenby Liberty's department store went on to specialize in fine fabrics such as lawn – a lightweight cotton material printed with floral motifs. In its history, Liberty has both reflected and contributed to sartorial changes, from the costume associated with the Aesthetic Movement of the 1880s to the fashion revolution of the 1960s.

☞ Bousquet, Fish, Muir, Nutter, Quant, Sassoon, Wilde

Arthur Lasenby Liberty. b Chesham (UK), 1843. d Lee Manor (UK), 1917. **'How To Kill Five Stones With One Bird'.** Photograph by Norman Parkinson, *Queen*, 1964.

Lindbergh Peter Photographer

Shot in 1990, this photograph gathers together the reigning supermodels wearing their off-duty uniform of bodies by Giorgio di Sant'Angelo and Levi's jeans. Peter Lindbergh's name is closely intertwined with those of Naomi Campbell, Linda Evangelista, Tatjana Patitz, Christy Turlington and Cindy Crawford, who partly discovered their singularity through him. The image's stark, grainy quality reveals Lindbergh's trademark lack of artifice and calm directness, rooted in the unadorned greyness of the industrial scenes of his childhood in Germany. He was twenty-seven when he picked up a camera for the first time. Ever since, his photographs have appeared in every major fashion magazine. The key influence that classical portraiture plays on Lindbergh gives his work a timeless allure. As Karl Lagerfeld said, 'His photographs will never be regarded with any condescending emotion in thirty or forty years' time.'

☛ Campbell, Crawford, Evangelista, Kawakubo

Peter Lindbergh. b Duesburg (GER), 1944. **Naomi, Linda, Tatjana, Christy and Cindy.** British *Vogue*, 1990.

Lloyd Alison (Ally Capellino)

Designer

Alison Lloyd describes her work as 'something which is fashionable, but which doesn't go out of fashion very quickly'. Here, she uses shot organza for a transparent over-dress. Its stiffness gives the shape a defined form and the visible seams take the appearance of a frame. It certainly defies fashion's usual proclivity for styles that can be easily dated. Lloyd is inspired by a passion for simple organic textiles, bright colours and wearable, enduring shapes. Lloyd and fellow Middlesex Polytechnic graduate Jono Platt set up Ally Capellino in 1979, initially selling hats, jewellery and accessories. (The name, they thought, was Italian for 'little hat'; to their amusement they later discovered that it means 'little head'.) Lloyd became a fashion designer in 1980. Her creativity never overwhelms her desire to produce clothes which can be worn by women of any age.

☛ Arai, von Etzdorf, Isogawa

Alison Lloyd. **b** London (UK), 1956. (Ally Capellino.) **Silk organza dress shot with metal.** Photograph by Aldo Rossi, 1996.

Loewe Enrique   Accessory designer

Supple, lavender leather distinguishes a strapless dress modelled on a handbag by Loewe, which has created such bags since 1846. Loewe is fabled for its ability to make animal skin behave as fabric. It was founded in the Calle del Tobo area of Madrid, a centre for leather artistry, where Enrique Loewe sold snuff boxes and purses alongside his bags. As a company, Loewe entered the fashion sphere in 1947 when it acquired the rights to sell Christian Dior's New Look in Spain. By the 1960s it had begun to design its own fashion collection, one that used the company's proclivity for draping and gathering, as well as producing classic working shirts in suede. In 1997, Loewe modernized its image by appointing Narciso Rodriguez as its house designer. In 2001 Rodriguez was replaced by Jose Selfa whose designs have been well received. Rodriguez left Loewe to design a house of his own.

☛ Hermès, Rodriguez, Vuitton

Enrique Loewe. b (GER), 1829. d (SP), 1919. **Lavender leather dress. Autumn/winter 1983.** Photograph by Rafael Roa.

Louboutin Christian

Shoe designer

Gold embroidery, black ribbon and blue mosaic heels: a jumble of shoes reveals Christian Louboutin's love of creating forbidden fantasies. His seductive shoes, with their trademark red soles, are inspired by tropical birds, flowers and gardens. He describes them as a cross between 'a work tool or weapon and an *objet d'art*', and individual commissions are intensely personalized. Love letters, petals, locks of hair and feathers have been encased within his heels. His obsession began in 1976 when, aged ten, he visited a Parisian museum. Far from being inspired by its contents, *bébé* Louboutin couldn't forget the impression made on him by a huge, red high heel worn by another visitor. A meeting with French shoe master Roger Vivier changed his outlook. 'I never thought to do it as a job,' he said. Catherine Deneuve, Inès de la Fressange and Princess Caroline of Monaco would be barefoot without him.

☛ Ferragamo, Pfister, Vivier

Christian Louboutin. b Paris (FR), 1963. **Autumn/winter 1998.** Photograph by Mark J. Curtis.

Louis Jean   Designer

'There NEVER was a woman like Gilda!' was the caption above Rita Hayworth's picture on the poster from the 1946 film. Sheathed in a satin dress by Jean Louis, she played a seductive *femme fatale*. The bodice which supports Hayworth's body hides an intricate construction of boning and padding, although she maintained that it stayed up 'for two good reasons alone'. Having started his career as a sketch artist for Drecoll, Jean Louis moved to New York where he designed for Hattie Carnegie. He brought the drama of his film work to a couture business which excelled at creating lavish gowns. The potency of this made Hayworth America's dream mistress and her wardrobe the blueprint for sexy, yet illusory dresses which is still followed today. Hayworth later sadly reflected on her broken relationships with men, saying, 'Every man I ever knew had fallen in love with Gilda and woken up with me.'

☞ **Carnegie, Galanos, Head, Irene**

Jean Louis (Jean Louis Berthault). **b** Paris (FR), 1907. **d** Palm Springs, CA (USA), 1997. **Rita Hayworth.** Still from *Gilda*. Photograph by Bob Coburn, 1946.

Lutens Serge

Make-up artist

Every element of this surreal advertisement for Shiseido was created by Serge Lutens, from the make-up and styling to the photograph itself. Lutens grew up wanting to be an artist. School bored him and he spent all his spare time performing makeovers on his friends, then taking their pictures with a Kodak instamatic. In 1960 he met his partner, Madeleine Levy, and together they launched a 'test salon' in Paris for make-up, hair, jewellery and furniture. In 1968 he was invited to look after the image and product creation of Christian Dior cosmetics, leaving to join Shiseido in 1980. Lutens does not regard his images as schemes that should (or even could) be copied by women. Fantastical in the extreme, they have the surreal spirit of Salvador Dali's fashion work. He advocates that women should develop their own creative effects with make-up, whether they want to look natural or artificial.

☛ Nars, Page, Uemura

Serge Lutens. b Lille (FR), 1942. **'Absolutely Amazing' campaign for Shiseido.** Photograph by Serge Lutens, 1998.

McCardell Claire Designer

Claire McCardell, who pioneered American sportswear, conceived this empire-silhouette 'baby dress' in 1946. The black wool jersey, suggesting an update of Chanel's little black dress, used nonchalant tying in the manner of the casual lifestyle design she championed. Tying and wrapping were not only apt for the active woman, but they also accommodated the inexact sizing and fit of ready-to-wear apparel. Cultivating such traits in soft, relatively inexpensive garments, McCardell made clothing that had a loyal following among women who wanted independence from corporeal restrictions or dictates from Paris. Instead, versatile separates and the use of materials from menswear, lingerie and childrenswear promised an adaptable, flexible lifestyle akin to the garment itself. Projecting her own desires into design, McCardell never forgot a woman's need for pockets. Her speciality was leisurewear, including playsuits and swimwear.

☞ **Cashin, Connolly, Dahl-Wolfe, A. Klein, Leser, Steele**

293

Claire McCardell. **b** MD (USA), 1905. **d** New York (USA), 1958. **Drawstring dress.** Photograph by Louise Dahl-Wolfe, *Harper's Bazaar*, 1946.

McCartney Stella Designer

An embroidered, miniature evening dress of satin bears the richesse associated with traditional French fashion, but the proportions belong to the modern age. Chloé showed the first collection by Stella McCartney, appointed designer in 1997 at only twenty-five, in the opulent setting of the Opéra Garnier in Paris. Even though Yves Saint Laurent beat her by a few years (he was just twenty-one when he took over at Christian Dior), McCartney's appointment was seen as a precocious one. She worked briefly for Lacroix and was influenced by finds made in the Portobello Market. On Friday and Saturday mornings McCartney would garner antique buttons and vintage clothes, which explains the romantic strand of her style. The other, tailoring, is attributable to a short, unofficial apprenticeship with Edward Sexton, a Savile Row tailor. McCartney has said, 'Anyone who has seen my work knows I am not about shock tactics.'

☞ Lenoir, Lacroix, Chloé

Stella McCartney. b London (UK), 1971. **Miniature satin evening dress for Chloé.** Photograph by Perry Ogden, 1998.

McDean Craig   Photographer

Model Guinevere, wearing nothing but artfully undone hair and make-up by Eugene Souleiman and Pat McGrath, appears from behind traditional wallpaper in an advertisement for Jil Sander. That this photograph is representing a fashion and make-up company would make it surreal, except that this is an example of selling a mood rather than a product. McDean's work appeared in the 1990s at a time when his realist photography stood out against the fashion for photographs which presented a limited number of scenarios. He has said, 'I want to appeal to everyone, not just the fashion world,' but it is primarily those in fashion who appreciate his work, which is subtly challenging. It is modern and each photograph, deliberately accidental, is stark and voyeuristic, seemingly capturing a dream-like moment. McDean is part of the neo-realism school dubbed 'Heroin Chic' by US President Bill Clinton in 1997.

☞ Berardi, McGrath, Sander, Sitbon, Souleiman

Craig McDean. b Nantwich (UK), 1964. Guinevere. Jil Sander publicity campaign. 1996.

Macdonald Julien Designer

With hairstyle and make-up to match, Jodie Kidd wears a tight-fitting sheath of gossamer-fine yarns and beading which decorate her body like calligraphy on skin. Seductive and opulent, Julien Macdonald's work takes the girlishness out of knitwear. He spins out fiery fantasies like this from his trusty knitting machine. With loosened screws and bent parts, it becomes an instrument for creating the tactile surfaces he desires. Karl Lagerfeld, who hired him as knitwear designer for Chanel in 1996, declared to *Vogue*, 'Julien plays with his machine like Horowitz plays on his Steinway.' While regarded as a master of innovation, Macdonald does pay homage to the traditional craft, making it modern by using new-fangled, fluorescent yarns and luminous mohair (an idea sparked off by metallic Nike trainers). Macdonald graduated from the Royal College of Art in 1996 and designed knitwear for Alexander McQueen and Koji Tatsuno.

☛ S. Ellis, Keogh, Lagerfeld, Tatsuno

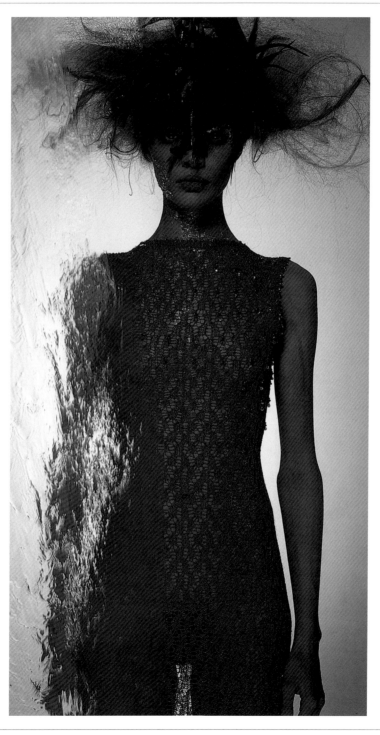

Julien Macdonald. b Merthyr Tydfil (UK), 1972. **Jodie Kidd wearing a red knitted dress.** Photograph by Sean Ellis, 1998.

McFadden Mary   Designer

While Mary McFadden will probably always be remembered principally for her pleated dresses *à la* Fortuny, she has not only made outfits for Grecian maidens, but has also brought global artistry to the comfort of easy sportswear. Hand-painted skirts, dresses and jackets are informed by McFadden's acute awareness of international design traditions, with a special leaning towards Southeast Asia and Africa. Textile scholarship and crafts luxury are, however, mediated by McFadden's unerring sense for modern comfort and poise. Inspired by decorative traditions and her pleasure in textiles, McFadden has rendered both Klimt and the *Book of Kells* in sumptuous coats, seized details from Portuguese tiles and understood the rich batiks of Southeast Asia. She straddles the art-to-wear movement and the pragmatic fashion industry. Likewise her clothing strikes an urbane formality for daywear and a wearable ease for evenings.

☛ Fortuny, Lancetti, Lapidus, Lester

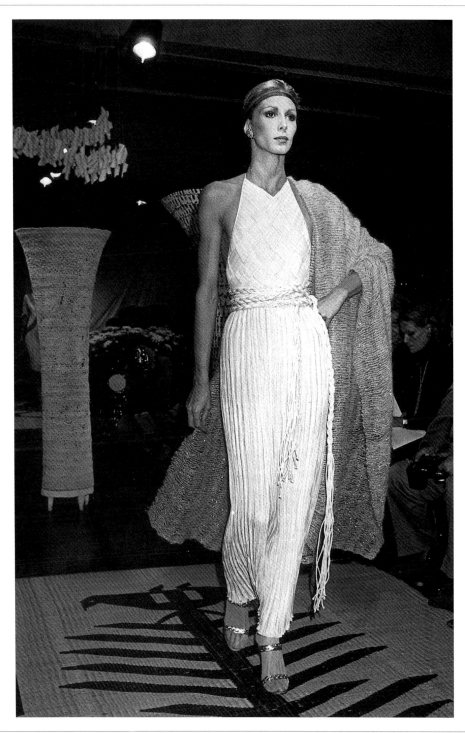

Mary McFadden. b New York (USA), 1936. **Finely pleated dress and throw.** Photograph by Pierre Scherman, *Women's Wear Daily*, 1977.

McGrath Pat   Make-up artist

Pat McGrath heightens the dramatic potential of make-up by using it as a brilliant focus, isolating dense blocks of colour in a parody of one accepted scheme. Here, red lipstick is the single feature on an otherwise undecorated face. In a customary twist on the *i-D* cover (established with the magazine's inception in 1980), model Kirsten Owen's eye is shrouded by her hat.

Her fiery mouth is the dominating focal point. McGrath, in partnership with hairdresser Eugene Souleiman, works with Steven Meisel, Paolo Roversi and Craig McDean to push the boundaries of beauty, and her directional vision has been used to flavour catwalk collections by Prada, Comme des Garçons and Dolce & Gabbana. Her innovation has released make-up from

the framework of facial contours since her patterns of colour are daubed seemingly randomly.

☞ McDean, Prada, Rocha, Roversi, Souleiman, Toskan

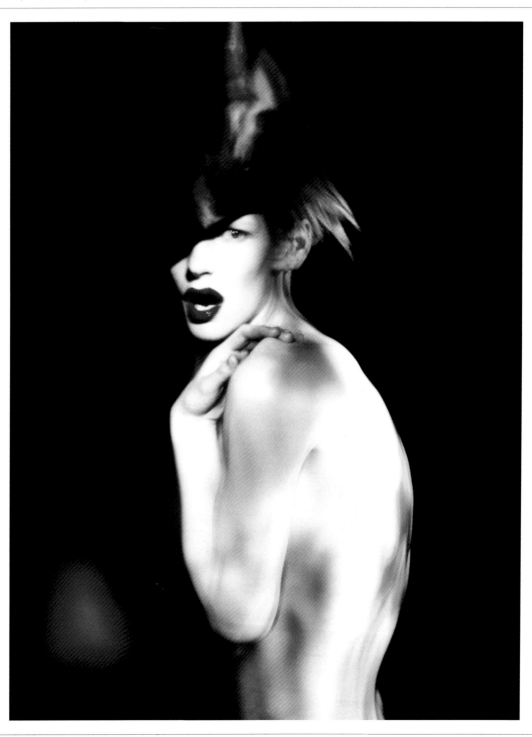

Pat McGrath. b Northampton (UK), 1966. **Kirsten Owen.** Cover of *i-D*, May 1998 (The Supernatural Issue). Photograph by Paolo Roversi.

Mackie Bob   Designer

Mackie offers a rhinestone cowgirl, a marvel in swinging fringe and bold motion and dressed in his signature style (reminiscent of the all-singing, all-dancing films of old Hollywood). Coming to fame as a television designer for *The Sonny and Cher Comedy Hour* (1971–4) and *The Carol Burnett Show* (1967–78), Mackie presented a hyperbolic form of showbiz glamour which was effective, even at television scale, in conveying large-screen and Las Vegas opulence and extravaganza. It was a tour de force achieved by letting the dress, or a few dresses, serve as the embodiment of a grandiloquence. By the advent of MTV, Mackie was too much associated with old-style theatricality to be popular there, but he was responsible for establishing brilliant costume for the medium of television. This was his contribution to fashion, the championing of beading and sequins for gowns, swimwear and loungewear.

☛ Leiber, N. Miller, Norell, Oldham, Orry-Kelly

Bob Mackie. b Monterey Park, CA (USA), 1940. **Black fringed, beaded dress.** Photograph by Steven Klein, British *Vogue*, 1988.

McKnight Sam   Hairdresser

Three women wear gamine hairstyles by Sam McKnight. The 'extreme gelled girls' illustrate his highly-polished, sharply-defined work. This sleek look, achieved by his 1920s-inspired styles, equals the make-up for dramatic effect, thus providing a fine balance. 'Hair is like clothes', says Mcknight, 'you should look as though you wear it with ease, that's the sexiest hair.' He is known for nonchalant glamour, and it was this he gave to Diana, Princess of Wales, when, on a shoot for *Vogue* in 1990, she asked him, 'What would you do if you had a free rein with my hair?'. 'Cut it short,' was McKnight's reply. And he did, becoming the architect of her later, modernized look. Trained in a salon that eschewed electrical appliances, he learned to create uncontrived hairstyles and still maintains that hair should not look forced. A woman, he believes, should always look approachable and should never risk fashion at the expense of her comfort.

☞ Antoine, Diana, Pita

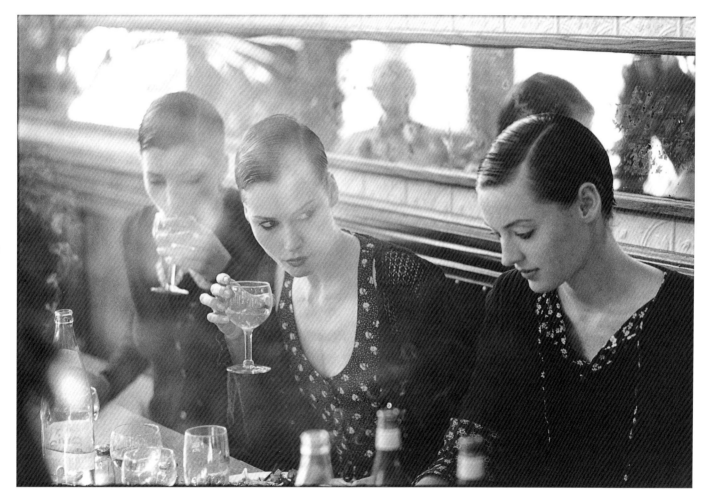

Sam McKnight. b New Cumnock (UK), 1959. **Extreme Gelled girls, hanging out.** Photograph by Arthur Elgort, Italian *Vogue*, 1993.

McLaren Malcolm   Designer

Malcolm McLaren delivers his manifesto wearing the rubber clothes sold in his shop, Sex, for the film, *The Great Rock 'n' Roll Swindle* (1978). A maverick entrepreneur and music aficionado, McLaren is credited with shaping the punk movement. In 1971 he and his partner, Vivienne Westwood, took over the running of a vintage shop, Let It Rock. Within three years they were selling bondage and fetish clothing, renaming the shop Sex in 1975. The graphic anti-monarchy and pseudo-porn images by Jamie Reid caused outrage (the shop was regularly raided by police). The same year McLaren managed a US band, whose pre-punk music inspired him to return to the UK to form his own band. The Sex Pistols was cast from customers and named after the shop. The band was effectively a public relations exercise which exploded; McLaren later confessed, 'Punk was just a way to sell trousers.'

☞ Rotten, Van Beirendonck, Westwood

Malcolm McLaren. b London (UK), 1946. **Malcolm McLaren wears rubber all-in-one.** *The Great Rock 'n' Roll Swindle*, 1978.

McLaughlin-Gill Frances   Photographer

This picture could be placed in any year since the one it was taken: 1948. The subject, Carol McCarlson, dries herself on a Florida beach; it is a picture that uses the blur of her oscillating towel to lend a naturalness for which its photographer is known. In 1941, Frances McLaughlin-Gill and her twin sister Kathryn entered a photography competition in *Vogue*. Both were finalists and Kathryn landed a job with *Vogue* photographer Toni Frissell. It was she who recommended that Frances should be introduced to her art director Alexander Liberman. He hired McLaughlin-Gill in 1943 and she came to illustrate the lives of the new young market for *Glamour* and *Vogue*, making relaxed depictions of real scenes the context for the burgeoning teenage and American sportswear markets. McLaughlin-Gill also added a spirit of informality to the stiff, grown-up couture of the 1950s.

☛ Campbell–Walters, Dessès, Frissell, Griffe, Shrimpton

302

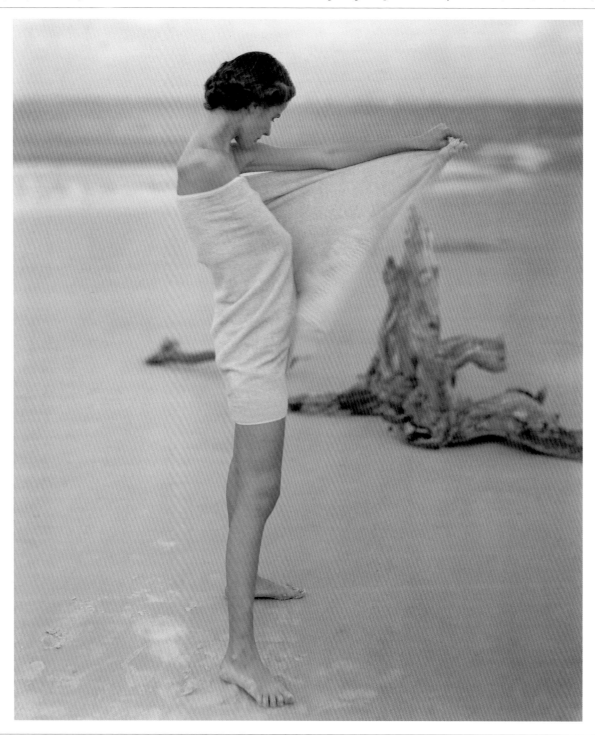

Frances McLaughlin-Gill. b New York (USA), 1919. **Carol McCarlson on the beach, St Augustine, Florida.** American *Vogue*, 1948.

McQueen Alexander Designer

'Bumsters' were Alexander McQueen's iconoclastic challenge to fashion. Just as women were getting used to wearing hipsters in 1995, he urged their trousers ever lower in the style of a builder's drooping waistband. From the moment McQueen graduated from Central Saint Martin's College of Art and Design in 1992, with a collection entitled 'Jack the Ripper Stalking his Victims', he used an aggressive approach towards design. 'Eclectic verging on the criminal' is how he describes his work, and no taboo has been ignored as he wields that banner. 'Highland Rape', a 1996 collection, dressed women in bloodied, tattered lace dresses. Savagery is usually close to the surface, although McQueen's work for Givenchy sometimes shows glimpses of a mellow McQueen – usually sharp, but often elegant. While McQueen has been accused of bad taste, it hasn't prevented his work from influencing that of the generation following him.

☛ Bowie, Chalayan, Galliano, Givenchy, N. Knight, Pearl

303

Alexander McQueen (Lee McQueen). b London (UK), 1969. **Brocade 'bumsters'.** Photograph by Phil Poynter, 1996.

Madonna

Icon

Madonna wears Jean-Paul Gaultier's famous pink satin corset for her 'Blonde Ambition' tour in 1990. A very real master of fashion's seasonal about-face, she has a unique and dynamic propensity for continually reinventing herself. Her impact as a vocalist and fashion icon in the early 1980s was undeniably heightened by the timely introduction of a new visual format of music, namely Music Television (MTV). But it was her ability to assume various, often controversial, personas with each new video release which set her apart from other artists. She has variously embraced lace and torn denim, a trashy, sexy, punky image for the release of her premier album in 1983; a glamorous, blonde Marilyn Monroe lookalike in 'Material Girl' in 1986 (complete with spray-on dress and Harry Winston diamonds) and a sophisticated persona as Eva Perón in the 1997 film *Evita*, wearing 1940s-inspired couture.

☞ Baron, Galliano, Gaultier, Pita, Testino, Versace

304

Madonna (Madonna Louise Ciccone). b Detroit, MI (USA), 1958. Madonna wears pink basque by Jean-Paul Gaultier. 1990.

Mainbocher

Designer

During the 1940s, Natalia Wilson (Mrs John C. Wilson, Princess Paley) was manager of Mainbocher's New York salon and his main vendeuse. She often posed for fashion magazines wearing his clothes, in this case a sumptuous evening outfit that would have been worn to a dinner party or to the theatre. Mainbocher was celebrated for his lush evening suits which consisted of a long dark skirt and contrasting jacket decorated with trimmings such as fur. With the distinctive beauty of Natalia Wilson modelling these suits, Mainbocher won acclaim and went on to become the first American designer to open a maison de couture in Paris. Mainbocher's earlier career had included sketching for *Vogue*. Like many others, he was influenced by Madeleine Vionnet's bias-cutting technique, a method he used for the Duchess of Windsor's wedding dress.

☛ Hoyningen-Huene, Ricci, Vionnet, Windsor

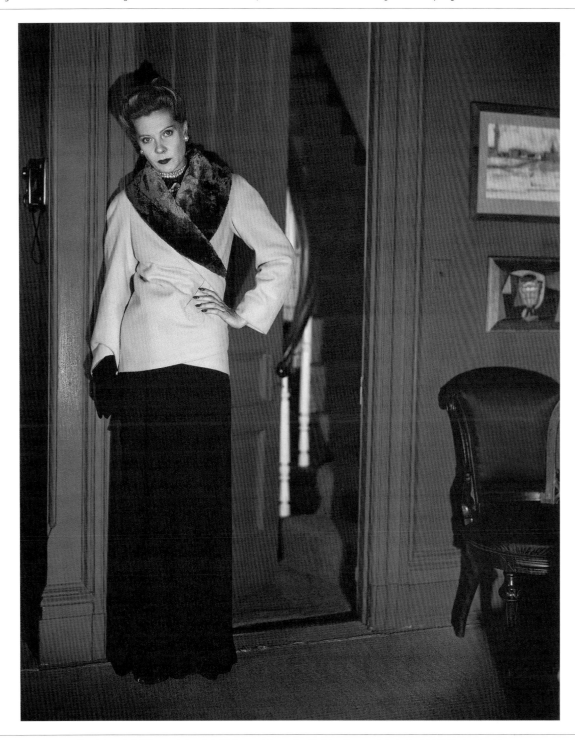

Mainbocher (Main Rousseau Bocher). b Chicago, IL (USA), 1890. **d** New York (USA), 1976. **Princess Natalia Paley.** Photograph by Louise Dahl-Wolfe, American *Vogue*, 1944.

Maltézos Madeleine and Carpentier Suzanne (Mad Carpentier) Designers

The very anonymity of the design team who created this dress is testament to their desire to remain on the conservative side of fashion, at a time when their colleagues were using shocking innovation as an advertisement for their houses. Upon the retirement of the legendary Madeleine Vionnet, two of her staff (Mad Maltézos and Suzie Carpentier) established a new fashion house. After the Second World War, Mad Carpentier was known for luxurious dresses and coats favoured by a restrained clientele not likely to go to the 'hot' fashion houses such as Dior, Fath or even Balenciaga. Rather, what Mad Carpentier distilled was an essence of the past, always harking back to Art Deco and the streamlining of the 1920s and 1930s. Dresses were demure and coats were elegant and comfortable. They were also more or less timeless and nameless, recognized mainly by New York's garment district, Seventh Avenue, which copied their saleable good taste.

☞ Connolly, Morton, Simpson, Vionnet

Madeleine Maltézos and Suzanne Carpentier (Mad Carpentier). (Active 1940s–1950s.) **Shawl-collared dress.** French *Vogue*, 1949.

306

Mandelli Mariuccia (Krizia)

Designer

Sharp pleats are thrown into black-and-white relief, capturing an atmosphere of drama and amusement, which conveys almost a circus mood in Mariuccia Mandelli's design for her company Krizia. There is a strong sense of architecture expressed in the geometric lines formed by the pleats of the outfit. When the wearer moves, these pleats form a rolling wave. Mandelli explained her distinctive style thus, 'There is often a sense of architecture in my clothing...one of my collections was inspired by the Chrysler Building.' Krizia, named after Critias, a Greek politician and poet commemorated in one of Plato's dialogues, was formed in Milan in 1951. Historically, it is noted for experimental construction and an irreverent approach to glamorous clothes, and was at one point dubbed 'Crazy Krizia' by the press. In the 1970s, Mandelli's eveningwear included sporting garments and those usually worn for daywear.

☛ Capucci, Miyake, Venet

Mariuccia Mandelli. b Bergamo (IT), 1933. (Krizia.) **Pleated lamé frills.** Photograph by Giovanni Gastel, 1998.

Man Ray

Photographer

Photographer Man Ray was one of the central figures in the Surrealist movement in Paris. He was fascinated by women's lips as objects of desire. Other artists and fashion designers have ventured to portray the lips of Surrealism: Dalí designed a sofa modelled on Mae West's lips, Saint Laurent created a Lip Dress and Elsa Schiaparelli used lips as a pocket (the hand inserted between them). In 1921 Man Ray left New York for Paris, where he took up photography to finance his painting. An introduction to Poiret, who was looking for a different sort of photographer, brought him into fashion, a field which united his experimentation with a commercial product. In the 1920s his work for *Vogue* and *Harper's Bazaar* extended fashion photography from posed formality into the sphere of collaborative art. He asserted that 'inspiration, not information, the force that binds all creative acts' is at the root of great fashion.

☛ Bernard, Blumenfeld, Dalí, Hoyningen-Huene

Man Ray (Emmanuel Rudnitsky). **b** Philadelphia, PA (USA), 1890. **d** Paris (FR), 1976. **Lips on Lips.** 1930.

Maramotti Achille (MaxMara) Designer

'For us to be considered fashionable would be very dangerous,' said MaxMara's former managing director, Luigi Maramotti. 'It is not chic for a woman to move violently from one way of dressing to another.' MaxMara is the epitome of Italian fashion: good quality and cut, in classic styles, while managing to interpret trends in a very wearable way. The camel-coloured wrap coat shown here is pure cashmere, and although the design seems pared down, attention to detail is impeccable. One of Italy's largest and oldest fashion companies, MaxMara was founded in 1951 by Doctor Achille Maramotti, a lawyer turned dressmaker. His first collection consisted of just two outfits: a suit and an overcoat. This brevity of design has always been MaxMara's signature, and the collections still focus on these key items of tailoring. It concentrates on easing the transition through trends for a clientele that requires good taste.

☛ Beretta, Paulin, Venturi

309

Achille Maramotti. **b** Reggio nell'Emilia (IT), 1926. (MaxMara.) **d** Albinea (IT), 2005. **Linda Evangelista wears MaxMara camel coat.** Photograph by Steven Meisel, 1997.

Margiela Martin   Designer

The construction of Martin Margiela's black jacket becomes clear in the negative image. It uses the deep-set armholes, raised shoulders, wide lapels and raised waistline often seen in his tailoring. Margiela designs in the manner of an avant-garde artist, rather than following fashion's accustomed desire to please. He deconstructs clothes (putting the lining material on the outside), uses doll's clothes as models for adult clothing (complete with giant buttons), recycles unlikely materials and makes sweaters out of socks. Having graduated from Antwerp's influential Royal Academy of Arts, Margiela became a design assistant to Jean-Paul Gaultier – his work takes off from Gaultier's fashion shocks and conceals clever techniques of tailoring and dressmaking. Rather than being rejected by traditional houses, Margiela's iconoclastic methods were accepted in 1997 when Hermès hired him to oversee its design studio.

☛ Bikkembergs, Gaultier, Thimister, Van Noten

310

Martin Margiela. b Louvain (BEL), 1957. Fitted jacket. Photographs by Ronald Stoops, 1989.

Marteans Dr Klaus (Dr Martens)

Shoe designer

In a stunning duality of purpose the Dr Marten ('DM') boot has been a symbol of aggressive, anti-fashion cults for three decades. It is also worn by most uniformed, establishment figures. It began life as an orthopaedic aid. Designed in 1946 by Klaus Marteans, a Bavarian doctor who had broken his foot while skiing and wanted something to relieve the pain, the boot was an overnight success. In 1959 the British bootmaker R. Griggs was granted permission to use Marteans' air-cushioned sole on his steelcapped workmens' boots; the compound was changed to granular PVC (resistant to fat, oil, acids and petrol) and has remained unchanged ever since. The 'Famous Footwear AirWair, with bouncing soles' was born. In the mid-1960s, the eight-eyelet boot in black or cherry red became a uniform for skinheads; in the 1980s, DMs became an essential part of British 'street style' when they were worn with a pair of Levi's jeans.

☛ Cox, Jaeger, Strauss

Dr Klaus Marteans. b Braunschweiz (GER), 1915. d (GER), 1988. Policeman and skinhead wear Dr Martens. Southend, 1980.

311

Matsuda Mitsuhiro Designer

Mitsuhiro Matsuda arranges a variety of woven linens for an outfit which hardly resembles clothes at all. The fabrics themselves dominate the image, with checks and stripes loosely woven to form a semi-transparent material. Matsuda is one of the early greats in the tradition of Japanese fashion design that carried successfully over to a Western tradition and sensibility.

In the 1980s, his clothes were whimsical and romantic in the British style, often taking their inspiration from the costumes of historical England. Yet he maintained a practicality and wearability in his tailoring that was androgynous and sexy. His menswear was directional and elements of it were used for his womenswear. Matsuda's father worked in the kimono industry and

it was with that garment that he and his contemporaries, Kenzo and Yohji Yamamoto, examined the principle of Western clothes.

☞ Kenzo, Kim, Kobayashi, Y. Yamamoto

312

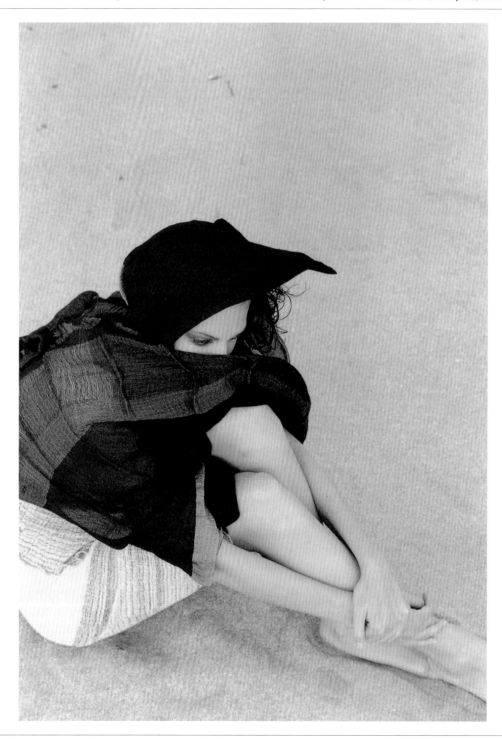

Mitsuhiro Matsuda. b Tokyo (JAP), 1934. 'Madame Nicole'. Mixed linens. Spring/summer 1996. Photograph by Mitsuhiro Matsuda.

Matsushima Masaki

Designer

'Fashion is necessary but I think it is of secondary importance,' says Masaki Matsushima. His suits for men and women show both sides of this argument at once. Inherently they deal with the pinstripe tradition, lending them a sober quality, and yet they have a fashion edge which is sharpened with broad shirt collars and a flamboyant buttonhole. But Matsushima feels that these styling touches are down to the individual who will make the clothes their own. 'I am trying to create a mass image,' continues Matsushima. 'That is why I don't think that creation means to force the designer's own personality on the people.' Matsushima graduated from Tokyo's famous Bunka Gakuen Fukushoku school of fashion in 1985. He designed costumes for conceptual singer Ryuichi Sakamoto and launched his own label. His clothes are by turns highly technical and instrumental in promoting the notion of conceptual streetwear.

☛ Bartlett, Dolce & Gabbana, Newton

Masaki Matsushima. b Magoya (JAP), 1963. **Reworked pinstripe suits.** Photograph by Satoshi Saikusa, 1998.

Maxwell Vera   Designer

'Buy a Share in America' declare the wartime posters, and Americans did – even in fashion. During the Second World War, European fashions, in particular those from Paris, were not available, so America turned to its own designers. Vera Maxwell was one of the designers who came to the fore at this time. Her separates – simple shapes in humble fabrics – adhered to wartime restrictions as well as being conscious of the pressures and new-found responsibilities of women workers. Maxwell often reinterpreted men's workwear shapes – this jacket is based on a man's lumberjack shirt. In 1970, Maxwell discovered Ultrasuede which was to become a durable yet sophisticated staple for women's tailoring, championed especially by Halston. In 1974 she designed her first Speed Suit – an elasticated dress that could be quickly slipped down over the head for busy women. It was a precursor to Donna Karan's ethos a decade later.

☛ Dahl-Wolfe, Halston, Karan, A. Klein

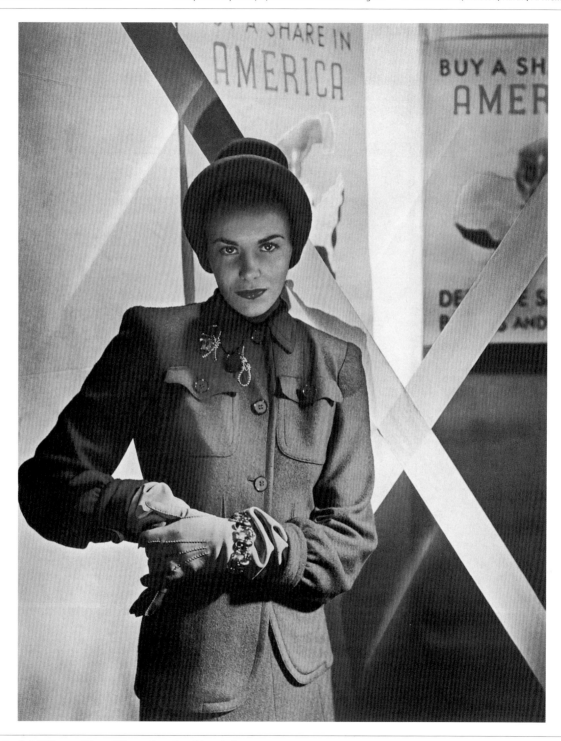

Vera Maxwell. b New York (USA), 1903. d Rincon (PR), 1995. **Co-ordinated day suit.** Photograph by Louise Dahl-Wolfe, *Harper's Bazaar*, 1942.

Mazzilli Tiziano and Louise (Voyage)

Designers

Wrinkled velvet ribbon sewn onto the neckline of a sheer T-shirt signifies the work of Voyage. Such clothes are designed to look like antiques and cast-offs and yet are recognizable as expensive garments to those in the know. Made from slub silk, linen, silk velvet and taffeta, each one-size-fits-all unstructured garment is hand-dyed, hand-painted and washed to 'authenticate' it. Voyage mixes colours in the same haphazard way, contriving to build an apparently careless look. Owners Tiziano Mazzilli and his wife Louise have fostered the label's image as an exclusive and expensive one. In 1991 they opened Voyage on London's Fulham Road. 'Our philosophy is to be unique,' says Mazzilli. 'We don't want to please everyone.' And they don't. Each visitor to the boutique must ring a bell, and undergo scrutiny before being allowed in, an example of fashionable exclusion surpassed only by a later move to introduce membership cards.

☛ von Etzdorf, Oudejans, Williamson

Mazzilli. Tiziano. b Udine (IT); **Louise. b** Brussels (BEL). (Active 1990s–) (Voyage.) **Velvet-trimmed T-shirt and cutwork pink skirt.** Photograph by Howard Sooley, *Joyce*, 1997.

Meisel Steven   Photographer

Steven Meisel's picnic illustrates a collection by Dolce & Gabbana. The sunny lighting contradicts the cold, dull background, giving the picture a surreal edge. Meisel calls himself 'a reflection of my times'. It is a phrase that equally applies to his work. His strength is as an image-maker, both in terms of his own image, and that of the designers' work he photographs and the models whose careers he has transformed – Meisel discovered Linda Evangelista and Stella Tennant. He has a sensitivity towards clothes and is able to adapt to each garment he photographs: 'I am always influenced by the philosophy of the particular couturier whose dress I am photographing.' American and Italian *Vogue* are Meisel's biggest arenas. In one Italian edition he has been given as many as thirty pages to depict a single story: a fact that makes him the undisputed emperor of fashion image-making.

☛ Evangelista, Garren, Gigli, Sprouse, Sui, Tennant

Steven Meisel. b New York (USA), 1954. 'Early fall picnic in Dolce & Gabbana'. Italian *Vogue*, 1998.

Mesejeán Pablo and Cancela Delia (Pablo & Delia)

The flower power youth revolts from Paris to San Martín and the resurgence of artisan crafting paved the way for Pablo and Delia's fantasies. Inspired by Lewis Carroll's stories, this shirred, floral-printed cotton top with a layered tulle, flower-shaped headband heralds the bloom of naïveté as a lifestyle. The mood of the times was summarized in Pablo Mesejeán and Delia Cancela's 1966 Manifesto, which proclaimed, 'We love sunny days, the Rolling Stones, tanned bodies, the *young savage look*, pink and baby blue, happy ends.' Upon the arrival in London in 1970 of these two art students from Buenos Aires, UK *Vogue* instantly featured a cover with Jean Shrimpton in their trademark rainbow-coloured, painted leather dress. Pablo and Delia's clothes were usually accompanied by their own dream-like illustrations of wizards and fairies wearing their creations. Since Pablo's death, Delia has concentrated on painting and illustration.

☛ Coddington, Gibb, Leonard, Shrimpton

317

Pablo Mesejeán. b Buenos Aires (ARG), 1937. d Paris (FR), 1986; Delia Cancela. b Buenos Aires (ARG), 1940. (Pablo & Delia.) Pink 'Petal Hat' and shirred dress. Photograph by Barry Lategan, British *Vogue*, 1972.

De Meyer Baron Adolph

Photographer

In balletic pose, Baron de Meyer's subject displays layers of opulent lace trimmed with silk satin ribbon. Her peignoir and dress are backlit to give them and her a luminous glow in a hugely romantic portrait of femininity. De Meyer's fashion photography was founded in the *belle époque* before the First World War. Having spent his childhood in Paris and Germany, he entered London's fashionable society at the end of the nineteenth century. He was hired by Condé Nast in 1914, becoming *Vogue*'s first full-time photographer and later moving to *Harper's Bazaar* in 1921. With their halos and fragile clothes, his subjects appeared too delicate to participate in vigorous modern life which included swimming, tennis, golf and the Charleston, and his style was replaced by dynamic experiments in movement. De Meyer left *Harper's Bazaar* in 1932, his place taken by Martin Munkacsi and his invigorating look.

☞ Antoine, Arden, Boué, Nast, Reboux, Sumurun

Baron Adolph de Meyer. b Paris (FR), 1868. d Los Angeles, CA (USA), 1949. **Romantic chiffon dress.** American *Vogue*, 1922.

Miller Lee

Photographer

A model, with her painted nails, lipstick, coiffed hair and bias-cut dress, is a tantalizing vision for the servicewomen she parades for. One stretches her arm to feel the cloth, the wearing of which, for most, would have been an impossible dream. Her unconscious touch renders the model as unreal as the image she projects. American photographer Lee Miller is known

for her poignant photographs taken during the Second World War as a member of the London War Correspondents' Corps. During this time, however, she also worked for *Vogue*. Her captivating photograph shows that Paris couture had lost none of its power during the war, and the city was well positioned to re-establish itself as a fashion leader. In the late 1920s

Miller was a model, photographer and writer for *Vogue* in New York. In 1929 she moved to Paris, where she lived and worked with Man Ray and was friendly with Picasso and the Surrealists.

☛ Arnold, Bruyère, Dalí, Man Ray

Lee Miller. b Poughkeepsie, NY (USA), 1907. d Chiddingly (UK), 1977. **Service women at a fashion salon, Paris. 1944.**

Miller Nolan   Designer

Nolan Miller, architect of the extravagant *Dynasty* look which defined the shameless glamour and camp of 1980s fashion, sits surrounded by the show's female stars. His studio generated twenty-five to thirty such outfits every week – with just two days to discuss a wardrobe and five days to create it. His 'bitch' wardrobe for Joan Collins (Alexis Colby), who wears a gleaming column of pink sequins here, was modelled on that worn by Joan Crawford in the 1940s. Her shoulders are exaggerated with vast outcrops of fuchsia ruffles. Next to her, Diahann Carroll (Dominique Devereaux) and Linda Evans (Krystle Carrington) also bear the inflated, squared-off shoulder line which was associated with masculine power. Miller moved to Hollywood in the hope of dressing glamorous women by becoming one of cinema's legendary costume designers. He arrived too late for that but in time to bring glamour to the small screen.

☞ Banton, Bates, Burrows, Mackie

Nolan Miller. b Burkbarnette, TX (USA), 1935. **Nolan Miller and his female cast.** *Dynasty*, 1985.

Milner Deborah   Designer

Deborah Milner's clothes are sculptural fantasies that defy the term 'fashion'. Indeed, this gauzy, full-length black coat featuring Milner's signature – a superb sweeping cowl neck and intricate textiles – could probably stand alone in an art gallery. Milner says, 'My work ranges from the avant-garde to the quite classic'. One of her former tutors describes her as having 'revived the art of couture by adapting her skills to work with everyday materials'. These include net, tape, film and coated wire. Milner had a strict Methodist upbringing and countered it by enrolling at art college where she discovered fashion. She began with a small couture studio in 1991, specializing in one-off, avant-garde fashion pieces for, among others, milliner Philip Treacy, who used them as foils for his climactic headgear. Here, his ergonomic glittered ellipse equals Milner's semi-sheer coat for drama.

☛ Hishinuma, Horvat, Treacy

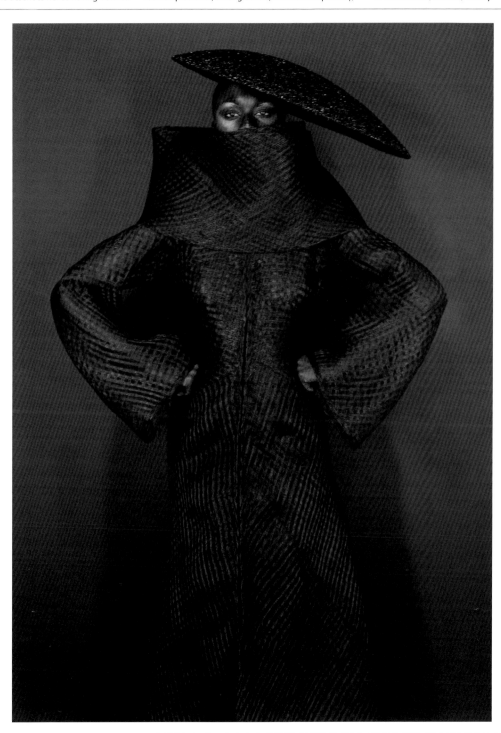

Deborah Milner. **b** Walton-on-Thames (UK), 1964. **Gauze coat.** Photograph by Mark Mattock, *i-D*, 1997.

Missoni Tai, Rosita and Angela

1971 or 2008? We rely on modern photography and styling for the answer because the enduring popularity of Missoni's colourful knitwear in basic shapes means their clothes have changed little over the years. Their strength and appeal lies in their simple beauty. Colour is the key to the Missoni look. The distinctive, flecked 'flame dye' effect is achieved by only partly immersing the yarn in the dye to leave a white mark or to allow the colour of the yarn to show through. The Missonis met at the 1948 Olympics in London, where Ottavio was competing in the 400-metre hurdles, wearing the team tracksuit that had been designed by his own small knitwear company. They married and their first collection was presented in Milan in 1966. In 1997 Ottavio and Rosita handed the business over to their daughter, Angela, who has inherited the Missoni sensibilities.

☛ Eula, Gibb, Khanh, Testino

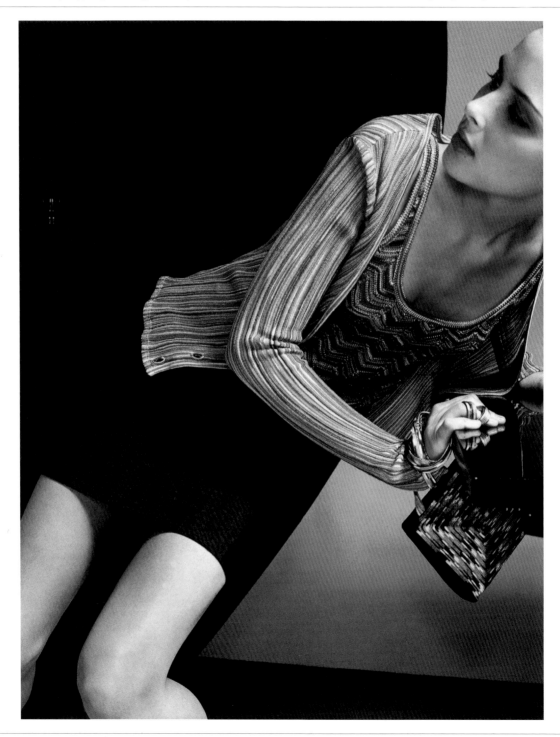

322

Missoni. Ottavio (Tai). **b** Ragusa (SYR), 1921; **Rosita. b** Golasecca (IT), 1931; **Angela. b** Milan (IT), 1958. **Chevron vest and striped cardigan. Spring/summer 1998.** Photograph by Mario Testino.

Miyake Issey   Designer

Peaking through torn tissue, a vivid pink shirt is displayed as though it were an installation. This intricately pleated garment has been created by carefully folding a length of polyester, twisting it tightly, then treating it with heat. This particular creation and other vividly coloured, highly innovative designs, often involving wrapping and layering fabric, are typical of the renowned Japanese designer, Issey Miyake. He served an apprenticeship first with Guy Laroche and then with Givenchy. He also worked in New York designing ready-to-wear for Geoffrey Beene, before returning to Japan in 1970 to found his own design studio at the age of thirty-two. Hugely influential, Miyake is a member of Japan's fashion elite, along with Rei Kawakubo and Yohji Yamamoto, and his clothes are admired and worn by artists, architects and intellectuals, so much so that a diffusion line, Pleats Please, has been devised.

☛ Arai, Givenchy, Hishinuma, Kawakubo, Mandelli

323

Issey Miyake. b Hiroshima (JAP), 1938. **Pleats Please pink shirt.** Photograph by Kazumi Kurigami, 1995.

Mizrahi Isaac   Designer

Isaac Mizrahi, wearing his customary headband, is photographed in his New York studio with model Amber Valetta, who is laid out on his pattern-cutting table. Beyond the scorching colour of her dress, designed for spring 1995, there is a rainbow of cottons stored on the wall and an intense mix of shades represented on a rail of samples behind them. They are all evidence that

Mizrahi is not a designer afraid of colour – pacific blue, cartoon yellow, bubblegum pink. 'I love Technicolor – it's wildly beautiful,' he says of his untrammelled taste in sunshine colours. He marries vibrant, unusual materials with shapes long used for American sportswear. This sense of comedy in his work and personality was aired in a docufilm, *Unzipped*, which followed the creation of his

autumn 1994 collection. It comes from his training at New York's High School for the Performing Arts prior to his entry into fashion.

☛ Beene, Kors, Moses, Oldham

324

Isaac Mizrahi. b New York (USA), 1961. **Isaac Mizrahi with Amber Valetta.** Photograph by Gilles Bensimon, American *Elle*, 1995.

Model Philippe   Milliner

Complex hats, such as this sculpted headpiece formed from interwoven, red velvet segments, have put Philippe Model at the forefront of French accessories design since 1978. It was then he left school and started his business from scratch by making haute couture hats. Shortly afterwards, Model was awarded the title *'Meilleur ouvrier de France'* (finest craftsman in France), a coveted prize for excellence which dates back to the Middle Ages. He moved to the heart of French fashion in the early 1980s, after working with Jean-Paul Gaultier, Claude Montana and Thierry Mugler for whom he accessorized avant-garde collections. Model doesn't limit his work to millinery – he is also a shoe designer whose neat, elasticated shoes became widely copied. Similar in idea to Hervé Léger's 'elastic bandage' dresses, they are formed from strips of stretch material and display a practical design talent.

☞ **Léger, Montana, Mugler, Paulette, Underwood**

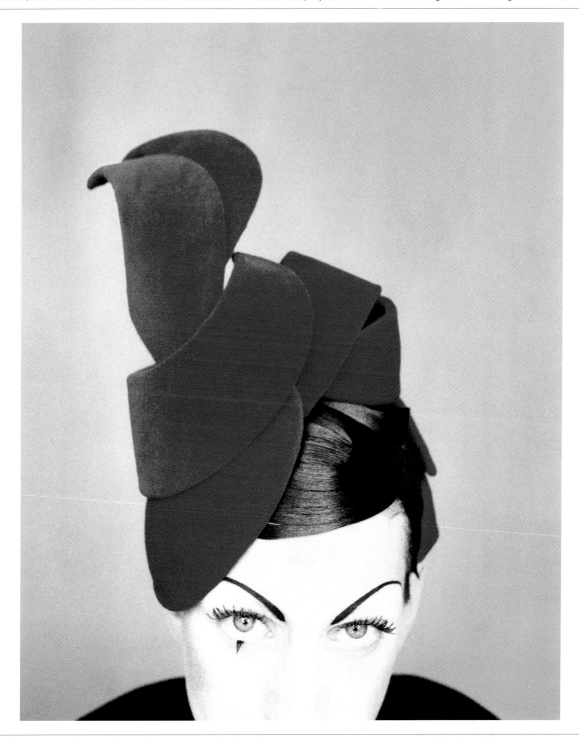

325

Philippe Model. **b** Sens (FR), 1956. **Spiral hat.** Photograph by Satoshi Saikusa, *Harpers & Queen*, 1988.

Molinari Anna   Designer

Anna Molinari believes that every woman has a dual fashion personality, widely known as the virgin/whore complex. In this editorial, model Trish Goff fulfils both by wearing a sheer shirt, brief satin shorts and a snowy tailored jacket for cooking. Molinari's work is always traditional in the way it deals with creating sexy clothes, often using a formula that marries brief hemlines with sheer fabrics. In doing so, she takes the clothes off the street and into the realm of a designer label. While mirroring current trends, Molinari attracts a following of ultra-feminine women. Her more romantic medium uses flouncy dresses, tutus and tops decorated with ruffles, frills and bows, which are always just decent. In 1977 she established the label in partnership with her husband, Gianpaolo Tarabini. At that time Molinari produced chiefly knitwear, a selection of which remains in the form of sweater-girl shapes trimmed with diamanté.

☛ van Lamsweerde, Thomass, Versace

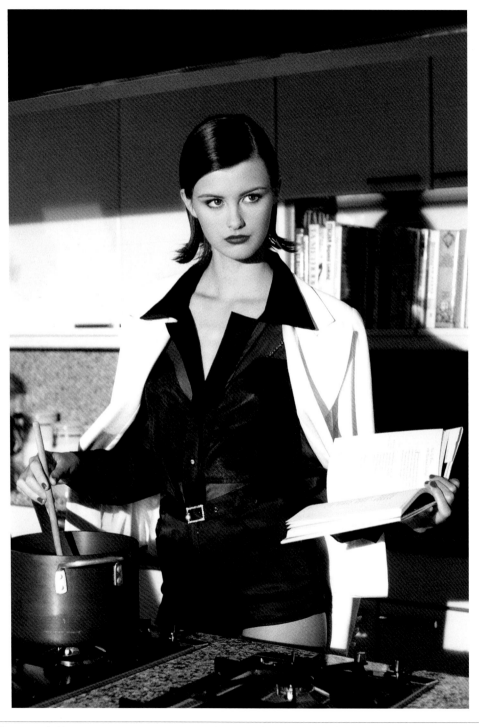

326

Anna Molinari. b Capri (IT). (Active 1970s–) **Trish Goff**. Photograph by Pamela Hanson, American *Vogue*, 1995.

Molyneux Captain Edward

Designer

A romantic look back to the silhouette worn by the Empress Josephine during the First Empire (1804–15) characterizes this evening dress. The empire-style dress has a high waistline, a square-cut neckline, short, puffed sleeves and rich embroidery. A draped, floor-length stole tapering into a train and long gloves completes the regal look. Such aristocratic grandeur made Molyneux a favourite fashion designer among royalty, society women and film stars. Princess Marina, Duchess of Kent, was one of his most famous and elegant clients. Trained under Lucile (Lady Duff Gordon), who in the early twentieth century designed empire-style gowns, Molyneux nevertheless walked a fine line between romantic revival and modernity. He was a fashion designer with a reputation for exquisite taste based on purity of line and cut. Christian Dior was known to have preferred Molyneux to any other couturier.

☛ Balmain, Dior, Duff Gordon, Griffe, Stiebel, Sumurun

Captain Edward Molyneux. b London (UK), 1891. d Monte Carlo (MON), 1974. **Embroidered satin, empire-line dress.** Photograph by François Kollar, 1939.

Montana Claude Designer

Aggressive jackets cut from leather epitomize Claude Montana's extreme style. Broad-shouldered, para-military shapes accentuated with epaulettes and cinched waists have dominated his work, the most powerful using leather, since his own label was launched in 1979. Montana understands a simple Constructivist shape with its straight, uncompromising lines and uses extreme styling in the way Pierre Cardin did in the 1960s. He relishes the act of 'building' his designs and was widely respected for those he created for Lanvin Couture from 1989 to 1992. Montana's career began in London, when he ran short of money on a visit and started designing jewellery, which was then featured in *Vogue*. After a year, he returned to Paris to work for the leather firm MacDouglas. In the 1980s his work symbolized a movement of women's fashion which dressed them as super-heroines.

☞ Flett, Lanvin, Model, Steiger, Viramontes

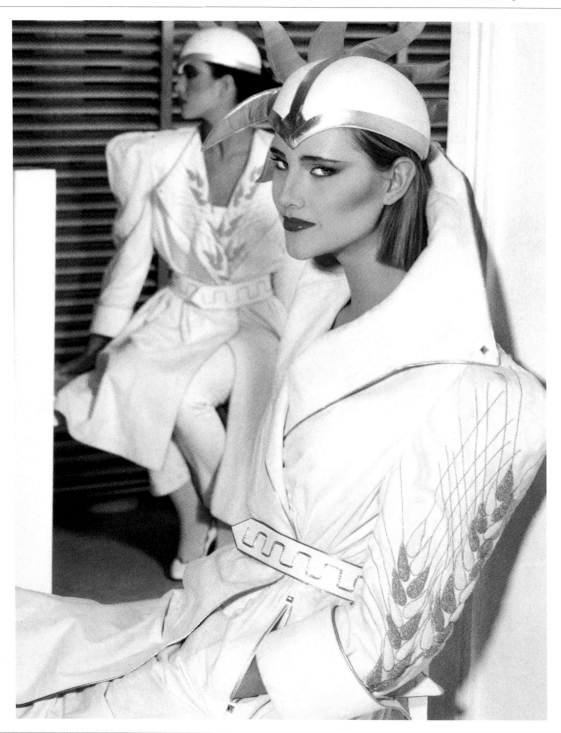

Claude Montana. b Paris (FR), 1949. **Embroidered, white and gold leather outfits for Idéal Cuir.** Photograph by Alain Larue, *L'Officiel*, 1980.

328

Moon Sarah   Photographer

A Sarah Moon photograph is almost always a dreamy, soft-focus trip back to the fashion mood of the 1920s and 1930s. When she photographed the Pirelli Calendar in 1972, it was a groundbreaking event: not only was she the first woman to do so (she was chosen to pacify objections from the feminist movement), but she was also the first to show fully exposed breasts. Moon spent much of the 1960s as a fashion model, but towards the end of that decade turned to photography. Her first assignment was an advertising campaign for Cacharel, which led to editorial work for *Nova*, *Vogue*, *Harper's Bazaar* and *Elle*. Subsequent advertising campaigns for Biba cosmetics summed up the fashion mood of the early 1970s. Moon has since moved beyond the constraints of fashion and into the sphere of fine art photography. Her work has remained muted, somewhat surreal, and always beautiful.

☞ Bousquet, Dinnigan, Hulanicki, Williamson

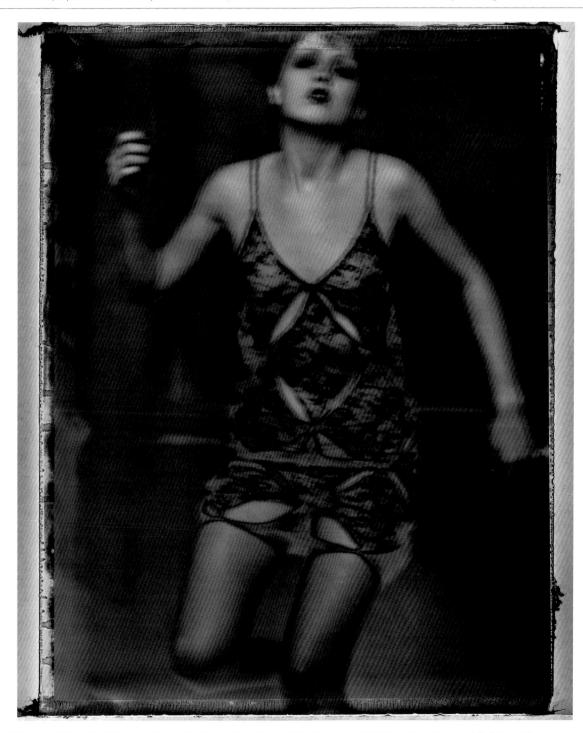

Sarah Moon. b Paris (FR), 1941. **Katia wears Enrica Massei.** *The Frankfurter*, 1997.

Morehouse Marion Model

The photographer Edward Steichen once declared that, 'Good fashion models have the qualities inherent in a good actress.' For Steichen, Morehouse was 'the best fashion model I ever worked with.' Fashion in the 1920s demanded a sleek and willowy silhouette, and Marion Morehouse had that archetypal figure. This, together with her commanding presence and seemingly effortless elegance, made her the ideal fashion model for the period. As Steichen said, 'She transformed herself into the sort of woman who really would wear that gown.' Morehouse was also frequently photographed by some of the other great photographers who began working in the 1920s, such as Horst P. Horst and George Hoyningen-Huene. She married the writer e.e. cummings, and later in her career also took up photography.

☛ Chéruit, Horst, Hoyningen-Huene, Steichen

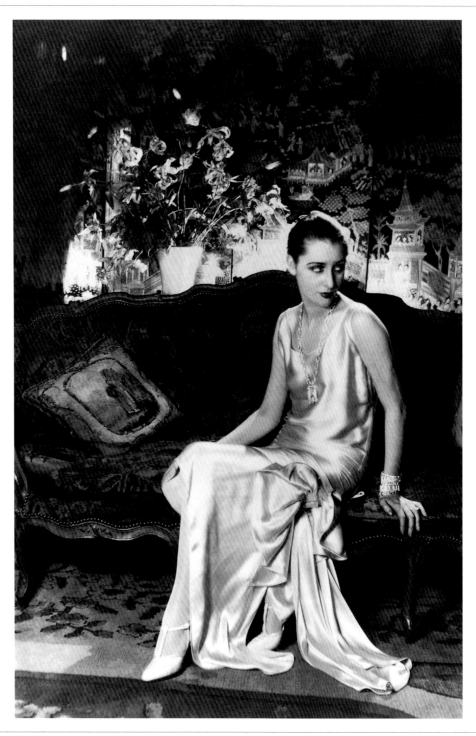

330

Marion Morehouse. b (USA), 1906. **d** (USA), 1969. **Marion Morehouse wears bias-cut satin dress.** Photograph by Cecil Beaton, 1929.

Mori Hanae   Designer

The radiant daylight catches Hanae Mori's favourite model Hiroko en route to her wooden pagoda retreat. Her bird-like frame, veiled in a tissue-soft, silk organza caftan printed with daisies, echoes Mori's restrained elegance and Japanese aesthetic. Kimono silk printed with cherry blossoms and butterflies, produced by Mori's husband Kei, Japanese asymmetry and obi belting are all indicative of her respect for her cultural heritage. Invariably balancing this with Western styling, Mori's feather-light creations are consistent and sensible, never enslaved to the dictates of fashion. A graduate in Japanese literature, Mori went back to college after her marriage and two sons to learn the fundamentals of dressmaking. She designed costumes for Japanese film and theatre, before setting up shop at Tokyo's shopping haven Ginza in 1955. She was admitted to Paris's Chambre Syndicale de la Couture in 1977.

☛ Hirata, Scherrer, Snowdon

Hanae Mori. b Tokyo (JAP), 1926. **Silk caftan.** Photograph by Snowdon, British *Vogue*, 1972.

331

Morris Robert Lee   Jewellery Designer

Three twisted, sterling silver bangles represent the sculptural work of Robert Lee Morris. The filing marks and beaten indentations lend them the natural spirit for which Morris is known. He says, 'I adore natural forms. I am a student of anatomy', and his designs forge elements of nature into a variety of objects, ranging from Africa-inspired breastplates to a lipstick holder

for Elizabeth Arden. Morris has used cork, rubber, granite and silicone in his work, but when New York's Fashion Institute of Technology staged a twenty-five-year retrospective for Morris's work, it was titled 'Metalmania'. His use of stark, urban metals brought him close to Donna Karan, whose cultivated designs are an ideal backdrop for dramatic modern jewellery.

Their work in the mid-1980s, often pairing navy fabric with elegant gold cuffs, created a uniform for white-collar women who wanted to escape the baroque excesses of that period.

☛ Arden, Barrett, Karan

332

Robert Lee Morris. b Nuremberg (GER), 1947. **Sterling silver Orbit bangles.** Photograph by Wolfgang Ludes, 1998.

Morton Digby   Designer

'Fashion is indestructible,' proclaimed British *Vogue* when it published this photograph by Cecil Beaton as London was bombed during the Second World War. Digby Morton provided leadership in British fashion during the war years. He specialized in tailored tweed suits. The example in this photograph has a hip-length jacket and a slightly flared skirt just covering the knees. Morton took the severity and masculinity out of the tailored suit. In 1928 he joined the house of Lachasse, quickly gaining recognition for his suits in exquisitely shaded tweeds, designed to be worn with silk blouses. He left in 1933 to start his own couture business and was succeeded at Lachasse by Hardy Amies. Morton was a member of the Incorporated Society of London Fashion Designers, a group of leading couturiers which promoted the British fashion industry in the face of wartime restrictions.

☞ **Amies, Beaton, Cavanagh, Creed, French, Maltézos**

Digby Morton. **b** Dublin (IRE), 1906. **d** London (UK), 1983. **Grey tweed suit.** Photograph by Cecil Beaton, British *Vogue*, 1941.

Moschino Franco Designer

Typical of Franco Moschino is this cheeky mockery of haute couture where, just for a second, the silhouette of a military jet is accepted as a couture hat in the grand French style. Moschino believed that fashion should be fun and he demanded laughs with the slogans he applied to clothes and advertising: 'Waist of Money' and 'Warning: fashion shows can be damaging to your health'. That his protest became fashion itself was testament to the garments they adorned: chic formal suits and evening dresses. As a boy, Moschino would go into his father's iron foundry and create images in the dust on the walls. He went on to study art and worked for Gianni Versace until 1977. In 1983 he launched the Moschino label. After his death in 1994, each garment was sold with a manifesto stating that environmental concern is 'the only true fashion trend'.

☞ Kelly, Steele, Versace

334

Franco Moschino. b Abbiategrasso (IT), 1950. d Milan (IT), 1994. **Silhouette of a Moschino Couture! cocktail dress, 1988.** Photograph by Fabrizio Ferri.

Moses Rebecca   Designer

A cartoon figure reclines in a classic bikini which represents Rebecca Moses' starting point for every piece of clothing: colour. The walls of her Italian studio are covered with plastic envelopes, each containing colour swatches in the form of materials, flowers and paper. They turn up on her cashmere sweaters with names such as 'Frozen Cranberries' and 'Robin's Egg'. Cartoon-like in their deep-dyed colours (thirty-five every season) and simplicity of shape, the clothes she forms owe nothing to transient fashion trends. 'I'm not saying fashion should stay still,' she says, 'but it should stop for long enough to consider the needs of modern men and women...I was fed up with fashion. There was just so much clothing out there – fashion was moving too fast and there wasn't any real life to it.' She refers to her clothing as 'mobile style' that can 'travel' between daywear and eveningwear, summer and winter and from outfit to outfit.

☛ Biagiotti, Jacobs, Mizrahi

Rebecca Moses. b New York (USA), 1956. **Magenta bikini, 1998.** Illustration by Rebecca Moses.

Moss Kate   Model

Every so often a special face appears, a face that changes the way we perceive beauty and which challenges our tastes. This is one such face scrubbed bare. Kate Moss was 'discovered' aged fourteen at JFK Airport, New York. Sarah Doukas, the spotter and owner of Storm modelling agency in London, felt 'she was going to be special'. She was. Kate Moss became the Twiggy of the 1990s; young and fresh, she symbolized the triumph of naturalness over artifice. Part of that charm is a naturally skinny frame that does not bear the fleshy undulations usually associated with beauty icons. Labelled a 'superwaif', her rise to fame coincided with the grunge phenomenon that celebrated an anti-designer look of uncoordinated clothes worn with rock-star attitude. Calvin Klein's unisex perfumes were one of the first products to literally bottle this attitude and make it a commercial product, leaving Kate Moss as the obvious choice of model.

☛ Day, Hilfiger, C. Klein, Kors, Sims

336

Kate Moss. b London (UK), 1974. **'cK be' advertising campaign for Calvin Klein.** 1997. Photograph by Richard Avedon.

Mugler Thierry   Designer

Thierry Mugler's photograph of his corset and latex trousers conjures up the themes of Aryan vamp and Pop Art dominatrix. Running through his work is a sexy 'anatomical vision' of moulded silhouettes, hand-span waists and exaggerated shoulders that have influenced Azzedine Alaïa and Hervé Léger. 'It's all about looking good and helping the silhouette...and it's all about

getting a good fuck, honey,' Mugler memorably informed Kim Basinger in Robert Altman's 1995 fashion film *Prêt à Porter*. Mugler made his first outfit for a female friend at the age of fourteen. Joining a ballet company, he moved to Paris at nineteen. In 1973 he launched his own label. Mugler's vision has been unswerving. Each season jackets are cut, padded and stitched to create his cartoon-like

ideal, a theme that also runs through his superhero menswear. Mugler re-shapes the body using seam and fabric; an uncompromising and total vision.

☛ Bergère, S. Jones, Léger, Model, Van Beirendonck

337

Thierry Mugler. b Strasbourg (FR), 1948. **Shaped bustier and latex pants.** Photograph by Thierry Mugler, 1996.

Muir Jean Designer

The minimalism of Jean Muir's jersey tunic and matching culottes presents a stark silhouette on Joanna Lumley (Muir's model in the 1970s). Simplicity was Muir's signature. She said, 'I am a traditionalist with a sense of evolution'. She inspired the respectful address 'Miss Muir', and always wore navy. Geraldine Stutz, president of Henri Bendel in New York, called her 'the most outstanding dressmaker in the world'. After working at Liberty, she designed for Jaeger, before setting up her own company in 1966. She made the 'little nothing' of a black dress a classic. But her designs were often deceptively simple – jackets could contain up to eighteen pattern pieces. The understated elegance of Muir's wearable designs have made them timeless classics. As the designer herself said,

'When you have found something that suits you and never lets you down, why not stick to it?'

☛ Conran, Jaeger, Liberty, Rayne, G. Smith, Torimaru

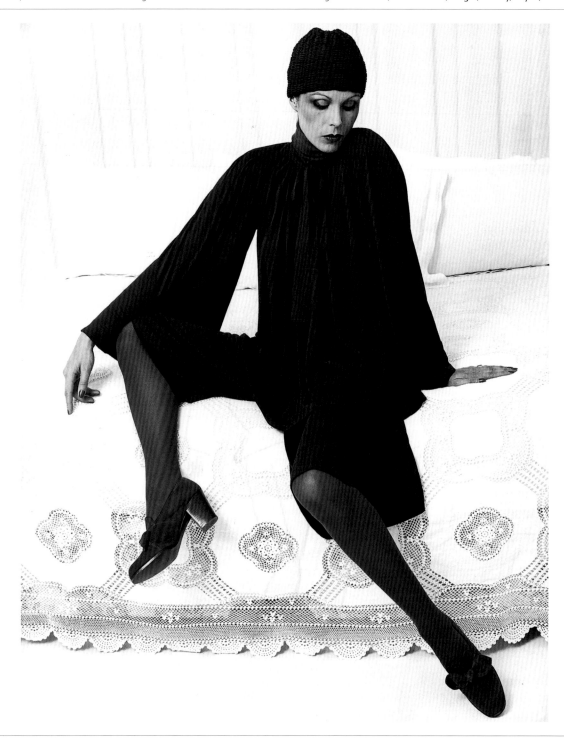

338

Jean Muir. b London (UK), 1933. d London (UK), 1995. **Joanna Lumley wears jersey tunic and culottes, Jean Muir's apartment.** Photograph by Michael Barrett, 1975.

Munkacsi Martin   Photographer

With her head high and arms swinging, Martin Munkacsi's subject is the personification of fashion liberation as she strides from the shadows into sunshine. Her bias-cut dress, blurred and flowing in the wake of her motion, moves with her body rather than restraining it. It is free of any detail that will date it and the sash is carelessly tied around her natural waist. It is this real-life spirit of spontaneity which Munkacsi brought to fashion photography when he joined *Harper's Bazaar* in 1932, encouraged by his mentor Alexey Brodovitch. As well as showing clothes in motion, thereby better describing the real potential of fabric once it is placed on the body, he shot fashion from new angles, giving the impression of a scene snapped rather than posed. Munkacsi's subjects always had a purpose beyond being a beautiful clothes horse, whether they were running on the beach or, as is shown here, enjoying an unaccompanied evening stroll.

☛ Brodovitch, Burrows, de Meyer, Snow

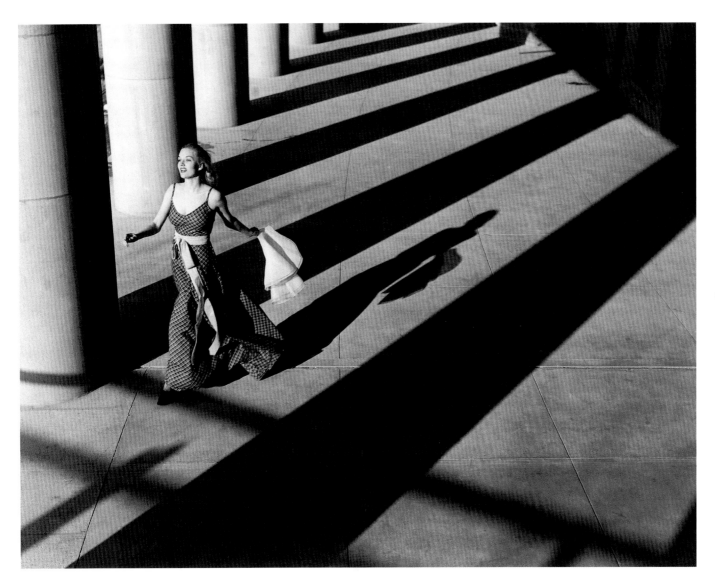

Martin Munkacsi. **b** Cluj (ROM), 1896. **d** New York (USA), 1963. **Marion Davies, San Simeon, California.** *Harper's Bazaar*, 1934.

Nars François

Make-up artist

Made-up and photographed by François Nars, model Karen Elson wears his signature make-up. Nars uses dense pigments to create rich blocks of colour. Against a snowy base, he isolates the eyes and lips with a striking, abstract method. 'The runway is my sketchpad,' says Nars who, like Bobbi Brown and Frank Toskan, belongs to a circle of directional make-up artists who have created signature make-up lines. For them, the catwalk is a public laboratory on which new directions are born. His company was formed on the catwalks of Versace, Dolce & Gabbana and Karl Lagerfeld, in his vivid Technicolor schemes that became the blueprint for each seasonal look. His work draws inspiration from old movies, exotic places and characters such as King Kong. Amongst his lines are a dark chocolate lipstick formulated to match the colour of the giant ape's fur, and Schiap, an exact match of Elsa Schiaparelli's classic shocking pink.

☛ Dolce & Gabbana, Lutens, Schiaparelli, Toskan

340

François Nars. b Biarritz (FR). (Active 1980s–) Karen Elson. Photograph by François Nars, 1997.

Nast Condé   Publisher

In one sideways glance, the Countess Divonne makes the first-ever photographic cover of *Vogue*. Her romantic pose and its artful styling preceded today's charismatic fashion covers. Following his 1909 purchase of *Vogue*, Condé Nast's transformation of the American social magazine into a high-class fashion glossy heralded a new era in international magazine publishing – starting with Baron de Meyer becoming the first full-time fashion photographer in 1914. With his editor, Edna Woolman Chase, Condé Nast exerted strict control at *Vogue*, and gave Carmel Snow and Alexander Liberman their first glimpse of fashion editorship and art direction respectively. Such a controlling policy did not always work: it fuelled Diana Vreeland's sacking in the 1960s, and caused *Harper's Bazaar* to poach de Meyer in 1921. Nast then hired Edward Steichen, Cecil Beaton and Harper's Christian Bérard, sparking a long-standing feud.

☛ **Liberman, de Meyer, Snow, Steichen, Tappé**

Condé Nast. **b** Montrose, CO (USA), 1873. **d** New York (USA), 1942. **First Vogue cover.** Photograph by Harry McVickar, 1893.

Newton Helmut   Photographer

The Scandinavian model Vibéké wears a superlative pinstriped suit and crepe-de-chine blouse by Yves Saint Laurent. Shot at night on a Parisian street, her hair is slicked to her head in the sexually ambiguous manner of Garbo and Dietrich, and she holds the cigarette as a man would. It is a scene conjured by Helmut Newton, whose work is always charged with sexual themes.

Preferring statuesque, Teutonic women, he places his subjects on the line between pornography and fashion photography – this is a tame, but nonetheless powerful example of Newton's work. Lesbian sex, breasts bared from behind a mink coat and the palpable suggestion of bondage are a few of the themes used by him in his depiction of fashion. His employment

of ring-flash photography lends a menacing mood to his scenarios, which have inspired debate for decades: does he objectify women, or doeshe invest them with a superhuman power?

☞ **Matsushima, Palmers, Saint Laurent, Teller**

342

Helmut Newton. b Berlin (GER), 1920. **d** Los Angeles (USA), 2004. **Tailored Yves Saint Laurent suit.** French *Vogue*, 1975.

Norell Norman   Designer

Propriety, the Norell hallmark, was never more evident than when all-over sequins, verging on the vulgar, were tamed by his application of them on to a gown of classic lines. An added layer of shimmer, perhaps an evening sweater, was justified as being warm protection for the shoulders on a wintry or Second World War night. From joining Hattie Carnegie in 1928 until his death in 1972,

Norell was an important figure in American fashion design and his work personified New York style. Norell's success resided in his simple silhouettes and pragmatism in the fickle world of late-day and evening dresses. With wool jersey dresses for evening, beaded sweaters matched to evening dresses and, later, trouser suits, Norell applied the ethos of sportswear to more formal

times of day. His uncanny capacity was to foster a comfortable, easy glamour which he achieved chiefly through an enduring fix on the 1920s.

☞ Carnegie, Ley, Mackie, Parker

Norman Norell. b Noblesville, IN (USA), 1900. d New York (USA), 1972. **Suzy Parker wears a red sequined dress.** Photograph by Milton H. Greene, 1952.

Nutter Tommy   Tailor

Mick Jagger marries Bianca Perez Moreno de Macias at the town hall in St Tropez in 1971. He wears a suit by Tommy Nutter, the man who opened the doors of Savile Row to a new generation (and also cut both John Lennon's and Yoko Ono's wedding suits). After studying architecture, he had answered an advertisement for a salesman at the Savile Row tailors G. Ward and Co.

In 1969 he opened Nutters in Savile Row. His three-piece suits were styled with narrow, square shoulders, wide lapels, tight waists, tightly crotched flared trousers, and waistcoats. Charming and shy, Nutter was a frontman for the company which, employing master cutters and tailors, made the Savile Row bespoke suitfashionable again. In 1976 he left the company and joined tailors

Kilgour French and Stanbury. He is still remembered with affection and respect by the tailors of Savile Row. 'He was a modern stylist,' said one. 'He brought fashion here.'

☛ Beatles, Fish, Gilbey, R. James, Liberty, T. Roberts

344

Tommy Nutter. b London (UK), 1942. d London (UK), 1992. **Mick and Bianca Jagger on their wedding day, St Tropez, 1971.**

Oldfield Bruce   Designer

Bruce Oldfield reclines next to his black silk crepe evening dress. The bodice is ruched with gold lamé and the mannequin wears shoes by Charles Jourdan; together they present a collaboration of deluxe fantasy. Oldfield once claimed, 'I can make any woman look better. That's what I do'. His starry clientele has ranged from aristocrats to soap queens; the Princess of Wales to Joan Collins.

The glamour could hardly be further removed from Oldfield's childhood in a Dr Barnardo's home. His foster mother was a seamstress and it was from her that Oldfield first developed his interest in fashion. He presented his first collection in London in 1975. His shop opened in 1984, attracting a strong following from the 'ladies who lunch'. Suzy Menkes, who selected his design as the Dress of the Year in 1985, praised 'his skills as a dressmaker, his belief in cut, line and silhouette, his standards of workmanship and his conception of women'.

☛ Diana, Jourdan, Price

345

Bruce Oldfield. b London (UK), 1950. Bruce Oldfield with a gold lamé and black silk crepe dress. Winner of the Bath Museum of Costume's 'Dress of the Year', 1985. Photograph by Nick Briggs.

Oldham Todd   Designer

Todd Oldham sits with one of fashion's more exotic muses – his grandmother Mildred Jasper. 'Granny's always been a huge inspiration to me. She does exactly what she wants, with great irreverence.' In this sitting for *Harper's Bazaar*, Mildred wears Oldham's hot pink, quilted satin jacket which comes close to being a boudoir robe. His family have long been connected to his career, which began at the age of fifteen when he turned a K-Mart pillowcase into a sun dress for his sister. Oldham always risks kitsch to achieve his distinctive style. Quirky colour combinations and textures are used for his down-home Texas style of flash and panache. His denim and bikinis are fringed, his midriffs bared and his skirts invariably short. Oldham creates a kaleidoscope of decorative pastiche for his own collection and, to a slightly lesser extent, for Escada, a label for whom he became a consultant in 1994.

☛ Eisen, Ley, Mackie, Mizrahi, de Ribes

346

Todd Oldham. b Corpus Christi, TX (USA), 1961. **Todd Oldham and grandmother.** Photograph by Gus van Sant, *Harper's Bazaar*, 1997.

Orry-Kelly

Designer

Orry-Kelly's hand-sewn, decorative costumes made him one of Hollywood's great designers, alongside Travis Banton and Adrian. On his first Hollywood movie, Orry-Kelly worked with Bette Davis and they formed a partnership that was to last for fourteen years. Orry-Kelly understood Davis's need for the drama in her wardrobe to match, but not overshadow, that of her on-screen acting.

They only fell out once when the studio insisted she be glamorized for *Fashions* of 1934, which she hated. The life and soul of many showbiz parties, Orry-Kelly was also a prima donna and an alcoholic. But his time with Warner Brothers ended on a high note after he dressed Ingrid Bergman in simple classics for *Casablanca*, before being drafted into the army. He later freelanced, winning

Oscars for Marilyn Monroe's sexy glamour in *Some Like it Hot* and Leslie Caron's colourful costumes in *An American in Paris*.

☛ Adrian, Banton, Mackie, Stern

Orry-Kelly (John Kelley). b Kiama (ASL), 1897. d 1964. **Marilyn Monroe wears diaphanous beaded dress.** Still from *Some Like it Hot*. 1959.

Oudejans Marie-Anne

Designer

Each season, Marie-Anne Oudejans produces dresses in just a few simple shapes but in many different fabrics and colours. The story of her label, Tocca, is similar to that of Lilly Pulitzer who, in the 1960s, became famous for her printed dresses. Oudejans was originally a stylist who wore her own little cotton dresses on fashion shoots; the supermodels who saw them begged for their own copies. Claudia Schiffer, Helena Christensen (pictured here) and Naomi Campbell were photographed wearing the dresses and customers started calling stores trying to find out how to buy them. 'It became a fashion by chance,' says Oudejans. Her dresses are unapologetically pretty and are cut from cotton or silk sari fabrics. Each season there are just a few styles to choose from, but many fabrics and colourways. Trimmed with broderie anglaise and sold in soft candy colours, they have a girlish quality that sits apart from mainstream fashion.

☞ Dinnigan, Mazzilli, Pulitzer, Williamson

348

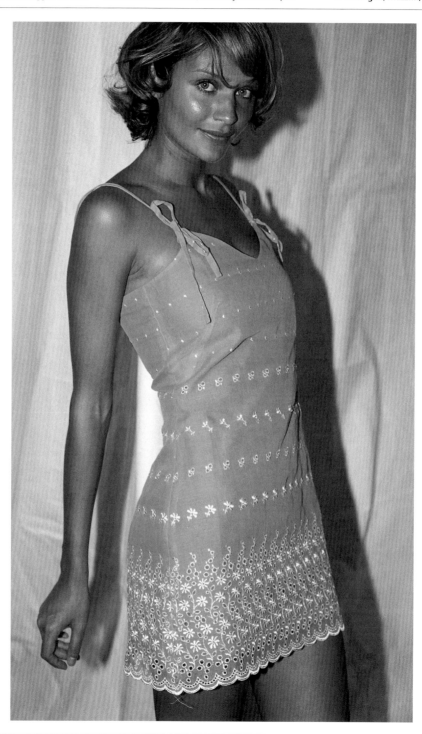

Marie-Anne Oudejans. b (NL), 1964. Helena Christensen wears a pink embroidered dress. Photograph by Niall McInerney, 1994.

Ozbek Rifat

Designer

Rifat Ozbek visited North Africa, India and his own Turkish roots for this eclectic, delicate outfit. A gauze cardigan is heavily braided and trimmed with cording. Underneath, a dress is embroidered with flowers, the raised waistband dotted with silver beads. Since setting up his own label in 1984, Ozbek has been inspired by the clothing and decoration of a variety of cultures, from American Indian and South African Ndebele to Eastern European gypsy and Haitian voodoo. Having been brought up in Britain, Ozbek worked with the seminal 1970s designer Walter Albini in Italy, before moving back to London to work for Monsoon, a chain store that specializes in designs manufactured in Indian fabrics. He has been heavily influenced by London street fashion.

Before moving his business to Milan in 1991, Ozbek designed his New Age collection. Using white and silver, it revealed a new-found purity in his work.

☛ **Abboud, Albini, Bowery, Hendrix**

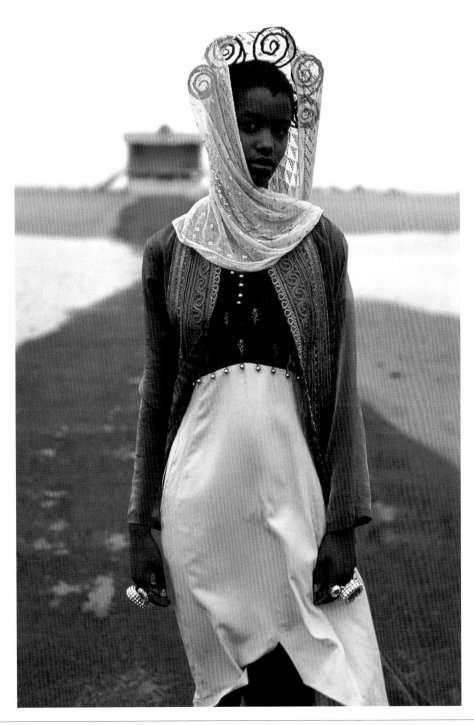

Rifat Ozbek. b Istanbul (TUR), 1953. **Embroidered jacket and dress.** Photograph by Gilles Bensimon, British *Elle*, 1989.

Page Dick

Make-up artist

Model Annie Morton sits in her apartment bare-faced and with dishevelled hair. The image is deshabille in the extreme. Make-up artist Dick Page did nothing to disturb her early morning beauty. Using this pre-shoot image, he contests the idea of what constitutes beauty, saying, 'There is no such thing as natural make-up. As soon as there is make-up on the face it is not natural'. This is the key to Page's ethos. While effecting transformations by giving skin a shiny surface, he rejects further artificiality and won't use make-up that regulates and reduces women to a uniform beauty – on one occasion even leaving spots as an 'undeniable part of the woman underneath'. Page's iconoclastic methods are unique in a business that is designed to sell make-up. However, he was a champion of the 'greasy, glossy' direction of make-up in the 1990s, a movement that, bizarrely, accelerated the sale of make-up.

☞ Brown, Day, Lutens

350

Dick Page.̓ b Gosport (UK), 1964. **Annie Morton in her apartment.** 1996.

Paley Babe

Icon

Babe Paley liked to look flawless; her clothes – twinsets, to-the-knee skirts and crisp blouses – always had to be just so. Here she decorates an exacting two-tone dress with an armful of costume jewellery in the style of another paragon of personal style, Coco Chanel. Truman Capote commented, 'Babe Paley only had one fault: she was perfect; otherwise, she was perfect.' Another friend, the socialite Slim Keith, called her style 'perfection in an era of casual convenience'. Paley was born Barbara Cushing into a middle-class family, with two elder sisters. All of the Cushing girls were trained by their socialite mother to snare wealthy husbands, which they did. Babe's second marriage was to Bill Paley, chairman of CBS. As a fashion editor of American *Vogue* in the 1940s, she was an arbiter of style and appeared in America's best-dressed list fourteen times. Her look is best described as effortless chic, achieved at great effort.

☛ Chanel, Lane, Parker

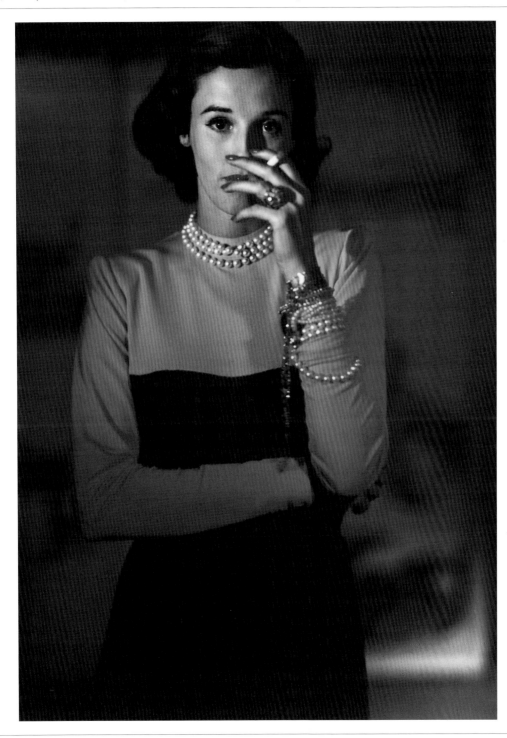

Barbara Paley. **b** Boston (USA), 1915. **d** New York (USA), 1978. **Babe Paley.** Photograph by Horst P. Horst, American *Vogue*, 1946.

Palmers Walter and Wolff Reinhold (Wolford) Hosiery designers

Nadja Auermann wears a pair of semi-opaque tights which were specially created for this photograph. In her right hand she holds a Polaroid, the chosen film of a voyeur, of herself in provocative pose. The Wolford company, founded by Walter Palmers and Wolff Reinhold operates from the small Austrian town of Bregenz, and creates four collections of hosiery and bodywear every year. For its 1996 advertising campaign to promote no-seam, 'second-skin' tights (which took four years to develop), Wolford chose photographer Helmut Newton, who places his subjects in a steely sexual context. Wolford has been associated with hosiery since 1949. The patronage of Vivienne Westwood, Helmut Lang, Christian Lacroix and Alexander McQueen, as well as devoted, style-conscious women around the world, has elevated Wolford to its position as the preferred hosiery of the fashion industry.

☞ Lang, Newton, Westwood

352

Walter Palmers. b Vienna (AUS), 1903. d Vienna (AUS), 1983. Reinhold Wolff. b Hard (AUS), 1905. d Hard (AUS), 1972. (Wolford.) 'Fatal Neon' tights. Photograph by Helmut Newton, 1996.

Paquin Jeanne Designer

It is five o'clock and Mme Paquin's salon is crowded with *vendeuses* (without hats) showing clients (with hats) bolts of fabric from which they will order their dresses. At the centre of the room one models a fur-trimmed gown for two ladies, one of whom is examining the embroidery on its skirt. Mme Paquin founded her own maison de couture in 1891. She was appointed

President of the Fashion Section of the Paris Exposition Universelle of 1900 and promoted spectacular displays of fur. It was from this time that fur appeared as a trimming or accessory in the collections of leading couturiers. Mme Paquin also made exotic and brilliantly coloured garments, blending her superb tailoring with drapery inspired by Iribe and Bakst. As soignée as her models,

Mme Paquin was the first couturière to achieve international fame, establishing further couture salons in London, Buenos Aires and Madrid.

☞ Boué, Dinnigan, Gibson, Redfern, Rouff, Van Cleef

353

Parker Suzy   Model

One hand holding a cigarette, the other thrown behind her head – both bear witness to Suzy Parker's reputation as someone who could never sit still. With high cheekbones, green eyes and red-gold hair, she became the most famous model of her generation, photographed extensively by, among others, Horst and Richard Avedon. It was while watching her sister Dorian Leigh model for Irving Penn in 1947 that Suzy was first discovered. Later she was taken on as the face of Revlon and of Chanel No. 5 (Coco Chanel became her friend and godmother to her daughter Georgia), before she set about becoming one of the MTAs (model turned actress). Although Suzy secretly married the playboy journalist Pierre de La Salle in 1955, it did not last and she later married the actor Bradford Dillman, for whom she put her modelling career aside for marriage and motherhood.

☛ Avedon, Bassman, Chanel, Horst, Norell

Suzanne (Suzy) Parker. b Long Island City, NY (USA), 1932. **d** Montecito, CA (USA), 2003. **Suzy Parker.** Photograph by Lillian Bassman, *Harper's Bazaar*, 1963.

Parkinson Norman Photographer

Norman Parkinson evokes the breathtaking thrill of Paris first seen from the air in this editorial picture taken in 1960. He was a realist who took fashion photography outdoors. After the Second World War, he embarked upon a successful career in fashion photography for *Vogue*, pioneering the use of colour. Parkinson had a feeling for the essentials of fashion, to which he brought great urbanity, charm and sophisticated wit. In colour and composition, his fashion photographs have often been compared to the paintings of John Singer Sargent. He was the official photographer for the wedding of Princess Anne and Captain Mark Phillips in 1973 and photographed the Queen Mother on her eightieth birthday in 1980. His wife, Wenda Parkinson, was a celebrated fashion model, whom he often photographed. Together they brought the new cosmopolitan spirit of intercontinental jet travel to the pages of *Vogue*.

☛ Fratini, Kelly, Levine, Stiebel, Winston

355

Norman Parkinson. **b** London (UK), 1913. **d** Singapore (SING), 1990. **Flying over Paris**. *Queen*, 1960.

Patou Jean Designer

Jean Patou's dress is influenced by two art movements: Art Deco and Cubism. Purity of line, a key element of Art Deco, was the hallmark of Patou's style. He also took inspiration from Cubism, creating sharp, geometric shapes and patterns in his fabrics. He worked closely with the textile firm Bianchini-Férier (where Raoul Dufy was under contract in the 1920s), in his search for materials that would best adapt to his design philosophy of simplicity and a streamlined, uncluttered silhouette. His long-waisted dresses with their luxurious designs were constantly described in the fashion magazines of the time as 'chic' and were worn by actresses such as Louise Brooks, Constance Bennett and Mary Pickford. Long strings of pearls and fur-trimmed coats added embellishment and also enhanced Patou's precision of cut. Tennis player Suzanne Lenglen was also dressed by Patou, setting a fashion for sleeveless jumpers.

☛ Abbe, Benito, Bohan, Eric, Frizon, Lacroix, Lanvin

Jean Patou. b Normandy (FR), 1887. **d** Paris (FR), 1936. **Sequined dress.** c1927.

Paulette

Milliner

Lush silk roses adorn the brim of a summer hat by Paulette, who was one of France's leading milliners for thirty years. She began creating hats in 1921, and set up her own millinery salon in 1939 at the start of the Second World War. These straitened circumstances were to bring out her most creative talents, just as Ferragamo was forced to experiment with plastics. Paulette reinvented the turban, which became a symbol of wartime practicality, by accident. When cycling she would wrap her head, a simple solution that turned into the biggest fashion for a decade. The theme developed, with draped veils and fabric often featuring in her work. Paulette went on to create work for Chanel, Pierre Cardin, Ungaro, Mugler and Laroche, demonstrating the versatility and wide-ranging appeal of her designs – helped by Philippe Model, who trained with her.

☞ **W. Klein, Laroche, Model, Mugler, Talbot, Ungaro**

Paulette (Paulette de la Bruyère). **b** Le Tours (FR), c1900. **d** (FR), 1984. **Barbara Mullen wears hat decorated with roses.** Photograph by William Klein, 1956.

Paulin Guy   Designer

In 1987 the baby-doll grew up in the hands of Guy Paulin. The pin-tucked, big-pocketed, girlish style becomes womanly with its floral print reduced to a few scattered petals. An admirer of Claire McCardell, Guy Paulin's easy-going, vibrant style consciously blended office formality with the no-nonsense detailing of American sportswear. Fired by a two-year training with Jacqueline Jacobson at Dorothée Bis, he took his passion for knitting to New York in 1968, where he shared rails with Mary Quant and Emmanuelle Khanh at the boutique chain Paraphernalia. Having freelanced for MaxMara, he replaced Karl Lagerfeld as designer at Chloé in 1983. Paulin had a reputation for pleasing women with his brand of French chic and his intention was always to create clothes that would boost the wearer's self-esteem.

☛ Jacobson, Khanh, Lagerfeld, Lenoir, Maramotti

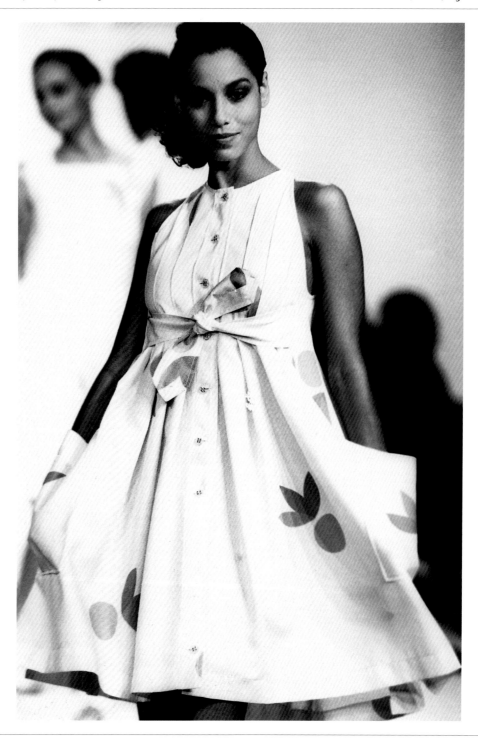

Guy Paulin. **b** Lorraine (FR), 1945. **d** Paris (FR), 1990. **Baby-doll dress**. *Women's Wear Daily*, 1988.

Mr Pearl

Designer

A child wears a garment designed to reduce an adult's circumference to that of a child. It is the highly crafted work of Mr Pearl, the man who made the corset a fashion item. Called the best corsetier in the world by Vivienne Westwood, he is famous for his own corseted eighteen-inch waist. Pearl left South Africa in the early 1980s for London and the costume department at the Royal Opera House, where his interest in the art of corsetry was aroused. His great-grandmother had been a fashionable dressmaker in the *belle époque* and he was inspired by photographs of the clothes she had made: 'The world used to be a more interesting place visually and I wanted to bring some of that visual stimulus back.' Pearl has worked on collections for Thierry Mugler, a designer famous for perfecting the hourglass silhouette. His work has also appeared on the catwalks of Christian Lacroix, John Galliano and Alexander McQueen.

☛ Berardi, S. Ellis, Galliano, Lacroix, McQueen, Mugler

Mr Pearl (Mark Erskine-Pullen). b (UK). (Active 1990s-.) **Black beaded corset.** Photograph by Sean Ellis, *The Face*, 1996.

Penn Irving

Photographer

Model Jean Patchett becomes an exercise in graphic perfection under the lens of a photographer whose work defined haute couture in the 1950s. The power and simplicity of Irving Penn's work made him the Balenciaga of fashion photography – a designer whose work was often shot by Penn. It has a natural solemnity which invests his subjects – a model, a still-life or even a sleeve – with a regal presence. Penn said, 'The camera is just a tool, like a wrench. But the situation itself is magical. I stand in awe of it.' Penn's black-and-white photography of the 1940s and 1950s captured the grandeur and drama of haute couture just before its pre-eminence was about to be threatened by the power of ready-to-wear. Of couture, Penn said, 'When I am working with the haute couture I think again and again of the beauty of women and the magic of Paris.'

☛ **Brodovitch, Dovima, Fonssagrives, Vreeland**

Irving Penn. b Plainfield, NJ (USA), 1917. **Jean Patchett.** Photograph by Irving Penn, American *Vogue*, 1950.

360

Peretti Elsa   Jewellery designer

Like so many of Elsa Peretti's designs, this apparently molten silver cuff, with its smooth, tactile lines, was inspired by her love of organic forms; in this case, the irregular contours of bones. A renowned craftswoman, Peretti creates jewellery and home accessories with a unique rhythmic sense of the natural world. She seizes the figurative essence of something as simple as a bean or a teardrop and translates it into a beautiful, sculptural, timeless piece of body art. She presented her inaugural pieces alongside Giorgio di Sant'Angelo's collection in 1969 and later designed for Halston. Her other designs, sold by Tiffany & Co, have included the famous Peretti 'Open Heart' pendant and 'Diamonds by the Yard' – a simple chain interspersed with diamonds which became a classic worn by Liza Minnelli in the 1970s and in the 1990s by Naomi Campbell, who threads hers through her navel ring.

☛ **Halston, Hiro, di Sant'Angelo, Tiffany, Warhol**

Elsa Peretti. **b** Florence (IT), 1940. **Silver 'bone cuff'.** Photograph by Hiro, 1989.

Perint Palmer Gladys

Illustrator

With its deft pen strokes and blocks of pastel colour, Gladys Perint Palmer's simple catwalk illustration resonates with fluidity and movement, accurately capturing not only Yves Saint Laurent's couture gypsy but also the women watching her. Like a cartoonist, Perint Palmer's work gives a humorous insight into the catwalk world. Subtle exaggerations, such as the model's extended neck which creates an imperious air, are just one step removed from reality. The close attention of Chanel's former model Inès de la Fressange, wearing a red jacket in the foreground, adds to an ambience that only a camera can record faithfully. Each picture is a microcosm of a show, illustrating the spirit of a collection and that of the spectators. Perint Palmer belongs to a tradition which is as old as fashion presentations. Sketch artists were once the only way for collections to reach the wider public before the clothes did.

☛ Chanel, Saint Laurent, Vertès

Gladys Perint Palmer. b Budapest (HUN), 1947. **Yves Saint Laurent catwalk show, 1992.**

Pertegaz Manuel   Designer

Henry Clarke's great attribute as a fashion photographer was his precision in defining a fashionable image, showing here how this haute couture coat was cut and how it hung. He has made the brilliantly tiled walls of the Villa Rosa, an elegant Madrid restaurant, the perfect backdrop for Manuel Pertegaz's vivid green, paper taffeta evening coat. Falling to mid-calf, it has an oval-necked shoulder yoke and three tie-fastenings. The most distinctive feature is its tent shape, flaring widely from the shoulders. One of the great Spanish fashion designers, Pertegaz earned a reputation for formal designs in the grand manner from his start in the early 1940s. The tent silhouette was first launched in 1951 by Pertegaz's compatriot, Balenciaga. Together they built up Spain's reputation for couture. In 1968 Pertegaz opened his Madrid boutique, selling couture, and in the 1970s launched a ready-to-wear collection.

☛ **Balenciaga, Clarke, Grès, Saint Laurent**

Manuel Pertegaz. b Aragon (SP), 1918. **Green taffeta evening coat.** Photograph by Henry Clarke, British *Vogue*, 1954.

Perugia André   Shoe designer

This decorative boot, based on turn-of-the-century spats, was the perfect complement to the attention-grabbing designs of Elsa Schiaparelli. Schiaparelli was a brilliant colourist. Shocking pink, which she made the predominant colour in the world of fashion in the late 1930s and throughout the 1940s, was her famous trademark. The sheer expanse of the surface of this boot, in black suede with a pink platform, enabled André Perugia to capture the essence of fantasy that was so much in accord with Schiaparelli's own creations. Despite its size, the boot was easy to walk in. Perugia understood balance, scale and the engineering of footwear, having been an apprentice at his father's shoe business in Nice prior to opening his own shop there when he was only sixteen. In 1920, he established his own salon in Paris. Perugia also designed footwear for Poiret, Fath and Givenchy, as well as Schiaparelli.

☛ Fath, Jourdan, Poiret, Schiaparelli, Talbot, Windsor

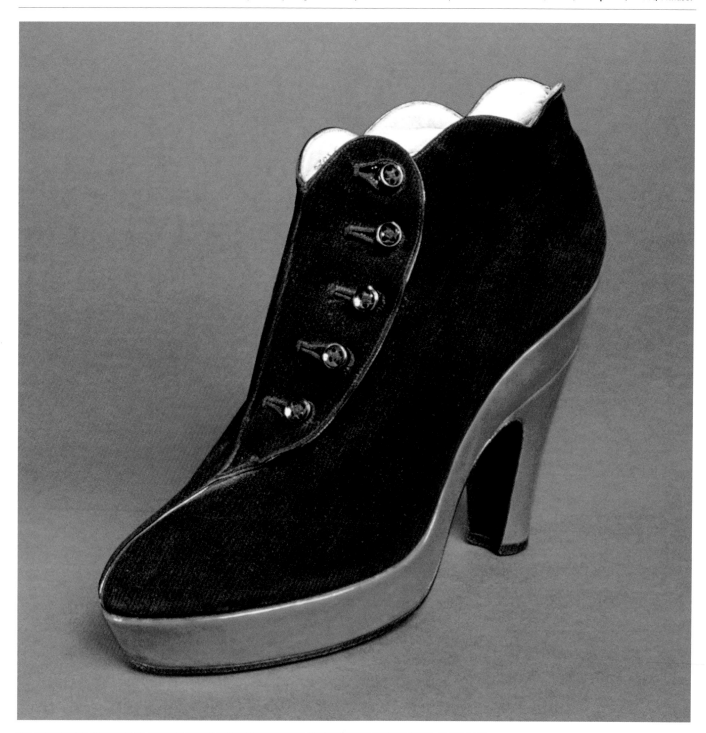

André Perugia. b (FR), 1893. d Cannes (FR), 1977. Buttoned boot with scalloped edging for Elsa Schiaparelli. 1939.

364

Pfister Andrea   Shoe designer

With 'Martini dry', a sunshine yellow sandal, Andrea Pfister evokes the cocktail culture of the mid-1970s. Its heel is shaped to resemble a martini glass embellished with a slice of lemon; a surreal object which demands attention. Pfister treats his shoes as a centrepiece rather than a distant accessory, and the foot, for him, is the start of the human body rather than its end. In 1964, having trained as an art historian, he moved to Paris where he designed footwear collections for Jean Patou and Lanvin. He moved on to design his own collections which became known for their humour. Pfister has appliquéd snakeskin penguins to the side of a boot, decorated the heel of a wedged mule with a three-dimensional frolicking sea lion and wrapped a black suede boot with clasping hands. The tradition of fantasy footwear in the twentieth century remained vigorous; from Perugia's pink platforms to Pfister's leather martini glass.

☛ **Ferragamo, Lanvin, Louboutin, Patou**

Andrea Pfister. b Pesaro (IT), 1942. **'Martini dry' kid sandal.** Photograph by Joël Garnier, 1975.

Piguet Robert　Designer

Horst has photographed Robert Piguet's outfit in a Surrealist manner. At first glance, we see the sitter wearing a well-cut bodice with the emphasis focused on the white sleeve. Miss Zelensky's other sleeve becomes a shadow, together with her Tyrolean hat and skirt. Horst has created an illusion for the designer. Having trained with Redfern and Poiret, Piguet understood the decorative importance of the hat, and has used it here as a witty punctuation mark to his garment. Piguet's work was admired for its uncluttered yet flamboyant shapes, an element greatly supported by contributions from talented freelance designers, including Dior and Balmain before the Second World War and Bohan after. Here, it is represented by the sleeve with its head raised to meet Miss Zelensky's cheekbone. The purity of Piguet's outfit is simplified further by Horst's impeccable style.

☞ Balmain, Bassman, Bohan, Castillo, Galanos, Horst

366

Robert Piguet. **b** Yvedon (FR), 1901. **d** Paris (FR), 1953. **Doris Zelensky wears puff-sleeved jacket.** Photograph by Horst P. Horst, 1936.

Pinet François   Shoe designer

The dainty flower design and distinctive Louis heel of this delicate, white satin boot – a finer version of the lowish, wasp-waisted heel worn in the reign of King Louis XV of France – are typical of the designs by the French shoemaking firm, Pinet. Established in 1855 by François Pinet, the Paris company soon became known for creating elegant footwear for the most fashionable members of society, shoes that would be worn underneath the grand gowns by Charles Worth. Shoemaking was a family concern for Pinet; he had learnt his craft from his father and, when he retired in the early years of the twentieth century, his son took over and continued to expand the firm, opening shops in Nice and London. Roger Vivier later supplied designs to this prestigious firm, which has become known for demonstrably expensive shoes, such as women's court shoes entirely covered with rhinestones and animal skin footwear for men.

☛ Hope, Pingat, Vivier, Worth, Yantorny

François Pinet. **b** Château-le-Vaillère (FR), 1817. **d** (FR), 1897. **Women's embroidered boot, 1867.** Photograph by Elisabeth Eylieu.

Pingat Emile   Designer

This navy faille day dress from the 1870s, with its frills, ruching and cut velvet bodice, recalls the grandeur of Emile Pingat's work. He was a contemporary of Charles Frederick Worth, the father of haute couture. They were rival couturiers, with their names mentioned together in the guidebooks for female tourists visiting Paris in the second half of the nineteenth century. His own fashion house flourished from 1860 to 1896. He was known pre-eminently as a couturier who created fashions of delicate contrasts and for a perfect harmony of proportion, evocative of the current ideal of femininity. His striking ball gowns captured the fantasy and romance of the great festive occasions in Paris during the Second Empire and the Third Republic. Together with Worth, his creations reflected the fashionable silhouette and aesthetic of the Parisian world of haute couture from the mid- to the late nineteenth century.

☛ Pinet, Reboux, Worth

368

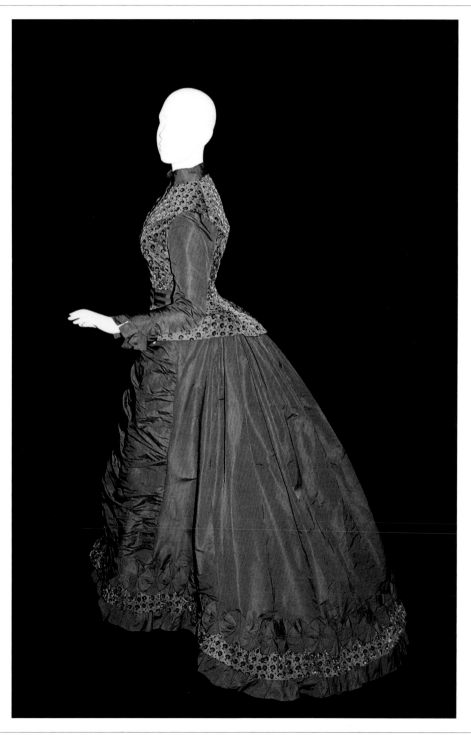

Emile Pingat. b (FR). (Active 1860s–1900s.) **Blue faille and silk velvet day dress.** 1870s.

Pipart Gérard Designer

Arlette Ricci, granddaughter of the couturière Nina, wears a luxurious astrakhan coat cinched with an elastic belt, an ironic conceit that displays modern use of a deluxe garment. It is the work of Gérard Pipart for the house of Nina Ricci, once described as a 'never too haute' designer. Pipart joined the house in 1964 after the departure of Jules-François Crahay. His education had been conducted in the houses of the great couturiers Balmain, Fath, Patou and Givenchy; consequently he creates simple Parisian chic rather than chasing seasonal trends. Pipart is also true to the tradition of maintaining 'house' styles, those which women can order each season with few alterations beyond a change of fabric. He never learned to cut fabric so he is unusual in working from precise drawings and making amendments straight onto the toiles. Pipart's style is one of conservative beauty that eschews gimmickry.

☞ Balmain, Crahay, Fath, Givenchy, Patou, Ricci

Gérard Pipart. b Paris (FR), 1933. **Arlette Ricci wears belted astrakhan coat for Nina Ricci.** Photograph by Peter Knapp, 1976.

Pita Orlando

Hairdresser

Model Shalom Harlow's hairstyle accurately reflects Orlando Pita's aesthetic approach. While creativity and subversion are critical elements of his vision, beauty still remains a priority. 'A hairstyle may be stunning, but I will have failed if it doesn't make a woman beautiful,' says Pita. This photograph displays his signature ethnic style, which was seen in the form of Hasidic *payos* on the Jean-Paul Gaultier catwalk and African-American braidings in videos for Madonna, one of his most loyal clients. Pita finds an ideal ground for experimentation in the diva, who allows him to break away from all stereotypes. 'There's no room for fantasy in the salon,' he says when asked why he concentrates on editorials and catwalk shows. Pita, who vehemently resists shampooing hair in the belief that its own sebaceous secretions have a natural cleansing function, has admittedly even used toilet rolls as curlers to achieve some of his Surrealist styles.

☛ Gaultier, McKnight, Madonna

370

Orlando Pita. b Havana (CU), 1962. **Shalom Harlow.** Photograph by Mario Testino, *Harper's Bazaar*, 1994.

Platt Lynes George

With her face turned away from George Platt Lynes' camera, the reclining figure presents herself as a living model in an art gallery setting. The drape of her crepe-de-chine dress mirrors that on the dress of her companion and the wavy print snaking along her body is a reminder of that fabric's propensity for liquid movement. These gowns, by Gilbert Adrian, are presented as vaguely Surreal *objets* by a photographer who followed that movement, explored during a friendship with Jean Cocteau. Platt Lynes started to publish his fashion work in *Town* and *Harper's Bazaar* in 1933 and became director of *Vogue*'s Hollywood studio in 1942. His later life was spent photographing male nudes (Platt Lynes was a charismatic, openly gay member of New York's artistic community). These, it is said, set precedents for the work of Herb Ritts and Bruce Weber, who apply simplicity and the artistic merit of a sinewy male physique to their work.

☞ **Adrian, Ritts, Weber**

George Platt Lynes. **b** NJ (USA), 1907. **d** New York (USA), 1955. **Adrian's 'Magic' draped silk dresses.** British *Vogue*, 1947.

Poiret Paul

Designer

The scope of Paul Poiret, 'The Sultan of Fashion', is illustrated in this line-up of models influenced by the Ballets Russes. In 1909 he introduced a fluid style of dress, inspired by the French *Directoire* and orientalism but also the sumptuous splendour in which he lived and worked. He gave fashion a theatrical spin by throwing lavish fêtes at his maison de couture, where the beau monde of Paris would wear Poiret-designed costumes – which became fashion overnight. He added a new dimension to fashion by parading his mannequins in the gardens of his house, at racecourses and on tours of Europe and the United States. Poiret opened his own salon after serving an apprenticeship under Doucet and working for Worth. He was one of the most creative fashion designers of the twentieth century, revolutionizing fashion design, reviving fashion illustration, establishing a school for the decorative arts and even diversifying into perfume.

☛ Bakst, Barbier, Brunelleschi, Erté, Iribe, Lepape

372

Paul Poiret. **b** Paris (FR), 1879. **d** Paris (FR), 1944. **Poiret's mannequins.** *L'Illustration*, 1910.

Pollock Alice Designer

The model sweeps down the catwalk in Pollock's crepe evening dress. Unadorned but for neat front buttoning, the design combines simplicity with femininity in keeping with the avant-garde of the 1960s. Challenging convention, Pollock created fluid and comfortable eveningwear. She opened Quorum, a wholesale and boutique business in London's King's Road, becoming the first to employ Ossie Clark, a stalwart of the 1960s Chelsea scene. Their designs often used fabrics designed by Celia Birtwell, Clark's wife. Together they produced clothes renowned for their sensuality – evident in deep necklines and wasp waists and in their luxurious trademark fabrics of crepe, chiffon, satin and close-fitting jersey. More than a designer, Pollock was an iconoclastic force in Britain's emerging fashion world who encouraged Clark and Birtwell, amongst others, to 'do their thing'.

☛ Birtwell, Clark, Jackson, Porter

Alice Pollock. b (UK), 1942. **White crepe dress.** Photograph by Annette Green, British *Vogue*, 1970.

Porter Thea

Designer

A printed voile headdress is weighted down with gold embroidery and bugle beads. Under it the model wears exotic make-up; kohl applied inside the lower lid, emerald eye shadow and ruby nail varnish. Her caftan top is made from a patchwork of rough Madras cotton and co-ordinating, semi-sheer voile. It all evokes the mixture of Middle Eastern influences that surrounded Thea Porter as she grew up in Damascus and later in Beirut. Porter took her international style to London's Soho in the 1960s where she opened a shop on Greek Street. It sold her own interpretation of Eastern clothing to an artistic clientele that included Elizabeth Taylor and Barbra Streisand. Porter concentrated on clothes which had an illusory element removed from real life: impressive robes embroidered with Arabic designs and evening dresses cut from silk brocade.

☛ Bouquin, Gibb, Pollock

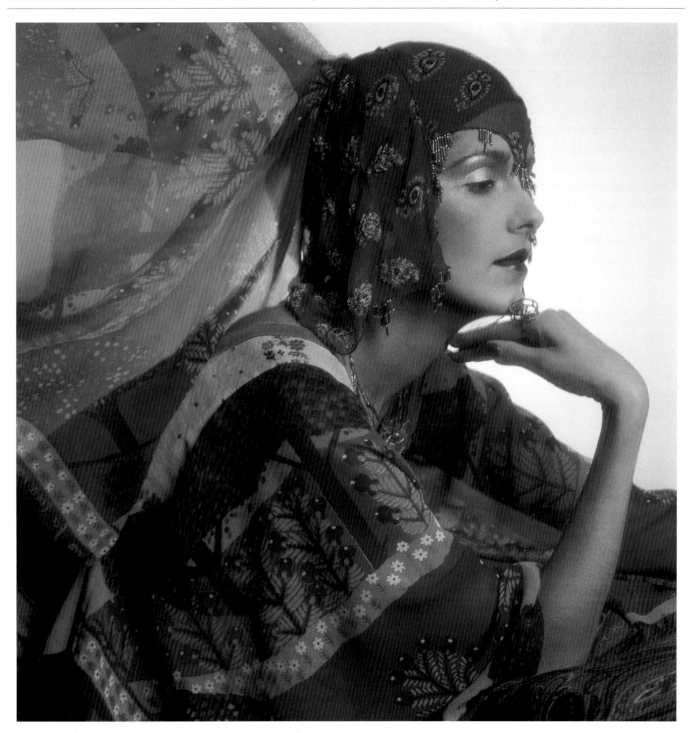

Thea Porter. **b** Damascus (SYR), 1927. **d** London (UK), 2000. **Eastern caftan and headdress.** Photograph by Barry Lategan, British *Vogue*, 1975.

POZO Jesús del   Designer

Jesús del Pozo adds substance to a drifting, cotton voile dress by piping its vertical seams. A natural, simple shape, it is a poetic garment, which becomes the focus of a dream-like image photographed in heightened colour by Javier Vallhonrat. Strong colour and simple shape is the backbone of del Pozo's style which has also cross-hatched a vibrant, melon slip dress with bold painted stripes. Del Pozo trained as an engineer, abandoning the discipline to study furniture design and interior decorating, before moving into painting, the influence of which is clear in his work; this dress resembles a sweep of paint. Del Pozo moved on once more, opening his first menswear store in 1974. Two years later his collection was being presented in Paris and worn by women who admired his soft, colourful menswear. Encouraged, he started to present womenswear in 1980.

☞ Dominguez, Sybilla, Vallhonrat

Jesús del Pozo. b Madrid (SP), 1946. **Handcrafted cotton voile dress.** Photograph by Javier Vallhonrat, 1997.

Prada Miuccia

Designer

Clutching the classic nylon bag upside down in an artless pose, model Kristen McMenamy models the unfettered look of Prada. Completely unadorned, save for the discreet triangular metal stamp, the bag articulates the 1990s notion of subtlety. The intelligence behind this cult label belongs to Miuccia Prada. Along with Gucci, her company redefined the image of Italian fashion in the mid-1990s. Prada had inherited her grandfather's leather luggage business in the 1970s and she revamped the label by introducing innovative fabrics. She pioneered the lightweight backpack in parachute nylon now popular among the fashion cognoscenti. Focusing on freedom of definition, rather than sex appeal, Prada experimented with 1970s furnishing fabrics in peculiar colour combinations and patterning that heralded the 1996 'geek chic' look. Prada managed to develop a line that is brave in spirit, controversial and desired above almost any other label.

☛ Lindbergh, McGrath, Souleiman, Steele

Miuccia Prada. b Milan (IT), c1950. **Kristen McMenamy. Advertising campaign. Autumn/winter 1995.** Photograph by Peter Lindbergh.

De Prémonville Myrène Designer

The jacket is given a dramatic cut by Myrène de Prémonville for a feminized business suit. Its long-line shape is softened with pockets which follow its curving hem. The shoulders are encircled with a strap which mimics an off-the-shoulder gown. De Prémonville's first designs for her own label in the late 1980s were a response to what she felt was missing from her own (and other women's) wardrobes. In the tradition of other female designers, such as Carven and Margaret Howell, de Prémonville started to design for her own needs. The results were sculpted, sassy suits which used unusual colour combinations, bright graphic appliqués and contrasting trims. She also designed a pair of classic black stirrup trousers because, as she says, 'No one else's felt comfortable.' By the early 1990s, de Prémonville had found an audience of working women who appreciated her meticulous attention to detail.

☛ Howell, de Tommaso

Myrène de Prémonville. b Hendaye (FR), 1949. **Day suit with banded yoke.** Photograph by Philippe Costes, 1984.

Presley Elvis   Icon

Presley's hip-thrusting style spoke eloquently to a new American phenomenon: the teenager. Wearing a loosely cut suit, black shirt and half-mast tie, he is the image of a young man who has rejected the formalities of dress of the older generation. This new, essentially working-class image scorned established ideas about status and redefined male attractiveness as youthful and overtly sensual. Presley started out as a truck driver and in 1953 recorded a few songs for Sun Records. Within five years he had made nineteen hit records and starred in four blockbuster movies. His hip gyrations would turn girls to jelly, earning him the nickname 'Elvis the Pelvis'. He was also known as 'The Hillbilly Cat', a reference to the 'hip cats' of the black jazz tradition – the song 'Blue Suede Shoes' denotes a cool dandyism synonymous with a certain black style.

☛ Bartlett, Dean, Hendrix

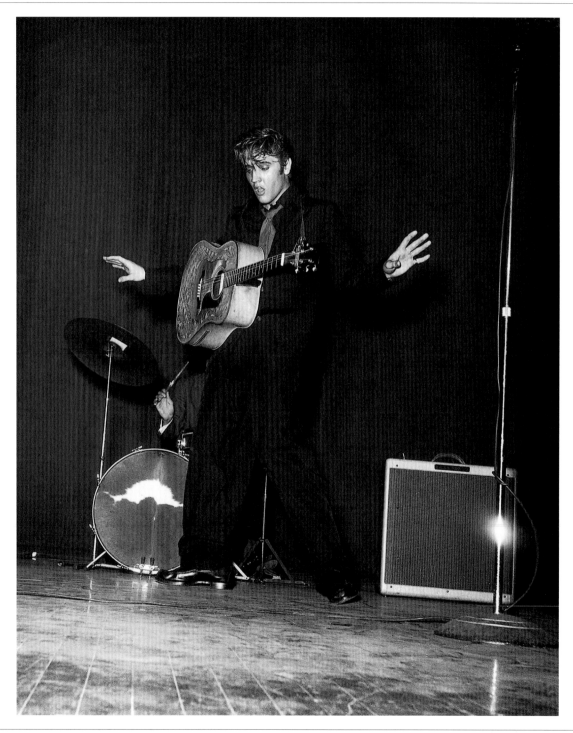

378

Elvis Presley. **b** Tupelo, MS (USA), 1935. **d** Memphis, TN (USA), 1977. **Elvis Presley. c**1957.

Price Antony   Designer

Antony Price is photographed with Jerry Hall, his friend and model. She wears a peplum dress of metallic and red French silk lace placed over lamé, an outfit worn for a benefit show in 1985. 'It wasn't the chicest or most subtle garment,' Price explains, 'but when Jerry moved under the lights she looked like a Siamese fighting fish in a vast blue tank.' It is a theatrical example of his potent eveningwear, designed, as he once said, by a man for a man. Price and Hall met when she was seventeen and modelling a blue mermaid frock for the cover of a Roxy Music album. In 1968 Price had designed a groundbreaking menswear show; its nostalgic 1930s and 1940s statement became a blueprint for the intellectual glam of Roxy Music. Launching his own label in 1979, Price consolidated his reputation for corseted super-heroine evening gowns made for 'women who go to serious parties'.

☛ G. Jones, Kelly, Oldfield

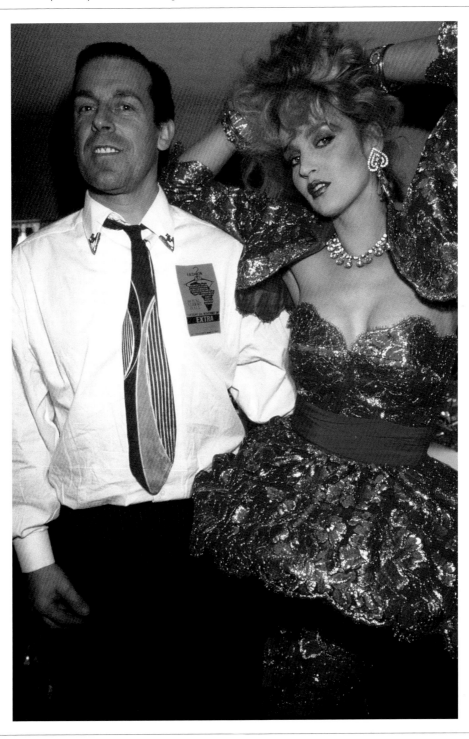

Antony Price. b Bradford (UK), 1945. **Antony Price with Jerry Hall.** Photograph by Richard Young, 1986.

Pucci Emilio

Designer

A skier is frozen in flight above a model wearing a classic Pucci design. The boldly patterned and brightly coloured jacket with plain, slim ski pants is typical of Emilio Pucci, the Marchese di Barsento, scion of an old aristocratic Tuscan family. He was a member of the Italian Olympic ski team and, after photographs of him on the slopes wearing his own designs appeared in *Harper's Bazaar*, he was invited to create winter clothes for women to be sold in New York. In 1951 he established his own fashion house in his Palazzo Pucci in Florence. He was celebrated for his 'palazzo pyjamas' in non-crushable, silk jersey which, worn by Grace Kelly, Lauren Bacall and Elizabeth Taylor, became a jet-set uniform. As a colourist of swirling patterns based on medieval Italian banners and an inventive user of fabrics, the 'Divino Marchese' captured the psychedelic mood of the 1960s. His look still inspires fashion revivals every few years.

☛ Ascher, Galitzine, Pulitzer

Emilio Pucci. **b** Naples (IT), 1914. **d** Florence (IT), 1992. **Ski jacket.** Photograph by Peter Beard, American *Vogue*, 1964.

Pulitzer Lilly Designer

The 'Lilly' dress, worn here by Rose Kennedy and her granddaughter Kathleen, suited every age. Like Pucci, Pulitzer found one style of pattern and kept with it. Her simple, summer shift dresses came in bright, colourful, floral cottons. Living in Florida's Palm Beach, Pulitzer knew what would make the perfect vacation-wear and she always claimed, 'The great thing about the Lilly is that you wear practically nothing underneath.' This wealthy resort area lent her clothes a certain cachet and her squiggly signature was on every dress. She had originally made one for herself to wear when, as a rich but bored housewife, she began selling freshly squeezed orange juice on the beach in 1959. The original dresses were made from cheap-and-cheerful cotton from Woolworths. She started selling her dresses on her stall and the 'Lilly' became an overnight success. John Fairchild dubbed it a 'little nothing' dress.

☞ Kennedy, Oudejans, Pucci

381

Lilly Pulitzer. b Roslyn, NY (USA). (Active 1960s.) **Rose Kennedy with granddaughter Kathleen, late 1960s.**

Quant Mary   Designer

Grace Coddington wears a jersey dress inspired by a footballer's strip. Fresh and youthful, Mary Quant's work democratized fashion, bringing an affordable version of couture to young working women. In 1955 Quant and her husband, Alexander Plunket-Greene, opened Bazaar, a Chelsea boutique that sold clothes which expressed an anti-establishment sentiment. The pair had met at art school and together they were members of a new society of design entrepreneurs that included Terence Conran and Vidal Sassoon. From 1962 Quant's hemlines were raised until, in 1964, skirts arrived at the era-defining mini length. It was dubbed the 'gymslip of the permissive society' and Mary Quant wore one at Buckingham Palace when collecting her O.B.E. in 1966. Her look also used matching pantyhose, a look inspired by dance rehearsal outfits. Ease, exercise and stretch; these elements add up to the foundations of modern fashion.

☛ Charles, Courrèges, Khanh, Liberty, Paulin, Rayne

Mary Quant. b London (UK), 1934. Grace Coddington wears a Mary Quant Ginger Group mini dress. 1967.

Rabanne Paco   Designer

Aluminium discs and panels linked together by wire using pliers have replaced conventional fashion created by threads and needles in this space-fantasy costume. Rabanne studied architecture at the École des Beaux-Arts in Paris but turned to fashion, supplying plastic buttons and jewellery to Givenchy, Dior and Balenciaga. Opening his own fashion house in 1966, it was his architectural training combined with the impact of space and space travel in the 1960s that inspired Rabanne to create such startling new styles. His space-age fashions using alternative, experimental materials were important in pushing aside the traditional parameters of what were acceptable clothes to wear on the street. Other fashion designers who travelled the space-age fashion route in the 1960s were Pierre Cardin, André Courrèges, Rudi Gernreich and Yves Saint Laurent.

☛ Bailly, Barrett, Dior, Gernreich, Betsey Johnson

Paco Rabanne. b San Sebastián (SP), 1934. **Aluminium chainmail dress.** Photograph by Gunnar Larsen, 1966.

Rayne Sir Edward   Shoe designer

'Ladies Day at Ascot. It simply mustn't rain,' reads the caption to this playful image. Rayne's lemon-yellow court shoes, striped with nylon mesh, are flirting with masculine polished riding boots and Oxford brogues. Impeccably crafted in a myriad of colours, from the day japonica pink to the evening jewelled jade, Rayne's shoes dressed Britain's well-heeled. Granted the Royal Warrant

for Queen Elizabeth, the Queen Mother, Rayne designed for Princess Elizabeth's wedding trousseau in 1947, draping her sandals in ivory silk with seed pearls. The family-owned business, H&M Rayne, was founded by his grandparents in 1889. Edward Rayne joined the company in 1940, taking over in 1951. He collaborated with couturiers Hardy Amies and Norman Hartnell, while still

keeping his eye on prevailing trends. Both Jean Muir and Mary Quant lent their talents to Rayne's fashion profile by designing youthful footwear.

☛ Amies, Hartnell, Muir, Quant, Vivier

384

Sir Edward Rayne. b London (UK), 1922. d (UK), 1992. 'Jaress' yellow shoe with mesh toe. Spring 1963.

Reboux Caroline   Milliner

Caroline Reboux was a milliner who excelled at structured simplicity. She avoided decoration and ornamentation. She liked working with felt – a strong and malleable material which she cut and folded on her clients' heads. For Mlle Conchita Montenegro, the milliner decorated the hat very simply with a lotus plant motif which reflected the line of the hat. This style of hat also complemented the tailored yet dramatic ensemble. Reboux designed hats for many couturiers and, later in her career, had a special relationship with Madame Vionnet, whose classicism matched her own. In the 1860s, Caroline Reboux's individual style caught the eye of Princess Metternich, who was credited with introducing Worth to the Empress Eugénie. She was soon making hats for the Empress and by 1870 she was established in the centre of fashionable Paris at 22 rue de la Paix, where she worked until her death.

☛ Agnès, Barthet, Daché, Hartnell, Pingat, Windsor

Caroline Reboux. b Paris (FR), 1830s. d Paris (FR), 1927. **Hat trimmed with broderie anglaise.** Photograph by Baron de Meyer, American *Vogue*, 1919.

Redfern John Designer

Mary Garden, the celebrated Scottish opera singer, wears a town dress made of pleated Rajah silk with a matching cape and a lace blouse. It evokes the fashionable silhouette of the *belle époque*: a high-necked, full bodice which gives a pouched effect, over a deep, tightly constricted waist. The skirt is cut straight at the front and filled out by pleats and extra fabric at the back which extends into a train. This style of dress became known as the S-bend. It reflected the taste for Art Nouveau. Redfern began as a ladies' tailor in Cowes on the Isle of Wight. The success of his tailored garments, especially his yachting costumes, led to his becoming a couturier, designing fashionable clothes for royalty, singers and actresses. In 1881 he established fashion houses in London and Paris, followed by branches in Edinburgh and New York. Redfern closed his houses in 1920.

☛ Boué, Drecoll, Gibson, Paquin

John Redfern. b Cowes (UK), 1853. **d** 1929. **Town dress of pleated Rajah silk and lace.** 1905.

De la Renta Oscar   Designer

Carla Bruni looks as though she owns, and plays, the grand piano on which she is perched. It is all part of the de la Renta image: sophisticated, lavish, grown-up. The svelte black bodice, which sweeps into a softly gathered skirt, is finished with flat bows on the shoulder. Known for ornamentation and extremely feminine silhouettes, de la Renta has cultivated clients among the rich and beautiful with whom he socializes. Following brief apprenticeships in Europe, de la Renta went on to design for Elizabeth Arden in New York, where his idealism of touches of European glamour applied to conventions of American dressmaking was crystallized. In 1993 he returned to Europe to design Balmain couture, while satisfying the chic American women who see de la Renta as a designer who makes flattering dresses and sophisticated suits, with a special gift for dress-up and evening glamour.

☛ Alfaro, Arden, Roehm, Scaasi, Steiger

Oscar de la Renta. b Santo Domingo (DOM), 1932. **Carla Bruni wears black cocktail gown.** Photograph by Arthur Elgort, 1992.

Revillon Théodore, Albert, Anatole and Léon (Revillon Frères)

Louise Dahl-Wolfe shoots a shawl-collared, sealskin cape draped around the shoulders like a wash of black ink; it is an image of a woman coated in wealth. The pioneers of this sort of fur fashion, the Revillon brothers – Théodore, Albert, Anatole and Léon – treated the pelt like silk, cutting it skilfully a century earlier. Were it not for their aristocratic father's neck-saving decision to change his name from Count Louis-Victor d'Argental during the French Revolution, such coats might not have existed. Louis-Victor had already taken fur beyond its practical use as a provider of warmth with much-coveted juxtapositions of exotic furs such as ocelot, chinchilla and Arctic fox, making Paris the fur capital of the world. On his death, the firm, renamed Revillon Frères by his four sons, became the first French global company with trading posts across Canada and Siberia and a museum opened in their name.

☞ Dahl-Wolfe, Fendi, Lauder

388

Revillon. Théodore. b Paris (FR). **d** (FR), 1920; **Albert. b** Paris (FR). **d** 1887; **Anatole. b** Paris (FR). **d** (FR) 1916; **Léon. b** Paris (FR). **d** (FR), 1915. (Active 1840s–1910s.) (Revillon Frères.)
Seal cape. Photograph by Louise Dahl-Wolfe, *Harper's Bazaar*, 1956.

Revson Charles (Revlon)

Sassy and liberated, Shelley Hack – the 'Charlie Girl' – strides across the page wearing a trouser suit and an expression that says, 'I've got it all'. Revlon captured the mood of a new generation of independent women with the image of its scent, Charlie, in the 1970s. Revlon was founded in 1932 by brothers Charles and Joseph Revson and a chemist named Charles Lachman. Charles Revson had the marketing brain. When Elizabeth Arden referred to him as 'that man' (because she thought he copied her ideas), he created a line of men's cosmetics named That Man. Success, however, was founded on opaque-coloured nail polish which supplanted clear tints and introduced women to matching nail and lip colour. They started with Fire and Ice, a strong red, with the ad slogan, 'There's a little bit of bad in every good woman'. Revson said he wanted his models to be like 'Park Avenue whores – elegant, but the sexual thing underneath'.

☛ Arden, Factor, Hutton, Venturi

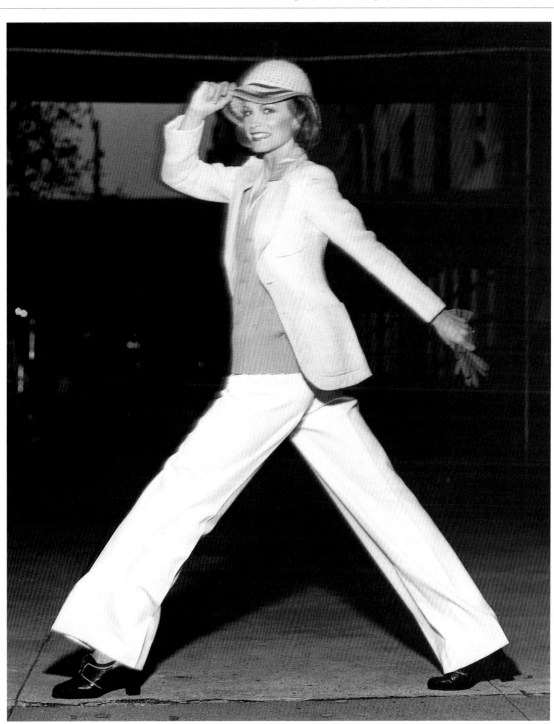

Charles Revson. b Somerville, MA (USA), 1906. d New York (USA), 1976. (Revlon.) **Shelley Hack modelling for Revlon's 'Charlie' perfume.** Photograph by Albert Watson, c1974.

Rhodes Zandra   Designer

Zandra Rhodes once said that she tried to achieve an ageless exoticism. As such, she is an original; her trademarks were slashed silk tatters, abstract beading, handkerchief points, squiggle prints, tulle crinolines and pleated fabrics edged with ruffles. The 'conceptual chic' collection of 1977, shown here, brought street style to couture using embroidered rips and safety pins

as jewellery. Her dresses used techniques that are still seen as subversive: exterior seams and 'winking' holes revealing erogenous zones and semi-sheer jersey. Rhodes studied fashion at the Royal College of Art, graduating in 1966. 'We were determined to live in a world of today, making it all ourselves, creating our own environment, a perfect world of plastic, perfectly artificial,' she

recalled. She cited Edith Sitwell as her inspiration. Her own image – multi-coloured hair and statement make-up – contributes to her aura of outrageousness.

☛ Rotten, Sarne, G. Smith, Williamson

390

Zandra Rhodes. b Chatham (UK), 1942. 'Conceptual chic'. Punk jersey dresses. Photograph by Clive Arrowsmith, 1977.

De Ribes Jacqueline Designer

In a pose of fragile elegance, the Comtesse Jacqueline de Ribes gazes out in a stark, black velvet dress, its rigorous cut softened only by a gentle froth of silk cloqué. Dubbed the 'Most Stylish Woman in the *World*' by *Town and Country Magazine* in 1983, the Comtesse was already appearing on the international best-dressed lists by the age of twenty-five, having consistently worn haute couture all her life. Because of a family history of French aristocratic wealth – which suggested fashion design was beneath her station – her longing to become a designer was not fulfilled until she was well into her forties. An innate sense of good taste meant success for her first collection in Paris and America in 1983. It catered for women of her ilk, who admired its aura of discreet grandeur and slender lines adorned by extravagant though simple shoulder detail.

☛ von Fürstenberg, de la Renta, Roehm

Comtesse Jacqueline de Ribes. b Paris (FR), 1931. **Jacqueline de Ribes, Paris.** Photograph by Victor Skrebneski, 1983.

Ricci Nina

Designer

In this advertisement from 1937, a slimline suit, the jacket trimmed with fur, is placed in the context of Nina Ricci's world; the centre of which was the place Vendôme in Paris. Unlike her contemporaries Coco Chanel and Elsa Schiaparelli, Nina Ricci did not set trends; instead, she concentrated on providing clothes for wealthy society women of a certain age, whose aim was to appear feminine, elegant and beautiful. It was a tradition that was continued by Jules-François Crahay and then by Gérard Pipart, both of whom respected Ricci's original tenet. She opened her Parisian couture house in 1932 and, with the help of her son Robert Ricci, rapidly established a reputation as a true couturière. She worked by draping fabric directly onto the body, gathering and tucking to emphasize her clients' attributes and disguise their imperfections.

☛ Ascher, Crahay, Frizon, Hirata, Mainbocher, Pipart

392

Nina Ricci. b Turin (IT), 1883. d Paris (FR), 1970. **Fur-trimmed jacket and skirt.** Illustration by Pierre Mourgue, 1937.

Ritts Herb   Photographer

Using his customary talent for black-and-white photography, Herb Ritts makes a drama out of Gianni Versace's already arresting dress. The funnel of black fabric, and that worn by the model, create startling geometric shapes that contrast with her pale skin and the desert backdrop. Born into a wealthy Los Angeles family in 1952, Herb Ritts lived next door to Steve McQueen and was exposed to a world of sophisticated beauty by his mother, an interior decorator. Photography started as a hobby, with portraits of friends and landscapes. In 1978 a picture he had taken on the set of Franco Zeffirelli's remake of *The Champ* was used by *Newsweek*. A friend, male model Matt Collins, introduced Ritts to Bruce Weber and fashion photography. Ritts's style was sexy and powerful, often homo-erotic and always fascinated by the texture of skin.

☛ **Platt Lynes, Sieff, Versace, Weber**

Herb Ritts. b Los Angeles, CA (USA), 1952. **d** Los Angeles, CA (USA), 2002. **Tatjana Patitz wears Versace.** *Le Mirage,* 1990.

Roberts Michael   Illustrator

Recalling the collage work of Henri Matisse, Michael Roberts accurately depicts Azzedine Alaïa's sculptural Sphinx dress. Bands of white paper emulate the elastic bands in Alaïa's trademark creation; a black paper silhouette accentuates these bands' curvaceous effect. Using a naïve, 'child-like' illustrative technique, Roberts keeps an outsider's perspective, while his humorous treatment hints at a deep knowledge of fashion's intricacies. A fashion writer, stylist, photographer, illustrator, video director and collagist, Roberts pokes fun at fashion icons. His outrageous sense of style and venomous pen found their way through his appointments at The Sunday Times in 1972, society magazine Tatler in 1981 and at UK Vogue and the New Yorker magazine. His provocative vision was acutely exemplified when, for an April Fool issue of Tatler, he transformed designer Vivienne Westwood into Margaret Thatcher.

☞ Alaïa, Ettedgui, Westwood

Michael Roberts. b Aylesbury (UK), 1947. 'Azzedine's Sphinx'. Paper collage, 1991.

Roberts Tommy (Mr Freedom)

Designer

Photographer Clive Arrowsmith puts Tommy Roberts' work into its kitsch Americana context for *Vogue* in 1971. The stretchy wrestler's dungarees are appliquéd with a bubblegum-pink satin heart and worn over a colour-blocked T-shirt. The grinning baseball team seals the story. This was fun fashion for the pop generation at a time when *Vogue* asked the question, 'Is bad taste a bad thing?' Designer Tommy Roberts was Mr Freedom, a man with an eye both for design and for the gap in the market. His cheerful T-shirts and tightly cut trousers were also decorated with camp symbols of 1930s and 1940s Hollywood – Mickey Mouse and Donald Duck adorned iconoclastic clothing for both sexes. In 1966 Roberts opened Kleptomania, a hippie emporium near London's Carnaby Street which was followed in 1969 by Mr Freedom, on the King's Road. It sold a fast-moving style that never took itself too seriously.

☛ Fiorucci, Fish, Nutter

Tommy Roberts. b London (UK), 1942. (Mr Freedom.) **Dungarees with pink appliqué heart.** Photograph by Clive Arrowsmith, British *Vogue*, 1971.

Rocha John Designer

Creative yet commercial, John Rocha says, 'Sex never comes into it. I'm interested in beauty more than anything else'. Here, his organza dress printed with vast orchids is thrown into relief by Pat McGrath's abstract cobalt-blue make-up. The dress is designed to stand proud of the body, creating a see-through sheath shadowed with flowers. Despite the hot mood of this picture, Irish references often influence Rocha's work. Natural fabrics, including linen, wool and sheepskin, are given the colours of a Celtic landscape: soft moss green, stone, slate grey. Rocha describes his clothes as 'free in spirit...a bit gypsy'. This description also fits the Portuguese-Chinese designer who moved from Hong Kong to London to study fashion. His Celtic-inspired end-of-year show was spotted by the Irish Trade Board who invited him to work in Dublin, where he has lived since 1979, producing clothes under his Chinatown label.

☛ Eisen, Kim, McGrath, Watanabe

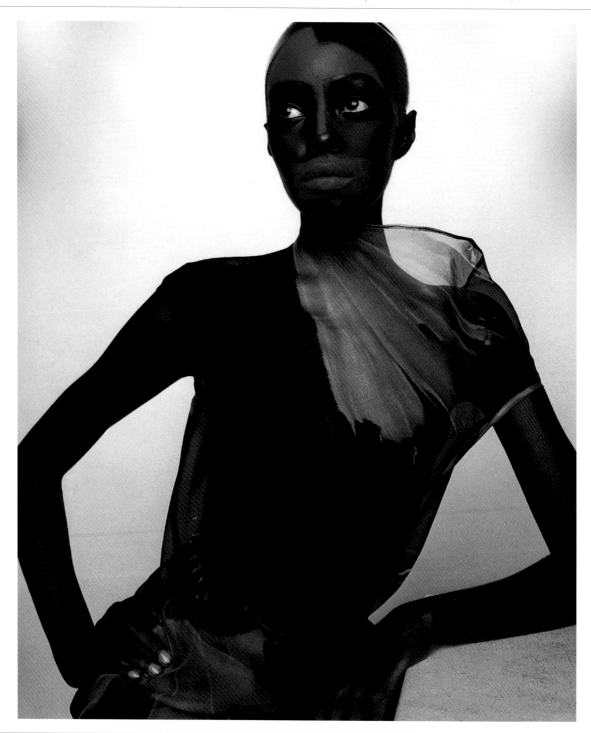

John Rocha. b Hong Kong (HK), 1953. **Organza print dress.** Photograph by Steven Klein, *Frank*, 1998.

Rochas Marcel Designer

Marcel Rochas oversees the fitting of a dress, conducted by his wife Hélène, while testing a fragrance sample. Mme Rochas pins and tucks the skirt into the New Look shape – a curvaceous silhouette that Rochas was credited with presaging in his film work for Mae West. In 1946 he launched the *guêpière*, a long-line strapless brassiere which enclosed the hips – a foundation garment that was to train figures for a decade. Counting Jean Cocteau and Christian Bérard among his friends, and with the encouragement of Poiret, Rochas opened his own maison de couture in 1925. He started to create black-and-white dresses that featured a white collar – one of which is photographed here. His creative innovations often featured a strong shoulder line, an element that Rochas considered 'a sign of the feminine'. In the 1950s, he transposed casual trousers into the context of women's suiting – another novelty.

☛ Bérard, Cocteau, Dior

Marcel Rochas. **b** Paris (FR), 1902. **d** Paris (FR), 1955. **Marcel and Hélène Rochas with model.** 1944.

Rodriguez Narciso Designer

Cerruti, for whom he designed this dainty, embroidered bodice, gave Narciso Rodriguez his first international platform as a designer of minimal fashion. However, it was the creation of a wedding dress that really brought his name to general attention. In 1996 Carolyn Bessette married John F. Kennedy Jr wearing one of his rigorously simple, bias-cut sheath dresses. 'I made a wedding dress for a really good friend and [it] brought a lot of attention to the work I was doing,' he said afterwards. Rodriguez learned the power of understatement while working for a succession of design houses, each of whose philosophy is based around clean, modern, luxurious and wearable clothes: Anne Klein, Calvin Klein (where he met Bessette) and TSE, a design label specializing in cashmere.

In 1997, Rodriguez launched his own label in Milan and was appointed to design for the luxurious Spanish label, Loewe.

☞ **Cerruti, Ferretti, A. Klein, C. Klein, Loewe**

398

Narciso Rodriguez. b NJ (USA), 1961. **Embroidered bodice and skirt for Cerruti.** Photograph by Carter Smith, *Harper's Bazaar*, 1997.

Roehm Carolyne   Designer

Carolyne Roehm, photographed at a gala event held by Bill Blass, is her own best advert. When she launched her own deluxe, ready-to-wear business in 1984, it was her tall, whippet-thin frame that starred in the glossy adverts and sold her feminine clothes. 'I wasn't so gung ho on the idea of being in the ads,' she said. 'I was told it would be a tremendous advantage.' And so it was. Roehm sold her society clothes to rich women who were either like her or wanted to be like her. She has been described as both 'driven' and 'highly organised' and it is these qualities that led her to Oscar de la Renta, for whom she worked for ten years as designer, house model and muse. Roehm mixes luxury with a practical awareness. Garments cut from lavish fabrics, such as a full-length, duchesse satin evening skirt, will be worn with a cashmere sweater to simulate the feel of sportswear.

☛ Blass, de la Renta, de Ribes, Wang

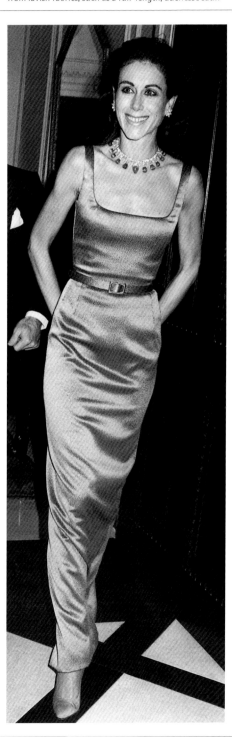

Carolyne Roehm. b Kirksville, MI (USA), 1951. **Satin cocktail dress.** Photograph by Daniel d'Errico, *Women's Wear Daily*, 1991.

Rosier Michèle

Designer

A mountain takes on the look of another planet for the backdrop to Michèle Rosier's space-age sportswear. The model's bug-eyed goggles and silver boots amplify the drama of Rosier's foil ski jacket and pants. Together with her contemporary Christiane Bailly, Rosier was a major player in France's burgeoning ready-to-wear market. With her young, accessible response to haute couture, she helped boost the export of French prêt-à-porter five-fold between 1962 and 1970. Rosier spent her childhood with her mother, publisher Hélène Gordon-Lazareff, in the United States, where the youth-orientated style was a formative influence. Rosier began her career as a writer for *New Woman* and *France-Soir*, but quit journalism to found V de V (Vêtements de Vacances) in 1962 with Jean-Pierre Bamberger. Rosier's use of sportswear fabrics, such as nylon fleece, paved the way for their adoption as part of everyday fashion clothing.

☛ Bailly, Bousquet, Khanh, W. Smith

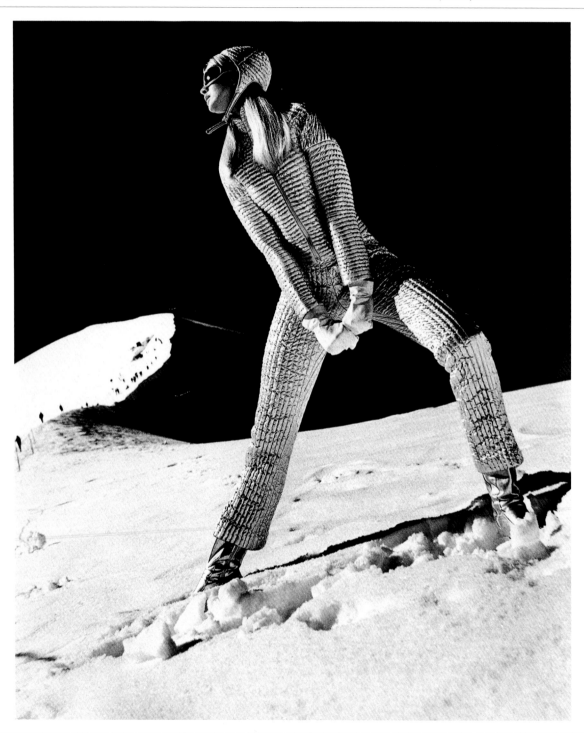

Michèle Rosier. b Paris (FR), 1929. **Quilted ski jacket and pants for V de V.** Photograph by Vernier, British *Vogue*, 1966.

400

Rotten Johnny   Icon

Created by Malcolm McLaren and styled by Vivienne Westwood, the Sex Pistols were a promotional tool for the pair's punk-defining London's King's Road shop, Sex. Johnny Rotten, lead member of the group, pronounced, 'The kids want misery and death. They want threatening noises, because that shakes you out of your apathy'. This uniform was designed as the sartorial equivalent. It was antipathetic to every dress code before it; even the individual protest clothes worn by hippies had proclaimed a mood of utopian collectivity, but punk was invented to alienate every other element of society by using sex and bondage as its themes. Rotten was surprised himself when Westwood gave him a rubber shirt to wear on stage: 'I thought it was the most repulsive thing I'd ever seen. To wear it as a piece of clothing rather than as some part of a sexual fetish was hilarious.'

☛ Cobain, Hemingway, McLaren, Rhodes, Westwood

Johnny Rotten (John Lydon). b London (UK), 1956. **Johnny Rotten wears tartan bondage trousers. c**1977.

Rouff Maggy

Designer

The East provides the inspiration for this evening gown. Rouff has incorporated Japanese influence into superlative modern tailoring: the long, loose pendant sleeves recall those of a kimono. Like Poiret and Bakst before her, Rouff has infused her design with a feel for the exotic, the Orient. She has achieved a perfectly wcut European gown. By using the bias-cutting technique, this dress takes on an almost seamless appearance, with a sweep of unbroken fabric reaching from the bodice to the cuff's hem. Rouff began her career as a fashion designer at Drecoll, where her mother, Madame de Wagner, was head designer. But it was Jeanne Paquin who was her main inspiration. Rouff founded her own fashion house in 1929, rapidly gaining a reputation for ravishing eveningwear and also for sportswear. In 1937 she opened her salon in London where her Parisian gowns were shown to her British clientele.

☛ **Agnès, Bakst, Drecoll, Paquin, Poiret**

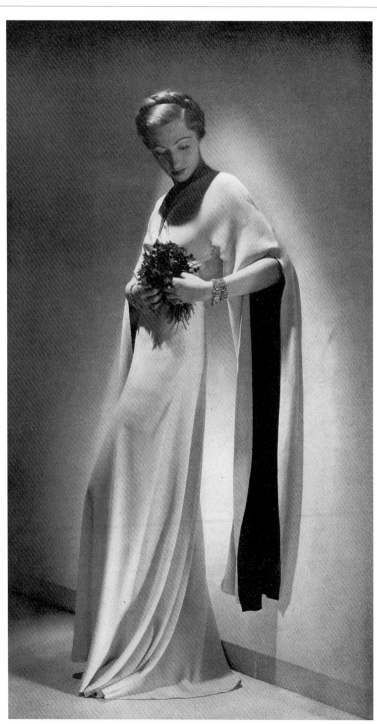

Maggy Rouff. b Paris (FR), 1876. **d** Paris (FR), 1971. **Evening dress with cut sleeves.** Photograph by George Hoyningen-Huene, 1935.

Roversi Paolo

Photographer

Paolo Roversi describes Kirsten Owen, his favourite model, as 'somewhere between an angel and a demon', which is how he captured her in this photograph taken for a Romeo Gigli campaign. Gigli, a long-term collaborator of Roversi's, believes the photographer 'succeeds in seizing a fleeting moment, a tremor of emotion which projects the women themselves into a timeless dimension'. Roversi's illusory work stands alone among late twentieth-century fashion photographers. He left his native Italy for Paris in 1973, and by the end of the decade had developed a distinctive style using double exposure and Polaroid film. Roversi's images are poetic, romantic and painterly, and by turns demure and slightly demented. He describes them as 'a very intense exchange', an attempt to 'capture a lot of their soul, a little of their personality'.

☛ Ferretti, Gigli, McGrath, McKnight

403

Paolo Roversi. b Ravenna (IT), 1947. **Kirsten Owen modelling for Romeo Gigli.** 1987.

Rubinstein Helena Cosmetics creator

'Life Red comes to life on your lips' claims Helena Rubinstein's fresh-faced advertisement from the 1940s. The healthy image promoted by Rubinstein's make-up and skin creams was born in a laboratory. She had wanted to study medicine but, denied her chance, left Poland to live with an uncle in Australia. She started to sell a face cream, Creme Valaze, brought from home to protect her complexion from the sun. A successful small skincare school followed and when one of her seven sisters joined her, Rubinstein studied with the best European dermatologists. Her white-coated approach to cosmetics resulted in several innovations, including the first skin cream to use male and female hormones in an attempt to delay the process of ageing. Her artistic credentials were also impeccable – in Paris she became friend and patron to Matisse, Dufy, Dalí and Cocteau.

☛ Cocteau, Dalí, Dufy

LIFE RED COMES TO LIFE on your lips

with Helena Rubinstein's new "LIFE RED" lipstick

Helena Rubinstein. **b** Cracow (POL), 1870. **d** New York (USA), 1965. 'Life Red' advertisement. 1940.

Rykiel Sonia   Designer

During a salon presentation, Sonia Rykiel's tailored knitwear is exemplified by cardigan coats and dresses accessorized with sequined roses and gold belts. Her attitude to the grand feasibility of knitted wool was explained when she said, 'Just as one woman looks fantastically erotic naked...another can seem the same in a polo-neck sweater.' The 'Queen of Knits' began designing in 1962 when she was pregnant and unable to find any soft sweaters. So she knitted her own, and also began selling them in her husband's fashion shops. Rykiel's style of elegant yet easy 'lounge' dressing is typically French. She calls her clothes *'le nouveau classicisme'*, their slim line owing much to the 1930s. Fluid jersey, wide trousers and raglan-sleeve sweaters in muted colours are her trademarks; her Lurex knitwear is sophisticated enough for evening. 'I love knit,' Rykiel says, 'because it is very magical. You can do so many things with just a thread.'

☛ Albini, Jacobson, Turbeville

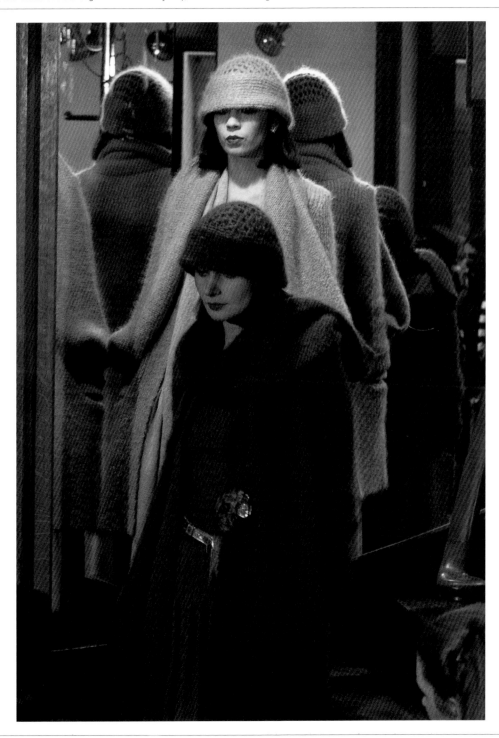

Sonia Rykiel. b Paris (FR), 1930. **Knitted co-ordinates.** 1974.

Saint Laurent Yves

Designer

Yves Saint Laurent dresses model René Russo in a polished evening suit, framing her face (simply made-up by Way Bandy) with feathers. Since the 1960s 'YSL' has been a directional and determining force in modern fashion. He introduced masculine tailoring for women, using military uniforms and variations on the tuxedo or 'le smoking', and took street styles and peasant costume and turned them into luxurious options for women. Saint Laurent has often referred to art, basing designs and embroidery on paintings by Mondrian, Matisse, Picasso and Braque, but always taking them as historical icons and making them current. Saint Laurent said, 'Like Proust, I'm fascinated most of all by my perceptions of a world in awesome transition.' Great fashion is about cutting those moments of transition out of cloth. He once described what he did as 'minor art' but later added the words 'maybe it is not so minor after all'.

☛ Bandy, Deneuve, Dior, Newton, Perint Palmer

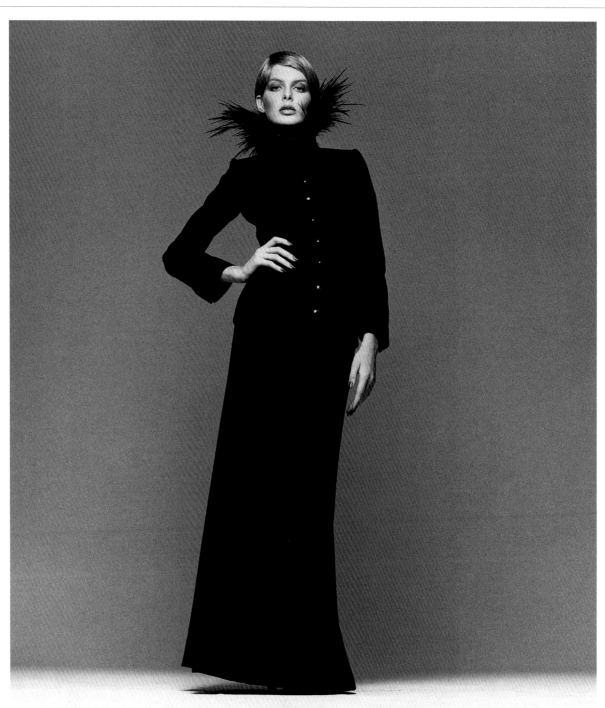

Yves Saint Laurent. b Oran (ALG), 1936. René Russo wears deep feather collar and skirt, Paris. Photograph by Francesco Scavullo, 1974.

Sander Jil   Designer

Sander began her career as a fashion journalist, but moved into fashion design. In 1968 she opened a boutique in Hamburg and five years later was showing on the catwalk. Sander perceived a need for understated clothes with a sense of quiet self-confidence, but which would provide the wearer with the ultimate in fit, quality and modernity. It was a prophetic vision: today, her clothes have become the byword for an ultra-modern, androgynous sensuality that is as uncompromisingly technical as it is beautiful. Her simplicity must not, however, be confused with classicism. As Sander told *Vogue*, 'A classic is an excuse, because one is too lazy to contrast the spirit of the time.' She rejects the clichés of femininity for the refinements found in the architecture of men's suits. This approach throws emphasis away from detail and onto the material, as can be seen here with a pair of trousers, the most striking aspect of which is the texture.

☞ Lang, McDean, Sims, Vallhonrat

Jil Sander. b Wesselburen (GER), 1943. **Angela Lindvall wears silk shirt and tweed trousers.** Photograph by David Sims, 1998.

Sant'Angelo Giorgio di

Designer

Veruschka's body is barely covered by a chain bikini by Giorgio di Sant'Angelo. Her hair is wrapped with gold lamé and her body encircled with gold chains. The 1960s was a decade devoted to the cult of youth and Sant'Angelo designed to make women aware of their bodies. Born in Florence, he trained as an architect and studied art, ceramics and sculpture, before winning

an animation fellowship with Walt Disney in Los Angeles. In the early 1960s, he moved to New York and worked as a textile designer, where his talent was spotted by Diana Vreeland, the flamboyant editor of American *Vogue*. She sent him to Arizona with an array of materials, scissors and Veruschka to 'invent' clothes for a spread in her magazine, of which this design is an example. In later life

Sant'Angelo found new customers with his wrapped, stretchy Lycra clothes designed according to the same principles.

☛ Bruce, Lindbergh, Peretti, Veruschka, Vreeland

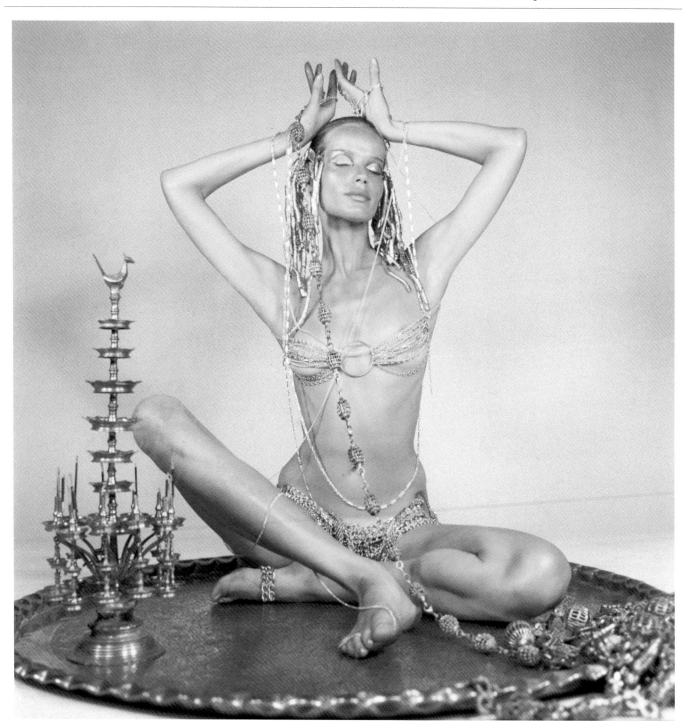

Giorgio di Sant'Angelo. b Florence (IT), 1936. d New York (USA), 1989. **Veruschka wears gold chain bikini.** Photograph by Franco Rubartelli, American *Vogue*, 1968.

Sarne Tanya (Ghost) Designer

A fine georgette fabric, traced over with a print titled 'ice river', is slashed into an asymmetrical dress; one that is of its season but at the same time unique to one label. Regardless of their style, which changes every season, Ghost's dresses are machine-washable, a practicality not usually associated with high fashion. Tanya Sarne, the founder and figurehead at Ghost, came up with the idea of developing a fabric that is hardy, yet sensuous against the skin. The result was a material woven mainly from viscose yarns and derived from specially grown soft woods. This is put through an intensive process of boiling and dyeing in an unusual palette of colours. This costly and time-consuming activity gives it a unique crepe-like texture and density. Such garments have longevity and require minimal attention – a fact that has made Ghost popular with women who travel. Ghost's fabric is used for everything from vests to complicated gowns.

☛ Clark, Dell'Acqua, Rhodes, Tarlazzi

409

Tanya Sarne. b Southgate (UK), 1945. (Ghost.) **Fuchsia 'ice river' printed georgette dress.** Photograph by Niall McInerney, 1997.

Sassoon Vidal   Hairdresser

'Hair is nature's biggest compliment and the treatment of this compliment is in our hands. As in couture, the cut is the most important element...haircutting simply means design and this feeling for design must come from within.' Vidal Sassoon's words explain the reasons for his simplified, Bauhausian haircuts which freed women from weekly beauty-parlour visits and the tyranny of curlers, lacquered shapes and other hair constriction. Sassoon's cuts – the geometric, the wash-and-wear perm, the bob (cut on a horizontal plane) and the Nancy Kwan – were low-maintenance high modernism, and he identified easy-to-care-for shapes that were adaptable for many women. Belonging to the generation of the Beatles and Swinging London, Sassoon took the cult of the natural to hair and elevated the role of the hairdresser, working in partnership with designers such as Mary Quant and Rudi Gernreich.

☛ **Beatles, Coddington, Gernreich, Leonard, Liberty**

410

Vidal Sassoon. b London (UK), 1928. **'Five-point' haircut.** Photograph by David Montgomery, 1964.

Scaasi Arnold

Designer

Saucer-sized black dots on a white silk dress, its colours reversed for the coat, was already a Scaasi signature in 1957. So were the waist-deep décolletage and the bell-shaped skirt. Scaasi was the first designer in America to do the snappy matching coat and dress look for evening. Having trained with Charles James, he left in 1956 to set up his own label, specializing in evening clothes for socialite functions. Scaasi was careful to include decorative 'table top' necklines and low décolletages, and he favoured large 'grand entrance' prints. In 1958 his polka-dot evening dress was the first formal evening outfit to end above the knee. His couture salon opened in 1964, producing short evening dresses and spectacular ball gowns. 'I am definitely not a minimalist designer!' said Scaasi. 'Clothes with some adornment are more interesting to look at and more fun to wear.'

☛ Deneuve, C. James, de la Renta, Schuberth

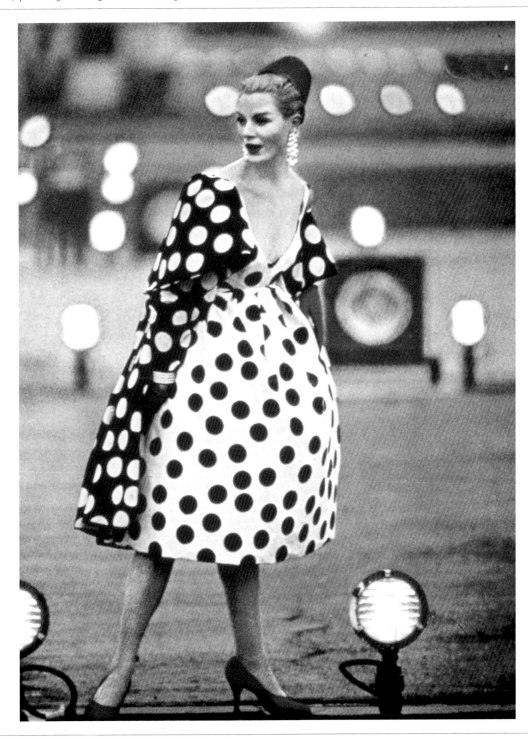

Arnold Scaasi. b Montreal, QC (CAN), 1931. **Polka-dot dress.** 1957.

Scavullo Francesco Photographer

The model Antonia plays a tourist in an epic fashion scene shot in the populated chaos of a Hong Kong marketplace, directed by the photographer Francesco Scavullo. Her flight bag crashes into her silk dress, oriental make-up and hat, dramatizing the outfit and dressing Antonia for her role. Scavullo's obsession with photography began at an early age: at nine he was making home movies and much of his early work has a filmic quality. He began his career at American *Vogue* and spent three years with Horst, before going to work on the new teenage magazine *Seventeen*. Scavullo's passion for photographing beautiful women was harnessed by American *Cosmopolitan*, whose unapologetically sexy covers he began to photograph in 1965. But his lasting legacy to fashion photography was undoubtedly his technical knowledge, particularly his use of diffused lighting designed to flatter the greatest 'cover' faces.

☛ Deneuve, Fonssagrives, C. Klein, Turlington

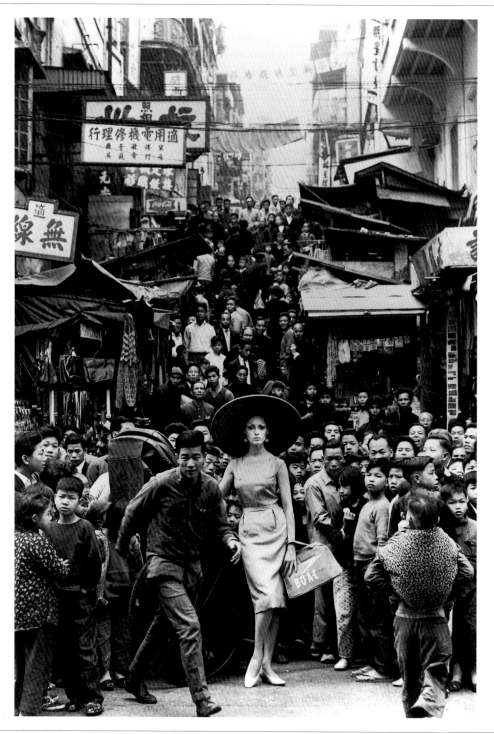

Francesco Scavullo. **b** Staten Island, NY (USA), 1929. **d** New York (USA), 2004. **Antonia, Hong Kong, 1962.**

Scherrer Jean-Louis Designer

This fantasy world of a Botticelli woman rising from a shell serves as the ideal medium for the revelation of a silk-chiffon dress with a waterfall collar and butterfly cape. Its luxurious yet dramatic qualities adorn Jean-Louis Scherrer's refined classicism. Scherrer moved into haute couture when, after the petrol crisis in the 1970s, he provided the wives of affluent Arabs with longer, covered-up fashions that satisfied the modesty requirements dictated by Islamic laws, while also proclaiming their wealth. Parisian ballrooms have witnessed Scherrer's sumptuous embroideries and glittering silks since he started as Christian Dior's assistant, after an accident finished his career as a dancer at the age of twenty. After Dior's death and the choice of Saint Laurent as his successor, Scherrer left and opened his own business in 1962.

☛ Lancetti, Mori, Ungaro

413

Jean-Louis Scherrer. b Paris (FR), 1936. **Print dress and straw hat.** Photograph by Angus McBean, *Harpers & Queen*, 1989.

Schiaparelli Elsa Designer

Is the woman wearing this 'Desk Suit', designed by Elsa Schiaparelli in 1936, going to the office or the beach? The suit features a vertical series of true and false pockets, embroidered to look like desk drawers with buttons for knobs. Dress designing for Schiaparelli was an art, and this Desk Suit is based on two Surrealist drawings by Salvador Dalí entitled 'City of Drawers'

and 'Venus de Milo of Drawers'. Surrealism was an art movement that flourished in the 1920s and 1930s, reacting against the rational and formal real world, and substituting instead fantasy and a dream world. Surrealism in fashion thrived in the 1930s, depicting psychologically suggestive garments. Schiaparelli's smart, sophisticated, witty clothes took the fashion world

by storm. She commissioned some of the best artists of the period, such as Salvador Dalí, Jean Cocteau and Christian Bérard, to design fabrics and embroideries for her.

☛ Banton, Cocteau, Lesage, Man Ray, Nars, Perugia

Elsa Schiaparelli. **b** Rome (IT), 1890. **d** Paris (FR), 1973. **'Desk Suit'**. Photograph by Cecil Beaton, 1936.

Schiffer Claudia   Model

In one of her most famous photographs, Claudia Schiffer becomes a sex kitten. Shortly after being discovered in a discotheque in 1987, Schiffer secured the Guess? advertising campaign and subsequently became one of the most sought-after models in the world. She has appeared on the covers of more than 500 magazines, including *Vanity Fair* which has an editorial policy that usually refuses to place any model on its cover. The first and only model to have a wax likeness in the Grévin Museum in Paris, Schiffer's appeal beyond that as a fashion model is an obvious one. As a member of the supermodel troupe, she represents natural blonde beauty – a modern, healthy look that dates back to Cheryl Tiegs. She modelled for *Sports Illustrated*'s swimwear issue in 1998, opening up the pin-up market for models. This became a lucrative avenue for women such as Schiffer and Cindy Crawford, whose beauty had a general appeal.

☛ Crawford, Thomass, von Unwerth

415

Claudia Schiffer. **b** Rheinberg (GER), 1970. **Guess? Jeans publicity campaign,1989.** Photograph by Ellen von Unwerth.

Schön Mila   Designer

This 1968 photograph, which features a perfectly cut, Mila Schön, white wool suit, represents several of her design signatures. Schön's favourite fabric was double-faced wool; she was a perfectionist who worked within a classical structure, to exacting specifications, and she also created modernist garments. She came from a family of wealthy Yugoslavian aristocrats who had fled to Italy to escape Communism. In 1959, Schön launched her business. She had gained her love of fashion as a couture customer at Balenciaga, and within her clothes can be seen his austerity of cut, together with the influences of Dior and Schiaparelli. By 1965, Schön had developed her own style and began showing on the catwalk. Construction of her tailoring is highlighted by its very simplicity – making details out of seams and darts.

☞ **Cardin, Cashin, Courrèges**

416

Mila Schön. b Trau, Dalmatia (CRO), 1916. **Benedetta Barzini wears double-face trouser suit and hat.** Photograph by Ugo Mulas, 1968.

Schuberth Emilio Designer

A ruched taffeta, puff-ball gown, inspired by a late eighteenth-century shape, flaunts a tiered underskirt decorated with a filigree print. The underlying flamenco theme is given cachet by the length of black ribbon adorning the model's chignon. As one of Rome's top couturiers in the 1950s, Emilio Schuberth was also one of the first to present his collection on the Italian catwalks in 1952. His signature touch, of undercutting serious evening crinolines with unexpectedly baroque embroidery, attracted the early fashion paparazzi, who were drawn to his double-sided skirts, which metamorphosed into capes strewn with appliquéd flora. Schuberth often created fantastical skirts decorated with rows of foaming tulle and dotted with silk flowers. His only known training was twenty years of atelier work within his own house prior to 1952, earning him an elite clientele, which included the Duchess of Windsor.

☞ **Biagiotti, Fontana, Scaasi, Windsor**

417

Emilio Schuberth. **b** Naples (IT), 1904. **d** Rome (IT), 1972. **Ruched taffeta evening gown.** Photograph by G.M. Fadigati, 1955.

Shrimpton Jean   Model

Although Jean Shrimpton had been modelling for a few years when she was pictured here, she retained a quality that prompted her to say, 'I was as green as a salad', of the day she joined London's Lucie Clayton modelling school in 1960. Later that year she was on a shoot for a cornflakes advertisement, when she met the photographer David Bailey. 'Duffy was taking her picture against a blue background,' recalled Bailey. 'It was like her blue eyes were just holes drilled through her head to the paper behind. Duffy said, "Forget it – she's too posh for you," and I thought, "We'll see about that".' In the course of her affair with Bailey, Shrimpton became a sex icon and top model; 'the Shrimp' was born. Shrimpton's gawky, urchin style was perfect for Courrèges' space-age look and Quant's mini. When the couple appeared in American *Vogue* editor Diana Vreeland's office, she exclaimed, 'England has arrived!'

☞ Bailey, Kenneth, McLaughlin-Gill, Mesejeán

Jean Shrimpton. b Buckinghamshire (UK), 1942. **Jean Shrimpton in Epping Forest.** Photograph by Frances McLaughlin-Gill, *Harper's Bazaar*, 1965.

Sieff Jeanloup   Photographer

Astrid wears a black pillbox hat by Halston and silk crepe gown by Bill Blass. Jeanloup Sieff said of this photograph, 'She had an aristocratic profile and a very inspiring back.' For him, fashion photography is, and has always been, more than the simple representation of clothing. Instead, it is about his passion for beauty and form. 'The simple pleasure of rendering certain shapes, those maddening lights...' he has said of his predominantly black-and-white images. Born in Paris to Polish parents, Sieff received a camera for his fourteenth birthday. By 1960, after a brief spell at French *Elle* and the Magnum picture agency, he was living and working in New York taking fashion pictures for *Harper's Bazaar*. His fame grew quickly, as did his disdain for fashion. In 1966 he returned to Paris where he remained until his death, occasionally dabbling in fashion, but staying true to his passion: capturing moments which cannot recur.

☛ **Blass, Halston, Ritts**

Jeanloup Sieff. **b** Paris (FR), 1933. **d** Paris (FR), 2000. **'Astrid's back'.** Palm Beach. *Harper's Bazaar*, 1964.

Simpson Adele   Designer

From Mrs Eisenhower to Mrs Carter, Adele Simpson's conservative versions of the current trends have delighted the wives of many leading US politicians. Her clothes, that could be co-ordinated into complete wardrobes, proved practical and suitable for the active and exposed lives of her clients. The ensemble shown illustrates this: though not a suit, the slim skirt and asymmetrically fastening jacket could easily match other elements of Simpson's collections. The first American designer to treat cotton seriously as a fashion fabric, she used this fibre for street dresses and full-skirted evening gowns. Cotton was also used in one of Simpson's most celebrated creations: a 1950s chemise dress with attached belts which could be tied at the front or the back. Reputedly one of the highest-paid designers in the world at the age of twenty-one, she bought her own company in 1949.

☞ Galanos, John-Frederics, Leser, Maltézos

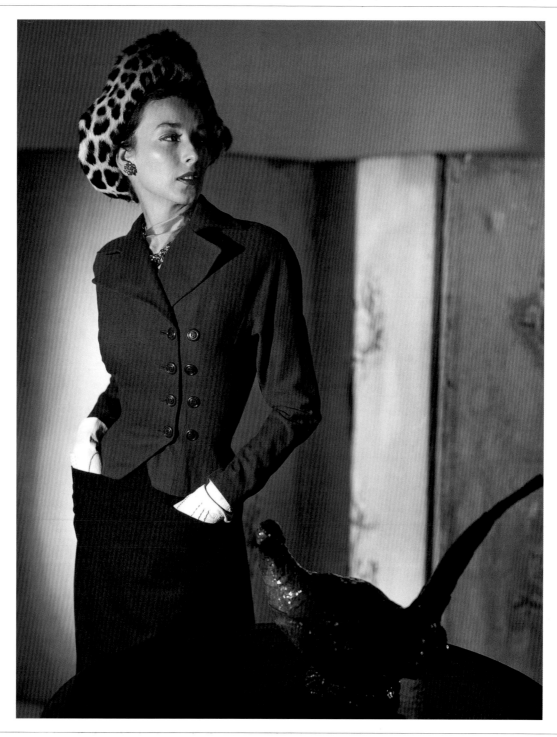

Adele Simpson. b New York (USA), 1903. **d** Greenwich, CT (USA), 1995. **Formal day suit.** Photograph by John Rawlings. 1947.

Sims David   Photographer

David Sims' stark, stylized fashion images have set agendas through their honesty. Here Sims chooses an utterly unstyled photograph, almost a snap of undressed hair and unclothed shoulders. In the early 1990s, after working as assistant to photographers Norman Watson and Enrique Badulescu, he began working with stylist Melanie Ward and models Kate Moss and Emma Balfour.

Together they helped to pioneer the grunge look, which gave them all an international platform between the covers of *Vogue*, *Harper's Bazaar* and *The Face*. Sims always tries to put the realities of daily life into his pictures, using either natural or edgy studio lighting, which illuminates quirky facial expressions and poses not seen in the realms of traditional fashion photography.

He is low-key about his contribution, saying, 'I think I've pushed the borders of fashion photography a bit.'

☛ Day, Moss, Sander

David Sims. b Sheffield (UK), 1966. **Strands of hair.** 1997.

Sitbon Martine   Designer

Wearing a splash-printed dress by Martine Sitbon, Stella Tennant crouches next to a surreal arrangement of wild animals. Sitbon herself started out as the wild child of French fashion, influenced by the rock scene inhabited by the Rolling Stones and the Velvet Underground (whose music was used as backing music for her first collection). As a teenager, Sitbon's early fashion education was gained in the flea markets of London and Paris, as has been the case for many designers before and since. Her passion for the English scene stayed with her as she worked first as a stylist, then as a designer. The art of pulling a look together from many inspirations is at the centre of Sitbon's style. In the mid-1980s she became known for feminized menswear, in particular fitted tail coats worn with slim trousers – suits inspired by those hanging on flea market rails.

☛ Kélian, Lenoir, Leroy, McDean, Tennant

422

Martine Sitbon. b Casablanca (MOR), 1951. **Stella Tennant wears devoré dress.** Photograph by Craig McDean, 1997.

Smith Graham   Milliner

A floral confection balances a formal hairstyle and co-ordinates with a powder-pink dress. It is a ceremonious hat made for the English season by Graham Smith who is noted for his royal millinery. He believes that a hat should appear to be part of the wearer, with particular emphasis on silhouette and scale. His lightweight, delicate textures create a hat that is showy yet well-mannered. Educated at the Royal College of Art, Smith's graduation collection achieved such acclaim that he was immediately appointed milliner at Lanvin-Castillo in Paris. In 1967 Smith launched his own label, at the same time collaborating with designers Jean Muir and Zandra Rhodes. Smith specializes in traditional styles, best shown by his designs for Princess Diana and the Duchess of York in the 1980s (he believes the Royal Family has saved British millinery). Smith is a master of balance and proportion, determined not to forsake flattery for fashion.

☛ Castillo, Diana, Muir, Rhodes

Graham Smith. b Bexley (UK), 1938. **'Small head, tiny roses, black-and-white chic'.** Photograph by Henry Clarke, British *Vogue*, 1965.

Smith Paul

Designer

At Paul Smith's party, men and women wear outfits that bear a contemporary blend of influences: unexpected materials mixed with traditional cloths, classic shapes cut with fashionable edge. In Smith's ranges, colour and print distinguish his wearable and individual work. Smith opened his first shop in Nottingham in 1970, expanding into London's Covent Garden in 1979 and Notting Hill in 1998. The first thing he ever sold was a Union Jack handkerchief and today his shops remain quirky, selling anything from toy robots to ties. It is this inspired eccentricity and a mind fine-tuned for marketing that has, unusually for a British company, turned Smith's label into a status one, particularly in Japan. In 1994 he launched Paul Smith Women, basing it on the same principles of cut, colour and fabric found in his menswear, with his androgynous suits finding a ready market for women who until then had to wear Paul Smith for Men.

☛ R. James, Nutter, Stephen

Paul Smith. b Nottingham (UK), 1946. **Paul Smith Men, Paul Smith Women. Autumn/winter 1997.** Photograph by Mario Testino.

Smith Willi — Designer

A jumpsuit, with functional zip, tie belt, large patch pockets and cuffed sleeves became extraordinary in the hands of Willi Smith, who decided to cut it out of silver-coated cloth in 1973. As a freelance designer he was already exploring the concept of putting fun into function. Then, in 1976, Smith launched his label Willi Wear. It produced well-priced, young, easy-to-wear, easy-to-care-for separates that brought designer fashion to a wider market. He used mainly natural fabrics and cut them with room for movement. For both men and women, Smith plugged the gap between jeans and stiff, formal clothes which meant nothing to the age group he was addressing. It was a market he was proud of, saying that he didn't design clothes for the Queen but for those who wave at her as she passes. Smith's style was founded on the concept of separates, at a time when the idea of traditional office dressing was being challenged.

☛ Bartlett, A. Klein, Rosier

425

Willi Smith. b Philadelphia (USA), 1948. d New York (USA), 1987. **Metallic jump-suit.** Photograph by Nick Machalaba, *Women's Wear Daily*, 1974.

Snow Carmel   Editor

The chic image of Paris is achieved through Louise Dahl-Wolfe's graceful composition of a model controlling her excitable poodles against a backdrop of the Sacré Cœur. Part of an illustrated fashion story, the picture accompanied Snow's 1955 Paris report for *Harper's Bazaar*, which concentrated largely on Balenciaga's and Dior's new silhouettes. Well before the rest of the press understood him, Carmel Snow was applauding Balenciaga's clean, sculptural lines, and she christened Christian Dior's New Look purely by accident in a letter to the designer. A major presence as American *Vogue*'s fashion editor, and then at *Harper's Bazaar* from 1932, it was said that if a dozing Snow awoke during a showing, the outfit appearing to her would be a hit.

For twenty years of her editorship-in-chief *Harper's Bazaar* mixed crisp fashion reportage with fresh visuals by Martin Munkacsi, Louise Dahl-Wolfe and Salvador Dalí.

☞ Balenciaga, Bassman, Brodovitch, Dior, Vreeland

426

Carmel Snow. b Dublin (IRE), 1887. **d** New York (USA), 1961. **Tunic and curled hat by Balenciaga.** Photograph by Louise Dahl-Wolfe, *Harper's Bazaar*, 1955.

Snowdon

Photographer

This 1957 fashion shoot by Snowdon, then Antony Armstrong Jones, for *Vogue* shows a new approach: the picture is infused with the energy inherent in the run-up to the 1960s. In fact, Snowdon's spontaneous moment was staged – the tumbling champagne glass was suspended on a clear thread and the model's thrilled greeting an act of theatre. He recalled, 'I made the models move and react, putting them in incongruous situations or performing incongruous feats. I made them run, dance, kiss, anything but stand still. Each sitting became a short story or miniature film strip'. This was the beginning of the language of contemporary fashion photography, a new naturalism and reality within artificial confines. In 1960 Armstrong Jones married Princess Margaret, prompting Cecil Beaton to call him 'the Cinderella of our time'.

☛ **Beaton, Fish, Mori**

Snowdon (Antony Armstrong Jones, 1st Earl of Snowdon). b London (UK), 1930. **Champagne glasses.** British *Vogue*, 1957.

Souleiman Eugene

Hairdresser

Eugene Souleiman's chignon is an amalgamation of traditional hairdressing and modern styling. The feathered hairpieces make it an avant-garde foil for her rococo gown by Valentino. Souleiman forges his own path through the world of hairdressing, often working with make-up artist Pat McGrath. Frequently contentious, he scorned the New York scene as boring and has fought with designers in his drive to develop new looks for the catwalk. In defiance of their expressive outfits, Souleiman has sent models along Prada's catwalk with belligerently unstyled hair, a typically contrary idea. He quickly tires of one look and, with the help of hairpieces, experiments with hair textures to reinvent the discipline on a monthly basis. Artificial or natural, Souleiman is one of the hairdressers who have made the manipulation of hair an indivisible element of fashion.

☛ McDean, McGrath, Prada, Valentino

Eugene Souleiman. b London (UK), 1961. **Taffeta gown.** Photograph by Craig McDean, Italian *Vogue*, 1998.

Sprouse Stephen   Designer

A design-school dropout, Sprouse arrived in New York in 1972 and soon made all the connections he needed for a career in fashion. Debbie Harry introduced him to Andy Warhol who introduced him to Halston who took him on as an assistant. But Sprouse's artistic interests distracted him and he and Halston parted company. In 1984, the photographer Steven Meisel persuaded him to launch his own label. Warhol's influence was always obvious – from Sprouse's silver showroom to his claim that Edie Sedgwick was his 'favourite meteor'. In 1997, when he relaunched his label, he used Warhol's artwork as prints on dresses. (Sprouse had exclusive rights to use the famous Pop Art images in clothing designs.) His work in the 1980s was largely influenced by the pop music scene: cut-out minidresses were printed with video images, Day-Glo 'hip hop' style graffiti was sprayed onto dresses.

☛ Halston, Meisel, Warhol, K. Yamamoto

429

Stephen Sprouse. **b** OH (USA), 1953. **d** New York (USA), 2004. **'Partytime' tank and sequined skirt.** Photograph by Rainer Hosch, *i-D*, 1998.

Steele Lawrence   Designer

Working on the lingerie theme, with a pin-tucked, chiffon camisole worn over a satin petticoat skirt, Lawrence Steele demonstrates his love of luxuriously simple clothes. His restraint is inspired by the work of Charles James and Claire McCardell. Born in Virginia, Steele had a military upbringing which took him to different cities throughout the United States, as well as Germany and Spain. Elements of this upbringing have been worked into his collections, including direct references such as epaulettes applied to the shoulders of shirts and jackets. Steele trained with Moschino in Milan, before moving on to Miuccia Prada's then relatively new womenswear line. He brought it forward with his simple, modern style, which blends American and European influences, then left in 1994 to continue his development under his own label.

☞ C. James, McCardell, Moschino, Prada

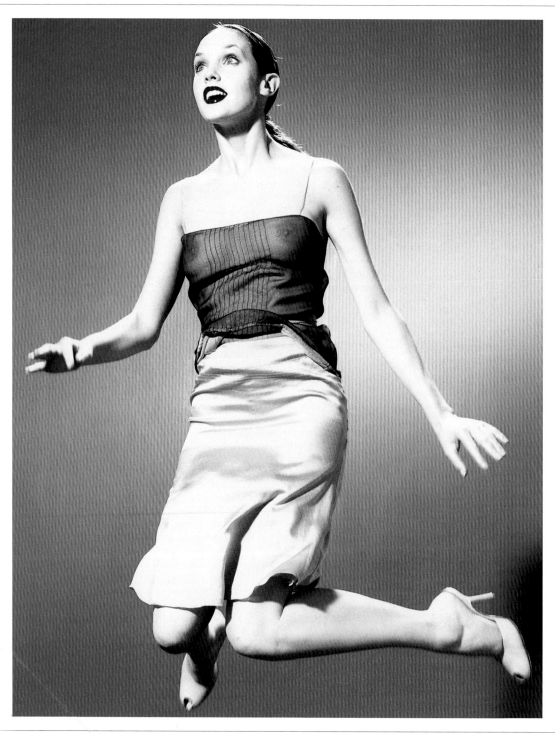

Lawrence Steele. b Hampton, VA (USA), 1963. **Strapless, pin-tucked camisole with skirt.** Photograph by Miles Aldridge, 1998.

430

Steichen Edward   Photographer

Gloria Swanson confronts the camera head-on. She wears a cloche, the tight-fitting, helmet-like hat which was the characteristic fashion headwear of the 1920s. In 1963, Edward Steichen recalled the circumstances surrounding the taking of this photograph. He and Gloria Swanson had a long session, with many changes of costume. At the end of the session, he took a black lace veil and hung it in front of her face, causing her hat to mould to her head and give a streamlined appearance. Her eyes dilated and her look was that of a leopardess lurking behind leafy shrubbery watching her prey. Steichen, a thoroughly modern fashion photographer, was noted for his settings which conveyed atmosphere and structure anchored to current fashions, a mood he took to *Vogue* in 1923. His working relationship with the model Marion Morehouse was the first such collaboration between mannequin and photographer.

☛ Barbier, Daché, Morehouse, Nast

431

Edward Steichen. b Luxembourg (LUX), 1879. d West Redding, CT (USA), 1973. **Gloria Swanson**. Photograph by Edward Steichen, American *Vogue*, 1924.

Steiger Walter Shoe designer

For Walter Steiger, the composition of a shoe is just as important as the aesthetic appeal of its exterior. Distinctive designs have been those with heels like many-sided cones or with triangular structures, an approach that was particularly popular in the 1970s and 1980s. Swiss-born, Steiger followed family tradition by undertaking an apprenticeship in shoemaking at the age of sixteen, after which he found employment at Bally in Paris. He moved to London in the early 1960s, where he designed lavish shoes under the Bally Bis label, as well as for Mary Quant. He also opened a successful studio in 1966 but felt Paris more appropriate for his first shop, which he opened in 1973. The sophistication of Steiger's highly innovative shoe construction met the demands of several couturiers with whom he subsequently collaborated, including Karl Lagerfeld, Chanel, Chloé, Montana, Oscar de la Renta and Nina Ricci.

☛ Bally, Kélian, Lenoir, Montana, de la Renta, Ricci

432

Walter Steiger. b Geneva (SW), 1942. **Heeled pump.** Photograph by Sheila Metzner, American *Vogue*, 1984.

Stephen John   Tailor

Photographed with his dog Prince, John Stephen wears the pristine suit, with Italianate 'bum-freezer' jacket, of a late 1950s buck. Known as the 'Million Pound Mod', Stephen revolutionized the way menswear was sold when he opened Carnaby Street's first swinging boutique in 1958. He would watch his teenage customers for inspiration – when he noticed them fluffing up their collars as they tried jackets on, he realized they were looking for wider lapels, which he produced and sold by the thousand. Stephen introduced extravagant details into the dusty realm of menswear, including flares, fly-fronted shirts inspired by dress shirts and suits cut from tweed treated with a lustrous finish. He had an early understanding of how quickly fashion would begin to change over the following decades and would not commit himself beyond eight weeks ahead, saying, 'In this world, change is violent. Anything can happen in two months.'

☛ Fish, Gilbey, P. Smith

433

John Stephen. b Glasgow (UK), c1936. d 2004. **John Stephen and Prince.** *Daily Mail*, 1957.

Stern Bert   Photographer

Bert Stern was the last person to photograph Marilyn Monroe, seen here wearing Christian Dior. This stroke of luck made him world famous and left the world with a series of sensitive portraits that transcend the duty of fashion photography. Stern taught himself photography while working as art director for the American magazine *Mayfair*: 'I was always moving around and reframing things in front of me.' His desire to capture the perfect image led him to a career in commercial photography, where he worked on print advertisements for Pepsi-Cola, Volkswagen and, most famously, Smirnoff. His 1955 picture of a martini glass in front of one of the pyramids at Giza became legendary, as did his image of Lolita wearing heart-shaped glasses for the 1962 film. He worked on fashion and portraiture throughout his career, photographing the most famous and most beautiful women of the time.

☛ Arnold, Dior, Orry-Kelly, Travilla

434

Bert Stern. b New York (USA), 1929. **Marilyn Monroe wears Dior.** British *Vogue*, 1962.

Stewart Stevie and Holah David (Body Map)   Designers

'Gawky but sexy' is how David Holah and Stevie Stewart defined their fashion sportswear in 1984. Body Map, their label, was named after a 1960s artwork by Italian artist Enrico Job which mapped a man's body with two thousand photographs: 'It seemed to sum up our approach to pattern cutting,' explained Holah. The partnership created sawn-off sweatshirts worn over striped tube skirts in a *mélange* of layers and knitted fabrics under absurd collection titles such as 'A Cat in a Hat Takes a Rumble With a Techno Fish'. Body Map designed a sporty and flexible wardrobe. Smith's stylized compass motifs were interwoven with abstract technological designs to produce graphic fabrics. The shapes were designed for London's uninhibited clubland which Body Map inhabited by night and brought to the catwalk. The sight prompted *Women's Wear Daily* to ask if it were all 'an outrageous pretension or merely a pretentious outrage'.

☛ Boy George, Ettedgui, Forbes

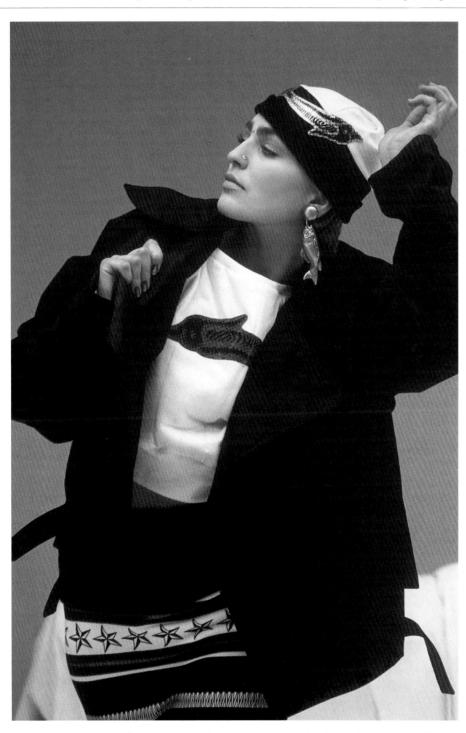

Stevie Stewart. b London (UK), 1958; **David Holah. b** London (UK), 1958. (Body Map.) **'Cat in a Hat' collection. Autumn/winter 1984.** Photograph by Andy Lane.

Stiebel Victor   Designer

Three women are snapped by Norman Parkinson en route to an Ascot race meeting. They are dressed and hatted by Stiebel in his romantic style, with their vast cartwheel hats dominating soft, feminine dresses with hemlines that stop eight inches from the ground. As a favoured designer of society women, Stiebel carefully considered his accessories, regarding them as part of his total look.

Stiebel studied architecture at Cambridge before being encouraged to enter fashion by Norman Hartnell. Having served as an apprentice at Reville & Rossiter, he became an accomplished British fashion designer and a member of the Incorporated Society of London Fashion Designers, together with Hartnell, Hardy Amies and Edward Molyneux. Stiebel also dressed actresses and members

of the British Royal Family, including Princess Margaret for whom he designed the going-away outfit for her marriage to Anthony Armstrong Jones.

☛ Amies, Hartnell, Horvat, Molyneux, Parkinson

Victor Stiebel. **b** Durban (SA), 1907. **d** London (UK), 1976. **Dresses and 'Cartwheel' straw hats.** Photograph by Norman Parkinson, *Harper's Bazaar*, 1938.

Storey Helen   Designer

Helen Storey has loved texture since childhood. Here she applies sequins to leggings with the intention of glamorizing what, at the end of the 1980s, was a basic garment usually cut from black Lycra. Her womenswear had the intention of putting forward a new mood of aggressively sexy feminism. Her bras were decorated with dangerously sharp gemstones and her metal minidresses and black patent leather chaps were equally challenging. 'Clothes made by women don't deny what's underneath – we dress the essence, not the male-inspired dream,' Storey said of this work. She trained with Valentino and Lancetti, both designers famous for their feminine sensibilities. After a partnership with designer Karen Boyd in the 1980s, Storey continued her explorations alone. In 1996, she collaborated with her sister to produce a sci-art project, *Primitive Streak*, which used magnified human structures as a basis for textile designs.

☛ Lancetti, Rosier, Valentino

Helen Storey. b London (UK), 1959. **Sequined leggings.** Photograph by Eamonn J. McCabe, British *Elle*, 1990.

Strauss Levi   Designer

A septuagenarian teacher invites her young audience to grapple with its preconceptions in an advertisement for Levi Strauss. 'I wish I had invented blue jeans', Yves Saint Laurent once said. 'Jeans are expressive and discreet, they have sex appeal and simplicity – everything I could want for the clothes I design.' The real inventor was Levi Strauss, a Jewish-Bavarian immigrant pedlar who followed the Gold Rush to sell his goods. When his customers asked for trousers, he cut up tents to make them. In 1860 Strauss discovered an equally tough fabric called *serge de Nîmes* (denim), from France. Jeans were named after the Genoese sailors' trousers on which the original 501 style was based. First brought to Europe by GIs during the Second World War, jeans were glamorized by the 1950s rebels James Dean and Marlon Brando. In the 1980s, a pair of Levis worn with Dr Martens shoes became the enduring uniform for an entire generation.

☛ **Benetton, Dean, Fischer, Hechter, N. Knight**

Levi Strauss. **b** Bavaria (GER), 1829. **d** San Francisco, CA (USA), 1902. **'Josephine, 79, teacher, Colorado' wears 501 jeans.** Photograph by Nick Knight, 1996.

Sui Anna

Designer

Nadja Auermann appears on Anna Sui's catwalk as Greta Garbo in sequins, trilby and boa. The key to Sui's look is the eclectic way she mixes her clothes, rather than the individual garments themselves. As shown here, she has a modern take on most fashion periods. This retro-reworking is typical of 1990s fashion, and Sui's versions are more wearable than many. She attended Parsons School of Design in New York and worked as a stylist – a skill that can be appreciated in the way she brings a look together from several directions. While studying, she teamed up with a classmate, photographer Steven Meisel. She also worked briefly as a designer in a sportswear company, before setting up on her own in 1981, after Macy's began stocking her designs.

Her inspiration comes from some forty years of magazine cuttings, stored away in what she calls her 'Genius Files'.

☛ Garbo, Garren, Meisel

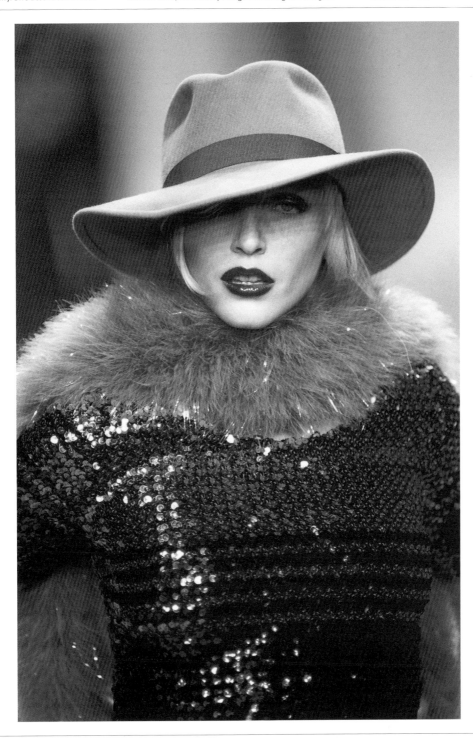

439

Anna Sui. **b** Dearborn Heights, MI (USA), 1955. **Nadja Auermann wears a sequined sweater and boa.** Photograph by Chris Moore, 1995.

Sumurun

Model

When Edward Molyneux left Lucile to open his own couture house in 1919, he hired Vera Ashby as his head mannequin. He named her Sumurun, the Enchantress of the Desert, and she became the highest-paid model in Paris (crowds would gather to see her enter and exit the Molyneux establishment). She was photographed by Baron de Meyer and drawn by Drian. This photograph shows Vera in the Molyneux studio dressed for the *Coucher du Soleil* (sunset) ball. Inspired by her exotic, oriental look, Molyneux created a harem dress of silver tissue worn under a sleeveless tunic of gold lamé. He concealed electric bulbs in the ruby jewels that decorated her outfit. As the house lights were dimmed, she pressed a button to light up her outfit, causing men to whoop and cheer. After retiring, Vera became a *vendeuse* at Molyneux, later moving to Norman Hartnell where she was appointed *vendeuse* to the Queen.

☛ **Drian, Hartnell, de Meyer, Molyneux**

Sumurun (Vera Ashby). b London (UK), 1895. d Victoria, BC (CAN), 1985. **Sumurun wears costume by Molyneux.** Photograph by Jean Desboutin, 1921.

Sybilla

Designer

'Travelling Clothes' is the title of this image by Javier Vallhonrat of Sybilla's autumn/winter 1989–90 collection. The incongruous title reflects the designer's Spanish sense of humour – these clothes are suited to a walk in the rain rather than international travel. Sybilla creates surreal designs and marries opposites in her work: extravagance with subtlety, humour with elegance. Here, a coat has the spirit of both a traditional belted trench coat and an opera coat by her fellow countryman Cristóbal Balenciaga. Sybilla grew up in Madrid and moved to Paris in 1980 to work at Yves Saint Laurent's couture atelier. After one year she dismissed Paris as too snobbish and cold, returning to the fun and laid-back atmosphere of her home city. In 1983 she launched her own label and swiftly became renowned for her use of soft colours and quirky, sculpted shapes in her clothing, shoes, bags and, latterly, furniture.

☛ Toledo, Vallhonrat

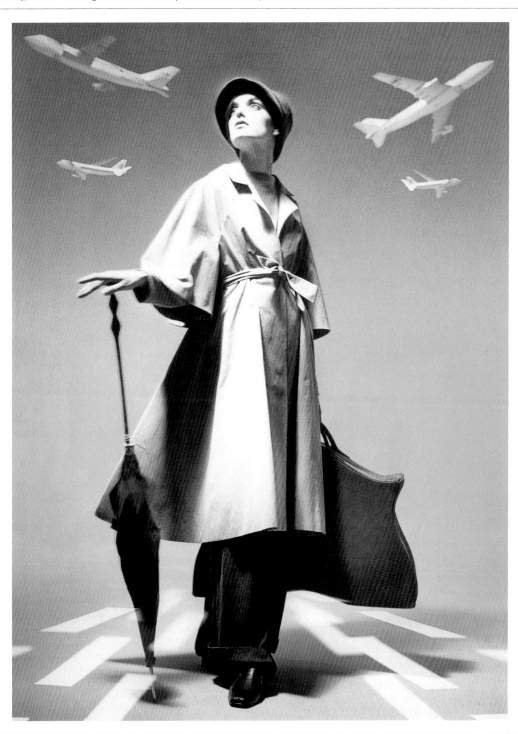

441

Sybilla (Sybilla Sorondo–Myelzwynska). **b** New York (USA), 1963. **'Travelling Clothes', 1989.** Photograph by Javier Vallhonrat.

Talbot Suzanne   Milliner

'Talbot would send us out to dine in public looking as exotic as the Wicked Queen in *Snow White* – easily the most chic vamp the films have ever evolved.' The caption that accompanied this picture takes us into Suzanne Talbot's charmed world. Talbot had long since died (her own powers being at their peak in the 1880s) but her spirit lived in the house's close alliance with the fashion world. The Talbot premises were part of the rich fashion map of Paris in the 1920s and 1930s, which included those of hairdresser Antoine, couturières Chanel and Schiaparelli and shoe designer André Perugia. This black silk jersey hat, embellished with a golden spike and embroidery, included a veil. Such theatrical French millinery was greatly admired by the American market. With Paulette, Mme Agnès and Lilly Daché, who moved to New York having trained at Talbot, it was a house whose work moved in parallel with the fashions for clothes.

☛ **Agnès, Antoine, Daché, Paulette, Perugia**

442

Suzanne Talbot. (Active 1880s–1900s.) **Embroidered, silk jersey hat for Bergdorf Goodman.** Photograph by George Hoyningen-Huene, *Harper's Bazaar*, 1939.

Tappé Herman Patrick Designer

Mary Pickford, 'America's Sweetheart', wears the wedding dress chosen for her marriage to Douglas Fairbanks. It was originally made by Herman Tappé for Natica Nast, Condé's daughter, to wear for a *Vogue* sitting published in 1920. Tappé had been upset that he should be asked to make it in such a tiny size, but that was before Pickford had seen and selected it for her high-profile nuptials. The silk tulle wrap, worn over a plain, strapless dress, is trimmed with ruffles edged with silk organdie. Elsewhere, the tulle is formed into rows of tight gathers. Wedding dresses, and those for bridesmaids, formed the core of Tappé's exclusive, expensive work. He was known as the Poiret of New York for his individual and mysterious style. His was a romantic, feminine view, and he became a creator of robes de style – quixotic dresses based on costumes found in paintings.

☞ Emanuel, de Meyer, Nast, Poiret

Herman Patrick Tappé. (Active 1910s–1940s.) **Organdie dress with ribbon-banding and matching bonnet.** Photograph by Baron de Meyer, American *Vogue*, 1920.

Tarlazzi Angelo   Designer

An asymmetric, taffeta evening dress perfectly details Angelo Tarlazzi's well-recognized skill: blending Italian imagination with French chic. Its bodice, caught on one shoulder, flows into a point, moving over a contrasting skirt. Tarlazzi abandoned his studies in political science to pursue a career in fashion design. He worked at the house of Carosa for a number of years, before leaving Rome for Paris to become an assistant at Jean Patou. By the late 1960s he was freelancing between Paris, Milan, Rome and New York, during which time he was affiliated with Laura Biagiotti. It was a mix which formed his appreciation of the international market. By 1972 he was back at Patou but this time as artistic director, a high-status position he held until he launched his own prêt-à-porter label in 1977. Tarlazzi's garments are amply cut from soft fabrics and often use such asymmetric drapes.

☛ Biagiotti, Patou, Sarne

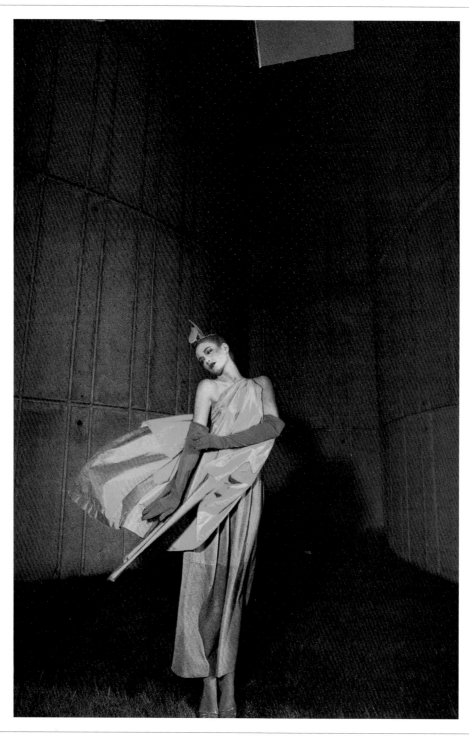

Angelo Tarlazzi. b Ascoli Piceno (IT), 1945. **Taffeta evening dress.** Photograph by Jean-François du Sel des Monts, *L'Officiel*, 1980.

Tatsuno Koji   Designer

Dress? Costume? Sculpture? Amid the acceleration backstage, the models stand motionless in orchestrated coils of fine mesh, trimmed with rows of flowers. Like sculptural relief, these lyrical compositions reflect Tatsuno's synthesis of modern technology and folkcraft. He has spent his career experimenting with rare craft techniques, initially from his bespoke tailoring establishment in London's Mayfair and now from his small gallery at the Palais-Royal in Paris. Completely self-taught in the most English art of tailoring, Tatsuno arrived in London as an antique art dealer in 1982. He co-launched the design label Culture Shock, based on the 1980s temperament of avant-garde Japanese fashion. Disillusioned by what he calls the 'corrupt and ephemeral', Tatsuno went on to pursue a more cerebral approach to fashion, developing his label in 1987, financially backed by Yohji Yamamoto.

☛ W. Klein, Macdonald, Y. Yamamoto

Koji Tatsuno. b Tokyo (JAP), 1964. **Backstage at Koji Tatsuno's catwalk show.** Photograph by William Klein, 1992.

Teller Juergen   Photographer

Iris Palmer lies flat; her underwear, designed as a covering, is made superfluous by the camera's angle – an example of the 'sexual fashion photography' that Juergen Teller feels allies his work to that of Helmut Newton. For him a model should never be regarded as a clothes horse, rather he or she should be represented as the people they are. Consequently, Teller shoots clothes as part of an image rather than its focus. Primarily he is a diarist recording the lives of those he works and lives with, resulting in a sometimes uncomfortable real-life documentary of those working in fashion. His uncompromising style is also non-judgmental and Teller doesn't prettify those lives. Originally encouraged by Nick Knight, Teller's reportage work was advocated by stylist and partner Venetia Scott above that which is artificially posed. Together they have created distinctive images for Katharine Hamnett and Helmut Lang.

☞ Hamnett, N. Knight, Lang, Newton, von Unwerth

Juergen Teller. b Erlangen (GER), 1964. **Iris Palmer. Katharine Hamnett advertising campaign.** 1997.

Tennant Stella   Model

The six-foot figure of Stella Tennant is dressed in Helmut Lang. Despite her model figure and superlative skin, Tennant's edgy looks originally fell outside the parameters between which models usually fall. She defied any stereotype and succeeded because of it. The art student who had pierced her own nose on a railway platform was propelled into modelling after being photographed by two leading photographers: as one of London's 'It' girls by Steven Meisel and as the granddaughter of the Duke and Duchess of Devonshire by Bruce Weber. Called the 'antithesis of the supermodel', Tennant was nevertheless picked up by Karl Lagerfeld for Chanel. Her slouching demeanour on the catwalk made the bouncing, pouty attitude of other models look passé. What she brought to fashion was cool. With characteristic nonchalance, Tennant finished the first chapter of her career by 'retiring' after just five years.

☛ S. Ellis, Lagerfeld, Lang, Meisel, Sitbon, Weber

Stella Tennant. b Chatsworth (UK), 1971. **Helmut Lang T-shirt and tiered skirt.** Photograph by Sean Ellis, American *Vogue*, 1998.

Testino Mario   Photographer

Nadja Auermann pulls her T-shirt from under her skirt. In doing so she exposes her legendary legs for Mario Testino, or 'Super Mario' as he is nicknamed. 'Fashion is all about making a girl look sexy,' he says, and it is his ability to orchestrate this mood that has made his photographs so powerful. In the case of his advertising images for Gucci, Testino imbues overtly sexy clothes with a dramatic quality, placing his models in the glamorous world in which he himself lives. He has photographed the most famous and iconic women of the late twentieth century, including Madonna, a friend, who was his model for an advertising campaign for Versace Atelier. Testino used his talent for best representing the women he adores when he became the last person to photograph Diana, Princess of Wales. Those pictures, which use a relaxed reportage style, are regarded as the most flattering and modern taken in her later life.

☛ Diana, Ford, S. Jones, Missoni, Versace, Westwood

448

Mario Testino. b Lima (PER), 1954. Nadja Auermann. French *Glamour*, 1994.

Thimister   Josephus Melchior   Designer

Surrounded by patterns and fabric, Josephus Thimister and his team work on a collection for Balenciaga, the label for which he designed from 1992 to 1997. Thimister was perceived by some as the natural heir to Cristóbal Balenciaga, sharing the pure vision of the Spanish designer often described as the Picasso of the fashion world. After one collection French *Elle* said, 'Balenciaga probably clapped in his grave.' Thimister used his detailed archives to create religiously simple clothes which have been called 'neo-couture' for their modern attitude. Educated at Antwerp's Royal Academy of Art, the training ground for Martin Margiela, Ann Demeulemeester and Dries Van Noten, Thimister describes his clothes, now designed under his own label, as being about 'light, fabric and shadow'. In showing his first collection, he studiously avoided fuss, cutting thirty dresses from black or blue-black fabric.

☛ **Balenciaga, Demeulemeester, Margiela, Van Noten**

449

Thomass Chantal Designer

Photographed against the masculine background of American footballers, Chantal Thomass's tartan-lined jacket flies away to reveal a co-ordinating bustier. Chantal Thomass provided frilly, coquettish underwear and outerwear for every Lolita or Vargas Girl in France. She described her designs as 'provocative, but not vulgar'; it is a delicate distinction and a line she treads carefully. Thomass did not train as a designer but began her fashion career in 1966 by opening a boutique, Ter et Bantine, in partnership with her husband. It sold tantalizing, flirtatious clothes and enjoyed patronage from Brigitte Bardot, among others. In 1975 the pair founded the Chantal Thomass label and designed a clothing range. Thomass trimmed jackets and evening dresses with lace but her name will forever be connected to lacy underwear, nightwear and stockings that combine fashion and sensuality.

☞ John-Frederics, Molinari, Schiffer

Chantal Thomass. b Malakoff, TX (USA), 1947. **Bustier and grey skirt suit.** Photograph by Bill King, French *Vogue*, 1982.

450

Tiffany Charles Lewis Jewellery designer

Audrey Hepburn's role as Holly Golightly in the 1961 film *Breakfast at Tiffany's* made the jewellery store, whose clients have included Queen Victoria, even more famous. In this photograph, Hepburn wears a Givenchy dress and the priceless 'Ribbon' necklace made by Jean Schlumberger, the celebrated Parisian jeweller, who worked for Tiffany & Co from the 1950s until his death in 1987. The centrepiece of the necklace, which is made from eighteen-carat gold, platinum and white diamonds, is the Tiffany diamond, bought by founder Charles Lewis Tiffany in 1877 for $18,000. Rather than selling it, Tiffany placed it in the window of his New York store. Charles's son, Louis Comfort Tiffany, Elsa Peretti and Paloma Picasso continued to keep Tiffany at the forefront of jewellery design. It is regarded as a fashion-friendly company for its broad range – providing both grandeur and delicate, modern pieces.

☛ **Cartier, Givenchy, Lalique, Peretti**

451

Charles Lewis Tiffany. b New York (USA), 1848. **d** New York (USA), 1933. **Audrey Hepburn wears the Tiffany 'Ribbon' necklace at a press reception for Breakfast at Tiffany's.** 1961.

Toledo Isabel   Designer

Latin flavour, surreal lines and futuristic content define Isabel Toledo's radical fashions sewn in the tradition of couture. Toledo, who speaks of herself as a seamstress rather than a fashion designer, creates in the manner of couturières such as Madeleine Vionnet and Madame Grès. Like them, she does not start from a flat sketch, but envisions clothing in three dimensions, always bearing a shape in her mind, usually a circle or a curved line. 'I love the maths behind the romance', she says of her so-called liquid architecture's craftsmanship. The crepe jersey that forms the body of this dress is suspended by the armholes and anchored at the hem (unseen) by a construction of lace, net, wool and felt; the effect is like that of water slowly pouring into a barrel. Toledo's husband, Ruben, known for his whimsical fashion illustrations, manages the business side of the New York-based company and acts as her creative alter ego.

☛ Grès, Sybilla, Vionnet

452

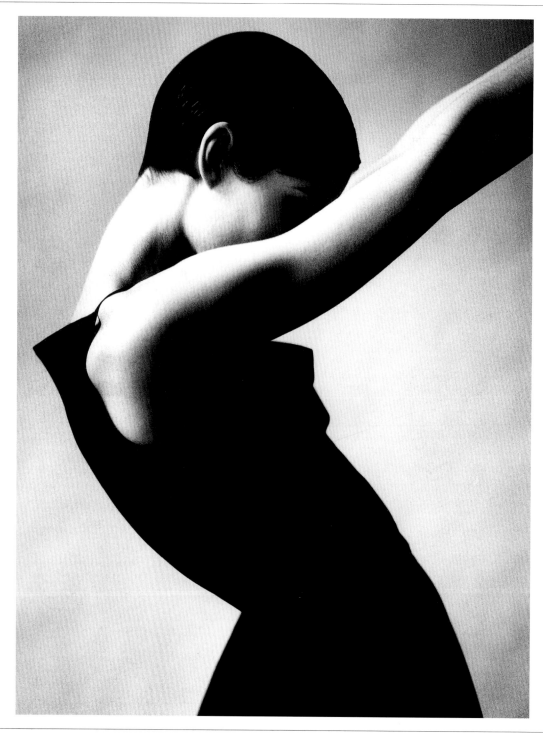

Isabel Toledo. b Camajani (CU), 1961. **Matte jersey 'Infanta' dress, spring/summer 1992.** Photograph by Ruven Afanador.

De Tommaso Carmen (Carven)

Designer

This immaculate striped cotton dress is designed specifically for a petite figure. The vertical lines which appear from pin-tucks above and below the waist will lengthen the figure while the dainty detail of bows and reversed stripes accentuate the hand-span waist. Carmen de Tommaso started designing because she was unable to find the clothes she wanted, in her case those that would fit her tiny figure. She studied architecture before founding the house of Carven in Paris in 1937 (a modification of her christian name). With her architectural training, de Tommaso excelled at adjusting the accessories to the exact proportions of her clientele. The dress below is an example of intelligent problem-solving, a vital aspect of good fashion design.

She diversified and enjoyed a successful career creating and marketing perfumes, of which Ma Griffe is the most enduring.

☛ de Prémonville, de la Renta

453

Carmen de Tommaso. **b** Châteauroux (FR), 1909. (Carven.) **White dress with green stripes.** 1945.

Topolino

Make-up artist

Conceptual make-up artist Topolino describes his influences as 'street, insects, nature, space, fairies, circus, cartoons and life', and his style as 'trashy trendy, fantasy but chic', which sums up this photograph. When asked about his technique, Topolino replied, 'It is more about imagination than technique.' Here, that imagination conjures nails embellished with rose thorns and lacquered.

The lips are half-coloured by feathered pencil lines. These methods are examples of the way Topolino explores the potential of make-up and uses it to accessorize fashion, in this case a fake fur jacket that begs such aggressive touches. He has a passion for Mickey Mouse, and has been described as a 'Puck-like figure' due to his diminutive size. He taught himself the art of make-up because of his interest in fashion, and began working in 1985. He has produced startling andinfluential catwalk work for designers Alexander McQueen and Philip Treacy.

☛ Colonna, N. Knight, McQueen, Treacy

454

Topolino. b Marseille (FR), 1965. **Nails decorated with rose thorns.** Photograph by Norbert Schoerner, French *Glamour*, 1994.

Torimaru Gnyuki (Yuki)

Designer

Jersey flows like water from a halter-neck bodice by Gnyuki Torimaru, formerly known as Yuki. He studied architecture, before becoming a textile engineer, an occupation that has dominated his work since. His love of vivid colour, purity and fluidity has remained a constant in Torimaru's work. He developed them to their fullest potential after discovering, in 1984, a luxurious non-crease polyester which could maintain long-lasting pleats. Using intricate pleating techniques, he created ever-more fantastical designs. Japanese-born, Yuki made London his permanent home in 1964, having worked for Norman Hartnell and Pierre Cardin, and launched his own label in 1972. He soon enjoyed a degree of fame for his one-size hooded or draped jersey dresses, often inspired by monastic garb. His dramatic cut often uses panels cut on a full circle – a luxurious technique that gives a garment the maximum fullness that can be achieved without seaming.

☛ Burrows, Muir, Valentina

Gnyuki Torimaru (Yuki). b Miyazaki-Ken (JAP), 1940. **Jersey halter-neck dress. Late 1970s.** Photograph by Richard Davis.

Toskan Frank and Angelo Frank (M.A.C)

Cosmetics creators

Frank Toskan is joined by drag queen RuPaul and singer k.d. lang who contort their bodies to form the words 'Viva Glam', the name of the lipstick that has championed M.A.C's (Make-up Art Cosmetics) Aids awareness campaign. Both celebrities epitomize the company's slogan, All Races, All Sexes, All Ages, that trailblazed the notion of unconventional beauty for the 1990s.

The catalyst for a cult beauty boom, M.A.C. started in 1984 in Frank Toskan's kitchen as a long-wearing foundation to meet the harsh demands of film, catwalk and stage work. As the owner of a national chain of hair salons, his business acumen complemented the creative expertise of the late Frank Angelo, an acclaimed hairstylist and make-up artist. Their beauty colourscape,

from the futuristic space tramp to the sun-buffed naturalist, has promoted the notion of make-up as complete freedom of expression.

☛ McGrath, Nars, Uemura

Frank Toskan. **b** Trieste (IT), 1950; **Frank Angelo. b** Montreal, QC (CAN), 1947. **d** Coral Gables, FL (USA), 1997. (M.A.C.) **'Viva Glam' lipstick advertisement.** 1996.

Tran Hélène Illustrator

A sedate, navy pyjama suit by Hardy Amies and crisp, organza shirt and skirt by Alistair Blair are put into a pastoral English scene by Hélène Tran. This was one of a series of images that illustrated the social summer season of 1987. Tran's easy, loose technique characterizes rich clothes and their languid wearers with broad washes of watercolour and baroque curls. Details such as Manolo Blahnik's shoes and sandals are picked out with fine brushwork. The picture recalls the social commentary by artists such as Marcel Vertès, who captured social situations in a way that photography cannot. Tran studied illustration at the École Supérieure d'Art Graphique in her native city, Paris. Her dramatic, and often humorous illustrations have been published in British and American *Vogue* and *La Mode en Peinture*. Tran has also illustrated for clients, including Jean Patou and Roger Vivier.

☛ Amies, Blahnik, Blair, Vertès, Vivier

Hélène Tran. b Paris (FR), 1954. **Outfits by Hardy Amies and Alistair Blair.** *Harpers & Queen*, 1987.

Travilla William   Designer

In one of film history's most famous moments, Marilyn Monroe's halter-neck dress is whipped into action over a city grille in the steamy comedy, *The Seven Year Itch*. The dress was designed by William Travilla, a favourite of Monroe's, who designed the costumes for eleven of her films. This dress is an adaptation of classical Grecian robes, with pleats mimicking draping and a bodice shaped by a crisscross tie. It actually came off the peg and remains a best-seller – resurrected every couple of years by retailers who are still profiting from its sexy allure. Travilla's appeal was his ability to flatter figures, including Marilyn's healthy hips and chest. His traditional assertion that 'femininity is the strongest weapon a woman can have' took him on to design the wardrobe for the early 1980s soap opera *Dallas*, in which the characters did indeed wield their womanliness like instruments of medieval battle.

☞ Head, Irene, Stern

William Travilla. **b** Avalon (USA), 1920. **d** Los Angeles, CA (USA), 1990. **Marilyn Monroe wears her famous white pleated dress.** Still from *The Seven Year Itch*. 1955.

458

Treacy Philip   Milliner

Philip Treacy's purple, melozine trilby, which historically belongs to the male hat rack, plays with both glamour and sexuality; the jaunty angle which conceals part of the face is reminiscent of Marlene Dietrich and the provocative cross-dressing common in 1930s cabaret style. Each season Treacy redraws the line of this style, an ever-changing classic worn by fashion icons as diverse as Chanel's creative director Amanda Harlech and Boy George. By comparison, many of Treacy's extravagant couture hats would be more appropriately called sculpture. The usual millinery fabrics are sometimes replaced with industrial plastics; a galleon is reconstructed, with correct rigging, then fixed to the head; and fluorescent satin ellipses shoot sideways from the crown for a full metre. Since he graduated from London's Royal College of Art in 1990, Treacy has redefined the role of millinery in fashion.

☛ Boy George, Conran, Milner, Topolino, Underwood

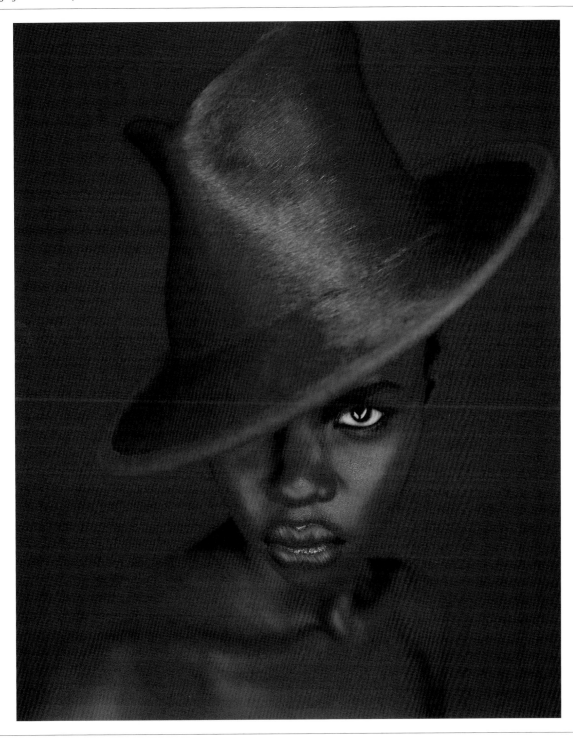

Philip Treacy. b Ahascragh (IRE), 1967. **Purple trilby.** Photograph by Christoph Sillem, the *Guardian*, 1997.

Tree Penelope

Model

Cecil Beaton photographs Penelope Tree's elfin face, an extraordinary one that made 'The Tree' a match for 'The Twig' in the 1960s. She was the rebellious daughter of a rich and serious-minded family who were disappointed in Penelope's original decision to embark on a career as a model. When she was first shot at thirteen by Diane Arbus, her father, a British multimillionaire, vowed he would sue if the pictures were published. By the time Diana Vreelend sent her to Richard Avedon, she was seventeen and her father had relented. David Bailey described Penelope as 'an Egyptian Jiminy Cricket'; in 1967 she moved into his flat in London's Primrose Hill which became a hang-out for spaced-out hippies who, Bailey recalls, would be 'smoking joints I had paid for and calling me a capitalist pig!' In 1974, Bailey and Tree split up and she moved to Sydney, Australia, far away from the focus of the fashion photographer's camera.

☛ Avedon, Bailey, Beaton, Vreeland

460

Penelope Tree. b London (UK), 1950. **Penelope Tree.** Photograph by Cecil Beaton, 1967.

Trigère Pauline   Designer

The structured tailoring on show here explains why in *Breakfast at Tiffany's*, Patricia Neal's character, an uptight girlfriend wearing Pauline Trigère, nearly proved a match for Audrey Hepburn's youthfully elegant outfits by Hubert de Givenchy. She represented grown-up and urban New York fashion. Born and trained in the family business of dressmaking in Paris, Trigère arrived in New York in 1937. After working with Travis Banton at Hattie Carnegie, Trigère opened her own business in 1942. More than fifty years later, she would demonstrate how she cut into luxury fabric directly from the bolt onto the mannequin to awestruck fashion students. Her cutting was sure, emphasizing wrapping and tying in the French tradition of magnificent scarves and idiosyncratic knottings. Trigère was the best model for her fashion: urban chic in luxury fabrics, coats robust and flowing, and rhinestone bras.

☛ **Banton, Carnegie, Givenchy**

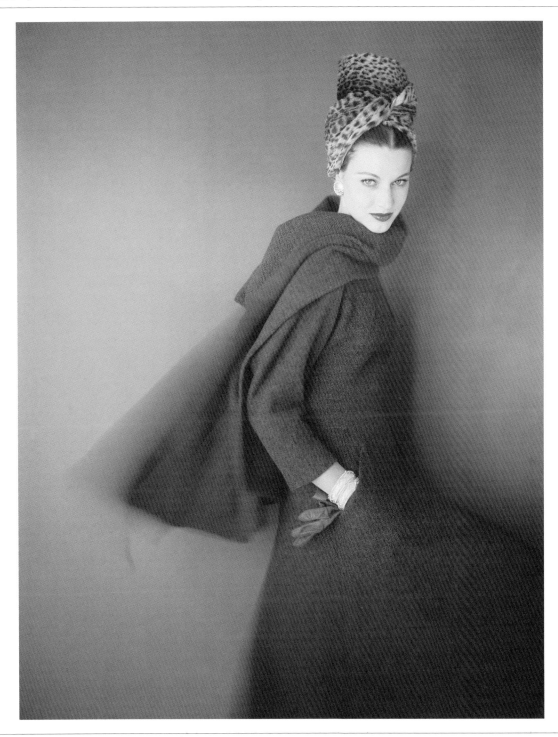

Pauline Trigère. b Paris (FR), 1912. d New York (USA), 2002. **Leopard-print turban and crimson coat.** Photograph by Karen Radkai, American *Vogue*, 1959.

Troublé Agnès (Agnès b.)   Designer

With her simple clothes, swept-back hair and classic black sunglasses, this model is the epitome of Parisian chic. The stripy black-and-white T-shirt shown is reminiscent of Jean Seberg's in *Breathless*, and the simple style of Left Bank beats. 'I don't like the word "fashion"; I say I design clothes,' says Agnès b. Her neutral-coloured wardrobe staples: crisp white shirts, plain knitwear and pared-down (often black) tailoring have survived precisely because they pay very little attention to fashion. She worked as a junior fashion editor at *Elle* magazine in France, and as a stylist at Cacharel and Dorothée Bis. She opened her first shop in 1975, during an eccentric era of flared trousers and platform shoes. From the outset, her designs, based on utilitarian clothing such as workman's blue overalls and undershirts, found a place as fashion's antidote.

☛ Bousquet, Farhi, Jacobson

Agnès Troublé. **b** Versailles (FR), 1941. (Agnès b.) **Black-and-white striped top.** Photograph by Darzacq, 1997.

Turbeville Deborah Photographer

Models Isabel Weingarten and Ella Milewiecz become part of Deborah Turbeville's dreamscape. A typical shot, it depicts motionless subjects who pose in a group but without relating to one another. Turbeville's career path was a tortuous journey through fashion, an experience that gave her a deep understanding of clothes. Having arrived in New York in 1956, she worked as a model and moved on to assist designer Claire McCardell. She then turned to magazines, becoming a fashion editor for *Mademoiselle*. In 1966 she changed course again. Turbeville became a freelance photographer for *Harper's Bazaar* after being inspired by a talk given by Richard Avedon. By 1972 she was working for the cult magazine *Nova* in London. Her haunting style was very different from other fashion photography of the time and yet it was intriguing rather than alienating.

☛ Avedon, McCardell, Rykiel

463

Deborah Turbeville. **b** Medford, MA (USA), 1938. **Isabel Weingarten and Ella Milewiecz.** 1978.

Turlington Christy Model

Christy Turlington's beauty is a versatile one. Here Francesco Scavullo makes hers a cover face in the traditional sense. But equally, Turlington has personified nude, unaffected beauty – representing Calvin Klein's fragrances since 1987. While modelling relies on the arts of lighting, make-up and retouching, a few women are able to achieve a perfect look through self-awareness; Turlington is one such woman. As she told *Vogue*, 'I know how to make every part of my body appear different than it actually is. I can make my eyes and my lips appear bigger by putting my chin down... You can manipulate everything for photography.' Called 'the most beautiful woman in the world', she feels it's all down to her full, symmetrical lips: 'I have gotten most of my advertising contacts because of them.' Turlington managed to make an easy transition from the haute glamour of the 1980s to the relaxed simplicity of the following decade.

☛ Ferre, C. Klein, Lindbergh, Scavullo, Valentino

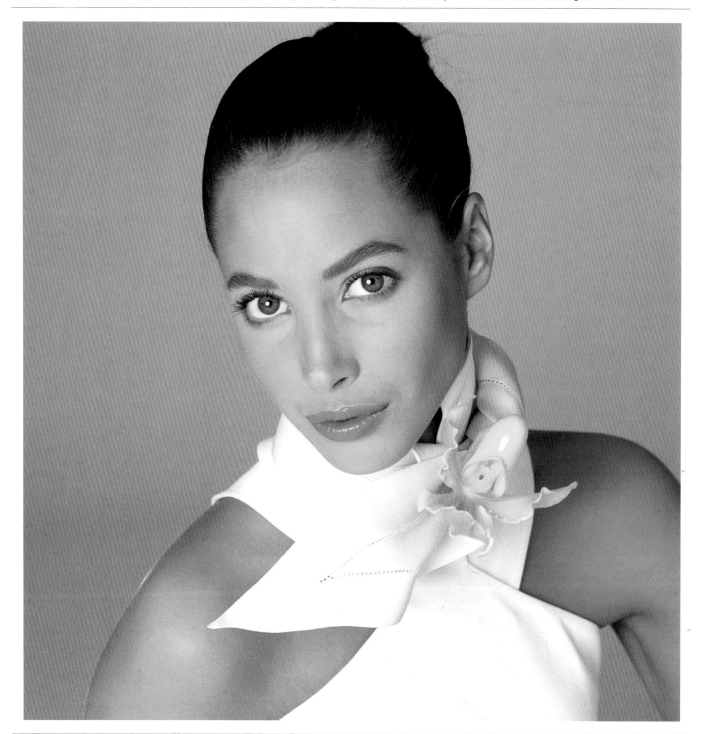

Christy Turlington. b Oakland, CA (USA), 1969. Christy wears Gianfranco Ferre. Photograph by Francesco Scavullo, 1988.

464

Twiggy

Model

Twiggy poses next to her mannequin lookalikes. It was the only way to replicate her powerful figure at a time when the whole world wanted to have a part of her magic. Lesley Hornby had come from the suburbs of London. At fifteen she met Nigel John Davies, then a hairdresser. He reinvented himself as Justin de Villeneuve and Lesley as 'Twig', later Twiggy. Just as it took a haircut to launch Linda Evangelista's career as a supermodel, twenty years earlier the potential of Twiggy's gamine charm was unlocked with a haircut by Leonard. With her elfin crop and teenage figure, Twiggy became the icon of young fashion and the first model to grow into a media personality, albeit a startled one. In response to one journalist's assertion that she earned more than the prime minister, she could only giggle, 'Do I?' Twiggy 'retired' at the age of nineteen.

☛ Bailey, Evangelista, Foale & Tuffin, Hechter

Twiggy (Lesley Hornby). b London (UK), 1949. Twiggy with mannequins by Adel Rootstein. Photograph by J. Drysdale, 1966.

Tyler Richard

Designer

Model Irina wears a shrunken, three-piece suit by Richard Tyler. He found success when Hollywood discovered his meticulous tailoring. Actress Sigourney Weaver said, 'Richard's clothes make you feel like a movie star'. Tyler became well known late in life, winning an award for best newcomer at forty-six. His fashion career, however, has been his life's work. He learned his craft from his seamstress mother and trained as a tailor, an education which became important to Tyler's work when he became a recognized craftsman of women's tailoring. He built his career designing stage clothes for Elton John, Cher and Diana Ross. A change of direction in the mid-1980s led to Tyler launching a menswear range with business partner and soon-to-be wife, Lisa Trafficante. This was followed in 1989 by womenswear. Both collections became successful through Tyler's reputation as a master cutter. 'I have no ego. All I have is my skill,' he says.

☞ Alfaro, Dell'Olio, Kors

Richard Tyler. b Melbourne (ASL), 1948. **Irina Pantaeva wears black three-piece suit.** Photograph by Chris Moore, 1995.

Uemura Shu   Cosmetics creator

With his design philosophy *'bien être'* (a sense of well-being), Shu Uemura freed the face from the shifting dictates of transient fashions and developed a notion of the inner sense of beauty, reflecting a mood of introversion and lack of artifice. Originally a hairdresser, Shu Uemura became a make-up artist to stars such as Shirley MacLaine and Frank Sinatra in 1950s Hollywood.

He raised the standard of make-up and made it into an art form, using superior cosmetics as his palette and the finest beauty tools as apparatus. These he stocked in his aesthetically modern Beauty Boutiques, which resembled art supply stores and heralded a cosmetics-counter revolution in the 1980s. After thirty decades, the natural style of his cosmetics, in soft, muted colours and distinct transparent packaging, is still relentlessly modern and very much a hallmark of twentieth-century design.

☛ Bandy, Bourjois, Factor, Lutens, Nars

Shu Uemura. b (JAP). (Active 1950s–) **Shu Uemura making-up a model's face.** Photograph by Morozumi, 1983.

Underwood Patricia

Milliner

The familiar stetson is given a modern twist: straw braid instead of suede, a wider brim and modest curve to create a feminine and elegant shape. The particular cock of the brim remains, hinting at the provocation the cowboy hat was noted for. Subtle, yet interesting manipulations of traditional hat shapes are characteristic of Underwood's millinery designs. Relying completely on shape and proportion, rather than fussy ornamentation, her hats are noted for their spartan modesty which makes them into one-statement sculptures for the head. 'A simplicity of design avoids the pitfalls of a hat becoming a distraction on the wearer,' she says. British-born, Underwood moved to New York in 1967 after a brief tenure at Buckingham Palace as a secretary.

Her understated aesthetics fit the New York look, where she works with designers Bill Blass and Marc Jacobs who mirror her modernist, abstract forms.

☛ Blass, Jacobs, Model, Sui, Treacy

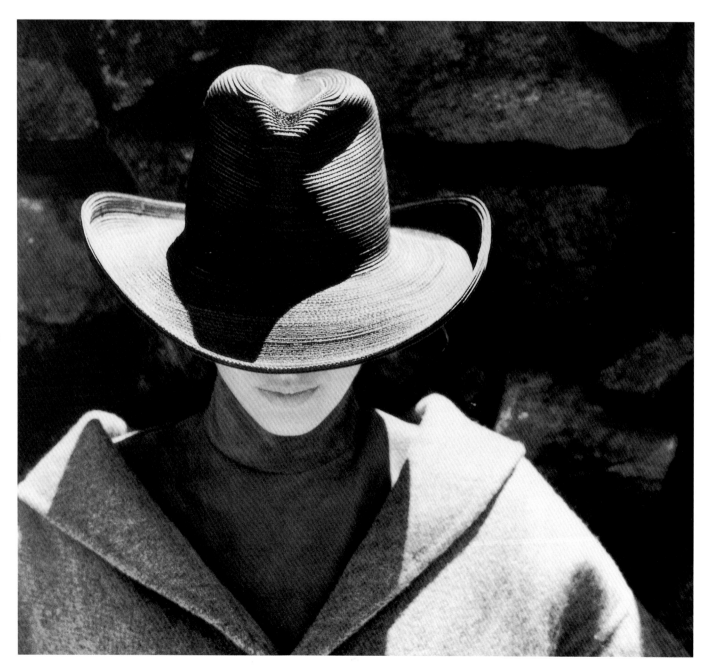

Patricia Underwood. b Maidenhead (UK), 1948. **Black straw stetson.** 1991.

Ungaro Emanuel Designer

This minidress by Ungaro shows him to be in touch with the flower power mood of the late 1960s and demonstrates his love of delicate fabric and surface detail. Yet the acute sense of cut remains. The son of an Italian tailor, Ungaro's favourite toy at six years old was his father's sewing machine and he became a tailor at fourteen. In 1955 he moved to Paris and was introduced to Balenciaga by Courrèges. He joined the Spaniard's house in 1958 and stayed for six years. Having learnt the master's rigorous attitude to cut, he opened his own couture business in 1965 with simple, bold garments such as blazers worn with shorts. Four years later, along with Cardin and Courrèges, Ungaro created a new nudeness in French fashion, but by the 1970s his style had softened. His 1980s eveningwear used vivid florals cut and ruched to form extremely ladylike, grown-up versions of his girlish dress from 1969.

☛ **Audibet, Balenciaga, Cardin, Courrèges, Paulette**

Emanuel Ungaro. b Aix-en-Provence (FR), 1933. **White, floral, trellis appliqué, lace dress.** Photograph by Peter Knapp, 1969.

Von Unwerth Ellen

Photographer

Wearing towering heels, stockings, silk underwear and corset, model Iris Palmer presents a traditionally provocative figure. Many observers are surprised to find that von Unwerth, the photographer, is a woman. She encourages her subjects to look sensual and her success stems from the fact that she projects these images from a female perspective. 'The models love to look sexy,' she says. 'They all like to be photographed in that way.' Von Unwerth 'discovered' the supermodel Claudia Schiffer in 1992 when she photographed her for Guess? Jeans. She has also famously created advertising images for Wonderbra, Katharine Hamnett and Gianfranco Ferre. Von Unwerth left her native Germany in 1974 to begin a modelling career in Paris, becoming a photographer ten years later. She has grown to be a key image-maker in the 1990s through her editorial work for *Vogue*, *The Face*, *Interview* and even *Playboy*.

☛ Hamnett, Schiffer, Teller

470

Ellen von Unwerth. b (GER), 1954. **Iris Palmer.** *The Face*, 1996.

Valentina

Designer

Madame Valentina, photographed here in triplicate, wears her own design: a dinner dress with a jewelled belt and collar. The dress was made in jersey, a material which swathes and clings to the figure, creating a sculptured look. The strong rosy-red colour provided an uninterrupted line, another key feature of the Valentina style. Colour to intensify line is enhanced by the fluid green cowl draped around her high-piled, chignon hairstyle and caught up in a belt. The whole aura is that of a Byzantine emperor's consort. The grand manner of Madame Valentina was rooted in her Russian heritage, even though she moved to Paris during the Russian Revolution and then to New York in 1922, where she set up her own establishment four years later. The costume also has a theatrical air, traceable to Madame Valentina's training for the stage. Her fashionable eveningwear was very popular with actresses.

☛ Grès, Torimaru, Vionnet

471

Valentina (Valentina Nicholaevna Sanina Schlee). b Kiev (RUS), 1904. d New York (USA), 1989. **Madame Valentina wears her jersey dress and cowl.**

Photographs by John Rawlings, American *Vogue*, 1945.

Valentino

Designer

Christy Turlington is worshipped wearing a beaded sheath dress from the spring/summer 1995 collection. Its designer, Valentino, has been called the 'Master of the Dress'. His clothes represent the romance, beauty, femininity and decadence of Rome, the city where he launched his own label in 1960. Valentino worked with Jean Dessès and then Guy Laroche, before becoming a couturier himself. Initially he made extravagant couture gowns for wealthy Italian socialites, but in 1968 he caused a sensation when he launched a radical, all-white collection. Jackie Kennedy wore an outfit from the collection when she married Aristotle Onassis. Fiery red, however, is Valentino's signature colour, used for precious lace gowns in his couture collection and beaded pyjama pants for ready-to-wear. His suave demeanour, impeccable manners and womanly, seductive clothes are about style, not high fashion.

☛ Barbieri, Dessès, Storey, Turlington, Viramontes

Valentino (Valentino Garavani). **b** Voghera (IT), 1932. **Christy Turlington. Advertising campaign.** Photograph by Herb Ritts, 1995.

Vallhonrat Javier   Photographer

Almost surreal, this dream-like image softly releases fashion of its social connotations. The model enjoys the company of the dolphins in aquamarine waves coloured with Vallhonrat's customary intensity. In his last campaign for John Galliano, in which nature is a source of harmony and fantasy, Javier Vallhonrat frees the clothes from their visual role. He agreed to work for

Galliano because, as he says, 'I felt identified with his aesthetic sensibility.' Vallhonrat, who has also collaborated with Martine Sitbon, Sybilla, Jil Sander and Romeo Gigli in their advertising campaigns, takes pride in only working for those designers whose creativity will serve as a ground for photographic research. His photographs, he affirms, never document fashion

but exploit its creativity to pursue autonomy in photography, which is Vallhonrat's main academic concern. Having worked for all European *Vogue*s from 1984 to 1994, Vallhonrat now lectures and exhibits.

☛ **Frissell, Galliano, Gigli, del Pozo, Sander, Sybilla**

473

Javier Vallhonrat. b Madrid (SP), 1953. **Beaded chiffon 'Dice' vest by John Galliano.** 1986.

Van Beirendonck Walter (W & LT)

Designer

Van Beirendonck's bright, futuristic clothing could have stepped straight from a computer game. His label, W & L T ('Wild and Lethal Trash'), first shown in 1995, humorously mixes high-tech fabrics with bright colour combinations and bold graphics. They reflect the carnival atmosphere of the clubs for which they are designed. Milliner Stephen Jones describes Van Beirendonck's clothes as 'such fun, so upbeat, such wild clubwear... like Gaultier in his early days.' He has Gaultier's rebellious, anti-fashion aesthetic and eclectic, visual references. The W & L T slogan, 'Kiss the Future!', suggests youthful optimism (and his promotion of safe sex) and his obsession with science fiction. He uses synthetics and innovative fabrics for his clothes, from inflatable rubber jackets to fuzzy nylon suits or stretchy tops with holograms. He claims, 'Young people want to wear something that defines them as different and that articulates their attitudes.'

☛ Bowery, Gaultier, S. Jones, McLaren, Mugler

474

Walter Van Beirendonck. b Brecht (BEL), 1957. (W & LT.) **Printed T-shirt and rubber trousers.** Autumn/winter 1995/6. Photograph by Jean-Baptiste Mondino.

Van Cleef Alfred and Arpels Charles, Julien & Louis   Jewellery designers

This illustrated magazine cover, featuring a faceted ruby and platinum cuff typifies the Van Cleef & Arpels customer of 1942. Her high turban, squared shoulders and fur wrap are worn with grand jewellery in a defiantly glamorous response to the occupation of Paris. Alfred Van Cleef and his three brothers-in-law, Charles, Julien and Louis Arpels, founded their jewellery company in 1906. They were among the first craftsmen to move into place Vendôme in Paris, a square now lined with such jewellery companies. Van Cleef & Arpels introduced exotic themes inspired by the excavation of Tutankhamen's tomb and chinoiserie. They used characteristic mixtures of bright precious and semi-precious stones to create jewellery that paralleled the work of Poiret and Paquin. Impeccably chic stars of the screen, such as Marlene Dietrich and Joan Fontaine, were clients of Van Cleef & Arpels.

☛ Paquin, Poiret, Verdura

Alfred Van Cleef. b Paris (FR), 1873. d Yvelines (FR), 1938. Charles Arpels. b Paris (FR), 1880. d Le Vésinet (FR), 1951. Julien Arpels. b Marseille (FR), 1884. d Paris (FR), 1964. Louis Arpels. b Nancy (FR), 1886. d Neuilly (FR), 1976. (Van Cleef & Arpels.) Ruby, diamond and platinum cuff. Illustrated by L. Louchel for La Femme Chic, 1942.

Van Noten Dries Designer

Dreadlocks, suit and printed tie: Dries Van Noten's signature for men and women is his eclectic use of themes. Prints and embroidery decorate Eastern and Western garments: a sarong is placed over trousers, a sari under a double-breasted jacket – displaying both his interest in North Africa and his love of layering. Van Noten sees fashion as something light, to be relished for its own sake and his own work always has a fanciful edge, such as this example of a plain suit and coat given personality by its 'owner'. He graduated from Antwerp's Royal Academy of Arts in 1981, and started his own womenswear label in 1985. The following year he showed in London together with five other Belgian designers, including Martin Margiela and Ann Demeulemeester. They called themselves 'The Antwerp Six' and earned Belgium an enviable reputation for producing design talent.

☛ Bikkembergs, Demeulemeester, Forbes, Thimister

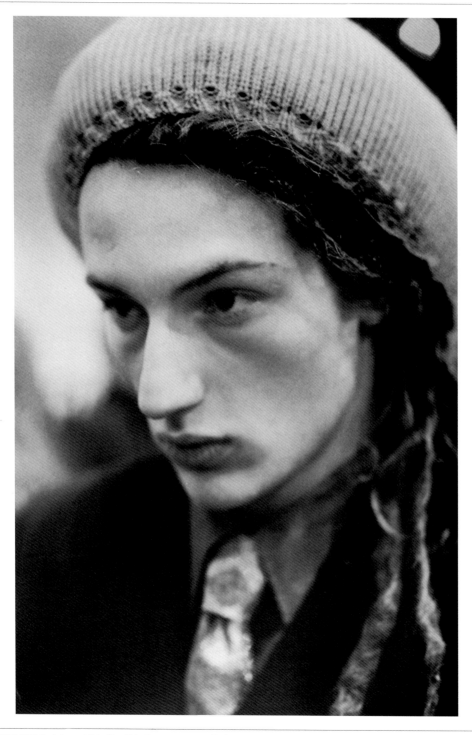

Dries Van Noten. b Antwerp (BEL), 1958. **Backstage at Dries Van Noten's menswear catwalk show.** Photograph by Olaf Wipperfürth, 1997.

Vanderbilt Gloria Designer

'Money is the symbol by which your peers judge you,' said Gloria Vanderbilt complacently. Heiress to one of America's biggest fortunes, Vanderbilt's gold-stitched signature logo on 'designer jeans' summed up the decadence of the disco decade. Here, they are put into the unlikely context of a cocktail party. A one-time actress, writer and poet, Vanderbilt was not a fashion designer, but was approached by Murjani International to license her name to their design of jeans. Vanderbilt was supposedly the company's second choice after Jackie Kennedy. By the early 1980s Vanderbilt's were the best-selling jeans in America. She was mobbed at in-store appearances, and made TV advertisements for 'the jeans that hug your derrière'. She didn't need the money but, she said, 'The only money that means anything to me is the money I make myself.' Her range later extended to dolls, greeting cards, soya-bean desserts, luggage and furniture.

☛ Adolfo, von Fürstenberg, Kennedy, LaChapelle

Gloria Vanderbilt. b (USA), 1924. **Jeans for Murjani, 1982.** Photograph by John Claridge.

Venet Philippe

Designer

A petal-like, organdie collar grazes Jane Birkin's face, extending down her back in a spine of ruffles, the red embroidered polka-dots sprayed like pollen. Venet explored floral themes like this to enliven his imaginative and deft tailoring, the hallmark of his creations. Apprentice to a Parisian couturier at the age of fourteen, Venet went on to work for Elsa Schiaparelli in 1950. Here, he met the young Hubert de Givenchy, who hired him as master tailor for his couture house in 1953. Venet's contributions were extensive during Givenchy's heyday in the 1950s, notably for dressing Audrey Hepburn in the 1954 film *Sabrina Fair* and conceiving her iconoclastic gamine look. He opened his own couture house in 1962, and became known for his tailored coats built on geometric silhouettes and organic lines, such as the triangle-shaped kite coats and oversized capes with dolman sleeves.

☛ **Givenchy, Mandelli, Schiaparelli**

Philippe Venet. b Lyon (FR), 1929. **Jane Birkin wears spotted organdie dress.** Photograph by Jean-Jacques Bugat, French *Vogue*, 1972.

478

Venturi Gian Marco Designer

A prominent designer in the Italian fashion scene of the 1980s, Venturi based his women's ready-to-wear label on sensuous, masculine tailoring. His dynamic, swingy designs reflected the elevated sportswear look of the time and had a distinctive Milanese feel in their artistic minimalism and architectural fluidity. Venturi was not formally trained in the field of design; instead he majored in business and economics at the University of Florence. He then spent many years travelling, embracing rich artistic and cultural Zeitgeists, before working as a designer/stylist. He was quickly noted for his classic, tactile separates in earthbound colours. He launched his own collection in 1979, favouring the bold, feminine look of a modern Louise Brooks dressed in a black snakeskin jacket, animal-printed capri trousers and dark aviator glasses.

☛ Maramotti, Revson, Wainwright

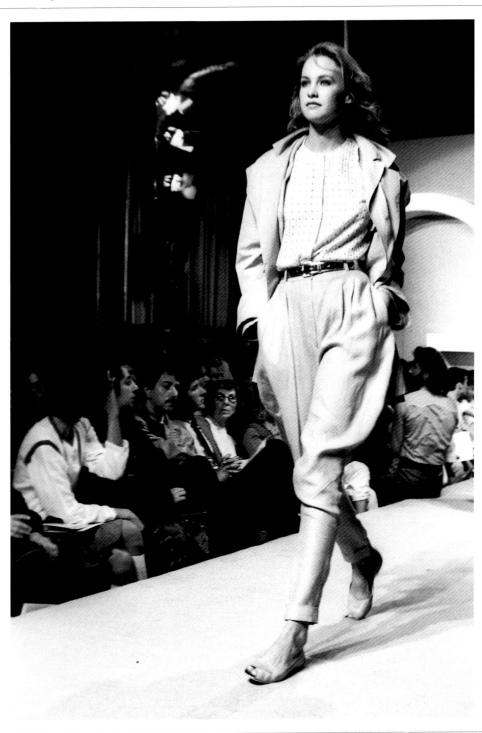

Gian Marco Venturi. b Florence (IT), 1943. **Jacket and jodhpurs.** *Women's Wear Daily*, 1981.

Verdura Fulco di   Jewellery designer

Diamond earrings and a gold bracelet are illustrated for 1950s America in a highly original composition. Their designer, whose own vision was equally original, was Fulco Santostefano della Cerda, Duke of Verdura, a widely influential, forward-thinking jewellery designer. Verdura worked for Chanel, before opening his own New York shop in 1939. Some of his designs were based on tassels from coats of arms and mariners' knots, but di Verdura found his greatest source of inspiration in nature, choosing themes such as wings, leaves, mermaids, pomegranates and especially shells for motifs. Jewellery designs evoked by nature were typical of his era, but, unlike many of his peers, he was far more experimental and eclectic in his design approach. Often using gold rather than platinum for mounts, he uncommonly melded semi-precious and precious stones in the same setting, using diamonds as an accent rather than as a centrepiece.

☛ **Chanel, Van Cleef & Arpels, Vreeland**

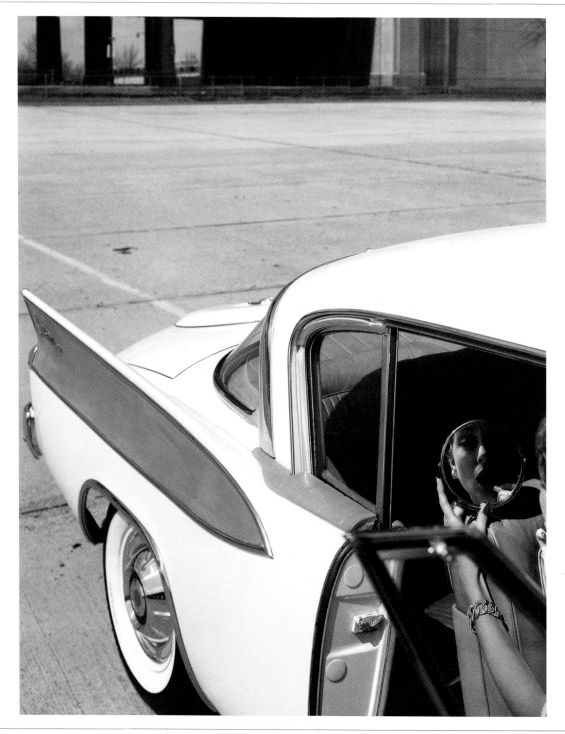

480

Fulco di Verdura (Fulco Santostefano della Cerda, Duke of Verdura). **b** Sicily (IT), 1898. **d** London (UK), 1978. **Gold bracelet and diamond earrings.**
Photograph by Karen Radkai, American *Vogue*, 1958.

Versace Gianni   Designer

'I like to dress egos, if you haven't got a big ego, you can forget it,' said Gianni Versace, who dressed the biggest personalities. Here, Madonna, a longtime friend and model for his work, wears a made-to-measure gown shaped with integral boning. Brightly coloured, sexually exuberant, celebrity-endorsed, Versace's clothes brought something of Hollywood glamour back to fashion. His sexy, extrovert designs were worn by the famously rich of both sexes, from rock stars to royalty; Elton John to Diana, Princess of Wales. One Versace dress could make a woman's career (as Elizabeth Hurley found out when she wore his safety-pinned column), and he is credited with fuelling the supermodel phenomenon with his flamboyant, baroque style. It often seemed out of pace with modern sobriety, but Versace celebrated the breadth of fashion. He said, 'I don't believe in good taste,' and then created a demure pastel suit for a princess.

☛ Fonticoli, Madonna, Molinari, Moschino, Nars, Ritts

481

Gianni Versace. b Reggio Calabria (IT), 1946. d Miami, FL (USA), 1997. **Madonna wears Versace Atelier. Advertising campaign.** Photograph by Mario Testino, 1995.

Vertès Marcel Illustrator

A woman wearing a black, bias-cut gown by Molyneux laments – has someone else also turned up in the same dress? Is her colour scheme hopelessly wrong? (Which might explain the imperious look on the face of her tormentor.) This drawing by Vertès demonstrates his flair for observing both the social life and the fashion of the Parisian beau monde. He sketched their foibles and vanities at the same time as illuminating the romantic dress of the period, here a trio of formal, bias-cut gowns worn with capes or a fichu. Vertès studied drawing and painting at the Academy of Fine Arts in Budapest. In 1921 he settled in Paris and his watercolours were exhibited at the Salon des Humoristes in 1925. Vertès' light fashion drawings portrayed high society and high fashion with a seemingly effortless lightness and grace, and were a major contribution to the graphic tradition of *Vogue*.

☛ Delhomme, Molyneux, Tran

482

Marcel Vertès. b Budapest (HUN), 1895. d 1961. **Molyneux evening gowns.** French *Vogue*, 1935.

Veruschka

Model

Rubartelli photographs Veruschka, the woman who put a face to 'hippie deluxe'. Her feathered waistcoat, painted make-up and beads represent fashion from the late 1960s, when her blonde hair and full lips were an ubiquitous element of fashion. From beginning to end, Veruschka's career was an unusual one. Her father, Count von Lehndorff-Steinort, was one of the group which conspired to kill Hitler. 'Little Vera' went on to study art in Hamburg and then Florence, where she was spotted and asked to model at the Palazzo Pitti collections. She became famous for her work with Irving Penn and Diana Vreeland, and for her role in Antonioni's cult 1960s movie, *Blow Up*. She retired in the early 1970s to do camouflage body art, where she would paint herself to blend in with her background. She described her art as a way of making herself disappear, 'working against my model career'.

☛ Bouquin, Kenneth, Penn, di Sant'Angelo, Vreeland

483

Vionnet Madeleine   Designer

Madeleine Vionnet's material does not hang on the models but accompanies them, following their natural lines, achieving a modern Grecian silhouette. To get this fluid movement, she dispensed with corsets and used the bias cut, which means cutting across the grain of the material to enable it to flow and cling into folds and drapes. To achieve this effect Vionnet commissioned fabrics two yards wider than usual. She created her designs on small dolls and those who were privileged enough to be allowed to watch likened her to a sculptress moulding designs to create these neoclassical dresses. Madeleine Vionnet, who refused to be called a fashion designer, preferring the title of dressmaker, reached the zenith of her fame in the 1920s and 1930s. She was a harbinger of modern styles, because these Grecian-draped dresses take their shapes from the body. Contemporary disciples of this fashion purist include Azzedine Alaïa and John Galliano.

☞ Alaïa, Boulanger, Callot, Chow, Galliano, Valentina

484

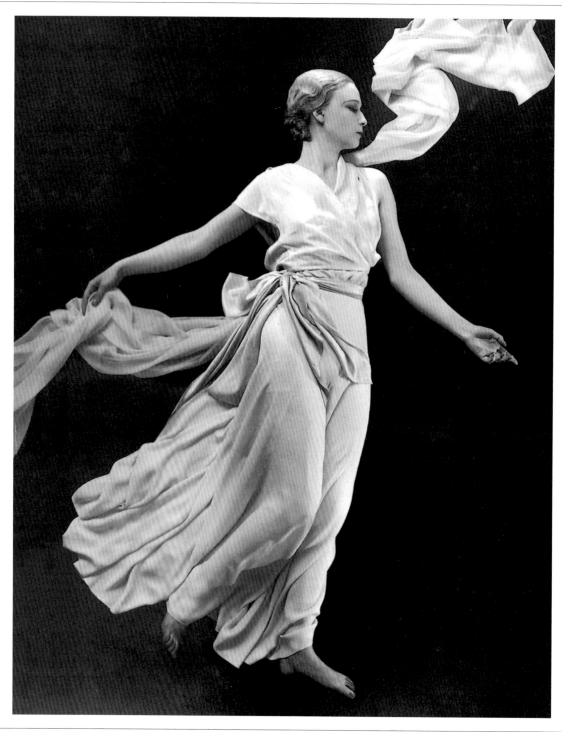

Madeleine Vionnet. b Aubervilliers (FR), 1876. **d** Paris (FR), 1975. **Bas-relief frieze.** Photograph by George Hoyningen-Huene, French *Vogue*, 1931.

Viramontes Tony   Illustrator

A waterfall of jersey in scarlet – Valentino's favouite colour – streams down the back of Tony Viramontes' subject. Her skin is a broad stroke of cobalt from naked head to waistband and the fabric is decribed with swathes of red gouache. Viramontes worked throughout the 1980s, capturing the vivid, angular attitude of the designers' work he illustrated – in particular Valentino and Montana. He also captured the highly colourful, romantic period of street fashion early in the decade; a time of fashion pirates with their heads wrapped with turbans and bodies decorated with elaborate costume jewellery. Viramontes settled in Venice and Paris, drawn to Europe by his love of fashion and art. Of the artists who inspired him, the most obvious influences were those of Jean Cocteau and Henri Matisse. Viramontes created line drawings similar in intention to Cocteau's figures and blocked them with oil pastel, ink or watercolour.

☛ **Cocteau, Montana, Valentino**

Tony Viramontes. **b** Los Angeles, CA (USA), 1960. **d** 1988. **Valentino Couture.** 1984.

Vivier Roger

Shoe designer

This pink satin evening pump, covered with embroidery and encrusted with glass beads and pearls, is as ornate and precious as a piece of jewellery. Roger Vivier's elaborate, sometimes heavily embellished shoes have been described as 'the Fabergé of footwear'. Vivier has always said, 'My shoes are sculptures'. Indeed, he studied that subject at the École des Beaux-Arts in Paris and is known for innovative heel shapes such as the rhinestone-studded 'ball' heel and the backward-bent 'comma', manufactured in lightweight aluminium alloy by an aeronautical engineering firm. Ava Gardner, Marlene Dietrich, Josephine Baker and the Beatles were all fans of Vivier's shoes and Queen Elizabeth II wore Vivier's gold kidskin pumps, studded with garnets, for her 1953 coronation. He worked at Christian Dior between 1953 and 1963, and has said of his shoes, 'They are quintessentially French, a Parisian alchemy in style.'

☛ Bally, Beatles, Dior, Lane, Louboutin, Pinet, Rayne

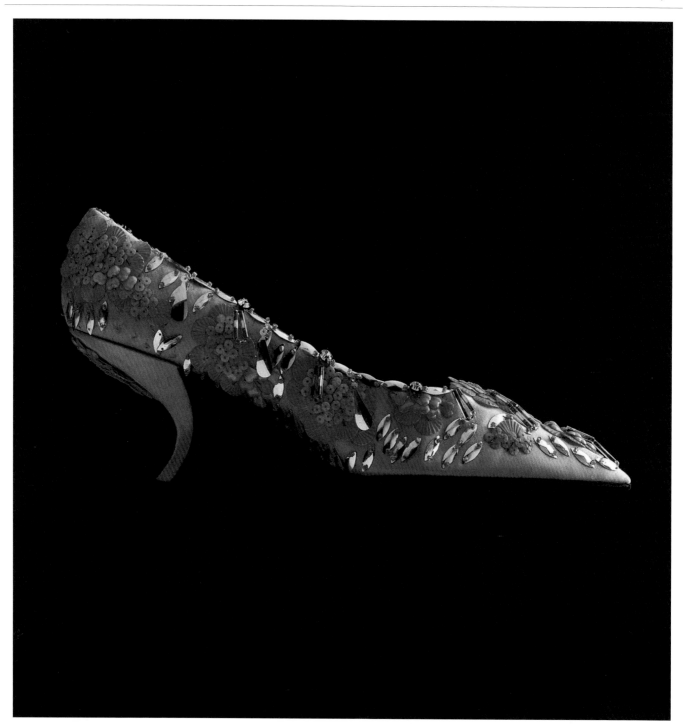

Roger Vivier. **b** Paris (FR), 1913. **d** Toulouse (FR), 1998. **Pink embroidered shoe with 'comma' heel, 1963.** Photograph by Jacques Boulay.

Vreeland Diana   Editor

The epitome of a *jolie laide*, Diana Vreeland was the beautiful swan and ugly duckling of fashion, complete with kabuki-like make-up. From 1937 to the 1980s, she was an arbiter of style, first as an editor-writer for *Harper's Bazaar* where she is most remembered for her short-lived but legendary 'Why Don't You...' column, which made insouciant suggestions in defiance of Depression-era gloom. Throughout her life, Vreeland had a way with words: her phrases (some sublime, such as 'elegance is refusal') and elegantly turned truisms (such as 'pink is the navy blue of India') have become fashion clichés. From 1962 to 1971, as editor-in-chief of *Vogue*, Vreeland gave the magazine the energy of the jet age and youth, making it a showcase for favoured photographers Richard Avedon and Irving Penn. In 1972 she became consultant to the Costume Institute of the Metropolitan Museum of Art in New York.

☛ Brodovitch, Dahl-Wolfe, Kennedy, Kenneth, Nast

487

Diana Vreeland. **b** Paris (FR), 1901. **d** New York (USA), 1989. **Diana Vreeland wears Verdura's cuffs.** Photograph by Horst P. Horst, 1979.

Vuitton Louis   Accessory designer

Colonial history and an exclusive lifestyle are evoked by this image of leisured travel. Louis Vuitton, the progenitor of the preferred luggage of such travellers, was the son of a carpenter. He moved to Paris in 1834 and crafted packing trunks for aristocrats at the court of the Empress Eugénie. He saw a general need for high-quality baggage and designed a flat trunk that could be stacked in the cargo hold of transatlantic ships or on the luggage racks of trains. His travelling wardrobe trunk, introduced in 1876, was accessorized with a rail and tiny drawers. It was a success and Vuitton's luggage and hand-luggage have symbolized privileged travel ever since – the 'Alma', a half-circular hand-held bag, was created for Coco Chanel in the1950s. Vuitton's chequerboard 'Daumier' canvas was first introduced in 1888 and the famous monogram, a perennial status symbol, was created in 1886 by Louis' son, Georges.

☛ **Jacobs, van Lamsweerde, Loewe**

Louis Vuitton. **b** Cons-Le-Saunier (FR), 1811. **d** Asnières (FR), 1892. **Monogrammed trunk.** Photograph by Sacha, 1991.

Wainwright Janice

Janice Wainwright brings the outdoors indoors with a pair of moiré taffeta jodhpurs – a widely used theme at the end of the 1970s. Sensuous fabrics cut with a feminine touch were at the centre of her work; here her silk crepe-de-chine shirt is given a fichu tie. Wainwright studied at the Royal College of Art in London, and worked with Sheridan Barnett before founding her own company in 1974. Throughout the 1970s she was known for soft dresses which were often cut on the bias. She produced clothes that, according to *Vogue*, '...obey the first rule of dress which is that clothes must be appropriate'. Wainwright's interest in textiles extended to her involvement with the design and colouring of the fabrics she used. Previous collections include dresses cleverly designed to spiral downwards around the body. Intricate embroidery, appliqué trimmings and accentuated shoulders are other distinctive hallmarks of her style.

☛ Barnett, Bates, Demarchelier, Venturi

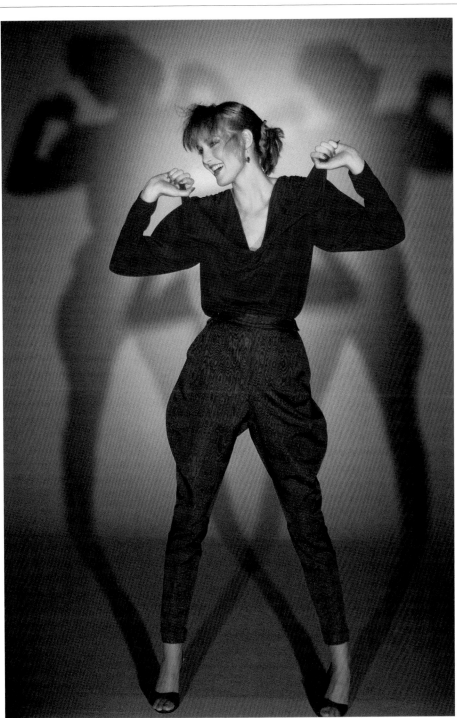

489

Janice Wainwright. **b** Chesterfield (UK), 1940. **Plum silk shirt and moiré jodhpurs.** Photograph by Patrick Demarchelier, British *Vogue*, 1980.

Wang Vera   Designer

A dress never works harder than on Oscar night or when it's worn by a bride. When Hollywood's daughters or the centrepiece of a wedding emerge from a limousine, they want a dress that will make the audience draw breath. This is what Vera Wang is famous for. She uses rich fabrics such as silk lace and duchesse satin in the tradition of Paris couture, and applies them to the simple shapes associated with American sportswear. Wang lives in the society she designs for. Born into New York's Upper East Side, Wang was forbidden to attend design school, becoming instead *Vogue*'s youngest fashion editor. Having worked for Ralph Lauren, she opened a bridal salon and couture business in 1990. Her appreciation of surface decoration, particularly beading, and the use of net to give the illusion of bare skin have also recommended her for the design of Olympic figure-skating costumes – another career she pursued before design.

☛ Jackson, Lauren, Leiber, Lesage, Roehm, Yantorny

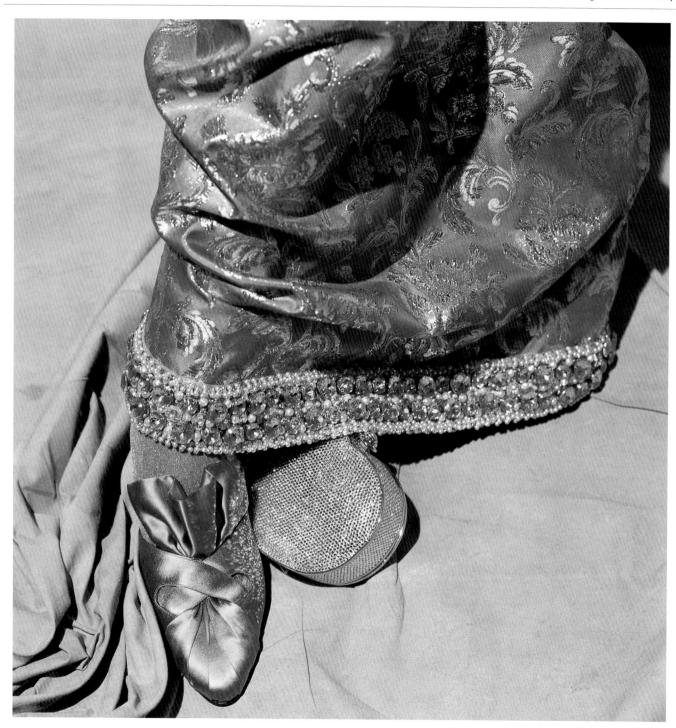

Vera Wang. **b** New York (USA), 1949. **Gold brocade couture gown, 1991.** Photograph by Victor Skrebneski.

Warhol Andy   Designer

Andy Warhol began work as an illustrator for fashion companies and magazines such as *Mademoiselle*, growing increasingly aware of the relationship between art, fashion and commerce. He then produced window displays for New York department stores Tiffany's and Bonwit Teller. By the early 1960s, Warhol had reinvented himself as a music and movies impresario and even

as a fashion designer. Here two women are hanging out in the Factory, his artist's salon, wearing his slogan dresses. Warhol began to wear rock-star leather jackets, satin shirts and a silver-sprayed wig and he used the superstar actresses from his films to model paper dresses printed with his Banana paintings. He also became friends with fashion editor Diana Vreeland and designer

Betsey Johnson, and in 1969 Warhol launched his experimental style magazine *Interview*, in which he profiled his designer friends Halston and Elsa Peretti.

☛ Bulgari, de Castelbajac, Garren, LaChapelle, Sprouse

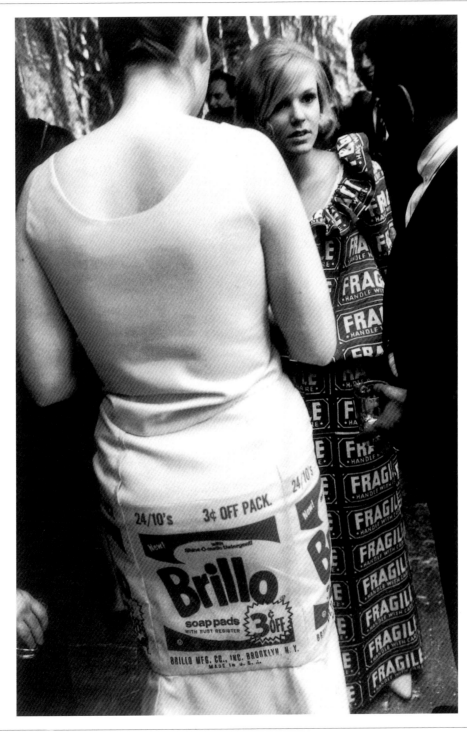

Andy Warhol (Andrew Warhola). b Pittsburgh, PA (USA), 1928. d New York (USA), 1987. 'Brillo' and 'Fragile, Handle With Care'. Photograph by Ken Heyman, 1962.

Watanabe Junya Designer

By extending the distances between each model as they tread the perimeter of his square catwalk, Junya Watanabe gives visual silence to his futuristic fashion. Glamour, sound and colour are notably absent; instead, an optical tautology of frugal, white cotton *khadi* presents this complex collection. Watanabe graduated from Tokyo's Bunka Fashion Institute in 1984 and joined Comme des Garçons, designing the Tricot line in 1987. As Rei Kawakubo's protégé, his creations reflect the intellectual Zeitgeist of the Japanese maestro. However, he takes a personal approach for his line, Junya Watanabe Comme des Garçons. He takes a successful stab at anything futuristic: from cellophane-wrapped neon punks and abstract oriental peasantwear, to poetic stark white. Giving his clothes an irregular touch through random tucking, pleating and ruching, he evokes the idea of the human aesthetic married with the future.

☛ Fontana, Kawakubo, Rocha

Junya Watanabe. b (JAP), 1961. **White dress and veil.** Photograph by Chris Moore, 1998.

Weber Bruce   Photographer

Chosen by Bruce Weber to represent his work, this photograph shows a girl, fresh and artless, peering from beneath a Charles James gown, itself the very example of constructed beauty. Such human subjects are, however, unusual. His historical paragon is the photographer Leni Riefenstahl, who extolled an exclusive and privileged male body. Weber was the most important photographer of redefined masculinity in the 1980s and 1990s. He created erotic images of muscular, natural bodies. One significant inspiration for Weber is Classical sculpture: his buffed, athletic heroes (seen in Calvin Klein's underwear advertisements) often recall Hellenistic sculpture. The chaos of real life never intrudes or spoils the mood; over the course of two decades his photographs for Ralph Lauren have created a privileged dream world of country houses, polo matches and safaris.

☞ C. James, C. Klein, Lauren, Platt Lynes, Ritts, Tennant

Bruce Weber. b Greensburg, PA (USA), 1946. **Girl beneath vintage dress by Charles James, 1991.**

Westwood Vivienne   Designer

Christy Turlington wears Vivienne Westwood in a photograph by Mario Testino for British *Vogue* in 1993. Westwood regards this outfit as typical of her work, even though it leaves out her waggish references to royalty (crowns set with paste jewels) and historical excess (mini-crinolines and bodices from which the wearer's bosom spills like a milk jelly). When Westwood began her confrontational fashion career in 1970, she would no doubt have laughed at the notion that her clothes would one day appear in an establishment fashion magazine on a famous model. In the intervening years she established herself as the only British designer who could not only explore extremes in dress, but also make sense of them. She did this most significantly with the punk movement during her collaboration with Malcolm McLaren. In 1981 she launched her catwalk collection, continuing her emphasis on eccentricity and subversion.

☛ Barbieri, McLaren, Palmers, Testino, Turlington

494

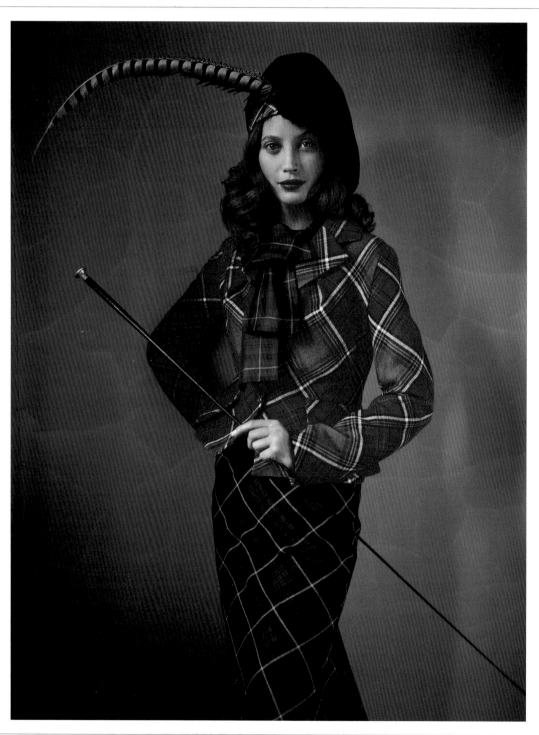

Vivienne Westwood. **b** Tintwhistle (UK), 1941. **'Anglomania': Christy Turlington wears a bias-cut tartan suit.** Photograph by Mario Testino, British *Vogue*, 1993.

Windsor Duke and Duchess of

Together the Duke and Duchess of Windsor symbolized opulence tempered by sartorial restraint. For their wedding day, Wallis Simpson chose a sapphire blue (dubbed 'Wallis' blue), crepe silk dress by Mainbocher, one of her favourite designers. Mainbocher preferred to 'blend mystery rather than to rant and rave with my shears', and he created an utterly simple, bias-cut dress and jacket which were worn with a matching hat by Reboux. Givenchy and Marc Bohan were other favourites. It was a discreet style that provided an ideal backdrop for her magnificent jewels, many of which were chosen by the Duke. His clothes were equally influential. At university he had championed the flapping trouser legs dubbed 'Oxford bags' and, rejecting the stiff, interlined clothing of his youth, he often flouted convention and pioneered new styles, such as the dark blue, double-breasted dinner jacket.

☛ Cartier, Ferragamo, Horst, Mainbocher, Reboux

497

Duke of Windsor. b Richmond (UK), 1894. **d** Paris (FR), 1972. **Duchess of Windsor. b** Blue Ridge Summit, PA (USA), 1896. **d** Paris (FR), 1986.
The Duke and Duchess of Windsor on their wedding day at the Château de Condé, France. 1937.

Winston Harry   Jewellery designer

Elizabeth Taylor wears a suite of diamonds by Harry Winston, the sparkling voltage of which is matched by the glint in her violet eyes for her favourite stone, after which her scent White Diamonds is named. When Marilyn Monroe sang about her favourite rock in *Gentlemen Prefer Blondes*, it was to the 'King of Diamonds' she appealed: 'Talk to me, Harry, tell me about it...' Winston's reciprocal love affair with Hollywood began when he assisted his father in their small Los Angeles jewellery store. At the age of twenty, he moved back to New York to found his own jewellery business. By the time he had incorporated his firm under his own name in 1932, Winston had become a leading retailer of exclusive diamond jewellery, renowned for using exceptionally large stones. In 1998, the Winston look was encapsulated in a pair of diamond-encrusted Ray-Ban sunglasses, designed for the Oscar ceremony.

☞ Alexandre, Hiro, Madonna

498

Harry Winston. **b** New York (USA), 1896. **d** (USA), 1978. **'Passion' perfume publicity campaign. Elizabeth Taylor wears diamond earrings and collar.** Photograph by Norman Parkinson, 1987.

Worth Charles Frederick Designer

Spangled silk tulle was typical of Worth's work in the 1860s. For Empress Elizabeth of Austria he chose gold to be scattered over her gown – a scheme extended by the golden stars in her hair. The dress's décolleté neckline, which exposes and embraces her shoulders, would be softened with the tulle held lightly around her hips. Winterhalter chronicled the work of Worth through such portraits and painted many similarly graceful compositions of the Empress Eugénie, Worth's most valuable client. The story of modern fashion began when Charles Frederick Worth, a young tailor, arrived at the court of Napoleon III. In his bid to re-establish Paris as the centre of fashionable life, the Emperor stimulated the luxury business and his wife Eugénie patronized it in fabulous style. Under that patronage, Worth drew on the history of costume to create lavish, expensive gowns which raised dressmaking to a new level called haute couture.

☛ **Duff Gordon, Fratini, Hartnell, Pinet, Poiret, Reboux**

Charles Frederick Worth. **b** Bourne (UK), 1825. **d** Paris (FR), 1895. **Empress Elizabeth of Austria wearing spangled tulle.** Painting by Franz Xaver Winterhalter, 1865.

Yamamoto Kansai Designer

Cartoon graphics and cotton netting were one of the wilder combinations offered by Kansai Yamamoto. Others included lush satin robes and pyjamas appliquéd with huge Japanese figures. Yamamoto married traditional Japanese culture and Western influences, set them to a music beat and put them in the realm of the performing arts. In the 1970s his fashion performance shows were huge events, attracting up to 5,000 people. After training as a civil engineer, Yamamoto left school in 1962 to study English, before moving on to fashion. He designed David Bowie's outrageous costumes for 'Ziggy Stardust' and 'Aladdin Zane' and, in 1975, he began showing in Paris, part of the first wave of Japanese designers who would have an impact on fashion through the following decades. Yamamoto's trademarks are a use of abstract colour sculpted into unique forms, which successfully blended ancient Oriental influences with modern sporty themes.

☛ Bowie, Sprouse, Warhol

500

Kansai Yamamoto. b Kanagawa (JAP), 1944. 'Kansai' graffiti shirt and mesh skirt. *Women's Wear Daily*, 1982.

Yamamoto Yohji Designer

This lean coat represents the traditions of both antique Western tailoring and those of contemporary Japan. In 1981 Yohji Yamamoto presented his clothes to a Western audience for the first time and effectively turned the notion of fashion as structured, sexy and glamorous on its head. Experts were shocked, labelling the collection 'Hiroshima chic'; it was composed of androgynous shrouds in several shades of black, worn with flat shoes, little make-up and a stern expression. But the shock turned to admiration. Yamamoto dropped out of a law degree to work for his widowed mother in her dressmaking shop. He followed this with a fashion degree at Tokyo's Bunka Fashion College, and set up his own label in 1977. He says, 'My clothes are about human beings: they are alive. I am alive.' His vision of women, and later men, as independent, intelligent, liberated artisans has elevated his status to that of a fashion legend.

☛ Capasa, van Lamsweerde, Miyake, Tatsuno

501

Yohji Yamamoto. b Yokohama (JAP), 1943. **Red hat and black tail-coat.** Photograph by Paolo Roversi, 1985.

Yantorny Pietro   Shoe designer

Pietro Yantorny's sumptuous custom-made shoes – in precious, milky silks and decorated with his trademark diamanté buckle – survive today as totems of unsurpassed grandeur. Over 300 of these shoes, each of them perching daintily on Louis-style heels, were made for Rita de Acosta Lydig, who never walked more than a few hundred yards. What little is known about Yantorny is partly attributed to a reputation that lasted only a few years, although in that time he enjoyed an international clientele sprinkled with royalty. Of East Indian origin, his own lofty aspirations – reinforced by the slogan used in his Parisian salon, 'The world's most expensive custom shoemaker' – did not deter clients, even when orders took two years to arrive. There was reason for their patience: Yantorny made painstaking measurements of each individual in order to make each shoe fit 'like a silk sock'.

☛ Hope, Lesage, Pinet, Wang

502

Pietro Yantorny. (Active 1910s.) **Trunk of evening shoes belonging to Rita de Acosta Lydig, c1915.** Photograph by Jack Carroll.

Zoran

Designer

Utterly simple, squared black shapes; the name Zoran is associated with minimalism and purity. Elements of his approach to design – mathematical precision-cutting and clean, simple shapes – hark back to his degree in architecture for which he studied in his home town, Belgrade. Zoran moved to New York in the early 1970s, launching his first capsule collection there to wide acclaim in 1977. His first collections were designed around squares and rectangles in silk crepe-de-chine. Zoran remains as unswayed by transient fads of fashion today as he was back in the 1970s. He prefers to design comfortable, practical clothing with longevity, in sumptuous fabrics, especially cashmere. Using an elemental palette of colours – mainly red, black, grey, white and cream – he also avoids using extraneous decoration. Even the practical details, such as cuffs, collars, zips and fastenings, are hidden away or banished where possible.

☛ Audibet, Coddington, Kim

503

Zoran (Zoran Ladicorbic). b Belgrade (YUG), 1947. **Black outfits.** Photograph by Goe Moe.

Glossary of movements, genres and technical terms

Aigrette

A decorative tuft, usually of heron, egret or osprey feathers, worn on hats or as a hair ornament.

A-line

A skirt or dress silhouette which flares from the waist or bust, forming the 'A' shape.

Alpaca

Formerly a fabric made from the wool of the alpaca (a South American mammal related to the llama) and cotton, today it describes a rayon crepe fabric.

Angora

The hair of the angora goat or rabbit. It is usually mixed with fabrics such as wool and used for knitwear. See mohair.

Aniline dyes

Vivid synthetic dyes, originally obtained from indigo, that were introduced in the late nineteenth century and widened the palette of colours available to designers.

Appliqué

A technique of creating surface decoration by stitching or gluing motifs, trimmings or other fabric onto the ground fabric.

Argyle

A block of diamond pattern, commonly seen on knitwear, which is an approximation of the tartan work by the Scottish clan Argyle.

Astraskhan

Originally the fleece of the karakul lamb of Russia, used as a trimming on collars and cuffs and for hats until the late nineteenth century. Today it refers to both the fleece and a heavy fabric, knitted or woven, with a pile imitating the shiny, black, tightly curled fleece. Also called persian lamb.

Atelier

The studio or workshop of a designer.

Baguette

A precious stone cut in an oblong shape with facets.

Ballets Russes or Ballet Russe

Sergei Diaghilev brought Russian dance to Western Europe with the Ballets Russes. For the first time, décor, costume and music were as important as the dance itself. Its first appearance in Paris, in 1909, shocked audiences with its unrestrained, brilliantly hued designs influenced by the Orient. The costumes consisted of harem pants, turbans, bold jewellery, painted linen, and appliqué on velvet and silk. Designed by Léon Bakst, they inspired Poiret – and subsequently much of early twentieth-century fashion – to discard the stiff corsetry and gentle colours typical of the period and to shorten skirts to ankle-length.

☛ Bakst, Barbier, Brunelleschi, Poiret, Sumurun

Bandeau

A strapless bodice usually made from a stretch fabric.

Barathea

A fine woollen cloth used for outer garments in the nineteenth century and now used for suiting.

Barège

A fine silky gauze, usually made from silk and wool, most often used for veils and head-dresses during the nineteenth century. Named after Barège in the South-West of France where it was originally made.

Batik

East-Asian textile craft of 'wax writing', in which liquid wax is used to draw designs which are protected from taking the dye.

Batiste

A generic term for a fine, sheer, lightweight fabric made from cotton or linen, with or without other fibres, wool, silk, polyester or rayon.

Batwing sleeve see Dolman sleeve.

Beat

First coined in 1958, the beat (or yé yé in France) was a progenitor of both mod and hippie, both in spirit and attitude. Having witnessed the ravages of the Depression, war and the atomic threat, the beat's distrust of politics, capitalism and uniformity provoked an aspiration to a simple, existential lifestyle. The tough, student uniform was, 'Any colour so long as it is black', usually a polo neck or turtleneck sweater and jeans. Beat was born at the University of Colombia which spawned a generation of philosophical writers such as Allen Ginsberg and Jack Kerouac – whose phrase 'Beat Generation' gave the movement its name. Its spirit spread to Britain and France where Juliette Greco and Jean-Paul Sartre made the Parisian Left Bank (Rive Gauche) a fashionable location. In the 1980s the beatnik look was revived as a minimalist fashion of black jeans and turtlenecks, Breton T-shirts and a pair of sunglasses.

☛ Bardot, Troublé

Belle Époque

The French phrase, meaning 'fine period', came to symbolize a comfortable, prewar society dressed in extravagant ruffles and out-sized hats for women and prosperous black tailoring for men. During this period the ideal female shape was no longer defined as small or meek, but voluptuous, majestic, and boasting a vast pigeon-bosom. That figure was covered with decorative flourishes intended to lend further richness. Lace, embroideries, ribbons, feathers, jewels and flowers all vied for space on figures trained into an S-curve. The froth of the Belle Époque was gradually replaced by a more rational style championed by modern women annoyed with its excess.

☛ Doucet, Drécoll, Paquin, Redfern

Bias cut

Fabric construction by which panels are cut across the grain, 45° to the edge of the cloth, giving it natural elasticity and drape.

Boat or bateau neck

Straight, boat-shaped neckline extending from shoulder to shoulder with the same depth at front and back.

Boater

Previously used in England as part of a late nineteenth-century punting uniform for men. Made of shellac-coated straw, the boater is a simple, circular hat with a flat top and brim.

Bolero jacket

Waist-length jacket worn open in front, with or without sleeves.

Boot-cut

Trousers cut slightly wider at the hem that can be worn over boots.

Bouclé

French for 'buckled' or 'curled'. A fabric or yarn which has a looped or knotted surface.

Box pleat

A pleat consisting of two parallel creases turned inwards towards each other.

Braid

A narrow, decorative band used for trimming or binding.

Brocade

A heavy dress and furnishing fabric woven with a jacquard loom, in which all-over patterns of flowers and foliage are raised from the surface cloth.

Broderie anglaise

A type of traditional embroidery consisting of petal shapes and eyelet holes cut out and finished with buttonhole stitching at the edges.

Brogue

A stout, lace-up stitched leather shoe with ornamental perforated bands originating in Scotland or Ireland.

Bugle beads

Long, tubular-shaped glass beads in black, white or silver often used as dress trimming.

Bust bodice

A heavily boned, padded and taped undergarment based on the camisole, which was replaced by the bra.

Bustier

A close-fitting, boned bodice.

Cable knit

A raised knitted pattern resembling twisted rope or cable.

Caftan

A rectangular-cut, ankle-length garment with a front opening, side splits and sometimes a cummerbund, probably originating from Mesopotamia. Once made in striped or brocaded silk, velvet or cotton, its predominance as a 1970s fashion item ensured versions were made in almost all kinds of fabric.

Calico

A coarse cotton fabric named after the city and port, Calicut, in India, from which it was originally exported.

Camel hair

A fabric made from the soft undercoat of the camel. Has also come to mean material made from cashmere and wool which has been dyed the colour of natural camel hair.

Camisole

Formerly an undergarment, based on the bodice, with fine straps, it is now also worn as an outer garment. It is generally made from lightweight silky fabrics and often trimmed with lace or ribbon.

Capri pants

Close-fitting trousers, tapered to the mid-calf, named after the Italian island of Capri.

Caracul, karacul see astraskhan.

Cashmere

The undercoat hair of the Kashmir goat, originally from India, now raised in Afghanistan, Tibet and China. An expensive fibre, it is often mixed with wool to reduce its cost.

Challis

A lightweight, soft woven fabric usually made from a blend of wool, cotton and rayon, and chiefly used as a dress fabric.

Chamois

Supple, fine, yellow-hued leather from the skin of the chamois goat, used for gloves. Not to be confused with chamois cloth, an imitation made of cotton.

Charmeuse

A lustrous lightweight fabric, developed in the twentieth century, made from synthetic or silk fabrics of satin weave.

Chenille

From the French, meaning 'caterpillar', because of its protuding, velvety tufts. Made of silk, rayon, cotton or wool, the yarn can be knitted or woven through the warp threads.

Chiffon

A lightweight, gossamer-sheer fabric, printed or dyed, made of silk or synthetic fibres.

Chinoiserie

From the French 'chinois', meaning Chinese. An embroidered or brocaded pattern showing Chinese motifs or qualities. An alternative French meaning is 'hair-splitting' which, if also applied to such embroidery, describes its fine intricacies very well.

Circular cut

A skirt or cape pattern piece cut in one curve or circle.

Cloche

A soft, felt hat with a deep crown and narrow brim occasionally pushed back to frame the eyes. Sometimes trimmed with a deep ribbon band.

Cloqué

A treated fabric with a blistered surface appearance, obtained by weaving a double-cloth consisting of yarns with varying degrees of shrinkage.

Combination jacquard

An updated version of jacquard weaving, in which computerized systems create highly complex jacquard patterns as well as incorporating yarns of various thickness and twist into the cloth.

Coq feathers/plumage

Iridescent black and green feathers of the barnyard cockerel.

Cravat

A scarf tied round the neck in front with its ends tucked inside a shirt.

Crepe

A fabric given a crinkled texture by heat and a particular weave. Made of silk, cotton, rayon or wool, its draping qualities make it most suitable for formal day dresses or eveningwear.

Crepe de chine

Very soft China silk crepe.

Satin-back crepe

Crepe fabric with a smooth satin surface on the reverse side.

Crinoline

From the French 'crin', meaning horsehair. In the early 1840s, the crinoline was a petticoat corded and lined with horsehair. It changed in the 1850s to a quilted petticoat with whalebone and several starched muslin layers underneath, flounced and tucked, eventually becoming a cage-like frame of flexible steel hoops.

Cut velvet

A variation of velvet, where the pile loops are cut to create tufts, either plain or patterned.

Panné velvet

Shiny shimmery velvet with the pile pressed in one direction to create a lustrous, smooth appearance.

Cut work

Originally a type of embroidery consisting of small openings made to form a pattern. Modern application includes figured cut-outs on leatherwear.

Décolleté

A deep neckline revealing the cleavage, neck and shoulders.

Delphos

The name given to a column dress of lustrous, intricately pleated silk designed and patented by Mariano Fortuny in 1909. Its simple, tubular shape was based on sculpture of the sixth century B.C. and resembled the Ionic chiton worn by the Delphic charioteer of Ancient Greek legend, hence its name.

Devoré

A technique used on velvet to create a patterned effect by chemically dissolving fibres using pattern plates.

Diamanté

Fake jewels or decoration, such as rhinestones, that imitate the sparkle of diamonds.

Dolman sleeve

A wide 'batwing' sleeve cut in one piece with the bodice, creating a deep armhole that reaches from the waist to a narrowed wrist.

Donegal tweed

Originally a hand-scoured, homespun, slubbed fabric made by Irish peasants using uneven yarns. Today it is a machine-made tweed with coloured slubs woven in.

Dress Reform

In 1851, at a time when Charles Frederick Worth was still dreaming of his future as a dressmaker to royalty, American Amelia Jenks Bloomer began a campaign to encourage women to wear trousers. Her bulbous pantaloons (a skirt divided and gathered at either ankle) were the ancestor of the tight hipsters worn in the 1960s. Throughout the last 150 years, fashion has been energized by the example of dress reformers. Dr Gustav Jaeger – whose 'Sanitary Stockingnette Combinations' were worn by George Bernard Shaw and other intellectuals – famously crusaded to dress the body entirely in wool. His efforts resulted in the first streamlined, truly rational fashion in the early decades of the twentieth century.

☛ Jaeger, Wilde

Empire-line

A lean dress or coat silhouette, usually in velvet, silk or lingerie fabrics, with its skirt gathered underneath the breasts, a low neckline and occasionally tiny, puffed sleeves. So named because it was popularized by Empress Josephine during the French Napoleonic Empire of 1804–1814.

Eton crop

An extremely short, severe haircut with longer hair on top slicked back. Typically a cut favoured by boys attending the English public school, Eton College, it became an androgynous fashion for women in the 1920s.

Façonné

French for 'fancy weave', describing patterned fabrics with scattered motifs or patterns woven into the cloth.

Faille

Close woven cotton, rayon or silk with a slight sheen, identified by the rib effect in the cross grain of the fabric.

Fedora

Felt hat with a tapered crown and medium-sized brim, and a centre crease.

Fichu

Small lace scarf or shawl knotted loosely around the shoulders with the points falling onto the chest.

Flapper

With their hair shorn into an Eton crop or shingle, leaving their necks and ears exposed, flappers symbolized a spirit of independence partially discovered in the absence of men during World War I. Fashion dressed that mood. In particular, Jean Patou's uncluttered, plumb line dresses, adorned by long, spare strings of pearls, and Chanel sporty jersey outfits were a pivotal influence in the 1920s. Because of public antipathy towards bared legs, designers fought against rising hems with elaborate creations that drew attention away from the bared ankle. In 1921, *Vogue* wrote 'One cannot help wishing for a less independent, less hard, more feminine product than the average twentieth century girl'. The reactionaries were disappointed in their hope but it wasn't until 1924 that the female knee showed itself for the first time. Skirts jumped from floor to knee-length and the flapper, coined earlier in the century for a young woman whose hair flapped free rather than being neatly pinned, took on her new role as a nightclub habitué with a taste for Martini cocktails and an ear for jazz. The new length caused a hemline controversy that would only be superseded by that of the mini forty years later.

☛ Abbe, Antoine, Chanel, Chéruit, Patou

Foulard

A soft twill weave silk used for making plain or printed scarves.

Frogging

A decorative fastening of long, braided or corded loops and buttons.

Frieze

A warm, coarse woollen fabric with a shaggy or 'friezed' pile for jerkins and overcoats.

Gabardine

A hardwearing twill worsted fabric, used for coats, riding habits and uniforms. In cotton it can be preshunk and made water-repellent.

Gauze

A thin, sheer fabric, made of cotton, silk, linen or rayon, first made in Gaza, Palestine.

Gingham

From the Malayan 'ginggang', meaning 'striped'. A checked, striped or solid colour cotton fabric of a plain weave, using pre-dyed yarns. Originally from India.

Grunge

Grunge was born in Seattle's music scene at the end of the 1980s. Youth developed a slacker lifestyle with a dependence on television and computers for entertainment. Their boredom was reflected in a dishevelled, lazily thrown together look of army trousers, unkempt hair and army boots or plimsolls. Grunge empathized with the horizontally-relaxed hippie attitude and was used by designers such as Marc Jacobs and Calvin Klein to market anti-fashion nonchalance as a fashion in itself.

☛ Cobain, Day

Gossamer

An extremely fine gauze or silk fabric. Its name, a combination of the old French 'gos', meaning goose, and 'somer', meaning summer. Its name probably refers to the fact that it appeared during the season when geese were ready for consumption.

Guêpière

A mini corset used to cinch the waist. Constructed of bone and elastic inserts, and laced in at the back or front.

Haute couture

An industry of established couturiers, or dressmakers, protected by the law and governed by the Chambre Syndicale de la Couture Parisienne with rigid regulations and emphasis on craftsmanship. Haute Couture specifically refers to the manufacture of made-to-measure garments, an industry that employs a small group of highly skilled craftspeople. In terms of revenue, haute couture no longer pays its way but is still shown twice a year (in January and July) as an exhibition of luxurious fashion for the purpose of selling the couture houses' perfume.

☛ Cardin, Dior, Lanvin, Lelong

Hippie

In 1967 and the 'Summer of Love', America's West Coast became the centre of the universe for a convergence of people detached from society – each with their own fashion. Hippies, their collective term, had been coined in the 1950s to describe 'uncool' people who tried hard to be, but the new breed had a relaxed attitude. So did their clothes; a mish-mash of psychedelic prints, Indian cotton, ponchos and caftans either picked up on their travels or imported and made to look as though they had been. The hippie look was transformed into a couture version, called 'hippie-deluxe', by designers who were also inspired by global travel. In using silk gauze instead of muslin and crepe rather than cheesecloth, the couturiers strayed far from the hippie's empathy with the cultures whose clothes they wore, but in doing so they ended the 1960s with an unrestrained and divergent style.

☞ Bouquin, Hendrix, Porter

Jacquard

A raised motif weave made on a jacquard loom used for damasks and brocades.

Jodhpurs

Riding breeches, christened after a former colonial Indian state. Traditionally full to the knee and tight from knee to ankle, with a strap passing under the boot, and with knee patches.

Khadi

Handspun Indian cotton yarn, or rough-surfaced Indian paper, strongly associated with Mahatama Gandhi, who suggested a return to a cottage industry in Khadi as a protest against the industrialisation brought with the British Empire.

Kid leather

Leather made from the skin of a baby goat.

Kimono

A national Japanese costume, consisting of a wrap-over, chinoiserie satin or silk gown with extremely long sleeve cuffs, fastened by an obi (see below).

Kitten heel

A low sculptured heel curved sharply inward along the sides and back, then flared slightly at the base.

Knee breeches

Breeches fitted to the knee, or knickerbockers with some fullness.

Lamé

Any fabric interwoven with (not necessarily real) gold or silver threads.

Leatherette

Imitation leather, produced by treating cloth to produce the grain and texture of real hide.

Loafer

Tailored low-heeled slip-on shoe fashioned after moccasins.

Lounge suit

An informal, plain style suit with no waist seam, single- or double-breasted; it fastens with one or two buttons, placed low at the front. Also called a sack suit, it appeared in the 1850s.

Louis heel

Named after Louis XIV of France, it then referred to a method of making the sole and heel in one section. It is better known as a thick heel, often covered, that curves in at the mid-section before flaring out.

Lurex®

Trade name for metallic thread, produced in various colours by thinly coating plastic sheets with aluminium on both sides. Used as a sewing thread, in embroidery, and can be woven into fabric for shimmery effect.

Lycra®

Trade name for the two-way and three-way stretch fabric manufactured by du Pont.

Mantilla comb

A Spanish hair decoration in the shape of a high tortoiseshell or ivory comb with four very long teeth. Traditionally used with a mantilla, a black or white lace scarf or veil.

Mantle

A loose cloak or wrap, usually without sleeves.

Matte jersey

Plain or ribbed fabric with a dull surface as it is knitted from crepe yarns.

Melozine

A rabbit-hair fabric, with a texture similar to camel-hair.

Mesh

A woven fabric made semi-transparent by its open-mesh texture, used for underwear and sportswear. Made of cotton, linen, wool, rayon or more commonly nylon.

Microfibre

Very fine synthetic fibre, approximately sixty times finer than human hair.

Minaudière

Small metal evening bag. Usually set with jewels or hand-engraved and carried either in the hand or on a short chain.

Moccasin

A one-piece foot covering gathered around the foot and laced to an upper piece. Traditionally made by native Americans from deerskin.

Mod

The mod, or modernist, originated in 1950s Britain as a celebration of clean, modern taste. Purposefully young and energetic, the mod adopted a more enthusiastic, acquisitive taste than their forerunner, the beatnik, accumulating a wardrobe of Italian-cut suits for men and immaculate short skirts and stiletto heels for women that betrayed material aspirations. Obsessively neat and narcissistic, mods wore parka anoraks while riding on their Lambretta motorcycles to protect their expensive suits. A vigorous economy enabled mods to embrace consumerism with gusto. Coming at a time when art made you dance and both cars and skirts were minuscule, the mod was very much of the moment, elevating British youth to iconic status and generally bolstering London's standing as a pop capital.

☞ Stephens

Modelliste

French term for a designer who works for a maison, or design house, whose work is shown under the label of the house.

Mohair

Fibre from the hair of the Angora goat, usually mixed with cotton, silk or wool to produce a distinctively hairy texture. A popular men's suiting fabric in the 1960s particularly with 'Tonik' weaves.

Moiré

A fabric with a gleaming water ripple effect, made of silk or synthetic silk. The fabric is passed through engraved rollers to create the pattern. Also called watered silk.

Mule

A shoe with the back cut away to reveal the heel.

New Look

With its tight, wasp-waist bodices, full skirt and padded hips, the New Look was a style that harked back to the age of crinolines. It was lauched in 1947 by Christian Dior. It appeared outdated and irrelevant to the more practical-minded woman who had survived two world wars, but as a weapon with which Paris could retrieve its former standing as a centre of international haute couture, it was essential. The New Look arrived at a time when women were still struggling with acute fabric shortages and it became a symbol of both desperate want and despair. Only the very wealthy could afford the New Look but it filtered through to influence fashion at all levels, replacing practicality with cumbersome femininity.

☞ Carnegie, Dior, Rochas, Snow

Obi

A traditional wide Japanese kimono belt, usually made of embroidered or brocaded silk or satin.

Ombré

French for 'shaded'. Weaving term for fabric, woven or painted, with graduated hues of colour.

Organdie

The sheerest plain-weave muslin fabric, made of 100 percent cotton yarn which has been stiffened slightly.

Organza

Similar to organdie, but made from silk or polyester. A fine, stiff and wiry fabric.

Pailette

A metal or plastic circular spangle, slightly larger than a sequin. Used as a trimming for evening clothes and accessories.

Palazzo pyjamas

Loose evening trousers that resemble pyjamas.

Paparazzi

An Italian term named after a character in the film *La Dolce Vita* (1960). It is used to refer to freelance photojournalists who persist in taking pictures for newspapers, whether invited or not.

Parachute silk

A light, airy, tightly-woven silk formerly used for parachute canopies. Now used as a fashion fabric for ultra-light summer clothes.

Pavé

An 'invisible' jewellery setting, with the stones placed closely together so that no metal shows between them.

Pin-tuck

A technique whereby the fabric is pinched vertically or horizontally, and the pinch sewn into a fine, uniform, decorative fold.

Piqué

A firm silk or more commonly cotton fabric, used for shirts, which gives a ribbed or corded effect.

Platform shoes

Shoes on which both the heels and soles are given extra thickness for height.

Plexiglass

A clear plastic material imitating glass in texture and appearance, but with greater flexibility.

Polo shirt

A cotton jersey sports shirt, usually short-sleeved, with a ribbed Peter Pan collar and buttoned placket.

Pompadour

A coiffure with the hair brushed back, often over a pad, to a loose, full roll around the face. Named after the Marquise de Pompadour, mistress of Louis XV of France.

Poncho

A square of woollen fabric worn as a cape with a neck opening in the centre.

Prince of Wales check

A wool fabric which consists of a black check against off-white, with a larger windowpane overcheck in red or blue. Popularized by Edward VIII, then Edward, Prince of Wales, when he wore a double-breasted suit in this pattern in 1923.

Princess line

The cut of women's clothing defined by continuous vertical panels shaping the waist, and lengthening through the torso without a waistline seam.

Pump

A simple, low-cut, flat shoe without fastenings.

Punk

Soaring temperatures and rising unemployment gave rise to an aggressive London subculture in 1975. Disaffection was reflected in an apocalyptic style made up of painted leather jackets, Doctor Martens, studs, spiked hair and safety pins worn as jewellery. As a look, it was designed to repulse and offend. Protagonists included a tartan-suited Johnny Rotten and Vivienne Westwood who, together with Malcolm McLaren, dressed the movement from their confrontational clothes shop, SEX (after which the Sex Pistols were named) on London's Kings Road. Selling bondage trousers and PVC T-shirts, it became a meeting place for punks.

☞ McLaren, Rhodes, Rotten, Westwood

PVC (Polyvinyl chloride)

A high-gloss vinyl fabric used for clothes, shoes and bags.

Raglan sleeve

A full sleeve which extends to the neckline instead of stopping at the top of the arm. It is named after Lord Raglan (1788–1855).

Ready-to-wear

Designer clothes manufactured in a range of sizes, colours and shapes. The term is derived from the French 'prêt-à-porter'.

Reefer jacket

Double-breasted, thigh-length boxy jacket with a small collar, thin lapels and three or four sets of brass buttons.

Robe de style

A dress fashioned on those found in seventeenth-century paintings, with a tight-fitting bodice, an ankle- or floor-length bouffant skirt, and short or non-existent sleeves. It is famously associated with Jeanne Lanvin. Also called the 'Infanta' style.

Ruching

A technique of tightly crimping or pleating lace or gauze causing it to ruffle on both sides. Used as trimming or to add a decorative texture to a fabric.

Satin

A fabric made of silk, rayon or synthetic silk fibres, closely woven to give it its distinctive sheen.

Duchesse satin

A thick, heavy, extremely glossy satin, suitable for formal evening gowns. Also called duchess satin.

S-curve

The female silhouette of the Edwardian period (see Belle Époque). A corset was developed to push out the bust and derrière, leaving a tiny waist and forcing the wearer's figure into an imposing 'S' shape.

Sheath dress

A figure-hugging, straight, ankle-length evening dress, popularized by film stars in the 1920s and 1930s.

Shibori

A varied fabric-making technique, generally used in Japan, combining tie-dye, stitching and pleat-resistance.

Shawl collar

A long, continuous collar, without peaks or notches, that wraps around the coat, dress or blouse it is attached to like a shawl.

Silk gazar

Stiffened organza used mainly in evening dresses.

Silk-screen printing

A method of printing using separate screens to block colour patterns individually onto a silk fabric.

Slip dress

A silky, lightweight dress with fine straps resembling an undergarment.

Smoking jacket

A type of lounge jacket in a brocade, velvet or other dark-coloured fabric, trimmed in braid. Worn at home for smoking during the late nineteenth century, by the twentieth century it appeared in a silk version, similar to a dressing gown. See lounge suit.

Snood

A loose hair net, either knitted or openwork, or a fabric bag, which encases the hair at the back of the head. Fashionable during the 1930s and 1940s.

Spangles

Tiny pieces of metal designed to catch the light and used as fabric decoration. Famously used by Charles Frederick Worth on silk tulle.

Stetson

An American cowboy sombrero, nicknamed the 'ten-gallon' hat. So-called after John B. Stetson's quality cowboy hats in the 1860s, which were famously comfortable and durable.

Stove pipe/cigarette legs

Straight-legged, ankle-length fitted pants.

Taffeta

Plain, closely woven stiff silk fabric which is slightly lustrous.

Technicolor*

A trade name for a cinematic colouring process in which the three primary colours are recorded on separate films and then combined in a single print. Also a description of colours displayed in such a way that they dazzle the viewer.

Toggle

A wooden button secured to the cloth by a cord loop, which is pushed through another cord loop on the opposite edge for fastening. A common feature on duffle coats.

Toile

A calico or muslin mock-up of a garment, made to enable the designer to see how it will look before he cuts the intended fabric. Also a muslin or calico copy of a garment which a manufacturer buys for copying purposes.

Toque

A small, round, brimless woman's hat, made of jersey or any other fabric that drapes well, occasionally decorated with a plume or brooch.

Trilby

Soft, felt hat of Alpine shape, with a plush-like texture, a dented crown and a flexible brim.

Tulle

A very soft silk, cotton or synthetic net.

Tussore

A type of wild, strong silk which includes pongee and shantung. It is made from the tussah silkworm of India. Also called tussah, tusseh, tusser, tussur.

Ultrasuede

Synthetic suede fabric of polyester and polyurethane mix which is crease resistant and machine washable.

Vendeuse

A French word for a sales assistant.

Vichy check

Chequered fabric woven with two different coloured threads, made of cotton or linen.

Voile

A sheer, semi-transparent, plain fabric of a tight weave, made from cotton, silk, rayon or wool.

Wedge heel

A heel merged into the sole in one graduated shoe layer, flat on the ground from heel to toe. Sometimes made of wood, rubber or cork.

Windbreaker*

Trade name for a lightweight nylon zip-up jacket with an attached hood, fitted waistband and cuffs.

Windsor knot

A fat, complex knot that juts out from the throat, best worn with a cutaway shirt collar. Named after Edward VIII, the then Prince of Wales, who wore his knots thickened with wadding – although he never actually tied a Windsor knot.

Yarn

A thread of fibres with or without twist, used for knitting or weaving.

Yoke

A fitted portion of a garment covering the back between the shoulders, or an extended waistband curving downwards. Traditionally an integral upper part of a smock.

Youthquake

'Youthquake' was the term given to an explosive period in the mid-1960s when short, confrontational fashion was designed, modelled and photographed by young men and women. For the first time, fashion was directed by youth for youth. Twiggy, David Bailey, Mary Quant and Vidal Sassoon were a few of the key figures who made London the centre of 'youthquake'.

☛ Bailey, Beatles, Charles, Foale and Tuffin, Liberty, Quant, Rosier, Sassoon, Twiggy

509

Directory of museums and galleries

ARGENTINA

Museo Historico Nacional del Traje
Buenos Aires
✆ (54 11) 4343 8427

AUSTRALIA

Museum of Victoria
P.O. Box 666E
Melbourne VIC 3001
✆ (61 3) 9660 2689

National Gallery of Victoria
180 St. Kilda Road
Melbourne VIC 3004
✆ (61 3) 9208 0344

Museum of Applied Arts & Sciences
500 Harris Street
Ultimo
Sydney NSW 2007
✆ (61 2) 9217 0111

AUSTRIA

Modesammlungen des Historischen Museums
Hetzendorfer Strasse 79
1120 Vienna
✆ (43 1) 804 04 68

BELGIUM

Flanders Fashion Institute (opens year 2000)
Nationale Straat
2000 Antwerp
✆ (32 3) 226 1447

Musée du Costume et de la Dentelle
6 rue de la Violette
1000 Bruxelles
✆ (32 2) 512 7709

The Vrieselhof Textile and Costume Museum
Schildesteenweg 79
2520 Oelegem
✆ (32 3) 383 4680

CANADA

McCord Museum
690 Sherbrooke Street West
Montreal
Quebec H3A 1E9
✆ (1 514) 398 7100

Bata Shoe Museum
327 Bloor St. West
Toronto
Ontario M5S 1W7
✆ (1 416) 979 7799

Royal Ontario Museum
100 Queen's Park
Toronto
Ontario M5S 2C6
✆ (1 416) 586 8000

CZECH REPUBLIC

Um˘eleckopr˘umyslové Muzeum
Ulice 17, Listopadu 2
11000 Prague 1
✆ (42 02) 24 81 12 41

DENMARK

Dansk Folkemuseum
Nationalmuseets 3 Afdeling
DK-2800 Lyngby
✆ (45) 45 85 34 75

FINLAND

Doll and Costume Museum
Hatanpään kartano
Hatanpään puistokuja 1
33100 Tampere
✆ (358 3) 222 6261

FRANCE

Musée de la Chemiserie et de l'Elégance
Masculine
rue Charles Brillaud
36200 Argenton-sur-Creuse
✆ (33 3) 54 24 34 69

Musée des Beaux-Arts et de la Dentelle
25 rue Richelieu
62100 Calais
✆ (33 3) 21 46 48 40

Musée du Chapeau
16 route de Saint Galmier
42140 Chazelles-sur-Lyon
✆ (33 4) 77 94 23 29

Musée des Tissus
30-34 rue de la Charité
69002 Lyon
✆ (33 4) 78 38 42 00

Musée de la Mode
11 rue de la Canabière
13001 Marseille
✆ (33 4) 96 17 06 00

Musée Galliéra,
Musée de la Mode de la Ville de Paris
10 avenue Pierre Premier de Serbie
75116 Paris
✆ (33 1) 56 52 86 00

Musée de la Mode et du Textile
Palais du Louvre
107 rue de Rivoli
75001 Paris
✆ (33 1) 44 55 57 50

Musée International de la Chaussure
2 rue Sainte-Marie
26100 Romans
✆ (33 4) 75 05 81 30

GERMANY

Museum für Kunst und Gewerbe
Steinorplatz 1
20099 Hamburg
✆ (49 40) 42813427

Deutsches Textilmuseum
Andreasmarkt 8
4150 Krefeld
✆ (49 2151) 572046

Bayerisches Nationalmuseum
Prinzregenten Strasse 3
80538 Munich
✆ (49 89) 211241

Münchner Stadtmuseum
Jacobsplatz 1
80331 Munich
✆ (49 89) 23322370

Germanisches Nationalmuseum
Kornmarkt 1
90402 Nuremberg
✆ (49 911) 13310

Deutsches Ledermuseum/ Deutsches
Schuhmuseum
Frankfurter Strasse 86
63067 Offenbach/Main
✆ (49 69) 8297980

Württembergisches Landesmuseum
Schillerplatz 6
70173 Stuttgart
✆ (49 711) 2793498

GREECE

Peloponnesian Folklore Foundation
1 Vass. Alexandrou
GR-21100 Nafplion
✆ (30 752) 28947

IRELAND

National Museum of Ireland
Kildare Street
Dublin 2
✆ (353 1) 677 7444

ITALY

Galleria del Costume
Palazzo Pitti
50125 Florence
✆ (39 55) 238 8763

Civiche Raccolte d'Arte Applicata
Castello Sforzesco
20121 Milan
✆ (39 2) 869 3071

Accademia di Costume e di Moda
Via della Rondinella 2
00186 Rome
✆ (39 6) 686 4132

Museo Palazzo Fortuny
Camp San Beneto
3780 San Marco
Venice
✆ (39 41) 520 0995

JAPAN

Kobe Fashion Museum
2-9, Koyocho-naka
Higashinada-ku
Kobe 658
✆ (81 78) 858 0050

Kyoto Costume Institute
Wacoal Corporation
103, Shichi-jo Goshonouchi Shimogyo-ku,
Kyoto 600-8864
✆ (81 75) 321 9221

Nishijin Textile Museum
Imadegawa, Kamigyoku
Kyoto
✆ (81 75) 432 6131

Bunka Gakuen Fukushoku Hakubutsukan
3-22-1 Yoyogi
Shibuya-ku
Tokyo-151-0053
✆ (81 3) 3299 2387

MEXICO

El Borcegui Shoe Museum
Bolivar 27
Centro Historico
CP 06000 Mexico City
✆ (52 5) 512 13 11

THE NETHERLANDS

Rijksmuseum
Stadhouderskade 42
1071 ZD Amsterdam
✆ (31 20) 674 70 00

Haags Gemeentemuseum
Stadhouderslaan 41
2517 HV The Hague
✆ (31 70) 338 11 11

Centraal Museum
Agnietenstraat 1
3512XA Utrecht
✆ (31 30) 236 23 62

NEW ZEALAND

Canterbury Museum
Roleston Avenue
Christchurch 1
✆ (64 3) 366 5000

NORWAY

Kunstindustrimuseet in Oslo
St. Olavsgate 1
0165 Oslo
✆ (47 22) 03 65 40

PORTUGAL

Museu Nacional do Traje
Parque de Monteiro Mor
Largo de Castalho
Lumiar
P-1600 Lisbon
✆ (351 1) 759 03 18

SOUTH AFRICA

Bernberg Fashion Museum
1 Duncombe Road
Forest Town 2193
Johannesburg
✆ (27 11) 646 0716

510

SPAIN

Museo Textil de la Diputación de Barcelona
Parc de Vallparadis-Carrer Salmeron 25
08222 Barcelona
✆ (34 93) 785 72 98

Museo Textil y de Indumentaria
Calle de Montcada 12
08003 Barcelona
✆ (34 93) 319 76 03

SWEDEN

Nordiska Museet
Djurgardsvägen 6-16
S-115 93 Stockholm
✆ (46 8) 519 546 00

SWITZERLAND

Textilmuseum
Vadianstrasse 2
9000 St. Gallen
✆ (41 71) 222 1744

Bally Shoe Museum
Parkstrasse 1
5012 Schönenwerd
Zurich
✆ (41 62) 858 2641

UNITED KINGDOM

Museum of Costume
The Assembly Rooms
Bennett Street
Bath
Avon BA1 2QH
✆ (44 1225) 477173

The Cecil Higgins Art Gallery
Castle Close
Bedford MK40 3RP
✆ (44 1234) 211222

Ulster Museum
Botanic Gardens
Stranmillis Road
Belfast BT9 5AB
✆ (44 1232) 383000

Birmingham City Museum & Art Gallery
Chamberlain Square
Birmingham B3 3DH
✆ (44 121) 303 2834

Brighton Art Gallery & Museum
Church Street
Brighton
East Sussex BN1 1UE
✆ (44 1273) 292882

Museum of Welsh Life
St. Fagans
Cardiff CF5 6XB
✆ (44 29) 20573500

Grosvenor Museum
27 Grosvenor Street
Chester
Cheshire CH1 2DD
✆ (44 1244) 402008

The Bowes Museum
Barnard Castle
Durham DL12 8NP
✆ (44 1833) 690606

National Museums of Scotland
Chambers Street
Edinburgh EH1 1JF
✆ (44 131) 225 7534

Kelvingrove Art Gallery and Museum
Glasgow G3 8AG
✆ (44 141) 276 9599

Lotherton Hall
Aberford
Leeds LS25 3EB
✆ (44 113) 281 3259

State Apartments and Royal
Ceremonial Dress Collection
Kensington Palace
London W8 4PX
✆ (44 870) 751 5170

Victoria and Albert Museum
Cromwell Road
London SW7 2RL
✆ (44 20) 7942 2000

Gallery of English Costume
Platt Hall
Rusholme
Manchester M14 5LL
✆ (44 161) 224 5217

Costume and Textile Study Centre
Carrow House
301 King Street
Norwich NR1 2TS
✆ (44 1603) 223870

Museum of Costume & Textiles
51 Castle Gate
Nottingham NG1 6AF
✆ (44 115) 915 3541

Paisley Museum & Art Gallery
High Street
Paisley
Renfrewshire PA1 2BA
✆ (44 141) 889 3151

Rowley's House Museum
Barker Street
Shrewsbury SY1 1QH
✆ (44 1743) 361196

York Castle Museum
York YO1 9RY
✆ (44 1904) 687687

UNITED STATES

The Museum of Fine Arts
465 Huntington Avenue
Boston
MA 02115
✆ (1 617) 267 9300

Chicago Historical Society
1601 Clark Street at North Avenue
Chicago
IL 60614
✆ (1 312) 642 4600

Wadsworth Atheneum
Hartford
CT 06103
✆ (1 860) 278 2670

Indianapolis Museum of Art
1200 West 38th Street
Indianapolis
IN 46208- 4196
✆ (1 317) 923 1331

Kent State University Museum
Rockwell Hall
Kent
OH 44242
✆ (1 350) 672 3450

Los Angeles County Museum of Art
5905 Wilshire Boulevard
Los Angeles
CA 90036
✆ (1 323) 857 6000

The Brooklyn Museum of Art
Eastern Parkway
Brooklyn
New York
NY 11238
✆ (1 718) 638 5000

The Costume Institute
Metropolitan Museum of Art
1000 Fifth Avenue
New York
NY 10028-0198
✆ (1 212) 535 7710

The Fashion Institute of Technology
West 27th Street at 7th Avenue
New York
NY 10001- 5992
✆ (1 212) 217 7999

Museum of the City of New York
1220 Fifth Avenue
New York
NY 10029
✆ (1 212) 534 1672

Philadelphia Museum of Art
26th Street & Benjamin Franklin Parkway
Philadelphia
PA 19130
✆ (1 215) 763 8100

The Arizona Costume Institute
The Phoenix Art Museum
1625 North Central Avenue
Phoenix
AZ 85004
✆ (1 602) 257 1222

Acknowledgements

Texts principally written by Angela Buttolph, Tamasin Doe, Alice Mackrell, Richard Martin, Melanie Rickey and Judith Watt and also Carmel Allen, Rebekah Hay-Brown, Natasha Kraal, Fiona McAuslan and Melissa Mostyn.

The publishers would particularly like to thank Suzy Menkes for her invaluable advice and also Katell le Bourhis, Frances Collecott-Doe, Dennis Freedman, Robin Healy, Peter Hope-Lumley, Isabella Kullman, Jean Matthew, Dr Lesley Miller, Alice Rawsthorn, Aileen Ribeiro, Julian Robinson, Yumiko Uegaki, Jonathan Wolford for their advice. And Lorraine Mead, Lisa Diaz and Don Osterweil for their assistance.

And Alan Fletcher for the jacket design.

Photographic Acknowledgements

Photograph James Abbe/ © Kathryn Abbe: 4; Photograph Eric Adjani, Sygma/JetSet: 11; photograph Miles Aldridge, courtesy Lawrence Steele: 430; photograph Simon Archer: 101; photograph © Brian Aris, courtesy Boy George: 72; courtesy Giorgio Armani: 18; © Eve Arnold/Magnum Photos: 19, 269; photograph Clive Arrowsmith, courtesy Zandra Rhodes: 390; courtesy Laura Ashley: 21; The Associated Press Ltd: 210; courtesy Marc Audibet: 22; © 1978 Richard Avedon. All rights reserved: 23; photograph © David Bailey: 24; courtesy Balenciaga Archives, Paris: 143; courtesy Bally: 29; © Gian Paolo Barbieri: 34; courtesy Fabien Baron: 37; © Michael Barrett: 338; courtesy Slim Barrett: 38; © Lillian Bassman: 41, 354; photograph Peter Beard. Courtesy Vogue. Copyright © 1964 by the Condé Nast Publications, Inc: 380; photograph Cecil Beaton, courtesy Sotheby's London: 44, 65, 141, 171, 186, 330, 333, 414, 460; photograph Cecil Beaton. Courtesy Vogue. Copyright © 1945 by the Condé Nast Publications, Inc: 30; photograph Cecil Beaton. Courtesy Vogue. Copyright © 1952 by the Condé Nast Publications, Inc: 89; courtesy Marion de Beaupré, Paris: 298, 403, 501; photograph Bellini, courtesy Christian Dior: 136; photograph Gilles Bensimon/Elle NY: 324; photograph Gilles Bensimon/SCOOP Elle UK: 349; © Harry Benson: 235; © François Berthod: 53; courtesy Laura Biagiotti: 55; collection Biagiotti-Cigna, Guidonia/photo Giuseppe Schiavinotto, Rome: 28; Bibliothèque national de France: 94, 372; Bildarchiv Peter W.Engelmeier, Munich: 35, 458; Birks Couture Collection, Camrax Inc: 83, 368; courtesy Manolo Blahnik: 58; courtesy Bill Blass Ltd. Archives: 60; © Estate of Erwin Blumenfeld: 61; photograph Jacques Boulay/Musée des Arts de la Mode, Paris: 486; photograph Guy Bourdin/ © Samuel Bourdin: 67, 239; courtesy Bourjois: 68; photo © Nick Briggs 1998: 345; British Vogue/The Condé Nast Publications Ltd: 36, 103, 191, 197, 282, 299, 317, 331 363, 373, 374, 395, 400, 423, 489; courtesy Brooks Brothers: 74; photograph Kelvin Bruce/Nunn Syndication Ltd: 134; courtesy Burberrys: 80; courtesy Butler & Wilson: 82; Camera Press Ltd, London: 204; courtesy Carven: 453; courtesy Oleg Cassini: 92; courtesy Cerruti: 96; © Dave Chancellor/Alpha, London: 274; photograph Walter Chin, reproduced by Bobbi Brown Beauty – The Ultimate Beauty Resource by Bobbi Brown & Annemarie Iverson (Ebury Press, 1997): 75; photograph Walter Chin, courtesy Gap: 168; courtesy Chloé: 294; Christie's Images: 263; photograph John Claridge: 477; photograph Henry Clarke, courtesy Vogue Paris (Nov 1957): 104; photograph Henry Clarke, courtesy Vogue Paris (1970): 66; photograph William Claxton: 190; photograph Clifford Coffin. Courtesy Vogue. Copyright © 1947 by the Condé Nast Publications, Inc: 188; photograph Clifford Coffin. Courtesy Vogue. Copyright © 1949 by the Condé Nast Publications, Inc: 109; photograph Michel Comte, courtesy Dolce & Gabbana: 138; photograph Michel Comte, courtesy Dirk Bikkembergs: 56; photograph Bill Cunningham. Courtesy Vogue. Copyright © 1972 by the Condé Nast Publications, Inc: 6; photograph Mark J. Curtis: 290; Louise Dahl-Wolfe/courtesy Staley-Wise Gallery, New York: 121; photograph Darzacq, courtesy Agnès B: 462; Corinne Day: 124; © Jean-Philippe Delhomme: 127; © Patrick Demarchelier/courtesy Harper's Bazaar: 130; Daniel d'Errico/Women's Wear Daily: 399; © Philip-Lorca diCorcia: 131; courtesy Adolfo Dominguez: 139; photograph Brian Duffy: 57; Raoul Dufy © Bianchini-Férier (Musée Historique des Tissus): 145; © Arthur Elgort: 9, 31, 102, 222; photograph Arthur Elgort, courtesy Oscar de la Renta: 387; photograph Sean Ellis, hair Jimmy Ka, make-up Eli Wakamatasu: 447; photograph Sean Ellis, hair Jimo Salako, make-up Eli Wakamatasu, model

Camellia: 148; photograph Sean Ellis, hair Jimo Salako, make-up Eli Wakamatasu, model Harley: 359; photograph Sean Ellis, hair Jimo Salako, make-up Eli Wakamatasu, stylist Isabella Blow, model Jodie Kidd: 296; courtesy Escada: 284; photograph Jerome Esch, courtesy Fendi: 162; courtesy Etro: 153; © Joe Eula: 156; Mary Evans Picture Library: 140, 192; photograph Elisabeth Eylieu/Musée International de la Chaussure de Romans, France: 367; courtesy Max Factor: 159; photograph G.M. Fadigati: 417; Fabrizio Ferri, courtesy Bulgari: 79; Fabrizio Ferri, courtesy Moschino: 334; Joel Finler Collection: 223; © Don Freeman: 251; photograph Jill Furmanovsky: 170; courtesy Gallery Bartsch & Chariau: 15, 237, 250; photograph Joël Garnier: 365; Getty Images Limited: 13, 382, 497; The J. Paul Getty Museum, Malibu: 14; courtesy Tom Gilbey: 194; © Givenchy: 195; photograph Nathaniel Goldberg, Paris: 86; photograph Nan Goldin – 1996 A/W Matsuda ad campaign: 257; image © 1998 The Archives of Milton H. Greene, LLC. All rights reserved. # 541-997 4970 www.archivesmhg.com: 343; courtesy Gucci: 201; courtesy Annie Guedras: 107; photograph François Halard/Elle, NY: 496; courtesy Hamiltons Photographers Ltd: 178, 283, 286, 355, 436, 487, 498; © Pamela Hanson: 326; photograph Michael E. Heeg, Munich, courtesy Adidas: 123; photograph Terry Andrew Herdin: 440; photograph Ken Heyman: 491; © 1963 by Hiro. All rights reserved: 213; courtesy Yoshiki Hishinuma: 214; photograph Horst: 114, 234; photograph Horst/courtesy Staley-Wise Gallery, New York: 216, 366; photograph by Horst. Courtesy Vogue. Copyright © 1946 by the Condé Nast Publications, Inc: 351; photograph by Horst. Courtesy Vogue. Copyright © 1961 by the Condé Nast Publications, Inc: 271; photograph Horvat/courtesy Staley-Wise Gallery, New York: 217; photograph Rainer Hosch, model Heather Payne, hair Christaan, make-up Linda, as published in i-D magazine, Jan 1998: 429; House of Worth, London/Bridgeman Art Library: 353; courtesy Margaret Howell: 218; photograph Hoyningen-Huene, courtesy of UK Harper's Bazaar/Harpers & Queen: 8; courtesy Barbara Hulanicki: 220; Illustrated London News Picture Library/Tatler Magazine: 99; photograph Dominique Isserman/Maud Frizon for Ombeline: 181; photograph Katerina Jebb: 97; © Gerald Jenkins: 135; Tim Jenkins/Women's Wear Daily: 25; courtesy Norma Kamali: 240; photog raph by Art Kane. Courtesy Vogue. Copyright © 1962 by the Condé Nast Publications, Inc: 246; courtesy Donna Karan: 241; courtesy Stéphane Kélian: 243; © Christoph Kicherer: 449; Bill King Photography, Inc: 169, 450; © 1997 Calvin Klein Cosmetic Corporation/cKbe TM owned by CKTT: 336; photograph Kelly Klein: 160; photograph Steven Klein, courtesy Frank magazine: 396; © William Klein: 113, 173, 184, 244, 254, 357, 445; photograph Peter Knapp: 228, 247, 369; photo Nick Knight: 70; photo Nick Knight/ stylist Simon Foxton: 438; photo Nick Knight/Art Director Alexander McQueen: 255; The Kobal Collection: 291, 347; photo F. Kollar © Ministère de la Culture, France: 327; photograph Krizia, Milan: 307; photo Kublin. All rights reserved. Balenciaga Archives, Paris: 327; Kunsthistorisches Museum, Vienna: 499; photograph Kazumi Kurigami: 323; photograph Christophe Kutner: 279; photograph David LaChapelle (Elle UK), set design Kristen Vallow, hair Jorge Serio at Jed Root, make-up Ellie Wakamatasu, wardrobe Alice Massey: 231; photograph David LaChapelle (Stern Galliano Story), set design Kristen Vallow, hair Greg Everingham at Carole Agency, make-up Charlotte Willer at Carole Agency, wardrobe Franck Chevalier at Smashbox: 259; courtesy Lacoste: 260; photograph Karl Lagerfeld: 262; Inez van Lamsweerde and Vinoodh Matadin/A+C Anthology: 264, 273; photograph Sylvie Lancrenon, courtesy Louis Féraud: 163; photograph Andy Lane, courtesy Stevie Stewart: 435; courtesy Jeanne Lanvin: 268; photograph Gunnar Larsen, courtesy Galerie Dominique Weitz: 383; Laspata/Decaro Studio, courtesy Elite, New York: 157; photograph Barry Lategan: 278; photograph Thierry Ledé: 110; photograph Erica Lennard, model Lise Ryall: 147; © Alexander Liberman: 98, 285; The Library of Congress, Prints & Photographs Division, Toni Frissell Collection: 180; photograph Peter Lindbergh: 287, 376; Peter Lindbergh, courtesy Comme des Garçons: 242; Peter Lindbergh, courtesy Harper's Bazaar: 187; courtesy Loewe: 289; Lisa Lyon, 1984 copyright © 1984 The Estate of Robert Mapplethorpe: 76; photograph Eamonn J. McCabe/SCOOP Elle UK: 437; © Craig McDean: 49, 295, 422, 428; Tony McGee, London: 226; photograph Niall McInerney: 348; photograph Niall McInerney, courtesy Ghost: 409; courtesy Malcolm McLaren: 301; © Frances McLaughlin-Gill, New York: 54, 85, 133, 199, 302, 418; photograph Andrew Macpherson: 119; courtesy MAC: 456; Nick Machalaba/Women's Wear Daily: 425; photograph by Marcio Madeira: 233; photograph Gered

Mankowitz / Bowstir Ltd.1998: 209; photograph Mitsuhiro Matsuda – 1996 S/S Madame Nicole ad campaign: 312; photograph Mark Mattock: 321; courtesy Maxmara: 309; Steven Meisel/A+C Anthology: 193, 316; photograph Randall Mesden, courtesy Joseph Abboud: 5; © Sheila Metzner: 432; photograph by Baron de Meyer. Courtesy Vogue: 385, 443; photograph by Baron de Meyer. Courtesy Vogue. Copyright © 1922 by the Condé Nast Publications, Inc: 318; © Duane Michals, New York: 202; © Lee Miller Archives: 78, 319; courtesy Nolan Miller: 320; photograph Eddy Ming, courtesy Akira Isogawa: 225; © Ministère de la Culture, France/AAJHL: 116; Mirror Syndication International: 149, 304, 401; photograph Jean-Baptiste Mondino, courtesy Walter Van Beirendonck, W. & L.T: 474; photograph David Montgomery, courtesy Vidal Sassoon: 410; photograph Sarah Moon: 69, 329; © Chris Moore: 12, 42, 105, 128, 129, 146, 185, 211, 248, 270, 276, 439, 466, 492; courtesy Robert Lee Morris: 332; © Jon Mortimer: 249; illustration Rebecca Moses, creative direction Deborah Moses, animation & design Detour Design, NY: 335; courtesy Thierry Mugler: 337; photograph Ugo Mulas, courtesy Mila Schön: 416; © Joan Munkacsi, courtesy Howard Greenberg, NY: 339; Musée de la Mode et du Textile, coll. UFAC: 137, 142, 280, 364; Museo di Arte Moderna e Contemporanea di Trento e Roverto: 158; Museo Salvatore Ferragamo: 164; The Museum of Costume and Fashion Research Centre, Bath: 386; The Museum at F.I.T, New York: 198, 230, 281, 293, 306, 314, 388; © 1998 The Museum of Modern Art, New York. Gift of the photographer. Copy print: 431; photograph NARS: 340; by courtesy of the National Portrait Gallery, London: 495; © Helmut Newton/Maconochie Photography: 342; photograph Helmut Newton, courtesy Wolford: 352; photograph Fiorenzo Niccoli, courtesy Roberto Capucci: 87; courtesy L'Officiel: 50, 93, 206, 228, 444; photograph Perry Ogden: 111; photograph Kazuo Oishi, courtesy Gianfranco Ferre: 165; Bill Orchard/Rex Features: 71; © Mike Owen: 175; PA News: 203; photograph Dick Page: 350; photograph by Kourken Pakchanian. Courtesy Vogue. Copyright © 1973 by the Condé Nast Publications, Inc: 183; photograph by Kourken Pakchanian. Courtesy Vogue. Copyright © 1975 by the Condé Nast Publications, Inc: 252; courtesy Parfums Christian Dior: 200; courtesy Jean Patou: 356; photograph by Irving Penn. Courtesy Vogue. Copyright © 1950 (renewed 1978) by the Condé Nast Publications, Inc: 172, 360; © Elsa Peretti 1989. Photography by Hiro: 361; J.M. Perier/SCOOP French Elle: 189; courtesy Gladys Perint Palmer: 362; Photofest, New York: 7, 32, 125, 205, 378; photograph PICTO: 167; photograph George Platt Lynes. Courtesy Vogue. Copyright © 1947 by the Condé Nast Publications, Inc: 371; photograph Phil Poynter: 303; Private Collection, Italy: 151; courtesy Lilly Pulitzer: 381; photograph by Karen Radkai. Courtesy Vogue. Copyright © 1958 by the Condé Nast Publications, Inc: 480; photograph by Karen Radkai. Courtesy Vogue. Copyright © 1959 by the Condé Nast Publications, Inc: 461; photograph by John Rawlings. Courtesy Vogue. Copyright © 1945 by the Condé Nast Publications, Inc: 471; photograph by John Rawlings. Courtesy Vogue. Copyright © 1947 by the Condé Nast Publications, Inc: 420; Rave Archives: 484; courtesy Red Rooster PR: 208; Retna Pictures Limited: 106; Rex Features: 43; Rex Features/SIPA: 344; Rheinisches Bildarchiv, Cologne: 308; photograph Terry Richardson, courtesy The Katy Barker Agency: 258; Art Rickerby/Katz Pictures Ltd: 245; courtesy Paolo Rinaldi, Milan: 10; © Herb Ritts, courtesy Fahey/Klein Gallery, Los Angeles: 84, 393; © Michael Roberts/Maconochie Photography: 154, 394; courtesy Rochas Mode: 397; Tim Rooke/Rex Features: 117; courtesy Adel Rootstein: 465; photograph Aldo Rossi: 288; photograph François Rotger, courtesy Patrick Cox: 115; © Paolo Roversi, courtesy Giorgio Armani: 300; © Paolo Roversi, courtesy Alberta Ferretti: 166; photograph Paolo Roversi (i-D cover, May 1998), stylist Edward Enninful , make-up Pat McGrath for Aveda: 298; photograph by Rubartelli. Courtesy Vogue. Copyright © 1968 by the Condé Nast Publications, Inc: 408; courtesy Helena Rubinstein: 404; courtesy Sonia Rykiel: 405; photograph Satoshi Saikusa, courtesy Masaki Matsushima: 313; photograph Satoshi Saikusa, courtesy UK Harper's & Queen: 325; courtesy Arnold Scaasi: 411; © Francesco Scavullo: 91, 132, 182, 253, 406, 412, 464; photograph by Francesco Scavullo. Courtesy Vogue. Copyright © 1982 by the Condé Nast Publications, Inc: 236; Pierre Scherman/Women's Wear Daily: 297; photograph Norbert Schoerner, courtesy Lionel Bouard: 454; SCOOP Paris Match/Garofalo: 152; © Fred Seidman: 221; courtesy Shiseido: 292; photograph Jeanloup Sieff,

courtesy Akio Hirata: 212; © Jeanloup Sieff: 419; photograph Christophe Sillem: 459; photograph David Sims: 421; photograph David Sims, model Angela Lindvall, courtesy Jil Sander: 407; Skrebneski: 391, 490; photograph Carter Smith, courtesy The Katy Barker Agency: 398; © Snowdon: 427; Solo Syndication Ltd: 433; photograph Howard Sooley: 315; photograph Howard Sooley, courtesy Georgina von Etzdorf: 155; courtesy Spectator Sports Ltd: 232; photograph Edward Steic hen. Courtesy Vogue. Copyright © 1927 by the Condé Nast Publications, Inc: 100; photograph Edward Steichen. Courtesy Vogue. Copyright © 1936 by the Condé Nast Publications, Inc: 120; © Bert Stern: 434; photograph Ronald Stoops, Antwerp: 310; John Swannell/Woman's Journal/Robert Harding Syndication: 215; photograph Yoshi Takata, courtesy Pierre Cardin: 88; photograph Juergen Teller, courtesy Z Photographic: 267, 446; photograph Mario Testino, model Marie Sophie: 261; photograph Mario Testino, fashion editor Carine Roitfeld, hair Marc Lopez, make-up Tom Pecheux: 424; photograph Mario Testino, stylists Carine Roitfeld & Patrick Kinmonth, hair Marc Lopez, make-up Tom Pecheux: 322; photograph Mario Testino, fashion editor Carine Roitfeld, hair Marc Lopez, make-up Linda Cantello, models Georgina Grenville & Ludovico Benazzo: 176; photograph Mario Testino, fashion editor Lori Goldstein, hair Orlando Pita, make-up Laura Mercier, model Madonna: 481; photograph Mario Testino (British Vogue, Sept 1993), fashion editor Jayne Pickering, hair Marc Lopez, make-up Leslie Chilkes, model Christy Turlington: 494; photograph Mario Testino (French Glamour, May 1994), fashion editor Carine Roitfeld, hair Marc Lopez, make-up Tom Pecheux, model Nadja Auermann: 448; photograph Mario Testino (Harper's Bazaar, March 1994), fashion editor Tonne Goodman, hair Orlando Pita, make-up Kevyn Aucoin, model Shalom Harlow: 370; photograph Mario Testino (Harper's & Queen March 1998), fashion editor Hamish Bowles, hair Sam McKnight, make-up Leslie Chilkes: 238; photograph Mario Testino (Visionaire 'Chic', Sept 1997), fashion editor Carine Roitfeld, hair Marc Lopez, make-up Tom Pecheux, models Linda Evangelista & Shalom Harlow: 51; photograph Ian Thomas: 59; Tiffany & Co Archives. All rights reserved: 451; Wolfgang Tillmans, courtesy Maureen Paley/Interim Art: 227; Louis Tirilly © CARTIER: 90; courtesy Isabel Toledo: 454; photograph Oliviero Toscani, courtesy Fiorucci: 167; photograph by Oliviero Toscani. Courtesy Vogue. Copyright © 1974 by the Condé Nast Publications, Inc: 81; photograph Tessa Traeger: 112; illustration by Hélène Tran, courtesy of UK Harper's Bazaar/Harpers & Queen: 457; courtesy Mary Trasko, New York: 502; © Deborah Turbeville, courtesy Marek & Associates Inc: 463; photograph Deborah Turbeville. Courtesy Vogue. Copyright © 1975 by the Condé Nast Publications, Inc: 45, 62; courtesy Shu Uemura: 467; courtesy Patricia Underwood: 468; courtesy Ungaro: 469; United Colours of Benetton: 46; Ellen von Unwerth: 415, 470; courtesy Valentino: 472; courtesy Valentino Couture: 485; photograph Javier Vallhonrat: 473; photograph Javier Vallhonrat, courtesy Jesús del Pozo: 375; photograph Javier Vallhonrat, courtesy Sybilla: 441; courtesy Van Cleef & Arpels: 475; photograph Gus Van Sant: 346; Victoria & Albert Museum, London/The Bridgeman Art Library: 26; V&A Picture Library: 20, 47, 95, 108, 179, 196, 455; courtesy Vogue Paris (1931): 484; courtesy Vogue Paris (1934): 275; courtesy Vogue Paris (1935): 402, 482; courtesy Vogue Paris (1949): 30 6; courtesy Vogue Paris (1970) 483; courtesy Vogue Paris (1972): 478; courtesy Vogue: 341; courtesy Vogue. Copyright © 1933 by the Condé Nast Publications, Inc: 150; courtesy Vogue. Copyright © 1935 by the Condé Nast Publications, Inc: 118; courtesy Vogue. Copyright © 1937 by the Condé Nast Publications, Inc: 122; courtesy Vogue. Copyright © 1938 by the Condé Nast Publications, Inc: 48; courtesy Vogue. Copyright © 1945 by the Condé Nast Publications, Inc: 63; courtesy Louis Vuitton: 488; photograph Anton Want, courtesy Nike: 256; photograph Albert Watson: 389; © Bruce Weber: 272, 493; Weidenfeld & Nicolson Archives: 266; Westminster City Archives/Jaeger: 229; Winpluke Asian Museum, Seattle/photo courtesy Junichi Arai: 476; photograph Olaf Wipperfürth, courtesy Dries Van Noten: 476; Women's Wear Daily: 265, 358, 479, 500; courtesy WPR, London: 174; Richard Young/Rex Features: 379; courtesy Zoran srl: 503

www.phaidon.com

512